Reading Across the Pacific Australia–United States Intellectual Histories

Edited by Robert Dixon and Nicholas Birns

SYDNEY UNIVERSITY PRESS

Published 2010 by SYDNEY UNIVERSITY PRESS
University of Sydney Library
sydney.edu.au/sup

Sydney University Press
Fisher Library F03
University of Sydney NSW 2006 AUSTRALIA
Email: sup.info@sydney.edu.au

National Library of Australia Cataloguing-in-Publication entry

Title: Reading across the Pacific : Australia - United States intellectual histories / edited by Robert Dixon and Nicholas Birns.
ISBN: 9781920899660 (pbk.)
Notes: Includes bibliographical references and index.
Subjects: Comparative literature--American and Australian.
Comparative literature--Australian and American.
Other Authors/Contributors:
Dixon, Robert, 1954-
Birns, Nicholas.
Dewey Number:
809

Cover design by Miguel Yamin, University Publishing Service

Contents

Contributors

Michael Ackland holds the inaugural Colin and Margaret Roderick Chair of English at James Cook University, Townsville. He is currently researching a monograph on Christina Stead and her socialist heritage.

Bruce Bennett is Emeritus Professor of English at the Australian Defence Force Academy, University of New South Wales. His books include *Homing In* (2006), *Australian Short Fiction: A History* (2002), *The Oxford Literary History of Australia* (1998) and *Spirit in Exile* (1991). Current research interests include literature and espionage and expatriate Australian writers.

Nicholas Birns is Associate Teaching Professor at Eugene Lang College, The New School, New York. *Theory after Theory: An Intellectual History of Literary Theory from 1950 to the Early 21st Century* appeared in 2010, and his single-authored *Wiley-Blackwell Encyclopedia of Critics and Criticism* will be published in 2011.

Patrick Buckridge is Professor of Literary Studies in the School of Humanities, Griffith University, where he teaches courses on world literature. He has published widely on Australian literary history and the history of reading, and is currently working on a study of Australian reading culture during the interwar period, and a history of the publishing house of Harrap.

Lawrence Buell is the Powell M. Cabot Professor of American Literature at Harvard University. His recent publications include *Writing for an Endangered World: Literature, Culture, and Environment in the United States and Beyond* (2001), *Emerson* (2003), and *The Future of*

Environmental Criticism (2005). In 2007 he won the Jay Hubbell Award, Modern Language Association, American Literature Group, for lifetime contributions to American literary studies.

David Carter is Professor of Australian Literature and Cultural History at the University of Queensland. He has recently co-edited *Modern Australian Criticism and Theory* (with Wang Guanglin, 2010) and contributed to the *Cambridge History of Australian Literature* (2009). He is researching a history of American editions of Australian books.

Robert Dixon is Professor of Australian Literature at the University of Sydney. His most recent book, with Katherine Bode, is *Resourceful Reading: The New Empiricism, eResearch and Australian Literature Culture* (2009). In 2011, his two books on Frank Hurley will be published by Anthem Press, London: 'The Diaries of Frank Hurley 1912–1944' (edited with Christopher Lee) and 'Photography, Early Cinema and Colonial Modernity: Frank Hurley's Synchronized Lecture Entertainments'.

Paul Genoni teaches in the School of Media, Culture and Creative Arts at Curtin University. He is the author of *Subverting the Empire: Explorers and Exploration in Australian Fiction* (2004), and co-editor of *Thea Astley's Fictional Worlds* (2006). He is currently President of the Association for the Study of Australian Literature.

Paul Giles is Challis Professor of English at the University of Sydney. His most recent books are *Transnationalism in Practice: Essays on American Studies, Literature and Religion* (2010) and *The Global Remapping of American Literature* (2011). He is currently chief investigator of an ARC Discovery project entitled 'Antipodean America: Australasia, Colonialism, and the Constitution of U.S. Literature.'

Kevin Hart holds the Edwin B. Kyle Chair of Christian Studies in the Department of Religious Studies at the University of Virginia. He also holds professorships in the Department of English and the Department of French. He has recently accepted a visiting Chair of Philosophy at the Australian Catholic University, where he will teach in the Australian winter for the next five years. His most recent books are *The Exorbitant: Emmanuel Levinas between Jews and Christians* (2010) and *Clandestine Companions: Philosophy in the Narratives of Maurice Blanchot* (2010).

CAROL HETHERINGTON is currently employed as Content Manager of the database AustLit: The Australian Literature Resource and as an editorial assistant for *Australian Literary Studies*. She has worked for many years as a research assistant and bibliographer with the English Department at the University of Queensland, and as a librarian in the Fryer Library of Australian Literature, the University of Queensland. Her research interests include bibliography and book history, the crime fiction of Arthur Upfield and the American publication of Australian literature.

IVOR INDYK holds the Whitlam Chair in Writing and Society at the University of Western Sydney. He is the founding editor of *HEAT* magazine and publisher of the Giramondo book imprint. A critic, essayist and reviewer, he has written a monograph on David Malouf, and essays on many aspects of Australian literature.

DEBORAH JORDAN is a Research Fellow in the School of English, Media Studies and Art History at the University of Queensland. She is a cultural historian currently working on the University of Queensland Press archive, on the 'Australian Literary Publishing and its Economies 1965–95' research project with Ivor Indyk and others, and with David Carter on American editions of Australian books. She is particularly interested in the ways nation intersects with nature and the narratives of change.

PAUL KANE is Professor of English and Environmental Studies at Vassar College. He is poetry editor of *Antipodes* and the author of *Australian Poetry: Romanticism and Negativity* (1996). His most recent collection of poems is *A Slant of Light* (2008).

MARILYN LAKE is Professor of History at La Trobe University and President of the Australian Historical Association. Her most recent book is *Drawing the Global Colour Line: White Men's Countries and the Question of Racial Equality*, which was co-authored with Henry Reynolds and which won the Prime Minister's Prize for Non-Fiction, the Ernest Scott Prize and the Queensland Premier's Prize for History.

Kerry Leves is completing a PhD thesis on Randolph Stow at the University of Sydney. His most recent poetry collection, *A Shrine to Lata Mangeshkar* (2008), was shortlisted for the NSW Premier's Kenneth Slessor Award in 2009. His poetry reviews and critical articles have appeared in *Australian Book Review, Blue Dog, Boxkite, Five Bells, Overland* and *Southerly*.

Benjamin Miller recently completed his PhD at the University of New South Wales. He has published on representations of Aboriginality in Australian literature and cinema in the *Journal of the Association for the Study of Australian Literature, Studies in Australasian Cinema*, and *Altitude*.

Fiona Morrison is a Lecturer in English at the University of Sydney. Her latest book is a critical edition of Dorothy Hewett's selected prose. She is also the co-author of *Masters in Pieces* (Cambridge University Press, 2006).

Roger Osborne has a research background in print culture, book history and scholarly editing. He has published a number of articles on these topics in Australian and British contexts and he is co-editor of the Cambridge Edition of Joseph Conrad's *Under Western Eyes* (forthcoming in 2012). He is currently Project Manager of the Aus-e-Lit Project.

Louise Poland is the recipient of an ARC postdoctoral fellowship as part of an ARC-funded project on 'Australian Literary Publishing and its Economies 1965–95', led by the University of Western Sydney. She has worked in book publishing and her research has focused on the publishing industry. Her doctoral thesis, awarded by Monash University, examined feminist presses and publishing politics in Australia.

John Scheckter is Professor of English at the C.W. Post Campus of Long Island University, New York. He is a founding member and past president of the American Association of Australasian Literary Studies.

He is the author of *The Australian Novel 1830–1980* (1998), and is currently investigating early modern imperialism.

Ken Stewart is an Honorary Research Associate of the School of Letters, Art and Media at the University of Sydney. He has been closely associated since the 1960s with the development of Australian literature as a subject for university teaching and research, and in 1978 co-founded the Association for the Study of Australian Literature (ASAL). He is the author of *Investigations in Australian Literature* (2000), and was in 2009 the recipient of a Festschrift, *Serious Frolic* (ed. F. de Groen and P. Kirkpatrick). His most recent book, edited with Laurie Hergenhan and Michael Wilding, is *Cyril Hopkins' Marcus Clarke* (2009).

Elizabeth Webby is Emeritus Professor of Australian Literature, University of Sydney. She has published widely on nineteenth-century Australian literary culture and is currently working on critical editions of Henry Lawson, Charles Harpur and Patrick White's notebooks

Introduction

Reading Across the Pacific is the first book-length study of literary and cultural engagement between the United States and Australia from a contemporary interdisciplinary perspective. Previous studies have been specialised, un- or under-theorised, and spoke to a narrowly bilateral context. *Reading Across the Pacific*, by contrast, is fully enmeshed in contemporary methodological debates: it does not just link the United States and Australia in a one-to-one dialogue but brings in the ambient circumstances of the Pacific Rim and Oceania. Importantly, it participates in a clearly identified 'transnational turn' in the study of both American and Australian literatures to which it is designed as a both a response and a provocation.

The few books and scholarly articles previously addressing US–Australian literary and cultural connections are now the work of previous academic generations, and are out of print or limited in approach.[1] And yet, as evidenced by the torrent of American students visiting Australia, the continuing wave of Australian novelists publishing in the United States, the substantial presence played by Australia in international

1 See for example Don Anderson, 'Contemporary American and Australian Short Fiction', *Westerly* 25.1 (1980): 83–90; Joseph Jones, *Radical Cousins: Nineteenth-Century American and Australian Writers* (St Lucia: University of Queensland Press, 1976); Laurie Hergenhan, *No Casual Traveller: Hartle Grattan and Australia–US Connections* (St Lucia: University of Queensland Press, 1995); Brian Kiernan, 'Some American and Australian Literary Connections and Disconnections', *Antipodes* 1.1 (March 1987): 22–26; Joan Kirkby, *The American Model: Influence and Independence in Australian Poetry* (Sydney: Hale & Iremonger, 1982); and Andrew Taylor, 'Bosom of Nature or Heart of Stone: A Difference in Heritage (Some Thoughts on American and Australian Literature)', *The Literary Criterion* 15.3–4 (1980): 144–56.

popular culture, the academic excellence and growing international orientation of Australian universities, and the seminal role of Australian scholarship within the worldwide study of postcolonial Anglophone literatures (notably in Britain, Canada, South Africa, and South and East Asia), there is an urgent need for dynamic, sophisticated new research and criticism addressing US–Australian literary and cultural relations.

These trends were confirmed by the publication in 2009 of *The Macquarie PEN Anthology of Australian Literature*, which was launched simultaneously in Sydney and in two important centres of Australian Studies in the United States: Georgetown in Washington, DC, and the Australian Studies Centre at Harvard University. The anthology is published in Australia by Allen & Unwin and in the United States by Norton as *The Literature of Australia*. At nearly 1500 pages, this unprecedented survey of Australian literature presents selections of more than 500 primary sources by over 300 Australian authors, and is being widely adopted by schools, universities and university libraries in both the United States and Australia. *Reading Across the Pacific* addresses the new demand for freshly conceived critical, historical and interpretive material generated by the international success of the *Macquarie PEN* collection of primary sources.

In the twenty-first century, both American and Australian literatures are experiencing important new challenges to the very different paradigms of literary history and criticism each inherited from the twentieth century. In American studies, the long-prevalent belief in American exceptionalism—the sense that the United States has a unique mission and destiny, and thus, inferentially, that its literature is also distinct or embodies distinct archetypes and identities—has been countered by demonstrations of an extensive array of connections to other literatures and cultures; demonstrations that these external currents have indeed impinged on American texts and their producers. Although American exceptionalism is still a live factor in the larger culture—even President Obama, elected partially on his promise to pursue a more multilateral and dialogue-oriented foreign policy, has reaffirmed his belief in American exceptionalism, as if it were a necessary tenet of a US secular faith—its stranglehold over academia is not what it was in the days of the founders of modern American literary studies such as Leo Marx and R.W.B. Lewis. As Paul Giles observes, American literary space is ragged or porous at the edges and to understand such a space we need to extend its conceptual geography in a series of ellipses as it touches and overlaps with the space of other 'national' literatures and cultures.[2] In recent years, a number of studies have invoked the importance of America's transatlantic connections—Giles' own *Virtual Americas: Transnational Fictions and the Transatlantic Imaginary* (Duke University Press, 2002) and *Atlantic Republic: The American Tradition in English Literature* (Oxford University Press, 2006) are exemplary here, as is the work of Wai-Chee Dimock, Paul Gilroy, Joel Pace, David Shields, William Spengemann and Robert Weisbuch.[3] In this context, *Reading Across the Pacific* is unique in invoking the United States' Anglophone transpacific connections.

In Australian literary studies, too, scholars such as Nicholas Birns, David Carter, Leigh Dale, Robert Dixon, Ken Gelder, Graham Huggan, Philip Mead, Wenche Ommundsen and Gillian Whitlock, among others, have begun to see Australian literature in ways that exceed or evade the space of the nation.[4] Australian literary studies, unlike American

---

2 Paul Giles, 'Transnationalism and Classic American Literature', *PMLA* 118.1 (2003): 62–77.

3 Wai-Chee Dimock and Lawrence Buell, eds, *Shades of the Planet: American Literature as World Literature* (Princeton, NJ: Princeton University Press, 2007); Paul Gilroy, *The Black Atlantic: Modernity and Double Consciousness* (Cambridge, Mass.: Harvard University Press, 1993); Joel Pace, et al., eds, *Transatlantic Romanticism: An Anthology of British, American and Canadian Literature 1767–1867* (Longman, 2006); David Shields, *Oracles of Empire: Poetry, Politics, and Commerce in British America 1690–1750* (Chicago: Chicago University Press, 1990); William Spengemann, *A New World of Words: Redefining Early American Literature* (New Haven: Yale University Press, 1994); and Robert Weisbuch, *Atlantic Double-Cross: American Literature and British Influence in the Age of Emerson* (Chicago: Chicago University Press, 1986).

4 Nicholas Birns, '"So Close and Yet So Far": Reading Australia Across the Pacific', *Australian Book Review* 309 (March 2009): 50–52; David Carter, 'After Post-Colonialism', *Meanjin* 66.2 (2007): 114–19; Leigh Dale, 'New Directions in Australian Literary Studies? Introduction', *Australian Literary Studies* 19.2 (October 1999): 131–35; Robert Dixon, 'Australian Fiction and the World

literary studies, always acknowledged that Australian literature was comparable to others, but the cultural nationalist critics of the mid-twentieth century registered the relevance of individual literary works in so far as they expressed an emergent Australian national identity that would declare its uniqueness by its maturity or difference from the parent English literature. Yet the rise of the internet and the ideological world of post-communism in the 1990s, instanced by the multinational conglomerates that took over most Australian publishing houses, meant that any supposed independence of Australian literature was over. If Australian literature is now irrevocably imbricated in a wider world, then so should its criticism and historiography. Like Giles' formulation of American literary space, Australian literature is also ragged at the edges, best seen in a series of relations with other literatures, not least American. Huggan begins his recent overview of Australian literature with the observation that 'Australian literary criticism continues to be hindered by its reliance on national(ist) tropes'. And yet, he argues,

> the 'postcoloniality' of national literatures such as Australia's is always effectively *transnational*, either derived from the apprehension of internal fracture ... or from a multiplied awareness of the nation's various engagements with other nations, and with the wider world. [5]

In the twenty-first century, then, critics and historians of both American and Australian literature are being challenged to find languages

---

Republic of Letters 1890–1950', in Peter Pierce, ed., *The Cambridge History of Australian Literature* (Cambridge: Cambridge University Press, 2009); Robert Dixon, 'Australian Literature-International Contexts', *Southerly* 67.1–2 (2007): 15–27; Ken Gelder, 'Proximate Reading: Australian Literature in Transnational Reading Frameworks', *JASAL* (2010); Graham Huggan, *Australian Literature: Postcolonialism, Racism, Transnationalism* (Oxford: Oxford University Press, 2007); Philip Mead, 'Nation, Literature, Location', in Peter Pierce, ed., *The Cambridge History of Australian Literature* (Cambridge: Cambridge University Press, 2009); Wenche Ommundsen, 'The Quest for Chineseness in Australian Literature', *Cultural Studies and Literary Theory* 16 (2008): 90–109; and Gillian Whitlock, 'New Directions in Australian Literary Studies?' *Australian Literary Studies* 19.2 (October 1999): 131–162.

5 Huggan, pp. vii and ix.

that attest to these new, polyvalent dimensions while not becoming lost in the rhetoric of what Huggan calls 'globaloney', and while still attending to nuanced, responsive analyses of literary texts. The essays in *Reading Across the Pacific* are written at this turning point in perceptions of American and Australian literatures. Both a product of and response to these new challenges, they seize the opportunity to reassess and reconfigure the conceptual geography of national literary spaces as they are re-formed by vectors that evade or exceed them, including the transnational, the local and the global. One of these vectors we call the transpacific.

The United States–Australian cultural relationship has often simply been assumed rather than theorised or empirically grounded. *Reading Across the Pacific* examines the concrete interaction between the two nations, shifting the emphasis from the broad cultural patterns that are often compared, to the specific networks, interactions, and crossings that have characterised Australian literature in the United States, American literature in Australia, and the many mediations and adjacencies that have accompanied this interaction. This entails shifting the characteristic perspective from two monadic nations facing each another across the Pacific to understanding the Pacific as a thread across which the two cultures have read each other, and focusing away from matters of direct literary influence to a broader range of responses, provocations and dialogues. Taking advantage of new interdisciplinary and theoretical possibilities, the essays nonetheless emphasise reading as a practice, whether done individually or collectively as a consumer, reviewer, or editor; whether performed in a private or public context. Principal questions to be considered are: why has the relationship, though always close and in some ways very obvious, always seemed under-scrutinised? Why has Australia received so little attention in US literary circles? What cultural factors (assumptions, fears, and inhibitions) are in play here? How have they changed over time as affected by political changes, or stylistic or genre transformations?

While each essay is individually conceived, they are collectively designed to reflect—and reflect upon—the following key topics applied to Australian–United States intellectual histories:

- wars, politics, literature
- Cold War Orientalism
- publishing history, book history and editing
- institutional crossings
- intellectual histories of the right and left
- feminism and gender
- cultures of poetry
- African diaspora connections
- print and digital cultures
- theatre and performance histories
- literature and popular culture
- travel writing
- America and modernity
- US–Australian prosopography
- economies of ecocriticism
- Australasia and regional identities
- English department cultures: the state(s) of the discipline
- comparative nationalisms.

Like *Shades of the Planet: American Literature as World Literature* (2007), edited by Lawrence Buell and Wai-Chee Dimock, *Reading Across the Pacific* takes American and Australian literatures out of the nationalist frameworks of the past and looks at them in a global context at once broader and deeper, while remaining critical of euphoric clichés about global culture. The essays are divided into five sections:

1. Transpacific: National Literatures and Transnationalism
2. Poetry and Poetics
3. Literature and Popular Culture
4. The Cold War
5. Publishing History and Transpacific Print Cultures.

'Transpacific: National Literatures and Transnationalism' includes essays by Nicholas Birns, Lawrence Buell and Paul Giles, and is concerned with how cultures of literary communication across the Pacific transcend or transgress national boundaries, being linked by other vectors such as Anglophone imperialism, environmental and ecocritical convergences, and individual cultural ambassadors with the daring to breach fixed discursive borders, such as the Americans C. Hartley Grattan and John Hope Franklin, or the Australians Shirley Hazzard and Randolph Stow. Australian and American authors discussed range from Benjamin Franklin to Gerald Murnane, from Mark Twain to Thea Astley, from Mary Wilkins Freeman to Christina Stead and Peter Carey.

'Poetry and Poetics' includes essays by Kevin Hart and Paul Kane, and focuses on how avant-garde poetics have provided a particularly fecund current with which to ferry ideas across the reaches of the Pacific. Issues featured in this section include communication and miscommunication between literary networks in Australia and America; the role of Asian poetries in both literatures (essential in their relation to innovative practice); and the inspirational role played by the New York School in the poetry of the Australians John Forbes and John Tranter.

'Literature and Popular Culture' extends from Benjamin Miller's study of African-American entertainers in colonial Australia and Elizabeth Webby's study of the role of newspapers in transmitting nineteenth-century popular fiction, to Paul Genoni's essay on the presence of Elvis Presley in transpacific popular culture, showing how music, visual culture and performance have been a major medium of cross-hemispheric contact, even when literary communication was intermittent.

The fourth section, 'The Cold War', includes essays by Michael Ackland, Bruce Bennett, Robert Dixon and Fiona Morrison. Too often discussion of globalisation concentrates on either the present or on periods long established as nodes of literary and cultural history—such as the 'long' nineteenth century—and often sidesteps the nearer past, which is a crucial precedent of present-day interactions. The essays in 'The Cold War' reveal the covert yet fascinating role Australian discourses played in the Cold War: the left politics of Christina Stead; the relation of Shirley Hazzard's fiction to the growth of area studies and the post-1945 vision of 'Asia'; the relation of Christopher Koch's spy fiction, including *The Year of Living Dangerously* and *The Memory*

Room, to fears of Asian invasion and the strange relation between Australia and the United States in Cold War constructions of Southern Hemisphere geostrategic space.

The final section, 'Publishing History and Transpacific Print Cultures', shows how nationalist rubrics are being replaced by a methodology that Katherine Bode and Robert Dixon have termed 'resourceful reading' or 'the new empiricism': concrete studies of the production, circulation and reception of books that yet do not eschew a literary framework, the place of the aesthetic, or the mandate of reading closely.[6] Drawing on important new-empirical and archival research projects in transpacific publishing history, chapters by David Carter, Carol Hetherington, Roger Osborne, and Louise Poland and Ivor Indyk provide new maps of Australian–American literary space. Furthermore, they address the concrete reception of books within that space from historically informed perspectives.

Although the material contained in these essays is as vast as the territorial expanse of the two countries combined and the even vaster ocean between them, certain themes do emerge. One is an increasingly globalising Australia. However much Australia may have wished to avoid opening itself up to the Pacific, and rather seeking to garrison itself from it—from fears of Russian naval invasion in the 1890s to later fears about Japanese and Chinese expansion—the twentieth century saw the Pacific emerge as a powerful arena for globalisation, however reluctantly embraced by still-colonial Australian attitudes. But globalisation did not always bring a more liberal, more tolerant, or more understanding point of view.

A number of the essays here see a US bias against Australia which, though less obvious and less racially tinged than West–East condescension, is nonetheless palpable, and has seriously limited attempts to read across the Pacific in a fully ramified way. As David Carter illustrates, the 1980s was arguably the golden age of Australian visibility in the United States, and what comes before and after raises the

6 Katherine Bode and Robert Dixon, eds, *Resourceful Reading: The New Empiricism, eResearch and Australian Literary Culture* (Sydney: Sydney University Press, 2009).

spectre of an arid plain of publications that, however trumpeted at the time, possessed neither short-term nor a long-term impact. Birns' essay points to some encouraging macro-political developments that may in time alter these conditions. But the aspiration to read across the Pacific has had to contend not just against the misunderstandings always latent in cross-cultural encounters but also an additional factor of indifference, of benign neglect. One way out of this may be to ventilate its existence rather than, as has been done in the past, bury it in politeness. Australia and the United States have not understood each other well enough, and the relationship has often been one-way. This needs to change.

The essays in *Reading Across the Pacific* were first presented as papers at the international symposium, 'Reading Across the Pacific: Australian–United States Intellectual Histories', convened by the editors at St Andrews College at the University of Sydney, 14–15 January 2010. The conference was hosted by Australian Literature at the University of Sydney. We wish to acknowledge the intellectual generosity and enthusiasm of delegates to the conference. The editors also acknowledge the contributions of staff at Sydney University Press, Susan Murray-Smith and Agata Mrva-Montoya, and the research, editorial and administrative assistance given by Lachlan Brown, Maisie Dubosarsky, Georgina Loveridge, Stephen Mansfield and Sam Moginie.

Robert Dixon, University of Sydney
Nicholas Birns, Eugene Lang College, The New School

Section 1

Transpacific: National Literatures and Transnationalism

1

Antipodal Propinquities? Environmental (Mis)Perceptions in American and Australian Literary History

Lawrence Buell

Since the mid-1800s, American literati have evinced recurring pulsations of interest in Australian writing and in Australia generally, even if Australia culture has rarely been for them a primary concern. Herman Melville's second novel, *Omoo*, makes an Australian doctor his footloose autobiographical hero's closest companion. Marcus Clarke's *For the Term of His Natural Life* was reprinted by the leading American publisher almost immediately after its appearance in book form. Mark Twain, the first American literary celebrity to visit Australia, at the turn of the twentieth century, praised Clarke and others of his generation for having brought into being 'a brilliant and vigorous literature' that 'must endure'[1]–and understandably so, since Rolf Boldrewood's *Robbery Under Arms* (1882) had recently accomplished something like Twain himself by infusing national fiction with the twang of vernacular speech.

Elsewhere in this same book, *Following the Equator,* Twain makes much of what he takes to be the affinities between Australian and American character. The Australians he met, he declares, 'did not seem to me to differ noticeably from Americans, either in dress, carriage, ways, pronunciations, inflections, or general appearance.' Both, unlike

1 M. Twain, *Following the Equator*, in Roy Blount, Jr, ed., *A Tramp Abroad, Following the Equator, Other Travels (*New York: Library of America, 2010), p. 549.

the English, like to socialise 'without stiffness or restraint'.[2] All this would have been music to Yankee ears as well as to Australian, since the United States at this time was still suffering from almost as heavy a dose of postcolonial cultural legitimation anxiety, although—to adapt A.A. Phillips' famous distinction—it expressed itself more often as 'strut' than 'cringe'.[3] Even Bernard O'Dowd did not approach the decibel level of Walt Whitman's rhetoric at its most jingoistic.

Twain was referring to white Australia, of course. He claimed that he'd never even seen an Aborigine. Scrolling forward a century to the contemporary dispensation of 'multi-cultural'-mindedness, however, the *prima facie* cross-national analogies continue to look strong, however differently framed. Anne-Marie Willis' diagnosis of Australia as one of 'those European colonies of settlement that developed an unfulfilled attachment to the lands they settled, an inadequate peace with the peoples they displaced, and an incomplete break with the cultures that gave rise to them'[4] largely holds for the cultural history of the United States as well, even if not wholly.

Willis' first proviso speaks to the origin of my own interest in Australian literature in the 1980s, when as background for a book on the literary history during the long nineteenth century of America's New England region—the country's far northeast—I spent a great deal of time researching what Franco Moretti might call 'the atlas of the provincial imaginary' in the US, the UK, and the Anglophone world at large.[5] I was struck by the ubiquity of texts (especially fiction) from the mid to late nineteenth century onward about lives led in isolated locales remote from metropolitan centres imagined as culturally quaint and thin to the point of grotesquerie—caught in premodern time-warps.

---

2 Twain, pp. 495–96.

3 A.A. Phillips, 'The Cultural Cringe' (1950), rpt., in Nicholas Jose et al. eds, *The Literature of Australia* (New York: W.W. Norton, 2009), p. 440.

4 A. Willis, *Illusions of Identity: The Art of Nation* (Sydney: Hale & Iremonger, 1993), p. 31.

5 Franco Moretti, *The Atlas of the European Novel 1800–1900* (London: Verso, 1998).

Two early examples from Australia and the US that lodged in my mind as especially provocative counterparts were Miles Franklin's autobiographical novel *My Brilliant Career* and a short tale by the contemporaneous American Mary Wilkins Freeman, 'A New England Nun'—not that these two works are much alike stylistically. Franklin's narrative rhetoric is mercurial and tempestuous, like her narrator-protagonist Sybilla, whereas Freeman's is tightly modulated and understated, like her titular heroine, the fastidiously reclusive Louisa Ellis. Both texts share, though, with variations I needn't belabour, the motif of extruding the ultimately rejected suitor to the opposite antipodes—a plot device that by limiting its reference to that event to the most laconic of allusions further underscores the remoteness of both protagonists and their home contexts. The imagined patches of American and Australian ground are each made to seem like the ends of the earth, and even more so in each other's eyes: the American text's image of Australia, and vice-versa. Each in the imagination of the other might as well be Mars. America is little more than a vast space for Harry Beacham to rush around in after Sybilla rejects him; Australia is the place where Freeman's faithful Joe Daggett must toil for fourteen years to make his fortune—we never learn how—during which time Louisa basically forgets him. This terseness becomes, in turn, a marker of the limited mental horizons of the figures—and communities—in the foreground.

The trope of socio-environmental enclosure that drives this kind of provincial imaginary—the image of sometimes secure though always somewhat culturally impoverished personal and community isolation at or beyond the verge of modern society—continues to run strong in both literary histories down to this day, as suggested by the striking family resemblances between, say, Thea Astley's *Drylands*, co-winner of the 2000 Miles Franklin Award, and the winner of the 2008 Pulitzer Prize for fiction, Elizabeth Strout's *Olive Kitteridge*, both of which take the form of a series of interlinked tales in which the most prominent figure is a prickly, sarcastic, self-focused, yet also vulnerable and not unkindly aging woman: a thinking person simmering in a small town outback, perpetually disaffected by its small-mindedness and general barbarity.

The persistence of this formation in both literatures seems explicable at least in part as, first, an after-effect of Euro-settler diaspora conditioning its subjects to conceive themselves as denizens of a frontier or periphery rather than as a centre of anything. Beyond this, and I suspect relatedly, it seems to follow from a subsequent, partially shared socio-geographical evolution of the cultural imaginary such that the dramatic history of techno-economic transformation from hardscrabble beginnings to advanced metropolitan society gets conceived not as a cosmopolitan triumph—or not merely that—but as another kind of de-realisation. To state this more plainly, both the United States and—to a still greater extent—Australia have developed as countries where the great majority of people live in urban enclaves near some coast with vast sparsely populated hinterlands into which relatively few of those metropolitan denizens venture for very long. Yet in both cases, Australia perhaps especially, that hinterland, whether we call it 'the bush' or (as Americans do) 'the heartland', has persistently maintained an iconic status as definer of the national.

Indeed for this Yankee critic, the landscapes refracted in Australian literary texts often seem to present themselves as a kind of limit case in this respect—that is, as an iconic formation basically familiar to me but extended to unfamiliar limits. Consider for example the sardonically bifurcated schema of A.D. Hope's much-quoted poem 'Australia', of 'cities, like five teeming sores' contrasted with 'desert' so 'savage and scarlet as no green hills dare'.[6] Hope could hardly have picked a more backhanded way of affirming the hinterland as the place from whence future prophets might come. Aversion both to hinterland and to metropolis are familiar themes in US literary and intellectual history as well;[7] but one looks in vain in our canonical literature to find anything approximating this pitch of toxic intensity, except for some of H.L. Mencken's satirical asides or Thoreau's wry dismissal of the victims

6 A.D. Hope, 'Australia' (1939), rpt., in Nicholas Jose et al., eds, *The Literature of Australia* (New York: Norton, 2009), p. 524.

7 A. Hilfer, *The Revolt from the Village, 1915–1930* (Chapel Hill, NC: University of North Carolina Press, 1969); M. White and L. White, *The Intellectual Versus the City from Thomas Jefferson to Frank Lloyd Wright* (Cambridge, MA: Harvard University Press, 1962).

of the Puritan work ethic run to excess: 'From the desperate city you go into the desperate country, and have to console yourself with the bravery of minks and muskrats.'[8]

So far I've been discussing Euro-settler imagination exclusively, of course, for that's where the print culture history in each case effectively starts; but obviously that's not where it remains.

At first, the figures in the foreground, in canonical Australian writing particularly, appear racially quite homogeneous, meaning in most cases also white, with exceptions, like Barbara Baynton's 'Billy Skywonkie' and the fiction of Xavier Herbert. Quantitatively the same still holds for both literatures, *Olive Kitteridge* being a good example on the American side. But for the cultural avant-gardes if not the average citizenry of both countries whiteness has long since ceased to stand unproblematically as the 'unmarked' ethnicity any more than 'he' can be deployed unselfconsciously as the default pronoun for humankind at large. Much of the strong recent Australian fiction seems to have paralleled—whether or not intentionally—the multi-ethnic turn in modern and contemporary white American writing by using that old trope of the enclosed remote enclave of white settlers in ways that evoke the repressed history of violent aboriginal displacement to undermine its retrogressive solidarity—as in Thea Astley's *Drylands*, David Malouf's *Remembering Babylon,* and Andrew McGahan's *The White Earth*.

No less striking than the performance in these texts of the fragmentation from within, of the image of the closed community's tranquil or stagnant or asphyxiating self-containment is their co-ordinate strategy of reconceiving their chosen locale as networked within wider and increasingly multiplex loops, ultimately not just national but planetary, so as to create a kind of double vision whereby the remote place in the foreground oscillates between seeming the end of the earth and a nodal point at which world-historical force fields converge. In recent Australian literature, perhaps the *ne plus ultra* is Alexis Wright's *Carpentaria,* which parodistically plays upon the image of the woebegone northwest Queensland town of Desperance as one of those intractably provincial outposts that from the standpoint

8 H. Thoreau, *Walden,* J. Lyndon Shanley, ed. (Princeton: Princeton University Press, 1971), p. 8.

of the metropoli to the south scarcely exists, but reconceives it transformatively, first as the ancestral home ground of Aborigines like the Phantom family, threatened with displacement by the white encroachers; then as an the site of 'the biggest mine of its type in the world'[9] with repercussions that extend worldwide to the transnational conglomerate's headquarters in the ultimate metropolis of New York. After evangelist-incendiary Mozzie Fishman and his impetuous protégé Will Fishman blow up the mine, the locale metamorphoses yet again into a mythic prototype of anagogic proportions as the town gets swept away—amidst glimmerings of hope that a new generation might build better—by a gigantic cyclone and flood that is seen literally as the work of the region's notoriously volatile and extreme weather patterns but infused with a larger-than-life sense of the wrath of autochthonic deific forces and (or am I imagining things?) a hint of anthropogenic climate change.

Carpentaria's grandly extravagant transformation of the benighted remote community into the centre of the universe seems all the more notable to an Americanist grazing through the realm of Australian letters for its cousinship to such contemporary stateside classics as Leslie Silko's *Ceremony,* a cornerstone work of the so-called Native American Renaissance. In that novel, what at first seems an isolated case study of a traumatised, dysfunctional war veteran returning to a homeland nearly as remote and immiserated as the Aboriginal shantytowns on the periphery of Desperance is likewise made to blossom into a drama of epochal import and global scope—partly with the aid of an offbeat Native shaman reminiscent of the weird cross-cultural charisma of Alexis Wright's Fishman, with his 'Clint Eastwood face'[10] and his zest for popular American music, and partly by the historical contingency of the particular tribal lands in Silko's novel having once been the epicentre for another key extractive industry: uranium ore, for the atomic bombs dropped on Japan.

Even if the affinities in the deployment or inversion of the remote outpost trope in these two novels aren't a matter of influence, neither

9 A. Wright, *Carpentaria: A Novel* (New York: Simon and Schuster, 2008), p. 411.

10 Wright, p. 136.

are they happenstance. Among other significances they bespeak an increasingly confident and sophisticated grasp of the creative opportunities for writers aware of being positioned at what was traditionally thought to be the sociogeographical margins to become the leading figures in what one Americanist critic has called the new 'global literary pluralism'[11] by reconceiving the histories of place-based minoritised cultures in planetary and world-historical terms. Key to this process for both Silko and for Wright is an insurgent reinvention of aboriginalism. Such revisionist practice is by no means limited only to the US and Australia, either. Within Anglophone literature alone one could just as easily look to New Zealand (e.g. Keri Hulme), Western Samoa (e.g. Albert Wendt), India (Amitav Ghosh's *The Hungry Tide*)—indeed, all the way back to the first postcolonial Anglophone text to achieve classic status, Nigerian novelist China Achebe's *Things Fall Apart* (1958). Imagined indigeneity, however, surely need not be a requisite for all literary projects undertaking to renegotiate 'margin' as 'centre'. As Wright herself states in her essay on how *Carpentaria* came to be, although

> the characters are Indigenous people in this novel, they might easily have been any scattered people from any part of the world who share a relationship with their spiritual ancestors and heritage, or for that matter, any Australian–old or new.[12]

Thinking similarly about the ultimate horizon of possibilities for place-centric fictions of an ecocultural memory built upon a sense of dispersal or displacement, one wonders if it might prove to be the case that writers across the board from a country like Australia where the dominant cultural group remains conscious of the effort required of settler culture to free itself from the long-embedded practice of thinking of 'home' as elsewhere might be especially well positioned to take the lead in this way of re-imagining the global stakes of the local.

---

11 M. McGurl, *The Program Era: Postwar Fiction and the Rise of Creative Writing* (Cambridge: Harvard University Press, 2009), p. 329.

12 A. Wright, 'On Writing *Carpentaria*,' *Heat* 13 (2007): 84.

To that hopeful-sounding prognosis it might be replied that Australian literary culture has to deal with a second elephant in the room: the spectre of the US as the new imperium, which *Carpentaria* also acknowledges by locating the mining company's headquarters in New York. Although *that* book conjures up corporate America only to humiliate it, obviously American *cultural* capital is not so easily exorcised, nor such capital's attendant literary networking and publishing infrastructures. The eviscerating effect of such dependence is showcased in Peter Carey's hilarious but also rather mordant and hangdog tale 'American Dreams', a rueful allegory of Australians having to perform for American audiences, if they wish to get a hearing at all, by fashioning quaintly retro simulacra of bygone small-town life. In order to attract tourists from the America of their fantasies, the characters in the story contort themselves into nonstop reenactors of themselves in conformity with the eccentric Mr Gleason's amazing miniature model of the daily life of the community, which an enterprising local purchases from his widow and 'charges five American dollars admission' to behold.[13] Yet a special kind of originality might also be claimed for such self-reflexiveness: as more likely occur to an Australian writer than an American, where the propensity for reinventing paradigmatic bygone small towns in slightly satiric but basically straight-faced ways seems unstoppable, even to the point of generating actual planned community projects like the Disney Corporation's Celebration, Florida. Even when Americans import iconic Anglo-European place-forms wholesale, we seem to do so shamelessly—creating imitation German villages in Wisconsin; neo-Elizabethan Globe theatres in Stratford Connecticut, and elsewhere; and reassembling the original London Bridge stone by stone as the centrepiece for an imitation English theme park in Arizona.

Yet these pilferings also attest to a certain ongoing anxiety on the American side apropos the sufficiency of its own national iconography. Jean Baudrillard's cartoon reduction of the national landscape in his 1986 *America* to two paradigmatic place-forms—metropolis and desert—can't be dismissed simply as Gallic magisterial hauteur

13 Peter Carey, 'American Dreams,' in *Collected Stories* (St Lucia: University of Queensland Press, 1994), p. 180.

masquerading as high theory. It has its counterpart in a longstanding tendency among the American intelligentsia. A prime instance, which will be the springboard for the rest of these reflections is the dramatic shift since the turn of the twentieth century in the cultural imaginary of America's vast trans-Appalachian central plains—meaning much of the drainage basin of the Mississippi-Missouri river systems from Ohio and Indiana to the east, westward to the Rocky Mountains from western Colorado north to Montana. Roughly speaking, the story of the evolving national imaginary concerning the non-urban portion of this territory—which includes much of the national farmbelt as well as much of its arid land ranching country as you move farther west—is a story of drastic image-recoding as the twentieth century unfolds from virgin land of infinite promise not only as breadbasket but also as cultural and population centre to the image of cultural and potentially also ecological wasteland. So, for example, when the New England poet William Cullen Bryant—the so-called American Wordsworth, writing a little before his Australian counterpart Charles Harpur—beholds a prairie for the first time he conjures up a split image of 'unshorn fields, boundless and beautiful' and a future wave of well-behaved, energetic agriculturalists who 'soon shall fill' and cultivate 'these deserts', as he calls them.[14] A half-century later, Walt Whitman celebrated 'The Prairie States' in his poem of that title as:

> A newer garden of creation, no primal solitude,
> Dense, joyous, modern, populous millions, cities and farms,
> With iron interlaced, composite, tied, many in one,
> By all the world contributed—freedom's and law's and thrift's society,
> The crown and teeming paradise, so far, of time's accumulations,
> To justify the past.[15]

---

14 W.C. Bryant, 'The Prairies', in *Poems* (Philadelphia: Carey and Hart, 1845), pp. 218, 221.

15 W. Whitman, *Leaves of Grass: Comprehensive Reader's Edition.* Harold W. Blodgett and Sculley Bradley, ed. (New York: New York University Press, 1965), p. 402.

But since the 1900s, this image—which lay behind Chicago's aspirations at the time to become the nation's first metropolis—has been completely dethroned. Especially since Sinclair Lewis' 1920 novel *Main Street,* which satirically portrays his eastern heroine's misadventures trying to negotiate the small world of Gopher Prairie, Minnesota, the mid-continent plains region from Ohio westward to the Rocky Mountains has become stereotypically imaged as insipid, lonely, and retrograde. During my two decades of teaching American studies at Harvard, which is located on the North Atlantic seaboard and attracts an overwhelmingly bicoastal clientele, I've repeatedly contended against an entrenched skepticism of any meaningful cultural life in the vast expanse of territory that lies between the Appalachian Mountains of the east and the Sierra Nevadas of California, with the possible exception of a few urban pockets such as Chicago, Minneapolis and Denver. I exaggerate slightly of course, but not much. These prejudices have been seconded by generations of flat-country self-deprecations, by its literati: such as North Dakota-born William Gass' story 'In the Heart of the Heart of the Country' (1968), which begins with a wry inversion of Yeats' 'Sailing to Byzantium': 'So I have sailed the seas and come … to B … a small town fastened to a field in Indiana.'[16] Or Wright Morris' novel *Ceremony at Lone Tree* (1959), whose Nebraska landscape looks like this: 'To the east … a lone tree, a water tank, sheets of rain and heat lightning: to the west a strip of torn screen blurs the view … As a rule, there is nothing to see, and if there is, one doubts it.'[17]

The reasons for this image shift are multiple. One contributory factor has no doubt been land abuse and deterioration through overfarming and overgrazing, which of course applies to Australia too. As early as America's so-called Dust Bowl years of the 1930s, dramatised in John Steinbeck's novel *The Grapes of Wrath,* Australian biologist Francis Ratcliffe was prophetically warning that even the best-balanced Australian pastureland couldn't withstand 'the strain … placed on it

16 W. Gass, *In the Heart of the Heart of the Country and Other Stories* (New York: Harper, 1968), p. 142.

17 W. Morris, *Ceremony at Lone Tree* (Lincoln, NE: University of Nebraska Press, 1973 [1960]), p. 7.

by pastoral settlement'.[18] But a related and doubtless more significant long-run cause of the cultural recoding of the American plains is the demographic shift ensuing from transition from predominantly agricultural to industrial economy between the late nineteenth century and the mid-twentieth—of which authorial outmigration has been one tiny sliver. Industrialisation also contributed to the hyperconcentration of the Australian population in a handful of urban metropoli, although the extreme aridity of Australia's 'dead heart' ensured a much less serious hearing and shorter shelf life for the fantasy of an interior populated by numerous white settlers.[19] In the United States, where hinterland ecological conditions are less harsh, the transition from industrial to information economy combined with new-found oil and other mineral wealth has arrested and even reversed the outmigration effect in certain districts, but with little net benefit thus far for the central arid plains and still less for the 'plains imaginary'. Today a huge north-to-south oval district from the Canada line down through the western Dakotas and eastern Montana almost to Texas has become so depopulated as to have fallen below the two-person-per-square-mile density level required for the American frontier to be declared closed in 1890, leading to calls by one group of American environmentalists that a tract nearly half the size of New South Wales be set aside for nature preserve as the 'Buffalo Commons'.[20]

Little is likely to come of a plan so grandiose. It warrants mention simply as one instance of counter-cultural transvaluation of the American plains imaginary after the golden age of agriculture—or what was supposed to be such. The midwestern creative writers mentioned before actually participate in this to some extent, reacting as it were against the image of a vacant, featureless landscape where nothing

18 F. Ratcliffe, *Flying Fox and Drifting Sand: The Adventures of a Biologist in Australia* (New York: McBride, 1938), pp. 331–32.

19 D.T. Rowland, 'Theories of Urbanization in Australia,' *Geographical Review* 67 (April 1977): 167–68.

20 D. Popper and F. Popper, 'The Great Plains: From Dust to Dust', *Planning* (December 1987), n.p., available at: www.planning.org/25anniversary/planning/1987dec.htm [Accessed September 2010].

much happens that they themselves have helped perpetuate. They seek to convert that nothing into dreamscapes of various kinds—as with the opening scene of Morris' novel, which pictures an old man peering through a smudged window from inside the Lone Tree Hotel at the plains landscape beyond, but mainly beholding 'the scenic props of his own mind', such that 'the emptiness of the plain' becomes a 'metaphysical landscape'[21] of austere but surprising plenitude. This kind of move calls to mind the two contemporary authors from our two respective countries who seem to me to have done the most fascinatingly intricate work of plains re-imagination: the American environmental writer who publishes under the name of William Least Heat Moon (a.k.a. William Trogdon) and the Australian metafictionist Gerald Murnane.

Least Heat Moon's massive *PrairyErth* (1991) is the most ambitious literary effort of the past quarter century to take American rural Great Plains eco-culture seriously. It's a 600-page literary ethnography and natural history of a single, depopulated hardscrabble district in the state of Kansas: Chase County, which lies at the geographical centre of what we Yankees call the lower forty-eight states. For Murnane, the key books are of course *The Plains* and *Inland*, the former more widely read but the latter the one I especially wish to seize upon here, both as the more complex albeit less concentrated achievement and as recurringly invoking the same topography and almost the very same locales that Morris and Least Moon evoke, as *Inland*'s split-personality narrator imagines himself in correspondence or rivalry with various American counterparts, at one point even projecting himself vicariously into that setting.

As the foregoing mini-description of *PrairyErth* implies, its stylistic register differs sharply from *Inland*'s. It is encyclopaedic rather than minimalist; it leans toward neo-realist documentary rather than Calvinoesque fabulism; it's packed with anecdotes of encounters with earthy local characters granted far more autonomy than the spectral figures in Murnane's monodramas; and the narrative voice has a hearty, populist-vernacular twang quite unlike Murnane's fastidiously

21 W. Morris, *Ceremony at Lone Tree* (Lincoln, NE: University of Nebraska Press, 1973 [1960]), pp. 4–5.

intellectualised voice. Taken together, the two books tend if anything to exaggerate the (considerable) difference in the degree to which settlement of the two continental hinterlands was and remains dominated by an oligarchy of land barons. But all these discrepancies only add piquance to the complementarity.

An Australian literature specialist might at this point wish to delve into the paradoxes of Murnane being at once 'perhaps the most fully manifest example of a persuasive Australian Internationalism in fiction'[22] yet so tenaciously lococentric as to refuse almost all forms of travel; and, secondly, as idiosyncratic to the point of solipsism yet also exemplary in 'the extent to which he embeds his quest for self-discovery in images that convey a rich sense of meaning associated with being "Australian"'—'associated with landscape, exploration, space, emptiness, home.'[23] As an Americanist of ecocritical bent, though, what I shall pursue instead is the transnational eco-logic behind *Inland*'s palimpsest of converging plains narratives from around the world: most especially Hungary, the United States, and above all Australia.

Perhaps the book's recurring preoccupation with *American* landscapes, place names and, tangentially, literature might up to a point be diagnosed as a variant case of Peter Carey's Australians dreaming American dreams. But two related considerations suggest otherwise. First, the crucial landprint animating *Inland*'s sweeping vision of grasslands as the dominant terrestrial ecology is clearly the storied tract of Australian territory stretching northward from Victoria through western New South Wales and Queensland.[24] *Inland*'s primary, more autobiographical narrator makes a virtue of his self-positioning at the southern metropolitanised verge in the process of encroaching on this iconic territory, and thus peripheral both spatially *and* historically,

22 N. Birns, 'Introduction', in Gerald Murnane, *Inland* (Sydney: Sydney University Press, 2008), p. iv.

23 P. Genoni, 'Gerald Murnane', in Nicholas Birns and Rebecca McNeer, eds, *A Companion to Australian Literature Since 1900* (Rochester NY: Camden House, 2007), p. 302.

24 T. Griffiths, 'The Outside Country', in T. Bonyhady and T. Griffiths, *Words for Country: Landscape & Language in Australia* (Sydney: University of New South Wales Press, 2002), pp. 222–44.

which befits his project of fashioning a phantasmal version of that inland sharply different from, say, the native daughter approach of Jill Ker Conway's memoir *The Road from Coorain*, a no less haunting evocation of interior grasslands landscape in its own much more literal vein. Murnane's deployment of his narrator's marginal position *via* a strategy of discursive metafiction allows him at once to de-realise through the filter of suburban fantasy and to reinstate through the magnifying lens of balked desire this particularly iconic subset of native hinterland, such that in *Inland* physical territory montages into dream, yet dream opens up into grand fantasy of an all-encompassing planetary grassland.

A second and related consideration that argues against imagining Murnane as particularly daunted by American or anybody else's cultural capital is his extraordinarily idiosyncratic reading of American literature and film. Devouring western movies as a prepubescent, what fixated him—so he recalls—was the 'seemingly empty land' in the background 'all but overlooked by the makers of American films'. Later on, Jack Kerouac's *On the Road* hit him, so he writes, 'like a blow to the head that wipes out all memory of the recent past'; but the way Murnane actually read this book, or so he claims, was not for the fast-paced plot, not for the soft-porn Beat Generation bohemianism, but for the landscapes—and not the featured urban settings, either, but the wide open spaces the characters rush through glancing at occasionally, so that in his imagination Murnane placed Kerouac 'not in New York City or San Francisco but somewhere between the Mississippi and the watershed of the Rocky Mountains'.[25] This is a truly bizarre reading of *On the Road*. Even I, who also often raise collegial eyebrows by my insistence on looking disproportionately at setting relative to everything else in a literary text, can barely force myself to read Kerouac that way. But the point that deserves stressing here isn't the perversity of Murnane's reading but its congruence with *Inland*'s main narrator's vision of America as 'so vast and so richly patterned with streams and towns and prairies that I will never have time for sea'.[26] This seems to

25 G. Murnane, 'On the Road to Bendigo: Kerouac's Australian Life', in *Invisible but Enduring Lilacs* (Sydney: Giramondo, 2005), pp. 10, 12, 19.

26 G. Murnane, *Inland* (London: Faber & Faber, 1989), p. 47.

express not envy but delight at having found (as also on the plains of Hungary and the disparate fictional landscapes of Hardy and Emily Brontë, and with the same obsessiveness as when reading Kerouac) that *Inland* conflates the landscape into 'one huge grassland'[27]—an *ur*-landscape glimpsed beneath and past the human, re-engineered, actual landscape near home.

This comparative grasslands consciousness starts to make *Inland* look a bit like a latter-day counterpart to Mark Twain's *Following the Equator*—not for any assertion of national character parallels, which seemingly interest Murnane not at all, but for the perception of kindred landform. This landform possesses dual ontology as both phenomenological space –'prairie-grasslands [as the space] where you and I dream of coming into our own'[28]—and as ecological space that, when you begin to gaze at it, has a way of evanescing to the vanishing point. This is apparent in *Inland*'s lingering near the start and then at the very end on graveyards as remnant sites of once-virgin but now much-diminished prairie: first, the Hungarian narrator musing about his suppositious expatriate editor in a South Dakota graveyard looking for native species; then, in the final scene, the Australian narrator visiting the spot where he himself plans to be buried. But the phenomenological prairie of infinite promise and the vestigial factical prairie reduced by urban sprawl to a few plants in a graveyard also hint at *cultural* affinity, insofar as they gesture both toward the history of frontier era grasslands as a site of infinite desire and to the ecological upshot of that desire, that is to say violent large-scale land transformation or land abuse. Unexpectedly relevant here is what the primary narrator claims to be 'the chief pleasure of my life': 'to see two places I had thought far apart lying … in one place'.[29] One way he indulges this pleasure is through toponymic puns, relishing for example that 'the name of a city north of Melbourne County might also be the name of … the county seat of Rock County, Nebraska'—which is true to geographical fact although the text doesn't state the

27 Murnane, p. 119.

28 Murnane, p. 64.

29 Murnane, p. 123.

actual placename: Basset.[30] Whether purposefully or not, such motions of the mind conjure up the prehistory of antipodal settler cultures consanguineously familiarising hitherto nameless landscapes by christening them with the same repertoire of placenames—and forcing their presence on the landscape in more exploitative ways in the process. A related settler fantasy that *Inland* evokes and incipiently subjects to metacritique is the stereotypical masculinist metaphorisation of land as female body anatomised by ecofeminist critics of American frontier discourse such as Annette Kolodny and Louise Westling—although *Inland*'s reminiscences of prepubescent sexual urges often seem more self-indulgent than ironic.

Turning now to *PrairyErth*, we find a much more emphatically outdoor book than *Inland* (or for that matter *The Plains*). Whereas Murnane's dreamers prefer to behold landscape from indoor sanctuaries, Least Heat Moon is a travel writer who has his persona saunter seriatim through the ten townships of Chase County, Kansas, site of 'the last remaining grand expanse of tallgrass prairie in America'[31]. Landscape takes on more topographical and also historical specificity than Murnane gives even to the near-home Melbourne neighbourhoods of *Inland*.

Yet in *PrairyErth* as well, landscapes have a way of continually dissolving into dream spaces proffered as counter-intuitively charismatic in the face of the orthodox aesthetic preference, as both writers see it, for seascape as opposed to dry flatlands. Rather like *Inland*'s narrators immured in their respective studies and surrounded by books about grasslands, *PrairyErth* starts each major section with a plethora of *Moby-Dick*-like extracts from what the persona calls the 'Commonplace Book', which immediately define landscape as an artifact of competing constructs. This point gets further reinforced throughout by hyperconsciousness of the landscape arrangements of today as the upshot of Thomas Jefferson's late-eighteenth-century survey of the trans-Appalachian US into an immense grid of rectilinear

30 Murnane, p. 85.

31 W. Least Heat Moon, *PrairyErth: A Deep Map* (Boston: Houghton Mifflin, 1991), p. 12.

land parcels—a quintessential act of Enlightenment hubris that created the checkerboard pattern of settlement everyone notices flying over the continental United States on a clear day. Chase County is microcosmic of this enormous macro-region, including its profoundly ambiguous ecological and civilisational effects—to which the book pays a combination of homage and parody by making the narrator's journey studiously follow the 'grain of the grid'.[32]

As a result, even though *PrairyErth* saturates the reader with lococentric landscape detail in a way quite unlike *Inland*, it too becomes a *mise-en-abîme*. Near the end, the persona achieves a flickering consummation in the form of momentary escape from settler-culture rectilinearity and linear historical time when he discovers a few traces of the aboriginal primordium. He meets up with the district's remnant Indian population and finds the old Native trail that cuts across the grid. For the first and only time he experiences a sense of liberation from it. But he's also forced to realise that his book has been driven much more by a mental 'gestalt' than by the *is*-ness of the place itself, and that 'Ninety-nine-point nine to the ninth decimal of what has ever happened here isn't in the book'.[33] This elusiveness he ascribes not only to his project but also to the region inherently. 'The prairie', he declares, 'is not a topography that shows its all but rather a vastly exposed place of concealment'.[34] So *PrairyErth* too becomes a book that simultaneously mystifies and de-realises the space it evokes.

Least Heat Moon's encyclopaedic documentary panorama offers a far more strenuous and complex engagement with environmental memory at the sociohistorical level than does Murnane, who leaves it almost wholly to the reader to posit the link between his solipsistic narrators' overcharged plains fixations and the lure of the plains for settler imagination. But *PrairyErth*'s accomplishment also comes at cost of hyper-concentration on the intra-national story of grasslands vicissitudes to the exclusion of *Inland*'s more cosmopolitan rendering of grasslands ecology and also grasslands topophilia.

32 Least Heat Moon, pp. 279–87.

33 Least Heat Moon, p. 615.

34 Least Heat Moon, p. 28.

Tim Flannery's compelling environmental history of Australasia *The Future Eaters* will help us begin to put these contrasts in a broader comparative frame. Like many other contemporary environmental historians and critics, Flannery rightly insists on historically nuanced ecological literacy as crucial to the fashioning of a viable sense of national identity for the future's sake. By this criterion, Least Heat Moon rates far above Murnane. But no less crucial to Flannery's argument is his insistence that eco-cultural imaginaries transcend national borders—as in this comment on the striking durability in Australian imagination of the mythic figure of the stockman.

> Give [the stockman] a moustache and maté … and you have an Argentinian gaucho. Give him fringed leggings and a six shooter and you have a North American cowboy. It is no coincidence that stockman, cowboy, and gaucho all come from newly settled continents. For just as the Australian grasslands were cleared of their diprotodons by the first invaders, the prairie and the pampas lost their native [animals] when the first Indians arrived … Thus, the grasslands of all three continents presented a bounty that had not been reaped for millennia. The stockman/gaucho/cowboy arose to take advantage of a particular, short-lived ecological niche which resulted from this situation.[35]

Murnane's forte is precisely the gift of envisaging this landscape of desire as a landscape at once national and planetary in scope, and furthermore with the power to maintain its hold as obsession that lingers on beyond the dispensation of the stockman into the dispensation of suburbia.

Perhaps fortuitously, these contrasts between our two grassland geniuses tally with the fact that the conference that served as launching pad for this symposium on 'Reading Across the Pacific' back and forth between Australia and the United States should have been held in Sydney rather than New York. For it is certain that American writers and American American-ists are both much more likely to be

35 T. Flannery, *The Future Eaters: An Ecological History of the Australian Lands and People* (Chatswood, NSW: Reed Books, 1994), p. 393.

oblivious to their Australian counterparts than vice-versa—with rare exceptions like environmental historian Thomas Dunlap on the subject of comparative parkland policy in the Anglophone world or ecocritic Tom Lynch, who studies the phenomenon of 'xerophilia', or attraction to dryland cultures, in both the US and Australia. As long as the relative political and cultural capital remains as it now is, this asymmetry will likely persist; but to the extent it does, the American literati and professoriat will likely be the losers, not only because of missing out on exceptional talents like Gerald Murnane, Alexis Wright, David Malouf, Thea Astley, and many others but also on the advantage of the aesthetic, psychosocial, and ecological revelations that come from seeing one's homeground even—or at times indeed especially—in so tantalisingly oblique and encrypted a way as *Inland* does through the lens of the antipodal other.

But it is misleading to imply that the discrepant strategies of plains imagination in *Inland* and *PrairyErth* are finally understood as symptomatic of their respective national-cultural imaginaries. Quite apart from and extending beyond that, they suggestively anticipate turn-of-the-twenty-first-century debates as to the desirability and viability in a globalising era of place-attachment, whether on the local or the planetary scale. The valorisation of small-scale bioregional place-attachment by 'first-wave' 1990s ecocriticism is under challenge from advocates of an 'eco-cosmopolitanism' that, as Ursula Heise puts it in the most forceful statement of this position to date, would 'attempt to envision individuals and groups as part of planetary "imagined communities" of both human and nonhuman kinds'.[36] On the face of it, *PrairyErth* might seem to be trying to model that traditional model of intensely local place-attachment, as against *Inland*'s much more abstruse and free-ranging reconnaissance of grasslands across continents. Yet the very opposite could be argued with even greater cogency. *Inland*'s primary narrator, for all his mental globe-trotting, remains far more doggedly attached to the Melbourne locale the text foregrounds than *PrairyErth*'s chronicler of Chase County—neither his birthplace nor his

36 U. Heise, *Sense of Place and Sense of Planet: The Environmental Imagination of the Global* (Oxford University Press, 2008), p. 61.

residence. In declaring primary and overriding ecological allegiance to grasslands neither text fits either within an old-style frame of traditional place attachment or an eco-cosmopolitan frame. On the contrary, what gives them special claim to extended examination here as representative acts of contemporary environmental imagination (despite their pronounced idiosyncrasies and their likely unfamiliarity to many who peruse this essay) is their sinuousness and inventiveness. They elegantly explore, without premature foreclosure, a number of questions about the meaning and ethics of place-attachment, of inhabitance, of environmental consciousness and belonging that are of the greatest import to those for whom neither the stolidity of lococentrism nor the abstraction of planetary citizenship will suffice.

2

Antipodean America: Charles Brockden Brown, New Holland, and the Constitution of US Literature

Paul Giles

For various historical reasons, the whole idea of an antipodean America has been largely neglected. When relations between the United States and Australia or New Zealand are considered today, it is more usually in the context of the supposed 'Americanisation' of the southern continent, and there has of course been a considerable amount of work on how Australia became Americanised in different ways after World War II.[1] But there are obvious power plays involved in such an assumption of one-way cultural traffic, with the Director of the Yale Center for British Art, Patrick McCaughey, introducing a 1998 exhibition of American and Australian landscape painting by claiming 'it would be difficult both imaginatively and organisationally to interest a major American art museum in an exhibition solely of nineteenth- or twentieth-century Australian art'. McCaughey continued by suggesting that in 'order for the antipodean voice to be heard, it has to come out of isolation and be ranged with other voices', since 'there is and perhaps always will be an imbalance in the intellectual and cultural relationship between Australia and the United States': Australians in general are familiar with American culture, he claimed, whereas '[o]nly a tiny minority of Americans know about Australia, let alone its art and literature'.[2]

1 See, for example: P. Bell and R. Bell, eds, *Americanization and Australia*, (Sydney: UNSW Press, 1998).

2 P. McCaughey, 'Likeness and unlikeness: the American–Australian experience',

McCaughey's assumptions would undoubtedly have been coloured by his own Australian provenance, but what such a one-dimensional perspective altogether overlooks is the fact that these two cultures have never been so entirely distinct. On the contrary, there are manifold ways in which Australasia has formed a shadow self in US national narratives, with the trajectories of the two countries having long been imbricated within each other.

The reasons for the relative invisibility of the southern continent within the culture of the United States are bound up not just with simple questions of population density but, more crucially, with the manner in which the intellectual matrix of American literature has long resisted its own postcolonial status. The emphasis upon declarations of independence that has been endemic to both literary and political aspects of US culture since 1787 has made the nation intellectually uncomfortable with its own former colonial incarnation, within which the claims of 'freedom' were not part of any constitutional framework. In this sense, the spectre of Australasia has haunted the United States as the colonial kingdom it might have been, but no longer was. Both the United States and Australia thus exist historically in a triangular relationship with Great Britain: the United States was the country that ceremonially detached itself from the mother country through General Cornwallis' surrender at Yorktown in 1781, while Australia was the colony invented by the British in 1788, at least in part, to atone for the loss of its North American colonies—and also because, with Virginia gone, it had nowhere else to send its felons. The purpose here, then, is not of course to claim that American and Australian literature run simply in parallel, but to suggest points of convergence and divergence between these former British colonies so as to elucidate ways in which they have both had to negotiate, implicitly or explicitly, with colonial legacies across two centuries.

Although this is to cast the subject of American literature in a different light, it is not to approach this field merely from a 'transpacific' perspective. While transpacific routes have played a significant part in

---

in E. Johns, ed., *New Worlds from Old: 19th Century Australian and American Landscapes* (Canberra: National Gallery of Australia and Hartford, CT: Wadsworth Atheneum, 1998), pp. 20–21.

US culture since the days of the nineteenth-century whaling industry, it is also important to recognise how America and Australia have frequently been bound together in more circuitous geographic ways. During the first half of the nineteenth century, the most common route from Australia to London or New York was westward around the Cape of Good Hope, across the Indian and Atlantic oceans; it was not until the middle of the century, after the publication of Matthew Maury's *Physical Geography of the Sea* in 1855, that it was generally realised how the eastward route around Cape Horn, though longer in terms of nautical miles, actually took considerably less time, on account of prevailing wind and ocean currents, and therefore saved money.[3] In the first half of the nineteenth century, Australia was thus linked to America as much through a transatlantic as a transpacific axis. This meant also that in terms of strategic world geography Australia became closely associated for America with its Indian trade, which flourished between 1790 and 1860. After the new United States had been cut off from West Indian commerce under the terms of the Paris peace treaty with Britain in 1783, it began to look elsewhere for new and profitable markets, and it was then that American trade with India became fully established.[4] Indeed, by 1792, President Washington had commissioned a consul for India to render aid to American ships and sailors, and by the 1850s the value of imports from India had increased dramatically, as had the number of voyages to America from the Indian Ocean. All this was complicated by the way America and India conceived of themselves historically as, in Susan S. Bean's words, 'odd step-siblings, brought together by the colonial ambitions of Great Britain'; the fact that General Cornwallis, notwithstanding his defeat at Yorktown, went on subsequently to serve for seven years from 1786 to 1793 as governor-general of India would only have heightened this sense of transcontinental irony.[5] If empires

3 For sailing times in the nineteenth century, see: R.D. Knowles, 'Transport Shaping Space: Differential Collapse in Time-Space', *Journal of Transport Geography* 14 (2006): 409.

4 On American trade with India, see: G. Bhagat, *Americans in India, 1784–1860* (New York: New York University Press, 1970).

5 S.S. Bean, *Yankee India: American Commercial and Cultural Encounters with*

are about interconnections and 'affinities', as David Cannadine suggests, the broader legacy of empire is also about ghosts and shadows, where icons that resonate in another world conjure up historical roads not taken.[6] The Salem East India Marine Society, which was founded in 1799 after fifteen years of direct trade with Asia, commissioned a portrait of Captain James Cook to hang in their meeting hall, and it was the spirit of this British explorer, the legendary 'founder' of Australia, that hovered over American dealings with Asia in the nineteenth century.[7]

There is, of course, a recognised pattern of cultural exchange between the United States and India in the nineteenth century that ran alongside this economic trade. Ralph Waldo Emerson's aunt is said to have introduced him to Sanskrit works in translation, while Henry David Thoreau in *A Week on the Concord and Merrimack Rivers* declared that the 'reader is nowhere raised into and sustained in a higher, purer, or *rarer* region of thought than in the Bhagavat-Geeta'.[8] Walt Whitman's poem 'A Passage to India' (1871) similarly hails the recent opening of the Suez Canal as an opportunity for the 'lands to be welded together' and for America to connect more readily with spiritual traditions of the East.[9] Yet nineteenth-century American transcendentalism tends to reify an apotheosised version of India centred upon its spiritual dimensions, while largely overlooking its more material traditions of empire and commerce. Part of the reason for this, I would suggest, is a covert desire on the part of the transcendentalists to repress their own implicit postcolonial status by keeping the untimely spectres of

---

India in the Age of Sail, 1784–1860 (Salem, MA: Peabody Essex Museum, 2001), p. 27.

6 D. Cannadine, *Ornamentalism: How the British Saw Their Empire* (London: Allen Lane, 2001), p. xix.

7 Bean, p. 79.

8 H.D. Thoreau, *A Week on the Concord and Merrimack Rivers*, ed. C.F. Hovde (Princeton, NJ: Princeton University Press, 1980 [1868]), p. 137.

9 W. Whitman, 'A Passage to India', in S. Bradley and H.W. Blodgett, eds, *Leaves of Grass* (New York: Norton, 1973), p. 412. On Whitman and the Suez Canal, see: A. Geffen, 'Walt Whitman and Jules Michelet—One More Time', *American Literature* 45.1 (1973): 109.

the Indian empire at bay. Emerson and Thoreau prefer to focus on the *Bhagavad Gīta* rather than on the political heritage of Warren Hastings or Cornwallis in order to annex India as a correlative to their own idiom of principled transcendence, where the social and economic forces circumscribing the emergence of an independent culture would simply fall away; indeed, in *A Week on the Concord and Merrimack Rivers* Thoreau quotes with approval what he calls Hastings' 'sensible' remark that 'the writings of the Indian philosophers "will survive when the British dominions in India shall have long ceased to exist." '[10] In this context it is not surprising that, for all of his interest in global reach, Whitman never wrote a poem called 'A Passage to Australia,' since that would have foregrounded a British colonial legacy that nineteenth-century American writers were attempting self-consciously to erase. Michael Warner has written of how US national culture 'began with a moment of sweeping amnesia about colonialism,' with Americans preferring 'to think of themselves as living in an immemorial nation, rather than in a colonial interaction of cultures.' Such amnesia has continued through to more recent times when, as Arif Dirlik has observed, a discourse of postcolonial criticism mediated through the rhetoric of hybridity has managed to assimilate itself relatively comfortably to 'an emergent consciousness of global capitalism' centred on the US market.[11] The widely recognised work of Indian-born intellectuals such as Homi K. Bhabha and Gayatri Chakravorty Spivak testifies to the ways in which an idiom of 'sly civility' and mimicry, encompassing both resemblance and menace, accommodates itself to US national narratives more readily than Australian cultural perspectives organised around what are, for Americans, the especially discomfiting and indeed oppositional formations of monarchical power, state collectivism, and liberal entropy.[12]

10 Thoreau, p. 137.

11 M. Warner, 'What's Colonial About Colonial America?', in R.B. St George, ed., *Possible Pasts: Becoming Colonial in Early America* (Ithaca: Cornell University Press, 2000), p. 63; A. Dirlik, 'The Postcolonial Aura: Third World Criticism in the Age of Global Capitalism', *Critical Inquiry* 20 (1994): 331.

12 H.K. Bhabha, *The Location of Culture* (London: Routledge, 1994), pp. 93–101.

The comparative invisibility of Australasia within US critical discourse, then, derives not from any lack of empirical evidence about the incidence of such cross-border conjunctions, but rather from widely held suppositions among Americanists about their relative unimportance and insignificance. This is the unexamined assumption, for example, that Jack London's transpacific wanderings and dealings with Australia should not be seen as particularly relevant to the subject of American literature, since the latter is grounded upon an ethos of liberal individualism to which London's socialist inclinations are, by definition, tangential. Sacvan Bercovitch has argued that professional Americanists have tended to be too heavily invested in the emancipatory potential of literature, imposing upon it a design of liberation that is not synonymous with the literary narratives themselves, but the concomitant expectation that naturalised conditions of American art should simply transcend the dogma of ideology—'a pillar of the old [liberal] consensus', as Bercovitch observed—now appears thoroughly exhausted.[13] In line with this, the familiar understandings among Americans of themselves as a people shaped by 'a profound anti-colonial temper' have, as John Carlos Rowe noted in 2000, been rendered moot.[14] David Harvey has discussed the resistance among Americans in the twenty-first century to conceiving of their country as an 'empire', and in terms of retrospective narratives there is a similar unwillingness to address the significance of colonialism to US history more generally.[15] This kind of reluctance to confront the circuitous byways of international engagement has been tied traditionally to a profound fear that such crossovers would undermine the special, exceptionalist qualities of US national identity. In *Culture and Imperialism*, Edward Said writes of how the work of 'Dickens and Thackeray as London authors' is necessarily 'informed by the colonial enterprises in India and Australia of which they were so aware', but he does not make the same claim for nineteenth-century

13 S. Bercovitch, 'The Problem of Ideology in American Literary History', *Critical Inquiry* 12 (1986): 639.

14 J.C. Rowe, *Literary Culture and US Imperialism: From the Revolution to World War II* (New York: Oxford University Press, 2000), p. 3.

15 D. Harvey, *The New Imperialism* (Oxford: Oxford University Press, 2003), p. 3.

American writers, who were generally assumed to be exempt from this colonial paradigm.[16]

Yet there are important ways in which nineteenth-century American literature and culture were deeply embedded in this colonial matrix. Because of the important strategic location of New South Wales, one that was relatively convenient for both the Asian interests of the East India Company and for the Royal Navy base at Valparaiso in Chile, Britain was keen quickly to develop a navigational and commercial network with Sydney at its hub. When François Péron called into Sydney during his exploration of Australia in 1802, he declared that he and his colleagues were 'completely astonished at the flourishing state in which we found this singular and distant establishment.'[17] Dorinda Outram suggests that by the 1790s the Pacific had already become part of 'an integrated system' of global trade, with a naval expedition being prepared in Britain as early as 1790 to take on board convicts from Port Jackson and members of the New South Wales Corps before proceeding to the north-west coast of America in order to establish a fur trading base.[18] Britain was keen to respond quickly to Captain Cook's report of the wealth of sea-otter furs to be found in the American Pacific northwest, and it saw the establishment of its new colony in Australia as a means to facilitate this potentially enriching business. American commercial exchange with Sydney also developed as a natural extension of its existing trade arrangements with China and the East Indies, and as early as 1792 four ships from the new United States put into harbour in Australia, two at Sydney and two at Shark Bay in Western Australia. The first American whaling ship to Australasian seas also visited New Zealand in 1804.[19]

16 E.W. Said, *Culture and Imperialism* (New York: Knopf, 1993), p. 318.

17 A Frost, 'The Antipodean Exchange: European Horticulture and Imperial Designs', in D.P. Miller and P.H. Reill, eds, *Visions of Empire: Voyages, Botany, and Representations of Nature* (Cambridge: Cambridge University Press, 1996), p. 71.

18 D. Outram, *The Enlightenment*, 2nd ed. (Cambridge: Cambridge University Press, 2005), p. 48.

19 L.G. Churchward, *Australia and America 1788–1972: An Alternative History* (Sydney: Alternative Publishing Co-operative, 1979), p. 9; K.J. Bertrand, 'Geographical Exploration by the United States', in H.R. Friis ed., *The Pacific Basin:*

As a specific example of how significantly Australasia enters into American literary consciousness during the period of the early republic, I want to focus on the work of Charles Brockden Brown, who as a member of the Federalist party was a political opponent of Thomas Jefferson in the first decade of the nineteenth century. Whereas Jeffersonian republicanism tended to operate with a linear, progressivist conception of history, the Federalists were generally more sceptical, both philosophically and politically, and consequently more attached to the cyclic conceptions of time that had been a common point of reference among conservative thinkers in the eighteenth century. The ideological perspectives of Federalism were more or less been written out of the American studies movement as it developed in the twentieth century, since the Federalists' more pessimistic prognosis for the future of the American republic did not accord with the constitutional optimism that came to dominate the subject in the eras of V.L. Parrington and Lionel Trilling, when the more utopian dimensions of Jeffersonian liberalism were held up, albeit in very different ways, to be paradigmatic of the US national experience as a whole. But this subsequent erasure of the Federalist point of view has had several detrimental effects on a just appreciation of US cultural politics at the turn of the nineteenth century. One, as Andy Doolen has observed, has been to downplay the significance of continuing global conflict between European empires in the formation of early US nationhood; rather than a benign belief in American exceptionalism, which would assume the new nation was exempt from these old European quarrels, the Federalists preferred to appropriate and continue the logic of the British Empire, as exemplified by their activities on the Caribbean frontier and by their design of the Alien and Sedition Acts in 1798 to circumscribe the political influence of German and Irish immigrants.[20] Another key feature of Federalist cultural politics was not just to be influenced by the European imperial model, but also to see the United States itself as a new kind of empire,

---

A History of Its Geographical Exploration (New York: American Geographical Society, 1967), p. 261.

20 A. Doolen, *Fugitive Empire: Locating Early American Imperialism* (Minneapolis: University of Minnesota Press, 2005).

one intent upon consolidating commercial markets, upholding the economic interests of slavery, and enforcing domestic security in what was thought to be the turbulent and uncertain world of the 1790s.

In this sense, Brown's novels derive their resonance from the way they engage in dialogue with everything that is extraneous to their domestic circumference so as to problematise the idea of an independent American republic. Puns on the word 'constitution'—'the moral constitution of man', 'a perverse constitution of mind'—appear frequently in Brown's first novel *Wieland* (1798), whose subtitle, 'An American Tale', deliberately links the protagonist's erratic state of mind with the uncertainties surrounding the new US Constitution. The descent of Wieland into madness and the disintegration of his family's stability under the malicious influence of the 'imp of mischief' Carwin, whose skills in biloquism induce murder and mayhem, thus come to appear allegorical of the inchoate political state of the new republic, where the 'known principles of human nature' do not accord with the country's abstract political theorems.[21] This fictional narrative is based upon interrogating rationalist epistemologies and scrutinising the whole idea of cause and effect, something which by extension would seem to cast doubt upon the rational premises of the US Constitution; but the idea of cyclic time and history repeating itself—with the Wieland family history fatalistically setting the parameters for Brown's story—also calls into question the progressive nature of Republican ideology. As Jane Tompkins observes, the fact that it is 'Wieland, the devout, well-educated farmer, the very epitome of the man on whom Jeffersonians staked their vision of Republican order' who murders his wife and children implies the kind of scepticism about the limits of human self-government that was part of the Federalist political agenda at this time.[22]

There is also a partially suppressed geographical consciousness in *Wieland*: we are told of how Wieland's 'brain seemed to swell beyond its

---

21 Charles Brockden Brown, *Wieland, or the Transformation: An American Tale; Memoirs of Carwin the Biloquist*, S.J. Krause, ed. (Kent, OH: Kent State University Press, 1977), pp. 3, 123, 235.

22 J. Tompkins, *Sensational Designs: The Cultural Work of American Fiction 1790–1860* (New York: Oxford University Press, 1985), p. 53.

continent', as though 'the extinction of a mind the most luminous and penetrating that ever dignified the human form' were linked to a process of spatial displacement.[23] But, as Nigel Leask observes, the 'utopian theme' of geographical exploration that is 'only a subliminal presence' in *Wieland* is much more explicit in Brown's unfinished *Memoirs of Carwin the Biloquist*, written in 1798 as a sequel to *Wieland*, although not published until 1803–05, when it appeared serially in Brown's *Literary Magazine*.[24] Here Carwin's 'perverse and pernicious curiosity' is couched in specifically geographic terms—'the world appeared to me an ocean on which my bark was set afloat, without compass or sail'—and this leads him into the orbit of the radical visionary Ludloe, who is committed to the kind of 'scheme of Utopian felicity' that became associated with Bougainville and other Pacific explorers of the eighteenth century. Since it is 'plain' to Ludloe that 'the nations of Europe were tending to greater depravity', he plans to look elsewhere to execute his 'plan of colonization'. Carwin finds in Ludloe's library copies of More's *Utopia*, Harrington's *The Commonwealth of Oceana*, along with 'voyages and travels of the missionaries of the sixteenth and seventeenth centuries' while he also discovers in Ludloe's atlas a mysterious hand-drawn map:

> It was drawn on a pretty large scale, representing two islands, which bore some faint resemblance, in their relative proportions, at least, to Great Britain and Ireland ... From the great number of subdivisions, and from signs, which apparently represented towns and cities, I was allowed to infer, that the country was at least as extensive as the British isles ... It is well known that the people of Europe are strangers to very nearly one half of the surface of the globe. From the south pole up to the equator, it is only the small space occupied by southern Africa and by South America with which we are acquainted. There is a vast extent,

23 Brown, *Wieland*, pp. 153–54.

24 N. Leask, 'Irish Republicans and Gothic Eleutherarchs: Pacific Utopias in the Writings of Theobald Wolfe Tone and Charles Brockden Brown', *Huntington Library Quarterly* 63.3 (2000): 357.

> sufficient to receive a continent as large as North America, which our ignorance has filled only with water. In Ludloe's maps nothing was still to be seen, in these regions, but water, except in that spot where the transverse parallels of the southern tropic and the 150th degree east longitude intersect each other. On this spot were Ludloe's islands placed, though without any name or inscription whatever.[25]

The 'transverse parallels of the southern tropic and the 150th degree east longitude' intersect at present-day Rockhampton, near the Queensland coast in Australia, so the author makes it easy for us to place precisely the site of Ludloe's imagined utopia. Although Carwin infers that Ludloe's 'geographical secret' had involved putting his 'plans for civilization ... into practice in some unvisited corner of the world', these precise spatial co-ordinates, along with the mention of a topographical resemblance to Great Britain and Ireland, drag this hypothetical realm—utopia as 'no place'—back into the land of the actual, where the bonds of British imperial authority hold sway. In a textual footnote attributed to the fictional editor of Carwin's *Memoirs*, Brown reminds the reader 'that the incidents of this narrative are supposed to have taken place before the voyages of Bougainville and Cook', and his narrative is based upon a retrospective exposure whereby the historical process of colonisation ironically unmasks the chimeras of hermetic prophecy.[26] By February 1805, when this section of the manuscript was written, these antipodean islands were no longer an empty space for the projection of transcendent visions, as Ludloe fondly imagines, but formed another part of the cyclic pattern of imperial time and space. As Hsuan L. Hsu observes, *Memoirs of Carwin* is thus 'a fragment in which both the forgotten voice of the colonized' and the repressed fact of America's continuation of Britain's imperial policy return with a vengeance; rather than working 'diligently to suppress the colonial origins of their critiques of modernity', as David Kazanjian argued, *Memoirs of Carwin* actually foregrounds the geographical *mise-en-abîme* whereby

25 Brown, *Wieland*, pp. 251, 268, 277–78, 298–99.

26 Brown, *Wieland*, pp. 299, 301.

British colonial developments in Australasia echo its colonial practices in Ireland and America, which were themselves echoed by the growth of an American empire in the 1790s.[27] For all of the ways in which, as Leask says, the 'late-eighteenth-century Atlantic imagination was thoroughly seduced by the utopian promise of a Pacific *Terra Australis*', Brown was enough of a hard-headed Federalist sceptic to hold in abeyance any prospect of a new world, either in pastoral America or the more distant antipodes, that might effectively position itself beyond the circumference of colonial power.[28]

In the last years of his life Brown spent less time writing fiction and more on political pamphlets, and his own involvement with the politics of colonisation manifests itself most directly in the *Address to the Government of the United States on the Cession of Louisiana to the French*, published in 1803. Here he argues indirectly that the United States has a right to the possession of the Louisiana Territory by ventriloquising in a Frenchman's voice the potential benefits to France from colonising these regions. As Jared Gardner notes, this turned out to be the most influential work of Brown's whole career, with the first edition selling out quickly and the second edition being published less than two months later.[29] What is most curious, though, is that a sizeable portion of the first edition—eight pages out of about eighty—was omitted when the pamphlet was reprinted, and all of this excised material deals specifically with New Holland: 'The editor has retrenched nothing new from the memorial', proclaims the 'Advertisement' to the second edition, 'but the passages respecting New Holland, which were thought to be no wise applicable to the present situation of our affairs'. Perhaps this was simply a matter of the economics of the publishing industry: the editor of the 'second impression' boasts of how it has been produced 'in a cheaper

27 H.L. Hsu, 'Democratic expansionism in *Memoirs of Carwin*', *Early American Literature* 35.2 (2000): 154; D. Kazanjian, *The Colonizing Trick: National Culture and Imperial Citizenship in Early America* (Minneapolis: University of Minnesota Press, 2003), p. 13.

28 Leask, p. 248.

29 J. Gardner, *Master Plots: Race and the Founding of an American Literature, 1787–1845* (Baltimore: Johns Hopkins University Press, 1998), p. 54.

and more convenient form.' But it is also the case that by agreeing to eliminate the discussion of New Holland, presumably in an effort to maximise his audience, Brown also implicitly altered the meaning of his argument. Acknowledging that 'little more than an hundred years ago, North America was a wilderness', the *Address* maintains the nation has 'become more compact, numerous, opulent, and enlightened' through the civilising processes of commerce, which have led to an 'increase of real wealth'. Brown thus portrays an empire constantly changing and evolving, whose foundations are linked inextricably to the exercise of power; talking of the desire to 'hold our footing against such powerful neighbours' as England and Spain, the French narrator concludes: 'We shall have no option but to destroy or be destroyed.'[30] The *Address* is accordingly predicated upon the inevitability of conflict between colonising powers, and the section on New Holland crucially balances out the American scene by describing how a similar battle for imperial mastery has recently been taking place in a 'new world in the eastern hemisphere,' which the narrator argues that France should also seek to bring into its dominions.[31]

It is, therefore, easy to see why New Holland in general played such a prominent role in Brown's literary and cultural imagination. In his 1804 essay 'Thoughts on the Probable Duration of the American Republic', Brown again compares the new American republic to other empires throughout history, ranging from the Assyrian, Persian, Macedonian and Roman empires to the more recent British model. Brown is optimistic that the 'American empire', which he says 'is formed by commerce and the arts of peace', and will be 'as durable as any empire the world has witnessed'; but he still acknowledges how 'this rising republic contains the seeds of internal destruction', both from its internecine political conflicts and from potential divisions 'between the eastern and western territories'. Despite his patriotism, then, Brown situates the United

30 Charles Brockden Brown, *An Address to the Government of the United States on the Cession of Louisiana to the French; and on the Late Breach of Treaty by the Spaniards*, 2nd ed. (Philadelphia: Conrad, 1803), pp. 2, 12, 16, 29, 33.

31 Charles Brockden Brown, *An Address to the Government of the United States on the Cession of Louisiana to the French; and on the Late Breach of Treaty by the Spaniards*, 1st ed. (Philadelphia: Conrad, 1803), p. 28.

States in a more abstract relation to cyclic time, whereby he envisages the common imperial fate of a rise and fall in power being visited in time upon his native country. He also expounds this cyclic vision by comparing America to another offshoot of the British Empire in a different part of the world:

> Besides having given birth to the United States of North America, a nation nearly as populous as itself, [Britain] is now forming settlements in New South Wales with a fortitude and perseverance surmounting all obstacles, and with the same unremitting watchfulness, toil, and labour, as attended the foundation of the United States. From the accounts of the salubrity, soil, and productions of New Holland, added to the advantage of its insular situation, very little doubt can be entertained of its becoming a more powerful empire than the United States, and in a more rapid progression.[32]

The manifestly inaccurate nature of Brown's prophecy here is of less importance than his concern to use the alternative British colony of New Holland to relocate America within a wider global orbit both spatially and temporally, a relativising strategy that is entirely commensurate with his Louisiana address published the previous year.

Whereas issues surrounding the Americanisation of Australia have become almost a cliché in twentieth-century Australian history, then, questions about the Australianisation of America are much less common. Yet both continents have experienced the history of empire, as an imperial power as well as a colonised society, and both are also familiar with the complications incumbent upon settler colony projects, particularly in terms of their relations with native peoples. But because these historical dynamics unfolded in different chronological frameworks—America being an explicitly colonial society through the eighteenth century and Australia through the nineteenth, with political independence coming to the United States in 1787 and Federation to Australia in 1901—one intriguing aspect of such cultural juxtapositions

---

32 Charles Brockden Brown, 'Thoughts on the Probable Duration of the American Republic', *Literary Magazine and American Register* 2.9 (1804): 215–19.

is the way they involve systematic correlations across different temporal as well as spatial dimensions. While transatlantic studies in their earlier incarnations tended to be relatively self-contained and self-allegorising, in the sense that they often focused on the Atlantic Ocean itself as a specific site across which different national (and ideological) forces faced each other, any reconceptualisation of US culture in terms of its antipodean imaginary necessarily involves wider and more complicated geopolitical juxtapositions, involving transatlantic as well as transpacific vectors. In this sense, the figure of antipodean America speaks not only to global geography, but also to the metaphoric inversion of US constitutional freedom by contrary impulses. Just as America displaced Britain, so Britain's former colony, Australia, displaces the United States through a process of intellectual exchange and mirroring that holds up the innate assumptions of the old 'new nation' to discomfiting scrutiny.

3

Transcendentalism, Emerson and Nineteenth-Century Australian Literary Culture

Ken Stewart

Transcendentalism in nineteenth-century Australian literature is the elephant in the library; literary historians either inexplicably fail to notice it, or do not wish to confront it. The word itself, not only in Australia, may carry a confusing variety of interrelated shades of meaning and contextual association. These may relate to: philosophical idealism, deriving ultimately from dialogue with Kant, often via Carlyle or Coleridge; aesthetic and literary idealism associated with Wordsworth or Ruskin, or German literary romanticism; spiritual awe evoked by landscape, landscape painting, or descriptive writing; the specific ideas of the American transcendentalist school, especially of Ralph Waldo Emerson; and a larger and more comprehensive American and metaphysical tradition extending beyond the early canonical and 'core' Emerson, and encompassing national, social and political ideas and practices, particularly republicanism. In Australia in the nineteenth century all these associations are at times pertinent; but a trap that must be avoided is the twenty-first century imposition of 'American transcendentalism' upon a colonial intellectual and literary world that assimilated and individuated 'transcendental' affinities and influences from Britain, Europe and Asia (particularly India) as well. The following discussion will focus on several colonial Australian writers whose 'transcendental' links, with both Europe and the United States, have been underestimated, but the approach taken will attempt to move outwardly from the individual Australian authors, rather than rigidly to impose the standard 'American transcendentalist' criteria on their literary texts.

There are several possible explanations for the neglect of 'Australian' transcendentalism, and of American affinities and influences, by Australian critics. They relate to: a lack of precise awareness of the issues themselves, sometimes brought about by a confusion of the discourses listed above; the 'Americanisation' of transcendentalism in literary criticism; an unwillingness among Australian literary critics and historians to place due emphasis on the significance of idealism within colonial literary culture; a greater perceived distance in Australia than in the United States between mainstream or popular nationalism and literary transcendentalism; the influence in Australia of colonial and imperial links with Britain; the critical difficulties of actually discerning 'transcendental' influences and affinities, and distinguishing them from orthodox Christian or traditional Romantic ones; and the problem of determining how adequately particular authors actually understand transcendentalism themselves.

By the 'Americanisation' of transcendentalism I mean the tendency to define it primarily or as a matter of course in American contextual terms and to relate it to American nationalism and nationality at the expense of underlining its global or universal historical and contemporary applications. The introduction of courses in American literature since the 1950s, in the United States as in Australia, has reinforced this dynamic, placing Emersonian transcendentalism (or simply 'Emerson') at the beginnings of American literary traditions and imaginaries. On the other hand, the growth of 'Australian literature', particularly as a body of knowledge for study, has established or drawn attention to certain narratives and discourses, like those of Russel Ward, A.A. Phillips, Vance Palmer, or those of recent feminists, post-structuralists, and Marxists, who (in every sense) fail to recognise colonial 'transcendentalism' within Australian literary culture.

We can witness an example of the latter in the critical reception of the verse of A.B. ('Banjo') Paterson, Australia's most popular poet for many years, who is rarely recognised for his romanticism, never as 'transcendentalist'; and always as a nationalist exponent of 'the masculine bush legend' and 'mateship'. Paterson's nationalism, that is to say, is rarely invested by literary historians with idealist, Romantic and individualist values; yet if we read 'Clancy of the Overflow', 'The Man from Snowy River' and 'Waltzing Matilda', arguably the most nationally popular Australian poems ever written, the 'vision splendid' is as transcendentalist as certain paintings of Arthur Streeton and Elioth Gruner. The phrase itself is purloined by Paterson from Wordsworth,[1] but translated from the experience of childhood and youth to the idealised Clancy's adult male experience of 'the sunlit plains extended', just as the title of Streeton's 'Still glides the stream, and shall forever glide' transposes a line from a sonnet by Wordsworth on the Cumbrian River Duddon to illuminate the 'transcendental' depiction of a very Australian watercourse. 'Clancy of the Overflow', in its simple quasi-folkloric way, registers a generalised disgust for industrialism, urban squalor, pollution and crowds, and endorsement of the nomadic (or modern American 'road') life of the independent individual. In 'The Man from Snowy River', the man, his pony, and the bush horses are from the (transcendental) mountains, a special mythical and super-natural site, and are graced with quasi-Olympian spiritual supremacy and physical skills, despite their stunted physiques; only in extraneous later versions (the film, and the 'novelisation') is the man given mates and a girlfriend. And in 'Waltzing Matilda' the hero is again a free-wheeling and in every sense mateless loner who dances only with a swag, and whose spirit inhabits and permeates Australian rural landscapes. The important point here is not that exclusive claims can be made for a quasi-transcendentalist reading of Paterson, but that commentators have apparently not been driven by a need to perceive such potentials.

---

1 The Youth, who daily farther from the east
   Must travel, still is Nature's Priest,
   And by the vision splendid
   Is on his way attended.

William Wordsworth, 'Ode. Intimations of Immortality from Recollections of Early Childhood', in *The Norton Anthology of Poetry* (Alexander Ward Allison, ed.), third edition, New York and London: 1983, pp. 551–55.

Affinities between transcendentalists and some colonial authors were explored by Joseph Jones in *Radical Cousins* (1976), which reaffirms (sometimes diffusely, as part of a wider consideration of Australian–American literary links) the 'American' circumstantial particularity of the Concord transcendentalists, yet rightly insists on derivative elements particularly from Coleridge, Carlyle, and German romanticism. Despite the book's originality and seminal importance, its effects are at times problematic, bestowing a primacy upon the 'American' element which decontextualises in some measure the Australian 'response' (physical, aesthetic, and metaphysical) from other local, national and global sources, and misrepresents local and national textual nuance. At times, in his discussion of Christopher Brennan, for example, the emphasis on American connections, which overlap with more central British or European links, seems disproportionate and misleading.

Conditions comparable to those experienced at Concord by Emerson in the 1830s, relating to population growth, industrialism, urbanisation and advanced literary institutionalisation (through universities, journals, newspapers, libraries, theatres etc.), were not in operation in Australia until at least the 1860s, following the gold rushes; and because a republican nationalism based on actual imperial separation was never locked into the status quo, the entire ideological mythology of American republican independence and its reinforcing links with Emersonian Self-Reliance had to be gently hybridised with monarchical patriotism, or at times belligerently separated from a theoretical ideal only practised elsewhere. Thus Emerson generally flourished more boldly and clearly, and in closer parallel, in Australian writing after the 1860s, though sometimes in an adapted or posthumously celebratory form.

The verse and prose of the (sometime) Unitarian idealist, Charles Harpur, Thoreau's senior and Emerson's approximate contemporary, provide a major exception. As early as the 1830s Harpur read and carefully assimilated Channing, Fuller and Emerson, for long periods in remote rural districts quite untouched in any direct way by industrialism and population growth. We might at first want to label Harpur a somewhat typical *American* transcendentalist, a contemporary representative of

Emersonian thought and aesthetics, and sometimes verse practice, and of Thoreauvian values and lifestyle. His life as a farmer, postman, would-be teacher in a one-man school; his politicking for liberal radical causes in local coteries; his pursuit of Wordsworth with some understanding of German romanticism; his explicit acknowledgement and apparent understanding of the importance for him of Emerson's Self-Reliance and his rejection of utilitarianism; and his use of the Emersonian Over-Soul as the metaphysical basis for cosmic argument in the long poem 'The World and the Soul', co-operate to make a claim for this brand of 'American' transcendentalism. But Harpur's transformations, whether from European or American idealism, Australianise, paradoxically by performing an assimilation and appropriation of 'sources' in exactly the way Emerson commends: he makes them his own, he doesn't care who said what first, he acknowledges mentors but not 'masters'. A measure of this individuality and independence is that, unlike with Bernard O'Dowd, we cannot tell what *is* derivative, and from whom or where. The 'transformations' of Harpur are themselves original; and the American original sense is cancelled.

In Harpur's writings, then, Australian themes are never displaced or monopolised by 'American' transcendentalism. Local and national or colonial content may be permitted to *converse* with American, but not to be Americanised, or globalised: the 'trans-national' is here really 'national'. Themes and topics such as the treatment of Aborigines, the quest for the republic, the rejection of 'Old World' follies, and the struggle for liberty against greed and mammonism or poverty and oppression, are from time to time related to American contextual counterparts. But the Australian Aborigine *replaces* rather than semantically 'joins' the indigenous American or the black slave counterpart. And Harpur's celebrated republicanism is an explicitly stated ideal and hope for the future rather than, as is often believed, an ideology available to immediate activation and practice.[2] Until the ideal republic is *ac-*

2 'But though utterly Republican in my politics, speculatively, I yet believe, that it will be best for Australia to continue during the present [i.e. nineteenth] century (at the very least) as part of the British monarchy. For even the state-butchers of Downing Street are full fifty years in advance of our present half-educated wool-kings.' From Harpur's 1847 note on his poem 'The Tree of Liberty' in Charles

tually established colonial monarchy is to be preferred to national republicanism. The Australian rural squatter stands in for the British or American 'captain of industry' (in Carlyle's phrase), and for British nobility; and the ordinary 'currency' population are merely hopeful or destroyed victims. For Harpur the squatter actually *is* the industrialist, literally: he owns and sells the wool that later turns the new Satanic mills of the Industrial Revolution. Harpur normally sifts from his writing, or subordinates within it, all other paradigms of the squatter figure: the wise, genteel Englishman; the quasi-aristocratic self-made man; the rapacious, ill-dressed scrooge; the struggling younger son; the ruthless explorer-land-taker; the acquisitive Anglo-Australian revenant are all possible types employed elsewhere in colonial literature, which for Harpur must remain secondary to the model of acquisitive selfishness who cruelly or meanly exploits his workers and feeds industrialism.[3]

For Harpur the Carlylean 'Age of Machinery' of steam, factories and locomotives, was more a literary concept than a local reality. Jerry's Plains was in the late 1830s a village sixty-seven kilometres from the second largest town in New South Wales, Maitland (which then had a population of about 2500), where a 'crowd',[4] however madding, was never numerically frightening or dangerous. Even distant Sydney was scarcely a 'city'.

The poem 'To the American, Emerson' illustrates Harpur's willingness to identify Emerson with American republican optimism. The title immediately distances, or 'others', Emerson by naming him as an American, and the reader must wait to decide whether this is derogatory or even slightly contemptuous, a familiar colonial attitude towards Yankee targets. But Emerson turns out to be a metonym, almost an emblem, of the ideal America, and at the same time 'the bard of

Harpur, *Selected Poetry and Prose*, Michael Ackland ed. (Ringwood: Penguin Books, 1986), pp. 21–23.

3 See, e.g. Harpur's verse play *Stalwart the Bushranger*, and his satiric poem 'The Beautiful Squatter'. The note cited above (in footnote 2) in its entirety pours further scorn on squatters.

4 See Charles Harpur, 'Crowds' (poem and note) in Adrian Mitchell, ed., *Charles Harpur* (Melbourne: Sun Books, 1973), pp. 143–44.

Self-Reliance', and a 'giant-minded mystic'. Nevertheless 'Self-Reliance' prompts Harpur, in a prose note, to be dourly skeptical of Emerson's optimism at its occasional rosiest, particularly here concerning the bardic life:

> I recd. some consolation the other day from a perusal of Emerson's Essay 'The Poet'. Some of the conditions he assigns as being inevitable in his lot are hard, but they must be accepted. I, at all events, have been accepting them all my life. 'The Poet must be content, (he says) to be thought either a fool or a madman for a long time. He must be baulked, hissed at, hooted, and be everywhere misunderstood & maligned. All this for a long time; but in the end he shall be known to his own, who shall console him with dearest love.' Let us see. There are many fine things in this Essay; but at the same time there is also in it, much transcendental trash.[5]

Harpur is also doubtful (and misunderstanding) of Emerson's endorsement of Kant's critique of 'pure reason'; and is, as Michael Ackland[6] has implicitly shown, generally a shade darker than Emerson, not so much on the question of human potential to avoid evil (true to standard Unitarian principles, he rejected original sin), as in his bleak awareness of human weakness, greed and oppression.

Harpur's most obvious deployment of Emersonian ideas takes place in 'The World and the Soul', his long, poetically charged and celebratory discourse based on a concept that seems very similar to the Over-Soul. But Harpur's exposition of both 'world' and 'soul' extends Emerson's ideas without his consent, taking into account evolutionary theory as it relates both to human history and prehistory, and to perceptions of God. In Harpur's poem stages of evolution are outlined, beginning with a primordial world in which 'No soul intelligent, save God alone' inhabited the universe, and the empty earth; followed by a period when, with the creation or evolution of humanity, 'soul' becomes pervasive

5 Charles Harpur, 'Emerson', in Mitchell, p. 175.

6 Michael Ackland, *That Shining Band* (St Lucia: University of Queensland Press, 1994), pp. 38–55.

and endemic, enabling man's potential divinisation simultaneously with evolution; until eventually, in an era yet unreached, man is overtaken by 'new successions in the scheme of life' and 'progressive changes in the sum/And increment' of the 'divine Idea'. Although Emerson's essay 'The Over-Soul', written long before Darwin's *Origin of Species*, provides no significant commentary on biological evolution, Harpur may have picked up some anticipatory hints of his own later perspective from Emerson's second 'Nature' essay (1836), which Lawrence Buell rightly describes as 'proto-Darwinian',[7] and which is introduced with these pertinent couplets:

A subtle chain of endless rings
The next unto the farthest brings;
The eye reads omens where it goes,
And speaks all languages the rose;
And striving to be man, the worm
Mounts through all the spires of form.[8]

Interestingly, Judith Wright, in the first serious examination of 'The World and the Soul',[9] failed to notice Emerson's influence, but did perceive affinities with Nietzschean *Übermensch*. Harpur's 'attempt to respiritualise' the Darwinian 'machine for physical evolution', however, is perceived by Wright as being far from Nietzschean: 'to Harpur the "intelligent soul" is not, as for Nietzsche, a law to itself, but is subject to and forms part of a larger whole, and bears the responsibility of its own immortality in God'. The soul, Harpur says, is complete:

In her sole being, evermore aspires,
An ultimate of all that went before,
A spirit of Thought, and thence a child of that
In which the world began and hath its end …

7 Lawrence Buell, *Emerson* (Cambridge, Massachusetts: Harvard University Press, 2003), p. 176.

8 R.W. Emerson, 'Nature' (1836) in *Essays and Other Writings* (London: Cassell, 1907), p. 360.

9 Judith Wright, *Charles Harpur* (Melbourne: Lansdowne, 1963), pp. 25–26.

Thus ancestrally a spark
From God's internal brightness, goes she forth
To die not, but to clothe for evermore
In robes of beauty and of use …

What Wright has unwittingly confirmed is Harpur's indebtedness, and Nietzsche's, to Emerson's doctrine of the Over-Soul; and also the significance of the gulf between Emerson and Nietzsche, which many recent American critics apparently fail to acknowledge.

* * *

Catherine Helen Spence was, like her (and Emerson's) Idealist mentor Thomas Carlyle, a lowland Scot who 'shook off the shackles of Calvinism and Presbyterianism, and emerged into … light and liberty.'[10] With her financially ruined but highly literate middle-class parents she had moved in early childhood to South Australia, the 'Paradise of Dissent' colonised on principles of freedom and equality: 'the presence of … so many ministers and preachers and so varied a swarm of sects, most of them with places of worship, created a record surpassing New England's first decade.'[11] Spence also saw the absence of convictism as freedom from a kind of societal 'original sin', which more readily nurtured the ethical potentials of free will as advocated in contemporary Concord.

Spence always described herself as 'unitarian', and not as 'transcendentalist'. Emerson and his colleagues she proudly designated in the same way. The label is for our purposes not so important as the views, affinities and roles they shared, as the 'brand' of unitarianism Spence herself accepted encompassed much of what Emerson came to endorse in his initial and later moves away from an 'established' Unitarian church. Like Emerson, she was for decades in today's terms a 'public intellectual' and 'human rights activist', an essayist, lecturer, journalist, critic, reviewer and, last and definitely least in her view, a novelist.

10 Susan Magarey, *Unbridling the Tongues of Women* (Sydney: Hale and Iremonger, 1985), p. 73.

11 Douglas Pike, *Paradise of Dissent* (Melbourne: Longmans, 1957), quoted in Magarey, p. 74.

The disregard of her connections with American transcendentalism may be accounted for in several ways: her best known novel, *Clara Morison*, least reflects her unitarian and transcendentalist beliefs and practices; her other fiction, with the exception of *An Agnostic's Progress*, tends towards the kind of political and utopian outlooks and activism favoured more perhaps by Emerson's radical and quasi-socialist later American contemporaries and successors, and by journals like *Arena* in the United States, than by Emerson himself; and twentieth century critical and historical emphases on Spence's feminism, utopianism, and their relative lack of focus or emphasis on Spence's direct writing and activities relating to Emerson and quasi-Emersonian doctrines. There is a tendency to compartmentalise the spiritual and the secular in her humanitarian political activities, and in her literary criticism: her religion becomes the 'inspiration' for her reforms whereas for her the reforms were part of her 'spiritual' practice. Her critical essay on (the atheist) George Eliot[12] (who received Spence at her home, and wrote to her later that she considered the essay to be one of the best she had read) should be (but usually isn't) regarded in the same way as Eliot regarded Carlyle's essays and Ruskin's *Modern Painters*: as the greatest of a kind to be respected and admired, but not metaphysically endorsed.

For Spence there are three unitarianisms, which must accept one another, and which comprehend the most liberal and transcendentalist positions: the purely secular, the spiritual, and the more literally and narrowly Christian.[13] Her essays and sermons reflect invariably unitarian principles that emphasise free will, soul and the nature of ethical commitment. Her first sermon typically endorses ethical responsibility, duty, and love; and the value of a subjective 'faith' that is 'not in ancient records, but in the relation of the human soul to the Infinite'. Science replaces miracles, and Beulah is gained not through 'grace' but by the spiritual infusion of duty with delight.[14]

---

12 Catherine Spence, 'George Eliot', *Melbourne Review* 1 (1876): 146–63. See also 'George Eliot's Life and Works', *Melbourne Review* 10 (1885): 217–44 (also written by Spence).

13 Excerpts from Spence's first sermon, in Helen Thomson, ed., *Catherine Helen Spence* (St Lucia: University of Queensland Press, 1987), p. 572.

14 Thomson, p. 572.

Spence's notion of Soul, which is similar but not identical to Emerson's Over-Soul, to which it is apparently indebted, is illustrated in a popular 'original parable' she composed, which refashions the Eden myth in a more 'transcendentalist' version:

> And it came to pass that after five days of Creation which were periods of unknown length of time that God took the soul, the naked soul, with which he was to endow the highest of his creatures in Eden ... And the soul could see, could hear, could understand, though there were neither eyes, nor ears, nor limbs, nor bodily organs to do its bidding. And God said, 'Soul, thou shalt have a body as these creatures that thou seest around thee have. Thou art to be King, and rule over them all. Thy mission is to subdue the earth and make it fruitful ... Which of all these living creatures wouldst thou resemble?

Soul then inspects the animals and chooses the ape who, though not beautiful, can 'stand and gaze upwards'. Then God says: 'Soul thou hast chosen well ... Thou shalt stand upright, and look upward and onward. And the Soul can create Beauty for itself, when it shines through the body'.[15]

The least known of Spence's prose fictional writings is *An Agnostic's Progress from the Known to the Unknown*, in which Bunyan's *Pilgrim's Progress* is rewritten and transvalued to accord with her unitarian and transcendentalist thought. The practice of reshaping Bunyan to fit a revised 'theology' was also followed by Alfred Deakin,[16] and by Christina Stead in parts of *The Man Who Loved Children*. 'To the modern pilgrim,'

15 Excerpts from C.H. Spence, *Catherine Helen Spence: An Autobiography* (Adelaide: W.K. Thomas & Co., 1910) in Thomson, pp. 448–49. The narrative of the years 1887–1910, which includes Spence's trip to North America, was written after her death in the first person by her close friend Jeanne F. Young, using Spence's notes. A scholarly collection of the autobiography, and of other material including correspondence, notes and diary, was published in 2005 as *Ever Yours, C.H. Spence,* edited by Susan Magarey with Barbara Wall (Adelaide: Wakefield Press, 2005).

16 Alfred Deakin, *A New Pilgrim's Progress* (Melbourne: W.H. Terry, 1877).

Spence writes, 'God reveals himself in Nature, in art, in literature and in history.' Society—Vanity Fair—ought not to be scurried through furtively and in disdain, but considered warmly as 'the world in which we have to do our work well.'[17] Spence's provocatively 'agnostic' title does not really conceal a world without 'soul' (though she makes no promise of an afterlife), but manifests her attempt to liberate herself from the lingering scars and stains of Calvinist 'evil', especially those left by the English children's writer Mary Martin Sherwood (1775–1851) in her quasi-Bunyanesque *The Infant's Progess*. This nightmarishly nasty little story tells how three children named Humble Mind, Playful and Peace are incessantly tempted on their journey from the City of Destruction to the Celestial City by a tenacious bullying imp named Inbred Sin, who is so determined that whenever a neighbour mentions a virtuous book or deed he wants the children to put their fingers over their eyes, to 'wallow with the swine', rather than 'give their hearts to any good.' For Spence (and the American transcendentalists) the doctrine of innate human depravity (original sin) was false and evil, and detrimental to moral improvement and social optimism:

> I wrote it to relieve my own mind. I wanted to satisfy myself that reverent agnostics were by no means materialists; that man's nature might or might not be consciously immortal, but it was spiritual; that in the duties which lay before each of us towards our own fellow creatures, there was scope for spiritual energy and spiritual emotion.[18]

In 1893–94 Spence visited Canada and the United States, where she was 'offered seven pulpits', 'went all over Harvard University', met the Unitarian pastor Gordon Ames, and preached for his Thanksgiving service. In Boston she stayed with immediate family descendants of Emerson's friend, the great abolitionist William Lloyd Garrison. She was introduced as well to Emerson's biographer Oliver Wendell Holmes, and

17 Spence in Thomson, p. 421.

18 Spence in Thomson, p. 455.

> had an hour and a half's chat with him in the last year of his long life. He was the only survivor of a famous brand of New England writers—Longfellow, Emerson, Hawthorne, Bryant, Lowell, Whittier, and Whitman were dead … I have often felt proud that of all the famous men I have mentioned … there was only one not a Unitarian, and that was Whittier, the Quaker poet of abolition; and his theology was of the mildest.[19]

* * *

'On! On! to transcendental faiths/And Young Democracies!'[20] urged Bernard O'Dowd, who was fond of exclamation marks. Jones' verdict, that O'Dowd was 'far and away the most transparent example of direct inspiration from American sources'[21] is an exaggeration: the problem with O'Dowd's 'transcendentalism' is that it becomes poetically confused with a pedantic classicism and with secular displays of knowledge and indignation. Unlike his idol Walt Whitman, who consistently and with some genuine learning and lyricism, infuses Emersonian notions of self and soul into his major verse to celebrate his 'American' self, and the God in man, O'Dowd allows his 'erudition' to become digressive, and it undermines the bardic authority of any philosophic or 'transcendental' role by leading the reader on trails of verbal ostentation, in 'learned' puzzles and conceits. His rejection of rolling Whitmanian cadence, and a frequent unwillingness to dispense with rhyme, seem more like failures of emulation than a declaration of independence. The problem is not only that, as Chris Wallace-Crabbe has observed, 'at every stage, his poems were limited in their general appeal by an Olympian diction that could seem knobbly, contorted, arcane and devastatingly abstract',[22]

---

19 Spence in Thomson, pp. 459–62.

20 Quoted by Joseph Jones, *Radical Cousins* (St Lucia: University of Queensland Press), p. 75.

21 Jones, p. 74.

22 C. Wallace-Crabbe, 'O'Dowd, Bernard,' in J. Ritchie, ed., *Australian Dictionary of Biography*, 11 (Melbourne: Melbourne University Press, 1988), pp. 62–63.

but also that such diction actually asphyxiates the bardic and *prophetic* voice of erudition.

The bright enthusiasm of the personal correspondence, beginning in March 1890, between the young O'Dowd and his Austral Club members and their ageing 'master' has sometimes dazzled from view more mature appreciations of Whitman by colonial contemporaries (particularly William Gay and Thomas Heney), and also of the emanations from and beyond O'Dowd of a youthful literary patriotism and democratic optimism more dubiously or distantly related to American transcendentalism. Moreover Emerson would probably have scorned or patronised from the grave the Master–Puppy relationship between 'Walt' and O'Dowd which entailed the kind of fawning literary servility and lack of Self-Reliance he detested, and was a desecration of his written ideal of friendship. O'Dowd's collection of small gifts and mementos sent by 'Walt', and his Bunthornean affection of leaves of grass in his lapel, would have seemed comically absurd.

Eventually Emerson became as important in O'Dowd's thought and message as Whitman, articulating more precisely specific concepts and doctrines, which required a less vague commitment. Evidently O'Dowd studied Emerson *after*, and as a result of, reading Whitman—a reversal of the expected order. Perhaps it was Emerson who inspired O'Dowd to make a closer study of Kant. In his sonnet 'To Immanuel Kant', which he claims 'sums up' the poems collected as *The Seven Deadly Sins*, O'Dowd writes:

O You, whose bridge invited me to span
Serene despair enamoured of his slough,
Ere gentle eyes became a lens to show
The loving Presence, and the perfect plan!
Copernicus who leaped the sophists' ban
In Konigsberg a hundred years ago,
And saw the adamantine cosmos flow
In opal streams WITHIN the mind of man.

Where now, abstracted, stellar spires you view,
Or teach Laplace young nebulae to plant,

Fill Berkeley's void, or Swedenborg pursue,
Or pick your steps 'mid Hume's agnostic gins,
Send here equipped like you another Kant
To gloss these Jekylls and their deadly sins!

This follows verses in the earlier series *The Silent Land* which are more explicitly Emersonian, for example:

Is there behind all men that live
  One all-containing Soul
  Whose symbols, apt for each one, give
    A transcript of the whole?

It is, as Hugh Anderson points out (quoting Emerson), the Unity 'within which every man's particular being is contained and made one with all other'[23] to which O'Dowd refers.

In 1952 O'Dowd returned to poetic composition after a long absence, during which he apparently retained some affinity with Emerson. He wrote two poems for the centenary of Unitarianism in Australia, in one of which he hopes to 'see our dream of Oneness realised'.[24] When he died the following year, his funeral service was Unitarian.

* * *

O'Dowd's longest and most intellectually productive epistolary dialogue was with his close friend Sydney Wheeler Jephcott, the poet, politician, conservationist and cattle farmer whose rarely studied life and writings offer another, quite different perspective on Australian 'transcendentalism'. Jephcott sought through poetry to open 'new avenues of sensation to Truth and Beauty' in order to cultivate public awareness of 'the vital Ideal in our national experience'.[25] O'Dowd acknowledged

---

23 Hugh Anderson, *The Poet Militant: Bernard O'Dowd* (Melbourne: Hill of Content, 1969), p. 94. For discussion of the paradoxical complexities of Emerson's affinities and disagreements with Kant, see Buell, esp. pp. 201–03.

24 Wallace-Crabbe, p. 63.

25 See Ken Stewart, 'Jephcott, Sydney Wheeler', in *Australian Dictionary of Biography*, 9 (Melbourne: Melbourne University Press, 1983), p. 483.

him as the source of his awareness 'of what poetry was both formally and substantially.'[26]

Jephcott was an actual 'man from Snowy River', in the Australian Alps. He never attended school but read widely from his father's library, evidently (as his poetry reveals) from Shelley, Wordsworth, Keats, Swinburne and Whitman. But 'the chief formative influence on his mind', so he claimed, was living alone in a tent in the Snowy Mountains for several years from the age of twelve.[27] Perhaps he took Thoreau's ideas on the virtues of a humble abode to an extreme, but his metaphysical, scientific and environmentalist absorption in Nature is easy to document. His father Edward had planted a large, still extant arboretum, and encouraged Sydney's scientific and botanical pursuits. When the eminent colonial botanist Ferdinand von Mueller sent an expedition to collect the plants of the Snowy Mountains region, the teenager Jephcott accepted the job of guide—not only to the terrain, but to some unclassified botanical species, of which *grevillia jephcottus* is one. When the principal colonial poet Henry Kendall, appointed late in his short life as Inspector of Forests by New South Wales Premier Sir Henry Parkes, eventually rode his horse to the Snowy region, in the course of his duties he met and befriended young Sydney, who decided then, he liked to claim, to become a poet. He also contributed botanical and scientific articles to the *Sydney Morning Herald*.

In poems such as 'With the West Wind' the narrator seeks to 'lose' his earthly soul within a greater one, intimated to him by Nature, especially wind and the 'immense and immanent snow' which 'like some space-centring spiritual sea' is 'past sight of all worlds and thoughts'. 'Love and Death, To-day' takes the traditional God away from a distant heaven, and argues for the creation of a new deity in humanity, created from the substance of 'all life's love', and 'shaped by the soul of Man today!'[28]

Jephcott's most ambitious poem, 'The Railway Train', attempts crudely but with *brio* to depict in writing the night-time journey of a locomotive as the symbolic representation of a vital spiritual energy

26 Anderson, p. 35.

27 Stewart, p. 483.

28 References are to Sydney Jephcott's personally proofed and amended copy of his *The Secrets of the South* (London: Reeves, 1892), in Mitchell Library, Sydney.

that encompasses and drives the sleeping human bodies within it. Written in the 1880s, its subject matter and incipient modernism anticipate Kenneth Slessor's poem 'The Night Ride', in which the dark night, the locomotive's force and the dream state of the passengers have been interpreted as manifestations of the Freudian unconscious, but which in Jephcott might also be read as Emerson's Over-Soul, or as an anticipation of the naturalised Jungian 'collective unconscious'. Certainly Jephcott follows both Carlyle and Ruskin, as well as Emerson and Thoreau and perhaps J.M.W. Turner in his great painting 'Rain, Steam and Speed', in his expression for the first time in Australian verse of a bitter-sweet ambivalence towards the dread locomotive 'monster' in an Age of Machinery which desecrates Nature.

* * *

Alfred Deakin, three times Prime Minister of Australia but also the first native born Victorian to publish a volume of verse,[29] was neither the first nor the most recent national leader to profess a profound debt to Ralph Waldo Emerson. Barack Obama has frequently extolled Emerson, and has placed him on his Facebook's list of 'favourite' authors, along with Martin Luther King and Gandhi. In his published *Inaugural,*[30] he also inserted Emerson's 'Self Reliance', and addresses by Lincoln. Some studies of Ronald Reagan argue a debt to Emerson.[31] Gandhi himself nominated Emerson, with Ruskin, and Hindu sacred books, among his most necessary spiritual guides. The Cuban revolutionary leader Jose Marti, and the Argentinian 'schoolmaster' President Sarmiento, were both (like Deakin) literary as well as political figures who acknowledged a primary debt.[32] Such a diverse list indicates not only Emerson's global

29 Alfred Deakin, *Quentin Massys* (Melbourne: Donaldson, 1875).

30 Barack Obama, *The Inaugural Address* (Penguin Books, 2009).

31 See, e.g. John P. Diggins, *Ronald Reagan: Fate, Freedom and the Making of History* (New York: Norton, 2007); Rainer Holl, 'Ralph Waldo Emerson and the Politics of Ronald Reagan', Termpaper, 2008. Available at: www.grin.com/e-book/135052/ralph-waldo-emerson-and-the-politics-of-ronald-reagan [Accessed September 2010].

32 Buell, pp. 327–29 and passim.

and transnational importance but also, probably, that interpretations of his works and preferred emphases are various.

Deakin wrote of himself, and of his academic and sometime parliamentary colleague C.H. Pearson, that both men had been 'saturated with the doctrines of [Herbert] Spencer, [and] Mill and Leckie, superimposed on an earlier and more durable foundation from Carlyle, Ruskin and Emerson'.[33] Pearson in fact had accepted an invitation to visit Emerson in Concord, and on political business in the United States in 1885 Deakin travelled hundreds of miles to visit Emerson's quite recent grave.

The dichotomy Deakin sets up is instructive: Emerson is the American, democratic link with the British idealist sages, and a potential foil to the incipient authoritarianism of Carlyle and radical Toryism of Ruskin. But he is also positioned in opposition to the utilitarian materialism of Mill and Spencer. As a politician Deakin knew, like Emerson himself in moments of cautious qualification, that 'utilitarian' compromise and ordinary tact and diplomacy were unavoidable social necessities; but it is likely, as we shall see, that in the contest with Mill and Spencer, Deakin's fundamental sympathies lay with Emerson's 'mystical' Self-Reliance, which is achieved by the pursuit of the divine universal discoverable within the self. Frequently in letters he applauds Carlyle's seemingly cantankerous invective as a cleansing and helpful honesty, despite his own political talents and charming affability. The reliance on discoverable truth through communion with the divine within the self is paramount.

La Nauze draws a simplistic line between the 'speculative' life, for which Deakin hankered, and the political world which he worked in professionally, and sought to escape.[34] Much of Deakin's longing to retreat to a 'speculative' realm was in fact the product of disillusion with self-interested conformists and fellow politicians, rather than with 'politics'. There is little evidence, I believe, that despite his continuing

33 Stuart Macintyre, *A Colonial Liberalism* (South Melbourne: Oxford University Press, 1991), pp. 188–89.

34 J.A. La Nauze, *Alfred Deakin*, 2 vols (Melbourne: Melbourne University Press, 1965), vol. 1, p. 70ff.

feelings of abject failure of ethical duty, he failed to value his own finer political triumphs as ethical victories or even spiritual achievements. To suggest, too, that philosophical abstractions were practically unimportant is to ignore that Deakin's mind and intellect contained his essential personal and political conceptual framework, his ethical map. He wrote intelligent juvenile essays on Mill and Herbert Spencer[35] (which he did not publish); and books that were founded on the idealism that propelled Carlyle and Ruskin, and particularly Emerson. They include unpublished studies of Swedenborg, Wordsworth and Shakespeare, and of poetry; a play influenced strongly by Carlyle[36] (*Sartor Resartus* was the first book he purchased as an adolescent, from his own pocket); studies of Indian culture and sacred art and architecture, and the Hindu sacred books;[37] a novel of spiritual 'progress';[38] and much political commentary. It is difficult to name an Australian contemporary with a more suitable background for the study of Emerson's canonical essays.

Deakin's hundreds of evocative unpublished prayers frequently reveal a painful, sometimes an elated, pursuit of what he sees as the God within the self:

> O God I approach Thee in spirit and in Truth with but dim knowledge and indefinite expectation and confessed doubt but with a longing for Thy inspiration, with a craving trust in thy will and power to help thy creatures and with a frequent though faltering reliance on my own intuitions.[39]

> How should we praise the infinite? Only in surrender to the best, only in the more perfect service of Thy will, only within ourselves, shaping ourselves in act and fact after Thy image

35 Deakin's unpublished essays and books are held by the National Library of Australia, Canberra, MS 1540.

36 See above, note 29.

37 Alfred Deakin, *Temple and Tomb in India* (Melbourne: Mullen and Slade, 1893).

38 See above, note 16.

39 La Nauze, p. 73.

> as presented to us in Jesus, most and dearest, in Buddha, Socrates and all Christ-like souls.[40]

La Nauze records how at the age of twenty-two Deakin, who had worked with Walter Lindesay Richardson (the model for his daughter's Richard Mahony) in the Spiritualist Sunday School, determined to become a vocational preacher, and consulted the only female minister in Melbourne 'to succeed her when she proposed to retire'.[41] Interestingly, La Nauze seems unaware that this 'lady preacher', Martha Turner, Australia's first female minister, (to a 'small and select' Unitarian congregation on Eastern Hill), was acknowledged by Catherine Spence as the most profound transformative influence on her spiritual and professional life.[42] Turner turned down Deakin's request for a preaching position, on the grounds that his views 'would not be approved by her congregation'.[43] Probably she was referring here to his current spiritualism: but he was at that moment, and probably in some sense throughout his life, a 'Unitarian' himself.

'After he had found his vocation in journalism and politics he continued to look wistfully to his roles, literary, religious, philosophical, but always didactic',[44] which he (but not La Nauze) believed he was best suited to play. The biographer here is, surely, presumptuous: Deakin's writings, speeches and political career, and his dialogue with the Harvard philosopher Josiah Royce, all suggest that Martha Turner may have unwittingly barred Deakin from the potentially successful 'Emersonian' career as a public intellectual, which she sparked and motivated in Spence.

* * *

In this preliminary investigation, which aims to discover questions and methods as well as answers, any conclusion will be tentative. But a

40 La Nauze, p. 74.

41 La Nauze, p. 71.

42 La Nauze, p. 71.

43 Magarey, p. 86ff.

44 La Nauze, p.71.

pattern of common preoccupations and responses, as well of individual variations, does appear to emerge among the authors I have discussed and may help to define some transpacific dialogues, commonalities and differences. The general picture may of course be altered after further study, both of texts and of other authors; but any such change would seem unlikely to challenge the particular importance of Spence, O'Dowd, Jephcott and Deakin even within a broader frame.

First we must accept that distance, however inconvenient, was never tyrannical in its effect on transpacific and British–Australian literary dialogue. The Americans, especially Emerson and Whitman, were known, read and discussed (but sometimes attacked) in Australia, through books (bought or borrowed), overseas journals and periodicals, syndicated essays and reviews, local commentary, lectures, and correspondence by mail. Colonial authors who refer directly or implicitly to Emerson and Whitman include, for example, Kendall, Clarke, J.D. Lang, Deniehy, William Gay, Catherine Martin, Brennan, James Smith, Miles Franklin and many others besides those discussed in this essay. Carlyle especially, and Ruskin and Wordsworth were also equally widely read, and fed into Australian colonial frames of reference. 'Transcendentalism' offered a metaphysical aesthetic position in opposition to other major colonial discourses and intellectual doctrines including: Benthamite and Millian utilitarianism; philosophical materialism; pessimism and fatalism (as adopted by A.L. Gordon); and any form of Christianity which affirmed original sin and the divinity and redemptive role of Jesus Christ. Many colonial readers and literati were Unitarians, or open-minded Christians like Ada Cambridge and her clergyman husband George Cross, for whom Emerson's skepticism and radicalism, and his departure from the Unitarian pulpit, were a source of appeal or interest rather than dissatisfaction. They explain a fascination that was at least as 'religious', but possibly less national and republican, than in the United States, or indeed in much of the later Emerson's writings. The 'mystic' Emerson was probably more prominent in Australia than America where Self-Reliance could be enlisted, for example by Henry Ford, as not merely national ideology but as capitalist propaganda.

Spence, Deakin and O'Dowd saw Emerson's Self-Reliance and the Over-Soul not as rebellious or seditious, but as potentially a speculative extension of their own faith. A transcendental optimism fed into their literary nationalism, as an aesthetic as well as a faith. Spence crusaded against Balzacian realism and 'the modern wave of pessimism in literature', which 'ignore[s] the joyousness of Australian life'. The tales told, 'While the Billy Boils', are 'not all tragedies'. Harpur and O'Dowd lay the heavy bricks of their bleak indignation on a foundation of spiritual hope; and Deakin, a product of the urban Victorian gold ethos, celebrated an 'Australian school' of bush poets as the young and invigorating deliverers of a national literary imaginary. At times both the intellectual essentials of literary idealism, and, (as Henry Lawson complained) the opportunity of a critical nationalism, were easily lost in the enthusiasm of a 'joyously' romantic aesthetic.

Nevertheless an Australian idealist literary tradition has endured, ironically achieving the (once) privileged status accorded 'the Great Australian Novel', comprising canonical works such as *His Natural Life*, *The Fortunes of Richard Mahony*, *The Tree of Man*, and *Voss*. That each of these Australian novels was also highly successful in the United States, winning (with the exception of the early Clarke book) prizes and awards, critical acclaim, 'Book of the Month' recognition, and substantial sales, is not entirely coincidental. In certain literary contexts each has also been labelled 'transcendentalist', and has been packaged in American editions to signal that quality (in dust-jacket illustrations, descriptions and blurbs). More recently, adopting the same métier, Australian novelist Geraldine Brooks was awarded a Pulitzer Prize for her novel *March*, a fictionalised version of the life of Concord abolitionist and transcendentalist Bronson Alcott. The protagonist in each of the above novels is a damaged metaphysical seeker in a destructive conformist philistine society, whose discovery of a spiritual and ethical integrity requires a 'journey into the self' that discovers spiritual 'truth' but is ironically paralleled by his own gradual material destruction. Although the novels do not themselves necessarily endorse a transcendentalist position, in each case a dualist or 'idealist' universe is established to debate and problematise the issues, and establish the fictional scheme.

The 'G.A.N.', whether Great 'Australian' or 'American' novel, is so well established in literary histories that any description of it today courts the stigma of the *demode*. There is, however, a difference between the American and the Australian G.N., within its respective national literary histories: for in Australia, literary transcendentalism in the twentieth century survived by finding in fiction a discrete moral high ground, detachable from popular culture and national discourses; whereas in the United States the relationship with mainstream individualism, however complex, various and at times incompatible with dominant social values, has been maintained in some degree by the synchronised and synonymous assertion of its own 'American individualism'.

4

Looking to American Manhood: The Correspondence of Alfred Deakin and Josiah Royce

Marilyn Lake

On the last day of December, 1888, Alfred Deakin, the young Chief Secretary in the colony of Victoria wrote a long and enthusiastic letter to his new found friend, Josiah Royce, a rising star in the philosophy department at Harvard University, who, some years after his death would be described in an article on the discipline of philosophy in the *Sydney Morning Herald* as 'the outstanding Idealist of America'.[1] The two men met in Melbourne, in early June 1888, courtesy of a letter of introduction from their mutual friend, Richard Hodgson, a Melbournian then working with William James at the Society for Psychical Research in Cambridge, Massachusetts.[2]

Deakin and Royce spent an intense and enjoyable week together walking and talking in the Blue Mountains near Sydney. Royce who had been suffering from depression appreciated Deakin's cheering companionship: 'I can't tell you how much you brightened me up'. Deakin replied that Royce's companionship was 'a source of unalloyed pleasure and profit' and added:

---

1 *Sydney Morning Herald*, 20 February 1926.

2 J.A. La Nauze, *Alfred Deakin: A Biography vol.1* incorrectly states that the two met on the train to Sydney. In fact they met in Melbourne when Royce brought his letter of introduction from Hodgson to Deakin after his ship *The Freeman* landed there after a voyage of three months. See Frank Oppenheim, *Royce's Voyage Down Under* (Lexington: University Press of Kentucky, 1980), pp. 6–13.

> Yours is the best trained and best informed mind in metaphysics and kindred topics that I have ever had the opportunity of enjoying. You showed me inter alia how much there is to be gained by the intellectual society of an older world than ours.[3]

An older world, but a democratic, vigorous and manly one. This was the appeal of the country Deakin liked to call 'the great republic'. He was then just thirty-two; Royce one year older. In appearance they presented contrasting types. Deakin was tall, dark and handsome; Royce short, stocky, red-haired and heavily freckled. In their intellectual and political interests, however, in their preoccupation with religious experience and their questing idealism they were as one. Though spending only a week together, they would remain friends for life, one becoming an eminent Professor of Philosophy and President of the American Philosophical Association, the other Prime Minister of Australia, their affectionate bond maintained through reading and writing, sending and receiving a variety of letters, articles, books, copies of Hansard and Federal Convention Reports.

The Rugged Power of American Literature

After they parted, in June 1888, they immediately exchanged books, Deakin sending Royce a collection of pen sketches, *Gum Boughs and Wattle Bloom, Gathered on Australian Hills and Plains* by Donald McDonald, a journalist at the *Argus* newspaper, which had been published in London, in 1887, just the year before. It was 'thoroughly faithful and genuine', Deakin had assured Royce: 'I trust it will reach you safely so as to supplement your knowledge of our natural scenery'.[4] Royce was planning to write some articles for American journals—*Scribner's Magazine* and *The Atlantic Monthly*—on his impressions of Australia.

Royce sent Deakin a package of his own early writings—despatched by his publisher—including a novel, *The Feud of Oakfield Creek: A Novel*

3 Royce to Deakin 21 June 1888, Deakin Papers, National Library of Australia, 1540/1/48; Deakin to Royce 30 June 1888, Deakin Papers, 1540/1/49.

4 Deakin to Royce 30 June 1888, Deakin Papers, 1540/1/49.

of Californian Life, a history of California and a philosophical work, *The Religious Aspect of Philosophy*. Royce, like Deakin had grown up close to raw and unruly gold rush communities and he wrote about their domestication through the coming of families, churches, communities and the rule of law. Deakin was thrilled to receive copies of Royce's works. He wrote from Melbourne to say that because they were 'a part of yourself and smack of your individuality' this increased their attraction.[5]

Deakin didn't presume to offer criticism, but wanted to say how they affected him. *Oakfield Creek* he thought had 'all the freshness, realism and vigor of the best American fiction dealing with America'. He elaborated on its American qualities of power and strength:

> It is as much Californian as 'The Prophet of Smoky Mountain'[6] is I suppose characteristic of Tennessee. California being much more like Victoria and having a glimpse of it I feel this vividness of its localism keenly. The chief quality of the whole is strength. The plot is strong and the chief characters are strong also ... Yours is a new world Tito Melema drawn from life and not copied. The whole book gives an impression of great and somewhat rugged power. The plot is in hand from the first page and the treatment is sure throughout.[7]

Deakin did presume to offer one small criticism: the novel was too long and could be halved as, they had agreed in their talks, should have happened in the case of the great Russian novel, *Anna Karenina*.

Deakin's warm appreciation of Royce's novel extended to his history, *California: A Study of American Character: From the Conquest in 1846 to the Second Vigilance Committee in San Francisco*, which had been

5 Deakin to Royce 31 December 1888, Deakin Papers, 1540/1/63.

6 *The Prophet of the Great Smoky Mountains* was written by Mary Noailles Murfee under the male pseudonym, Charles Egbert Craddock and published in 1885 by Houghton Mifflin. Set in the rural hills of the Smokies, contemporary reviewers praised it for its exploration of the tensions created by the encroaching Tennessee state authority on the mountaineers' lives.

7 Deakin to Royce 31 December 1888, Deakin Papers, 1540/1/63.

published in a series on 'American Commonwealths'. 'The History of California appears even more original in its treatment than the novel', wrote Deakin. It offered an 'invaluable political and social treatise'. He was particularly impressed by Royce's rendering of the coming of social order to California as 'a sociological example, more striking than any of its kind I have ever read of the true operation of moral law'.[8] Royce disapproved of the military conquest, thought it unnecessary and that it displayed a weakness in American national character. Americans tended to justify aggression by talking of it as God's will.

'You have reason to be proud of both your books', Deakin told Royce, 'and so has your literature'.[9] Royce thanked him for his kind words but protested that they were not key works of American literature, having only sold a few thousand copies: '"California" 2000 copies (a little less), Rel. Asp. Of Phil. 1000 copies and the novel ditto'. 'If you ask visiting Americans who I am', Royce suggested 'the wisest will greet you with a blank stare of surprise. I am quite an unknown young college professor, and you do far too kindly by me'.[10]

When during the following month he read *The Religious Aspect of Philosophy* (twice) he praised its kinship to Royce's other two books and its American qualities: 'Your style seems to me sinewy, fresh and graphic, but it is too composite'. This time Deakin thought the book too short and that its 'happy thrusts and telling paraphrases' tended to interrupt the necessary development of the argument and break the readers' continuity of thought.[11]

Deakin prided himself on his knowledge of American literature and saw in it an example that the nation-to-be that was Australia must surely emulate. He admired Hawthorne, Thoreau and Whitman and had undertaken a pilgrimage to Emerson's grave in Concord, Massachusetts, in 1885, probably at the suggestion of his mentor Charles Pearson, who had met Emerson in 1868 and written a review of his work when he died in 1883. Oliver Wendell Holmes Sr whom Pearson had also met

---

8 Deakin to Royce 31 December 1888, Deakin Papers, 1540/1/63.

9 Deakin to Royce 31 December 1888, Deakin Papers, 1540/1/63.

10 Royce to Deakin 28 February 1889, Deakin Papers, 1540/1/75.

11 Deakin to Royce 22 April 1889, Deakin Papers, 1540/1/80.

had famously praised Emerson's essay 'The American Scholar' as 'our intellectual Declaration of Independence'. Thomas Carlyle, who had introduced Emerson's essays in the English edition commended his 'man's voice'; he was 'a kinsman and brother', an 'original veridical man'. Emerson was a prophet of Self-Reliance, the 'best single key' according to his biographer Lawrence Buell, 'to his thought and influence'.[12] In his notebooks, Deakin often quoted Emerson on Self-Reliance, the importance of self-trust and the centrality of a strong will to manhood: 'A grand will, which when legitimate & abiding we call character, the height of manhood'.[13]

In a passage on 'Australian literature' in his notebooks, Deakin mused:

> In this new land we look to America ... Hawthorne Emerson ... The ideas of progressives & of the infinite perfectability of the human race belong to democratic ages. Democratic nations care little for what has been, but they are haunted by visions of what will be; in this direction then unbounded imagination ... [14]

When Royce wrote about Australia and Deakin on his return to Harvard, he recalled:

> a young man, nervously active in temperament, cheerful, enquiring, speculative, unprejudiced—unless it were in favour of the political tendencies of the country where he is Cabinet Minister—an admirer of America and of good scenery, a lover of life, of metaphysics and power.[15]

For Deakin the American republic represented masculine power; colonialism meant subjection to imperial rule, embodied by Queen Victoria

12 Lawrence Buell, *Emerson* (Cambridge: Harvard University Press, 2003), pp. 45, 49, 328.

13 Notebook on entries on subjects, Deakin Papers, 1540/3/11.

14 Deakin notebooks, Deakin Papers, 1540/3/1–2.

15 *Scribner's Magazine* IX.1 (January 1891): 78.

and her disdainful prime minister, whom Deakin had confronted in London, in 1887, the year before Royce's visit to Australia, with what he styled 'unrestrained vigour'.[16]

Harvard Manhood

Deakin was not alone in the late nineteenth century in looking towards America when shaping his democratic aspirations for Australia, caring little for what had been, but rather directing an unbounded imagination towards 'what will be'. Other Australian liberal democrats, such as Andrew Inglis Clark and H.B. Higgins, who also grew to manhood in the second part of the nineteenth century, were widely read in United States history, law and literature. Each was drawn to nurturing and stimulating American friendships, in particular with Harvard men, luminous examples of what historian Kim Townsend called in the book of that name, *Manhood at Harvard*.[17] The self-conscious mission of Harvard, as Charles William Eliot, president of Harvard between 1869 and 1909 saw it, was to prepare men for 'the strenuous competitions of the world, and win the mental power, the nervous power to succeed in them'.[18]

Charles Eliot Norton, the foundation professor of Fine Arts at Harvard, translator of Dante and editor of the *North American Review* was in the view of his contemporary, the historian Albert Bushnell Hart, a 'model for Harvard manhood'.[19] Norton was the ideal in that he considered that the true goal of education was not reached via study of any particular subject. Rather it was 'the consummation of all studies', 'the final result of intellectual culture in the development of the breadth, serenity, and solidity of mind … in the attainment of that complete self-possession which finds expression in character'.[20]

---

16 Alfred Deakin, *The Federal Story: The Inner History of the Federal Cause 1880–1900*, edited and introduced by J.A. LaNauze (Melbourne: Melbourne University Press, 1963), pp. 22–23.

17 Kim Townsend, *Manhood at Harvard: William James and Others* (Cambridge: Harvard University Press, 1996).

18 Townsend, p. 22.

19 Townsend, p. 82.

20 Townsend, p. 81.

Deakin's mentor at the University of Melbourne, Charles Henry Pearson, became one of Norton's many friends when he travelled from England to Boston in 1868, five years after he had first been to Australia. Personable and erudite, an outspoken supporter of the North in the Civil War, Norton combined in Pearson's admiring view 'refinement and scholarly taste' with pronounced sympathy with the 'democratic tone of American institutions'.[21] Recoiling from the brutality of British class inequalities and the entrenched privileges of landed aristocracy, Pearson was powerfully attracted to the promise of New World democracy. He wrote admiringly about the Australian example in the English collection *Essays on Reform* in 1867.

Andrew Inglis Clark, Chief Justice of the Supreme Court of Tasmania, also enjoyed a friendship with one of Harvard's luminaries, Oliver Wendell Holmes Jr, Chief Justice of the Supreme Court of Massachusetts, whom Clark met in Boston in 1890. Clark's love for all things American was well known. A letter of introduction commended him as 'a great admirer of the splendid manhood' of America.[22] Clark was a particular admirer of Holmes' classic work *The Common Law*, which was a constant reference for lectures and judgments. 'Your book on the Common Law continues with renewed charm to supply me with an annual course of instruction in first principles', Clark wrote to Holmes in 1892, 'and the whole substance of a lecture I delivered to a local association of law students'.[23] The copy of Holmes' *Speeches* he sent to Clark that year gave him 'very much pleasure'; they had 'vividly revived the memory of the very delightful time I spent in your company in Boston'.[24]

Another of Clark's correspondents was the Harvard historian Albert Bushnell Hart, Norton's admirer, who regularly quizzed Clark about the progress of the Australian federal conventions and requested copies of

---

21 Charles Pearson, 'The Story of My Life', in William Stebbing, ed., *Charles Henry Pearson: Memorials by Himself, His Wife and His Friends* (London: Longman, Green and Co, 1900), p. 92.

22 A.I Clark Papers, C4/C 391 (12), University of Tasmania Archives.

23 Clark to Holmes 20 January 1892, Clark Papers, C4/C211 (5).

24 Clark to Holmes 20 January 1892, Holmes Papers, Harvard Law School.

the reports so that he could use them in a course he was teaching on federal government. He wrote gratefully to Clark:

> The Debates and Journals of the Australian Convention duly arrived in time to be of much service to me and to a class in federal government. I have turned them over to the Harvard College Library who will send you due acknowledgment. The friends of good government throughout the world are rejoiced at the final accomplishment of your big task.[25]

The President and Fellows of Harvard College duly thanked Clark for these records of Australian Federation history, which can now be found in the Widener Library.[26]

H.B. Higgins, President of the Commonwealth Arbitration Court, also enjoyed a stimulating and encouraging friendship with the Harvard man Justice Felix Frankfurter, whom Higgins met when visiting in 1914. Frankfurter subsequently became a leading champion of Higgins' ideas about industrial relations as 'a new province for law and order', which had been published in the *Harvard Law Review* in 1915 and a regular correspondent with him.

Books Like Yours Are Hailed

Living thousands of miles from each other, these were for the most part epistolary friendships, thriving on the exchange of books and ideas and news of politics and society. On the Australian side letters were sometimes also expressions of deep longing. Thus did Andrew Inglis Clark write to Oliver Wendell Holmes Jr in 1901, the year of the inauguration of the Australian Commonwealth of whose Constitution he had been co-author, saying how much he longed to be in Boston. 'I suppose that you had a good time in England', he wrote, wistfully:

> I often wish that Australia was as near to California as Massachusetts is to England. I should then see Boston

25 Hart to Clark, Clark Papers, C4/C198.

26 President and Fellows of Harvard College to Clark 24 February 1892, Clark Papers, C4/C199.

> every three or four years, and would probably be preparing now for a journey there early next year. But I must bow to the geographical configuration of the earth and all its consequences and wait in patience until my time to cross the Pacific Ocean again arrives. [27]

In the first years after their meeting, Deakin yearned to hear from Royce, who confessed that he was not a good letter writer. 'You do not reply to letters and I am scarcely surprised at it', chided Deakin in 1891, 'though I should like to hear what you are doing and follow what you are writing'. He added that when in Sydney for the Federal Convention he took the opportunity to revisit the place of their meeting:

> I ran up to the Blue Mountains and took my Easter by myself in the same hotel and in the same haunts as those in which we passed hours that were among the pleasantest I have ever spent. [28]

Deakin also longed to hear of Royce's 'literary undertakings'.[29] Royce kept faith by regularly sending Deakin copies of his new books, beginning in 1892 with the collection of lectures on key thinkers including Spinoza, Kant and Hegel titled *The Spirit of Modern Philosophy.* Deakin praised its chatty colloquial style:

> It ought to be widely read for in it you have brought the Idealistic philosophy down into the marketplace and unless American wits are much denser than I suppose you are laying the foundations for a new growth of metaphysical thinkers under your influence.

And he thanked his friend for helping to clarify his own thinking:

> What a great help your book has been to me. In my blindfold way rather by faith than by intellectual sight I have reached

---

27 Clark to Holmes, 26 October 1901, Clark Papers C4/C211 (3).

28 Deakin to Royce, 8 July 1891, Royce Papers, Incoming correspondence to Royce, Box 1 of 5. HUG 1755.3.3, Harvard University Archives.

29 Deakin to Royce 8 May 1890. Ibid.

> some of the positions you attain by force of thinking … Disgust with the easy optimism of the moderns which you so powerfully dispose of gave me a zest for Carlyle's diatribes and I had even come by degrees to realise Kant's place and importance. These things were cloudy and disconnected beliefs—part of my world of appreciation—of which I could not have given a description. But now you have provided the means and have given form and substance to my dreams—and much besides … I can hardly conceive any more useful teaching for students at present time than the spiritual reading of Evolution and its meaning which you give.[30]

In late 1897 Deakin received a copy of *Conception of God*, which contained essays by Royce, Joseph Le Conte, his former teacher at Berkeley, and G.H. Howison. Royce's essay had been delivered as an address at his *alma mater*, the University of California, Berkeley, to whose academic community he expressed a deep sense of obligation.

Deakin wrote to him in January 1898: 'I was naturally greatly gratified to find myself remembered by you and in so handsome a fashion on receipt of the copy of your last book'.[31] He told Royce that he had recommended his various books to friends including the Rev. Charles Strong of the Australian Church, who was 'particularly impressed by them'. Once again Deakin praised Royce's book for its American qualities:

> Your method is so thorough and your style so simple and effective, pithy and graphic, that, coupled as these are with a bold frankness and sense of humour which appear to us to be 'American', it seems to me the combination ought to rehabilitate Anglo-Saxon metaphysics … [32]

30 Deakin to Royce 5 June 1892, Deakin Papers, 1540/1/159.

31 Deakin to Royce 14 January 1898, Deakin Papers, 1540/1/411.

32 Ibid.

Deakin also reported on his own political activities, especially with regard to the movement in the Australian colonies towards federation. Following the financial crash of the early 1890s, he had retreated to the sidelines of Victorian politics to work as a barrister, embarrassed by the economic collapse of the colony over which he had presided and by his own financial dealings. 'My one political hope', he confessed, 'lies in Federation to which I have devoted as much of my time as possible'.[33] He told Royce that he had sent copies of the convention records from Adelaide and Sydney, in case he had any curiosity as to that movement. He stressed the importance of the American example to the project of Australian federation ('it follows so largely the precedent of the United States') and how his thinking on the subject had been influenced by their conversation : 'In this field also I am free to admit that the political chats we had in the Blue Mts. affected my own opinion of your Constitution and system of Government very considerably'.[34]

More generally, Deakin expressed his gratitude for Royce's work in providing him with solace and strength. In such troubled times, with the strife of the modern industrial struggle, the clash of opposing political doctrines, and the collapse of financial institutions 'books like yours are hailed by many whose anchors are drifting, or likely to drift under the stress of trials and perplexities, personal and general, such as assail us all in these days of upheaval'. Thus from 'faraway Australia' Deakin asked Royce to accept a

> note of sincere thanks … just to say how highly your work is appreciated by those who if not qualified to be your jurors, are nevertheless encouraged, rallied and inspirited by the force and sincerity of your thinking, its scope and insight and the constructive conclusions that you so resolutely establish.[35]

At the end of 1898 Deakin wrote to thank Royce for the copy of his *Studies of Good and Evil: A Series of Essays upon the Problems of*

33 Ibid., 1540/1/412.

34 Ibid.

35 Ibid.

Philosophy and of Life which he had been 'duly studying' in the 'few intervals of leisure' available to him as he negotiated conflicts and mediated disputes between the delegates to the Constitution Conventions. Royce considered his essays in *Studies of Good and Evil* to be contributions to the comprehension of the ethical aspects of the universe. The collection contained reflections on a diversity of topics—a combination of literary and philosophical criticism, analysis of metaphysical and psychological problems and a historical study of 'a concrete conflict between good and evil tendencies in early Californian life'.[36]

Once again Deakin thanked Royce for the usefulness of his philosophical reflections in helping him deal with the practical problems of real life. From his office in the Victorian Legislative Assembly, Deakin wrote:

> [M]y chief debt as before is for the valuable and very helpful character of your reflections and the assistance you lend to those like myself too feeble to fly in the rare ether of Idealism without aid or support. In bringing your doctrine down from the heights into the practical realm of daily life you have repeated the feat attributed to Socrates … In dealing with present day problems or with ever present problems from your standpoint you certainly do much to bridge that gulf which appears to lie between abstract disquisitions upon metaphysical principles and the actual trials and difficulties of life.[37]

Perhaps thinking of his own recent political labours, Deakin added that he had sent Royce the latest Federal Convention reports—'not with any suspicion that you could or would look at them except to shudder at their bulk, but on the chance that someone in your acquaintance might wish to see them or some library find them a place'.[38] Harvard's libraries

36 Josiah Royce, *Studies of Good and Evil: A Series of Essays upon the Problems of Philosophy and of Life* (New York: D. Appleton and Co, 1898), p. v.

37 Deakin to Royce 27 November 1898, Deakin Papers, 1540/1/42.

38 Ibid.

were being inundated with documentation of the Australian federal story.

Ten years passed without any further contact between the two friends. Then in 1908, Deakin, by then Australian Prime Minister, prepared to receive the visit of the United States Naval Fleet, sent by Theodore Roosevelt in response to Deakin's personal invitation. To his delight he received in the mail a gift of Royce's latest and what would become one of his most highly regarded books, *The Philosophy of Loyalty.* Royce noted in his letter that his country's naval fleet was soon to visit Australia:

> I venture to send in advance of the fleet—vast and noisy as it is—my very tiny and silent book ... a word of greeting about our common ideals. If you have time to look at it some day—for an hour or two—remember that its author loves you.[39]

Royce apologised for his silence and wrote movingly of the continuing power of Deakin's presence in his life. Now aged fifty-two years, 'an oldish professor, who stoop[ed] a little and carr[ied] too many books around' he recalled the time and place they met twenty years before as young men:

> Few memories stand out more clearly and encouragingly, and more pleasingly in my life, than our meeting in 1888, our days together in the wonderland of your mountains, our talks, and your kindness, and the gracious cheer of all your hospitality. What a place the meeting and your presence and personality have since occupied in my life, I can hardly tell you.[40]

Royce believed that an individual's highest achievements were realised in a consciously chosen loyalty to a common cause or community. Deakin was encouraged to define their 'common ideals' as those shared by the Commonwealth and the Republic. In his speech

---

39 Deakin to Royce, 18 April 1908, 1540/1/1964.

40 Royce to Deakin, 18 April 1908, Deakin Papers, 1540/1/1964.

on the occasion of the Fleet's visit Deakin referred to 'Prof. Royce of Harvard' and spoke of the ideals of community and unity immanent in the ethic of loyalty. Ultimately they might look forward to the 'unity of mankind' as Royce had suggested, but in the meantime,

> Realising the riches of natural national relationships, we look, instinctively, first and most confidently, to you Americans, nearest to us in blood, in character, and in purpose. It is in this spirit, and in this hope, that Australia welcomes with open hand and heart the coming of your sailors, and of the flag, which like our own, shelters a new world under the control of its vital union. May the present accord between English-speaking peoples beget a perpetual concord of brotherhood between us ...[41]

The first draft of Deakin's speech had referred to 'the friendship between the Empire and the Republic' but this was deleted in favour of a more exclusive relationship between Australians and Americans, informed by the 'ardent hope of all our citizens ... that their friendship, strengthened as it now is among us by many new personal ties, may long endure and flourish on both sides of the Pacific'.[42]

Deakin's strong identification with and admiration for the United States found personal expression in his relationship with Royce, but by 1908, even at the height of their mutual accord, there was evidence of a significant political divergence. That year Royce published another book of essays based on talks he had given in the last three years called *Race Prejudice, Provincialism and Other American Problems* in which he denounced race prejudice as ignorant folly, destructive of community. Race prejudice, Royce said, was caused by our antipathies and based on illusions—it was common for people to cherish illusions, he wrote, but they should not 'sanctify them by the name of science'.[43] It seems that this was one of his books that Royce didn't send to Deakin, perhaps

41 Deakin Papers, 1540/15/3908.

42 Ibid. 1540/15/3910; 1540/15/3911.

43 Josiah Royce, *Race Prejudice, Provincialism and Other American Problems* (New York: Macmillan, 1908), pp. 26–66.

thinking its arguments would simply embarrass his friend, some of whose political efforts included the *Immigration Restriction Act* and the *Pacific Island Labourers Act*, legislation which would be later referred to as the White Australia policy.

Conclusion: Sister Republic or Daughter of Empire?

Historians have generally ignored the significance of Deakin's friendship with Royce and its broader context of fraternal yearning across the Pacific—his attraction to republican manhood. For example, J.A. La Nauze, Deakin's biographer, completely omits Deakin's pilgrimage to Emerson's grave from his two-volume account of Deakin's life and gives just two pages to his long friendship with Royce. And even then he, as we have seen, gets some of the facts wrong.

The ambitions of Australian progressives such as Charles Pearson, Andrew Inglis Clark, Alfred Deakin and H.B. Higgins were shaped by the example of the vigorous manhood of the great republic, but those aspirations have been lost in histories written in nationalist or British imperial frameworks. The historical amnesia about radical liberals' desire for republican manhood and the strength of identification with the United States, buoyed by the conceit of their common Anglo-Saxon heritage has been exacerbated in recent times by the promotion of the concept of 'British race patriotism' by Neville Meaney and his followers, who see it as definitive of Australian political culture across the nineteenth and twentieth centuries until its demise in the 1960s.[44]

In fact, British race patriotism is best understood as a new formation. It was a political response to Australians' identification with the United Sates, a reactionary force aimed at overcoming the powerful attraction to America before World War I, and aimed at locking Australia back into the imperial embrace. The threat posed to British interests at the turn of the century by the growing affinity between Australia and the United States—dramatically symbolised by the visit of the United States Fleet

44 James Curran and Stuart Ward, *The Unknown Nation: Australia after Empire* (Melbourne: Melbourne University Press, 2010); Neville Meaney, 'Britishness and Australia: Some Reflections', *Journal of Imperial and Commonwealth History* 31.2 (2007): 121–35.

to Melbourne and Sydney in 1908—was noted by Sir Charles Lucas. As head of the newly formed Dominions Office, Lucas wrote of his fear that the Dominions might break away from the Mother Country and form a new organisation 'having its roots in race affinity' that would directly challenge the idea of Imperial unity.[45]

Two voyages undertaken during World War I nicely symbolise the changing order. In 1915, at the time the Australian Imperial Force as part of a larger British force was invading Turkey, Deakin travelled across the Pacific to the still-neutral United States to receive an Honorary Doctor of Laws from the University of California, Berkeley, where Royce had undertaken his undergraduate degree and first worked as a lecturer. It was the only such accolade he agreed to accept, having refused honorary degrees from Oxford and Cambridge as well as a British knighthood. In inviting Deakin to accept the degree in 1915, the university president spoke of the high service he had rendered to government in 'our neighbour commonwealth across the ocean'. Deakin spoke in turn of his 'very deep sense of the proposed compliment'.[46]

In 1916, Sir Henry Rider Haggard arrived in Australia as an emissary of the Royal Colonial Institute, formed in London in 1915, to lock Australia into a vast imperial land settlement scheme. He toured the state capitals to persuade the premiers to make their lands available to his grand vision. As I wrote many years ago in my book on soldier settlement after World War I, the arrival of Rider Haggard in Australia in 1916 both symbolised and made real 'the British intention to reinvigorate the empire strategy'.[47] As Haggard wrote in his memorandum to the Premiers' Conference in May 1916:

---

45 Quoted in Marilyn Lake and Henry Reynolds, *Drawing the Global Colour Line: White Men's Countries and the Question of Racial Equality* (Melbourne: Melbourne University Press, 2008), p. 233.

46 President, University of California, Berkeley, 15 May 1915, Deakin Papers 1540/17/162; Deakin reply, 21 May 1915, 1540/17/166.

47 Marilyn Lake, *The Limits of Hope: Soldier Settlement in Victoria 1915–38* (Melbourne: Oxford University Press, 1987), p. 31. See also Peter Pierce, 'Rider Haggard in Australia', *Meanjin* 2 (1977).

> The Royal Colonial Institute and its sympathisers are of the opinion that the state of the Empire, with reference to its white population and otherwise, and the dangers by which undoubtedly it will be confronted in the future demand that its citizens should as far as possible dwell within its limits.[48]

This was the work required of 'British race patriotism'.

In the 1880s, Deakin and Royce had discussed their vision of Australia as a 'future sister republic' joining the United States as 'co-workers' in 'the cause of free civilization' but by the end of World War I, with the exploits of the Australian Imperial Force invoked as the basis of a new national tradition, Australia had succumbed to a reinvigorated vision of its place in the Empire.[49]

---

48 Ibid.

49 Josiah Royce, 'Reflections after a Wandering Life in Australasia', *Atlantic Monthly* LXIII (1889): 676.

5

American Friends: Clinton Hartley Grattan and W.W. Norton

Carol Hetherington

Numerous commentators have noted affinities between Australia and America. These observations differ in tone and focus but they are all strongly indicative of a perceived connection between two countries in the 'new' world, former colonies of an imperial power. The following quotations cover a range of voices over a period of time. In *Moby Dick* (1851) Herman Melville described Australia as that 'great America on the other side of the sphere';[1] Jack London commented in 1908 that 'Australia is first cousin to America. They have the same sort of patriotism';[2] P.R. Stephensen asserted truculently in 1933 that 'Americans are interested in us ... There is a real kinship, greater in essence than our carefully boosted up link with Britain'[3] and in 2002 Peter Carey's American editor Gary Fisketjon noted 'We former colonials enjoy a kinship that feels to me very natural and quite comfortable'.[4] David Malouf, writing in 2003, refers to 'The close relationship with the United States [which] has for Australians been there from the start'.[5]

---

1 Herman Melville, *Moby Dick* (New York: W.W. Norton, 1967), p. 99.

2 Quoted in Laurie Hergenhan, 'Jack London and the Never Never', *Overland*. 177 (2004): 88.

3 Stephensen to Hartley Grattan 27 May 1933, Grattan Papers, Harry Ransom Humanities Research Center, University of Texas, Box 35, file 1 (a), p. 3

4 Jason Steger, 'Book World Beats a Path to Our Authors of Success', *Sunday Age*, 5 May 2002, p. 8.

5 David Malouf, 'Made in England: Australia's British Inheritance', *Quarterly*

The connections suggested by these remarks have never been fully documented or analysed. There have been important historical, economic and cultural studies of the Australian–American relationship: Hartley Grattan's work *Introducing Australia* (1942) and *The US and the South West Pacific* (1961) would be part of such a list, as should Joseph Jones' *Radical Cousins: Nineteenth Century American and Australian Writers* (1976). What is missing is an examination of literary interactions and affinities. Indeed this is noted by Jones in his preface, where he describes his own work as 'not a definitive work of scholarship but rather a short reconnaissance'.[6] Numerous studies of such links between Australia and England exist, pitched at both the academic and the general audience. In the former category, Stephen Alomes' *When London Calls* documents the history of Australian expatriate writers in Britain. An example of the latter is Roslyn Russell's *Literary Links* (1997), which had its genesis in a major multimedia exhibition jointly sponsored by the British Council and the National Library of Australia in 1993.[7] No similar display or examination of Australian and American literary connections has ever been mounted. Apart from several articles on Jack London and Mark Twain by Laurie Hergenhan, and his 1995 biography of Clinton Hartley Grattan, *No Casual Traveller*, the area has been, until recently, largely unexplored.[8] The first large-scale, systematic examination of the area is currently in progress through David Carter's 2007 Australian Research Council-funded research project 'America Publishes Australia: Australian Books and American Publishers, 1890–2005'.

What will this investigation find? Will it reveal a continuing and definable thread or pattern running through this literary relationship?

Essay (Melbourne, Victoria: Black Inc., 2003), p. 4.

6 Joseph Jones, *Radical Cousins: Nineteenth Century American and Australian Writers* (St Lucia, Qld: University of Queensland Press, 1976), p. x.

7 Roslyn Russell, *Literary Links: Celebrating the Literary Relationship Between Australia and Britain* (St Leonards, NSW: Allen & Unwin, 1997).

8 See Laurie Hergenhan, *No Casual Traveller: Hartley Grattan and Australia–US Connections* (St Lucia, Qld: University of Queensland Press, 1995); 'Jack London and the Never Never', *Overland.* 177 (2004): 88–89; 'Beautiful Lies, Ugly Truths', *Overland* 187 (2007): 42–46.

Or will it point to a complex set of diverse personal and particular relationships between individual writers, publishers and audiences at different points in time? Existing research reveals great variety in the ways Americans have engaged with Australian literature and writers. Australian family sagas were popular in America in the 1930s and 1940s: G.B. Lancaster's *Pageant: A Novel of Tasmania* was first published in New York in 1931; *The Fortunes of Richard Mahony* appeared in 1931 and was reprinted in 1941 in a Readers Club edition with a foreword by Sinclair Lewis in which he focuses on parallels between the two countries' pioneering history; Barnard Eldershaw's *A House is Built* was published in 1941 and was a Book of the Month Club choice. These appealed, one suspects, to quite a different audience than that which eagerly purchased Norman Lindsay's more urbane, cosmopolitan novels like *The Cautious Amorist* (1932) and *Pan in the Parlour* (1933).[9] And are either of these the same type of audience who now reads David Malouf, Janette Turner Hospital and Peter Carey? Like the family sagas, *The Tree of Man* and *Voss* have pioneer and frontier themes, yet Simon During has attributed Patrick White's success in America to an American editor's receptiveness to their modernism and 'highly individuated ... art writing'.[10] Other publishers and their editors have taken up Australian authors not because of their Australian content, but because of the genres in which they write: cases in point are crime fiction writer Arthur Upfield (1890–1964), who had a long and successful career with the Doubleday Crime Club, and romance writer Maysie Grieg.[11] Genre

9 Norman Lindsay, stifled by conservatism and censorship in Australia, published five novels in New York during the 1930s. One of these, *The Cautious Amorist*, was first serialised in *Cosmopolitan* in 1932 and was so successful it was published in three hardback editions, in 1932, 1940 and 1946, and reprinted in paperback editions until the late 1950s. The novels were *Redheap* (as *Every Mother's Son*), 1930, *The Cautious Amorist*, 1932, *Pan in the Parlour*, 1933, *Mr Gresham and Olympus* (*Miracles by Arrangement* in England), 1932, and *Age of Consent*, 1938. For discussion of their success, see Patricia Holt, '"It's Enough to Drive a Bloke Mad': Norman Lindsay's Art and Literature', *Bibliographical Society of Australia and New Zealand Bulletin* 27.1–2 (2003): 62–81.

10 Simon During, *Patrick White* (Melbourne: Oxford University Press, 1996), p. 6.

11 See my 'Bony at Home and Abroad: The Arthur Upfield Phenomenon', *JASAL*

fiction appears to have an easier passage between national boundaries than does literary fiction. If there is a commonality to be found in the history of publishing and reception of Australian literature in America it should emerge from Carter's study, but I suspect that there will also be evidence of a significant number of unique situations and circumstances that defy generalisation.

In this context, I would like to look at two highly individual cases of Americans whose connections with Australian literary culture have been of significant and lasting importance: Clinton Hartley Grattan and William Warder Norton. One popular approach to exploring cultural connections has been to investigate the experiences and impressions of literary visitors to Australia, as with Russell's *Literary Links*, previously mentioned, and Susannah Fullerton's recent *Brief Encounters: Literary Travellers in Australia 1836–1939* (2009). As Fullerton notes, although many of these visitors have gone on to record their impressions of Australian culture and literature, they have almost without exception come here by chance. Mark Twain came here on a lecture tour because he was on the verge of bankruptcy; Jack London abandoned his Pacific odyssey on *The Snark* to receive medical treatment in Sydney and recuperate in Tasmania; Zane Grey came for the big game fishing at Bermagui. Twain's *Following the Equator: A Journey Around the World* (1897) contains fascinating insights and observations. Jack London wrote six articles for the *Sydney Star* and a short story based on his Australian experiences; he also recognised the importance of Mrs Aeneas Gunn's *We of the Never Never*, writing an introduction for a proposed American edition that was never published.[12] Zane Grey's *An American Angler in Australia* (1937) had at least a popular appeal and some interesting descriptions of landscape and scenery. Despite the interest and value of their accounts, these visitors were not motivated, in the spirit of Captain Quiros, to discover the literary equivalent of the

(Special Issue 2009), available at www.nla.gov.au/openpublish/index.php/jasal/article/view/869/1751

12 The manuscript, in Jeannie Gunn's handwriting, is contained in a book of letters written to William Peter Hurst; MS 6107, Box 169/1. William Peter Hurst papers, La Trobe Australian Manuscripts Collection, State Library of Victoria.

Great South Land: they were 'accidental tourists'. The same is true of Grattan and Norton. Neither came to Australia on a voyage of literary discovery, both came for other reasons and yet their time in Australia proved to be important both to them and to our literature.

Hartley Grattan, a New York freelance journalist and intellectual, arrived in Sydney in 1927. He was accompanying his new wife, actor and singer Beatrice Kay, who was starring in the musical comedy *Sunny* during its Sydney and Melbourne seasons. During their visit, which lasted almost a year, Grattan did pursue his intellectual interests even though they were incidental to his main purpose. He made contact with leading figures in the world of literature and journalism: the Palmers, L.A. Woolacott at *The Triad*, Frank Wilmot and Percival Serle. Grattan was to make six visits to Australia between 1927 and 1977 and his range of contacts and correspondents grew to include Miles Franklin, P.R. Stephensen and political figures such as Herbert Vere Evatt. His interest in Australian affairs widened to include economics, politics and foreign affairs and, as mentioned earlier, he produced major publications in these fields. Grattan was made an Honorary Doctor of Laws at the Australian National University in 1977. In his own words to Nettie Palmer, he had developed 'an entirely eccentric interest in your country'. He hoped to live long enough to attend the Australian bicentenary in 1988 but he died on 25 June 1980. He expressed a wish that his ashes be scattered in Sydney Harbour and in a private act his Australian friend Harold Bell 'distributed them ... on a fine evening roughly between the Opera House and Admiralty House.'

Grattan's importance for Australian literature lies primarily in his role in what Franklin described as 'interesting Australians in themselves' and in validating the worth of Australian literature. From 1927 onwards he wrote regularly about Australia and Australian literature for American newspapers. At the centre of this activity was his small pamphlet *Australian Literature*, published in Seattle by the University of Washington Press in 1929.[13] It was the first account of our literature by an overseas critic. Nettie Palmer in the introduction noted that while

13 Clinton Hartley Grattan, *Australian Literature*, University of Washington Chapbooks 29 (Seattle: University of Washington Bookstore, 1929).

a number of English literary visitors had written their impressions of Australia 'it has remained for Mr Grattan to examine us through our most significant books and to show the characteristic thread running through them. No English critic could have done this for our growing literature.'[14] Laurie Hergenhan has described the pamphlet as 'a call to arms in difficult times, a boosting of confidence in the cause if not the achievement of Australian literature.'[15] Grattan also played a pioneering role in Australian studies: from his first visit, he assiduously collected Australiana; these books formed the basis of what is now the Australian Collection at the Edward A. Clark Center for Australian Studies in the Harry Ransom Humanities Research Centre at the University of Texas.

From 1929, Grattan worked at promoting Australian books in the United States and at placing titles with American publishers. With this he had only some success—he was instrumental in the publication of Louis Stone's *Jonah* (as *Larrikin,* 1933) and wrote a glossary of Australian terms for it. It is through these activities that he came into contact with my second 'American friend', publisher William Warder Norton. At some point their shared interests in Australian literature must have coincided and Grattan worked for Norton as a publisher's reader. I have been unable to find details about their first meeting but by late 1929 they were well acquainted and Grattan refers in a letter to 'my friend Warder Norton'. Norton actively sought the American rights to Henry Handel Richardson's work, publishing *Ultima Thule* in 1929 and the complete Mahony trilogy in 1931; he also published two novels by Katharine Susannah Prichard, *Coonardoo* in 1930 and *Haxby's Circus* in 1931. Grattan's reader's report for this latter novel resulted, to Prichard's delight, in the inclusion in the American edition, entitled *Fay's Circus*, of some significant material omitted from the English edition.

Norton corresponded regularly with Richardson and Prichard and possibly through them, or through Grattan, established a relationship with Nettie Palmer, to whom he expressed his 'more than ordinary interest' in publishing Australian literature. In a series of letters, asking for her assistance in this matter, Norton repeatedly affirmed his genu-

14 Nettie Palmer, 'Foreword', in Grattan, *Australian Literature*, pp. 7–9.

15 Hergenhan, *No Casual Traveller*, p. 46.

ine desire to develop an 'Australian list',[16] stressing that he was 'most anxious to publish for Australian authors'. He hoped that *The Fortunes of Richard Mahony* would be only 'the beginning of our firm publishing for Australia.'[17] In 1930 a double-page spread in the Norton catalogue was devoted to Australian books.

As with Grattan, Norton's direct personal interest in Australia and its literature was the result of chance. He did not enter publishing until 1923. As a young man his career had had a quite different trajectory. After three years at Ohio State University, Norton became foreign sales manager at Kilbourne & Jacobs Manufacturing Company in Columbus. In 1916 he moved to New York to the English export firm of Harrisons & Crossfield Ltd., who had extensive interests in coffee, tea, rubber and palm oil plantations throughout Southeast Asia. It was almost certainly during his employment with this firm that Norton visited Australia. In a letter to Nettie Palmer he wrote, 'I was in Australia during the war—'16 and '17—made many friends in your country, have grown to love it, and it is to me a never-to-be-forgotten experience, that year'.[18] A later letter to Prichard refers to the 'happy months I once spent under the Southern Cross.'[19] When America entered the war in 1917 Norton returned home and enlisted; he took with him some cherished memories of a happy experience which were to inform his attitude to Australian writers in his publishing career.

Norton's letters to his Australian correspondents are full of warmth and fond recollections of a country he visited by chance for a short time. I have developed an affection for the W.W. Norton, of the letters—a warm, tactful, self-deprecating man with high ideals and standards.

16 Norton to Nettie Palmer 23 Oct. 1929, Palmer Papers, National Library of Australia, MSS 1174 (1/3391).

17 Norton to Nettie Palmer 30 Dec. 1929, Palmer Papers, National Library of Australia, MSS 1174 (1/3391).

18 Norton to Nettie Palmer 23 Oct. 1929, Palmer Papers, National Library of Australia, MSS 1174 (1/3391). When the United States entered the war in 1917 Norton returned home and enlisted, serving as ensign and assistant to the supply officer of the Naval Overseas Transport Service.

19 Norton to Prichard 11 July 1945, Prichard Papers, National Library of Australia, MSS 6201 Folder 9.

He dwells on the details of 'Australian' themes and scenes: he relishes the design of the cockatoos on the covers and endpapers of *Coonardoo*, experimenting with six different colour combinations to achieve the final result; he is intrigued by the boxing match in *Haxby's Circus*—we do not have the letter he wrote to Prichard but we do have her reply: 'The fight? I did write it myself from one that I saw, you know, although Jim [Prichard's husband] was a referee and an invaluable coach as to the details';[20] he corresponds with Jim Throssell, Prichard's husband, about their first-hand experience of life in the goldfields, regretting that he never had the opportunity to visit Kalgoorlie. There are two handwritten letters from Throssell in the Norton archive at Columbia and Norton's interest in this as a subject for a new novel is quite apparent in his replies. There seems little doubt that his willingness to support Australian writers had its roots in his own affection for the country expressed in the exchange detailed below between Norton and Henry Handel Richardson.

Richardson, referring to a review of *The Fortunes of Richard Mahony* by Grattan, wrote 'I have no desire to be marked for life as an "Australian writer" (though of course I keep this private) and quite agree with him [Grattan] that the way is open for a masterpiece by a "better Australian" than myself.' Norton replied:

> As to Mr Grattan's opinion and yours, I must disagree with you both. It seems to me that *The Fortunes of Richard Mahony* is inevitably an Australian book in that it paints once and for all, on a canvas which I believe will never fade, the way the frontier life beat upon the character of the European not fit for frontier life. But perhaps it might have been any frontier, so after all I may not be so sure of my opinion except that to me, who went to Australia for a year as a young man, it will always be the Australian masterpiece.[21]

---

20 Prichard to Norton 5 May 1931, Prichard Papers, National Library of Australia, MSS 2601 Series 10 Folder 9.

21 Richardson to Norton, 24 May, 1932; Norton to Richardson 2 June 1932, W.W. Norton Papers, Butler Library. Columbia University, New York.

With Richardson, Norton's enthusiasm went hand-in-hand with commercial interests—*The Fortunes of Richard Mahony* was a great financial success for his firm. The same was not true of Prichard's novels but Norton continued to believe in her abilities, 'her present work and future possibilities'.[22] His letters show a sensitivity and commitment to high standards, which seems somewhat unusual in an extremely competitive and sometimes ruthless business world: he aims 'to publish only good books … without sales consideration'.[23] His care for Prichard's writing and the production of her books is both personal and meticulous and he is rewarded by her thanks for the 'energy and courtesy' that he put into their presentation.[24] Unfortunately Norton was never to publish *The Roaring Nineties*, the first volume of Prichard's goldfields trilogy, or indeed any more works by Prichard. There were realities of the market place to be heeded. Prichard's next work, after *Haxby's Circus*, was a volume of short stories, a literary form considered unsuitable for the American market. Then war intervened, and Norton was absent from the firm on war duty (he was chairman of the Council on Books in Wartime for the benefit of men in service), and his sudden death in early November of 1945 put an end, prematurely, to his firm's dealings with Australian writers in any concerted way.

Norton's highly personal relationship with Australian literature came to an end, as it began, somewhat inadvertently. However, the relationship was to be brought to a completion in 2009. The firm he founded has added an anthology of Australian literature to its renowned stable of anthologies and is marketing the *Macquarie PEN Anthology of Australian Literature* worldwide as *The Literature of Australia*. As Mary Cunnane, a former Vice-President at Norton and Advisory Publishing editor for the Macquarie Anthology project has said:

---

22 Norton to Nettie Palmer 30 Dec. 1929, Palmer Papers, National Library of Australia, MSS 1174 (1/3416).

23 Norton to Nettie Palmer 30 Dec. 1929, Palmer Papers, National Library of Australia, MSS 1174 (1/3416).

24 Prichard to Norton 20 May 1930, Prichard Papers, National Library of Australia, MSS 6201 Folder 9.

> the serendipity of Warder Norton's interest in Australian literature all those years ago being realized some 70 or more years later in this anthology is quite a wonderful thing.[25]

Serendipity is the key word here. Between them, these two chance visitors, who would have been delighted to be labelled as 'Americans friends', have left some important legacies and landmarks in Australian literary history: the best editions of two novels by Prichard, an edition of *The Fortunes of Richard Mahony* which helped cement Henry Handel Richardson's reputation at home and abroad, a critical account of Australian literature which was a testament of support for a fledgling literature in difficult times and a collection which was the basis of a centre for Australian Studies in a leading American university. It is only appropriate that the contribution they have made should be mentioned in this place, and at this time—Sydney, 2009—when a major Australian literary publication, an affirmation of the value of our literature, has recently been published internationally by W.W. Norton; and a conference exploring Australian–US intellectual and literary connections is being held in Grattan's favourite city, not far from his final resting place.

---

25 Mary Cunnane, e-mail to author, July 2009.

6

Missed Appointments: Convergences and Disjunctures in Reading Australia Across the Pacific

Nicholas Birns

This essay will discuss both what the Australian–American cultural relationship has been built upon, and why that transpacific architecture has not been more foregrounded. I will begin by focusing on Americans who had transient relationships with Australia, but ones that yet impacted on their careers and were emblematic of patterns in the transpacific relationship. The traffic between the US and Australia these individuals represent indicates that beneath formal notice there exists a patchwork of encounters ramified in such a way as to provide a base for later criss-crossings. Yet, in each case, fissures are also revealed—'missed appointments'—that suggest why the potential transpacific 'rendezvous with destiny' was never actualised in the era where that above phrase had recent resonance.

Arlin Turner was a prominent Americanist who was born in 1909 and died in 1980. He was of the generation of Americanists who first put their own literature on the academic map, a real achievement in a discipline which, when founded, had been heavily built on Old English and Germanic philology and scholarship so positivistic as to be quasi-scientific. Turner was a literary historian of the American South who taught for most of his life at Duke University. He took a Fulbright year at the University of Western Australia in 1952 (actually from June to November of that year) where he lectured on both classic American literature (Emerson, Thoreau, and so on) and the (white) literature of the American South. Turner wrote a brief article, 'Scholars Discover the Commonwealth Literatures' for *Australian Literary Studies* in 1964, but did not engage in any kind of large-scale comparative scholarship on Australian or Commonwealth texts. Turner importantly worked on the novelist George Washington Cable, a Southerner who turned against the post-Reconstruction South, advocating civil rights for African-Americans. In the late 1950s, Turner edited a reprint of Cable's manifesto *The Negro Question* in a way that, with desegregation already afoot, was a tacit reorientation of American literary history towards a more progressive and emancipatory paradigm.[1] With Turner, we see the beginning of a trend away from the reliance on mutual whiteness that marked transpacific relationships in the days of the Great White Fleet and towards an understanding that the overcoming of racism, not its suppressed exaltation, was the most salient link between the two lands.

James Michener, the novelist, took an early interest in Australia, but it was never one of his major subjects, an attitude indicated as late as his memorable 1991 exchange with Barry Oakley on shipboard chronicled in the latter's *Diaries*. But Michener and his close collaborator A. Grove Day importantly redefined how America saw Australia. We all know that contacts increased between the two countries after Pearl Harbour, that Curtin's 'look to America' reestablished a commonality that had not been the same since the twin shocks of the construction of the Suez Canal and the American Civil War diminished the frequent cultural contacts occurring between the two countries. Before the 1860s, Tocquevillean America and Eureka-era Australia—what Manning Clark called 'the young tree green'—had genuine trade and cultural relations, which withered in the face of what the New Zealand historian James Belich has termed the 'recolonial' effect of the Suez Canal.[2] When relations sprung up again at the turn of the last century, whiteness and Anglo-Saxonism inevitably coloured them. In the wake of World War II Americans came to know Australia once again in a non-racist if not yet

1 George W. Cable, *The Negro Question: A Selection of Writings on Civil Rights in the South*, Arlin Turner, ed. (Garden City: Doubleday, 1958).

2 Kames Belich, *Paradise Reforged: A History of the New Zealanders: From the 1880s to the Year 2000* (Honolulu: University of Hawai'i Press, 2000).

post-racist way. But importantly they did so via Polynesia and the other South Pacific island peoples, whose terrain played a much more direct role in the 1941–45 fighting than Australia did. Michener's work, in both *Tales of the South Pacific* and *Return to Paradise,* linked Australia with the Pacific.[3] This tallied with the growing use of the term 'Australasia' in this era. In the 1890s, the Harvard Library catalogue widely used this term to cover 'Australia and New Zealand'. In the twentieth century the use of the term grew exponentially in the frequency of book titles (sometimes even including Antarctica!) that employed it. This reiteration eventually displayed a cultural drift as well, as 'Australasian' began to include Polynesian, Micronesian and Melanesian peoples. Despite the '-asia' suffix, though, the term never had anything to do with the actual Asia. In fact, by definition, it excluded Asia, being east of the 'Wallace Line' that separated Malay from Melanesian populations in the eastern part of present-day Indonesia. As a word, 'Australasia' is complicated. There is a disjuncture between its semantic and morphemic aspects. The '-as' element that makes 'Australasia' different from 'Australia' was meant as a doubling, an extension, of Australia northeastward and eastward, not at all an extension of Australia to include what later came to be called 'The Near North'. The Wallace Line as a boundary meant that Java, Sumatra, Borneo, even Bali were not at all part of 'Australasia'.

The valences of 'Australasia' as a term superintend how Michener's cross-cultural tolerance is notable but also limited. In a way, his work adheres to a very traditional American paradigm in which Polynesians were more culturally acceptable than Melanesians, Micronesians, or Indigenous Australians. Unlike these other groups, for instance, Polynesians were seen as 'white' in terms of their geneaological heritage by the Mormon Church, for example, and thus suitable proselytes during the early twentieth century, and the Maori scholar Peter Buck had a long tenure at the Bishop Museum in Honolulu in the 1920s and 1930s. Melanesians, Micronesians and Indigenous Australians were, though, in racial terms progressively less acceptable. Michener extended this acceptability to Melanesians and Micronesians, but he was not particularly sensitive towards Indigenous Australians, nor did he have much

3 James Michener, *Return to Paradise* (New York: Random House, 1951).

good to say about migrant or diasporic peoples in the South Pacific, such as the Indo-Fijians, about whom his comments are reprehensible. The anthropologist Margaret Mead, who necessarily passed through Australia many times on her way to New Guinea, had a less racialist cast to this approach, but fundamentally she, like Michener, was basically interested in non-white Pacific peoples in this order: Polynesians, Melanesians, Micronesians, and Indigenous Australians, followed by diasporic people such as Indo-Fijians. She certainly took more care to understand these people than did Michener, but the cultural hierarchy remained the same. The famous 'exposure' of Mead's Samoan research by Derek Freeman in the early 1980s represents perhaps the end of the Australasian paradigm.[4] That this was in many ways an attack from the Right, designed to delegitimate Mead's cultural relativism, shows that there were many positive aspects to the Australasian way of thinking about the Pacific. It was multiracial and got US–Australian dialogue out of its whites-only cocoon. Yet the 'Australasian' paradigm, emblematised by the touristic, tacky exoticism of the 1950s Tiki style in popular artifacts, excludes as much as it includes. Still, it remains the first articulation of a Pacific where common ties did not only mean common white ties.

John Hope Franklin was at the time of his death in 2009 the most famous African-American historian living. Franklin was already an established scholar in 1960 when he spent a Fulbright year in Australia. Remarkably, at a time before the Civil Rights movement in the US had gathered full steam, and nearly a decade before the 1967 referendum which first made Indigenous Australians citizens of Australia, a black man was an official US government representative in Australia. Importantly, Franklin's Fulbright grant was given under the Eisenhower Presidency in the US, and his visit to Australia occurred during the tenure of the Menzies government—both national leaders not terribly keen on civil rights, although history must accord Eisenhower the better record in this regard. To be understood, Franklin's visit to Australia has to be seen in the context of the very complex racial dynamic of that

---

4 Derek Freeman, *The Fateful Hoaxing of Margaret Mead* (Boulder: Westview, 1999).

era's transpacific relationship. Franklin did not extend his scholarship to cover Australian racial history, nor did Australia occupy anything more than a very peripheral place in his later work. Franklin was in Australia to represent *America* in the Cold War—in his autobiography, he speaks of the US government 'using me as an example of what was possible', and particularly, per H.V. Evatt's aspirations for Australia as a bridge to newly emergent states, to show the nations of Asia and Africa that America was not racist.[5] Franklin was not there to address Australia's racial problem, which in order to make Franklin's race visible to Asian and Africa had to be sidestepped if Australia was to be the bridge that this Cold War outreach projected. Intriguingly, Australia's role here was ideologically the opposite of the role it played in the Cold War in Asia, where its role as stanchion of American policy bolstered anti-Communist, often Christian Asian dictators such as Syngman Rhee, Chiang Kai-Shek and Ngo Dinh Diem. Franklin was there to prove a point to the Bandung-era nations, the nonaligned nations, not to be explicitly a part of what Christina Klein has termed 'Cold War Orientalism'.[6] But in both cases the US was, fascinatingly, using an Australia then far less multiracial than itself to serve as a concourse to the more multiracial world that the US needed to endorse in order to win the Cold War—a stance Jodi Melamed has recently characterised as 'mid-century racial liberalism'.[7] Fay Zwicky, in her poem 'Makassar, 1956' illustrates this:

> Decks buzzed with students going home, new
> Graduates from our Colombo plan, old hands form
> What was called the indies in *tempo dulu* ...[8]

The mention of the Sri Lankan capital and the Latin-Malay macaronics of the few words in Bahasa Indonesia acknowledge the new way in which

5 John Hope Franklin, *Mirror to America: The Biography of John Hope Franklin* (New York: Hill and Wang, 2005).

6 Christina Klein, *Cold War Orientalism: Asia in the Middlebrow Imagination, 1945–1961* (Berkeley: University of California Press, 2003).

7 Jodi Melamed, 'The Spirit of Neoliberalism: From Racial Liberalism to Neoliberal Multiculturalism', *Social Text 89* (Winter 2006): 1–25.

8 For the text of the Zwicky poem, see N. Jose, ed., *The Literature of Australia: An Anthology* (New York: Norton, 2009), p. 815

Asia was spoken now that it was a continent of independent nations. In this field, a black American was a potential bridge between Australia and Asia. John Hope Franklin stated that he was perceived in Australia simply as 'a distinguished American' (184) and that white Australians 'did not seem to draw any analogies' between African-Americans and Aborigines.[9] Franklin, though, did meet with Aboriginal delegations. Here, he was apprised as to the need for better communication between whites and Indigenous people by Sir Paul Hasluck, later Governor-General. A gloss on the preconditions of Franklin's time in Australia may be seen in this passage from the memoirs of Edward J. Perkins, the US ambassador to Australia during the 1990s, who was African-American:

> When my mother visited us in Australia, she asked 'Where are the people?' She meant black people. There were few to be seen. As a white nation, Australia was similar to South Africa, except that blacks are the minority in Australia. Aboriginal and Torres Strait Islander people total less than 2 percent of the Australian population.[10]

Aboriginality was not visible even after US multiracialism became an official part of the image the US presented in Australia; the plight of the Indigenous people of Australia was only a moral one with no perceived geostrategic potentiality. Australia, for America in the 1960s, was at the crossroads of a number of disjunctive racial discourses: Cold War Orientalism, appeals to the Third World nonaligned, and Polynesia-centred Australasianism, that could not in themselves coincide, and were so specific in their discursivity as not to be able to extend to a systematic championship of Indigenous rights. Even in the 1960s and 1970s, disjunctures still prevailed over convergences; appointments were still being missed.

* * *

9 J. Hope Franklin, p. 184.

10 Edward J. Perkins, *Mr Ambassador: Warrior for Peace*. (Norman: University of Oklahoma Press, 2006).

The 1960s and 1970s were the last era in which vestigial miscommunication still lingered in transpacific discourse, Constance Helmericks (1919–1987) was an aviator and adventure-travel writer who was a combination of, say, Amelia Earhart, Mary Kingsley, and Freya Stark, though garnering less publicity than any of these. Author of a number of books of adventure set in remote places such as Alaska, Helmericks, as she was about sixty and following a divorce from her former collaborator, took a tour with her two daughters of the more remote parts of Australia, centering on Queensland, Western Australia, and most extensively the Northern Territory. This produced a 1971 book, *Australian Adventure.*[11] Helmericks was ambivalent about Indigenous people in the text. Hailing their artistic achievements and speaking on behalf of a racially integrated society, she nonetheless used phrases which would not sit well with today's attitudes. Her characterisation of the Australian urban scene as greedy and materialistic can seem culturally insensitive today, after Australians have placed so much stress on pointing out to the world that, despite all the movies they have seen, most of the population resides in cities.

Helmericks, though, makes a real attempt to know the people and land of Australia on their own terms. On the environmental level, she is largely successful. On the literary level she is less so. She says that the four leading writers of Australia are Ernestine Hill, Mrs Aeneas Gunn, Daisy Bates and the only one then still living, Mary Durack.[12] There are laudable elements about this list. It is certainly feminist, and is perhaps a needed counterpart to the hyper-masculinity of the *Bulletin* era that laid the groundwork for most connections between US and Australian literature, even, and especially, on the Left. She does admit 'there are men writers too' and mentions Ion L. Idriess and Alan Moorehead in her bibliography. We can all be grateful she did *not* mention Nevil Shute. But there was an even bigger omission. In 1971, to omit mention of Patrick White—two years before his receipt of the Nobel Prize for Literature—is the ultimate in missed appointments, an unfortunate misrecognition

11 Constance C. Helmericks, *Australian Adventure* (Englewood Cliffs: Prentice-Hall, 1971).

12 Helmericks, *Australian Adventure*, p. 91.

of the lay of the land. This is not only because of White's prestige, then and now, but because White's novels address the land, its obduracy, and the struggle of Europeans and white Australians to come to grips with it, whether in terms of epic tragedy such as in *Voss*, pastoral determination as in *The Tree of Man*, or visionary reckoning in *The Vivisector*, would have resonated in the purview of Helmericks' angle of vision. As David Carter and Roger Osborne's recent work has suggested, it is as a pioneer writer of the land, not as a spiritual modernist, that White was often marketed in the US.[13] It might have provided a needed diversity to White studies had Helmericks seized on this more demotic aspect of him with the felt depth that she could have brought to it. It must also be said, though, that his omission from Helmericks' work is testament to how little-known Patrick White remained in the US in 1971.

Furthermore, it indicates that the mechanisms of being well known in 1971 were more inefficient than today, as, because of the huge publicity and wide reviews of contemporary Australian fiction in the US press, and the existence among the worldwide literati of such a category as 'Australian literature', no-one could now write a Helmericks-style book about Australia and not mention Tim Winton or Peter Carey. The White omission in Helmericks also, in a methodological sense, shows how ineffective high-literary periodical reviews—which White undeniably had—were to general popularity and popular awareness.

Helmericks' omission of White makes a powerful argument from negative evidence; yes, Patrick White was published by a prominent firm and received good reviews in US newspapers and magazines.[14] But, even after he won the Nobel, there was neither an intellectual vogue nor a popular craze for White's work. The omission is suggestive proof of this ceiling on White's appreciation, one of the most consequential of all the missed appointments between the US and Australia.

---

13 Roger Osborne, 'The Australian Accent in America's Middlebrow Library: The Book-of-the-Month Club and Australian Novelists, 1929–1959'. Paper presented at MLA conference, San Francisco, 29 December 2008.

14 See David Carter, *Dispossession, Dreams, and Diversity: Issues in Australian Studies* (Frenchs Forest, NSW: Pearson Education, 2006), for more on the distinction between cultural visibility and cultural impact.

The occurrence of this very symposium means that appointments between the two countries are less likely to be missed. The internet, in particular, has played an enormous role in making Australia more connected to and accessible to the rest of the world. Indeed, one may hypothesise that the first twenty years of the internet era saw a tremendous connection between world speakers of the same language that promoted global solidarity, and also reaffirmed the cultural power of former colonisers which gained new residual authority as a result of people communicating, in a monoglot fashion, across the internet: see the prominence of the Booker Prize in Britain, the Prince of Asturias Prize in Spain, and so on. This tendency was both recolonial, in that the old colonial centre gained more cultural capital, and postcolonial, in that former world peripheries became more visible as a result. One wonders, though, if this is less an inextricable structural feature of the information age but simply a phase of it; the burgeoning interest in translation in the US, and the sense that we should begin to learn more foreign languages, threatens to sideline Australia. But, even if this happens, the relationship between the US and Australia can no longer enjoy the safety of a purely bilateral context; the world is too much with both nations now. But the series of travellers to Australia who did not and could not achieve a full linkage should not be blamed for trying.

Their efforts, though, seem curiously quaint in the present era where transnationalism is all the rage and nationalism has been repudiated—that word is not, I think, too strong—by the advanced intellectual class. In Australia, from at least the *Bulletin* era onward, Australian literature was celebrated—because it was Australian, because it was infused by a certain categorical torque that testified to its Australianness. Certain authors, such as Patrick White, at once exemplified the phenomenon of Australian literature at its best, but also, since even *The Tree Of Man* was clearly about 'something else', fell outside the system and thus became the object of controversy. Outside Australia, Australian literature was ignored—equally, because it was Australian. Christina Stead, in a way, proved this with *The Man Who Loved Children*. Certain authors, such as Patrick White, with his clearly international aspirations, fell outside the system, and thus became the object of at least some world notice.

What we have now is an independence of this national template, an assertion that Australian texts can manifest themselves in less geographically confined ways. This is not to say the previous nationalistic approaches were ethnocentric or privileged the dominant powers—the nationalism here was liberal, progressive, inclusive—but in a way which conjoined emancipation with a discovery of a national identity that spurned colonial influences. Now the tables have been turned: the more external influences the better, even if those influences tug the nation back towards enmeshment with the former coloniser, that is seen as broadening and expansive. But what is interesting here is that the move beyond the nation has not gone beyond hierarchy entirely. There are still some nations that are more transnational than others. Just as in the founding days of American studies and the generation of Leo Marx and R.W.B. Lewis, the United States, say, was clearly more 'national' than Canada. With regard to Australia, the equation becomes interesting because Australia can be the *object* of transnationalism. It can receive Asian or Continental European influences, can have the previously suppressed British or American influences accentuated or retrieved. But Australia is not the agent of the global. It can be transnationalised, but it cannot globalise others. 'Cannot' in terms of how it is seen discursively; Australian writers certainly have transnationalised other national discourses, especially American ones. Delia Falconer, in *The Lost Thoughts of Soldiers* (2005) took a relatively overlooked figure in the frontier wars of the American West—Captain Frederick Benteen—and made him the nodal point for a reframing of war narratives, gender and body hierarchies, and white-versus-indigenous struggles that would be impossible without what from an American perspective is a minoritarian, Australian viewpoint. Rod Jones in *Billy Sunday* (1995) took the famous American evangelist and turned his life into a meditation on the frontier and on the chimerical desire for national and natural fulfillment. This is against a background of a long tradition—from Patrick White's *The Aunt's Story* (1948) to Gerald Murnane's *Inland* (1988) to Peter Carey's *Parrot and Olivier in America* (2010) and his *The Unusual Life of Tristan Smith* (1994), which celebrate the idealism and scope of America but do so very, very critically, to Thomas Keneally's highly underrated novel

Confederates (1979)—of Australian writers interrogating America from an alternative perspective. *Confederates* treats the Civil War with an uncanny sensitivity perhaps one half-step off in tone, a *méconaissance,* a not-quite-getting-it right in terms of speech patterns and phraseology—such as 'torpid swamps' in the very first paragraphs, or the very names Usaph and Ephephtha, crypto-biblical names only seen in this novel—as much as history—that haunts as it may be part of a built-in structural misunderstanding between an American and Australian set of imaginaries that can reach out to each other but never converge. Yet these writers are not seen as 'transnationalising' America. They are perhaps seen as providing a specifically Australian perspective, but not one that can reverberate back on how non-Australians see the US. Similarly, when Murray Bail contrasts European philosophy with the sheep stations of New South Wales in *The Pages,* when David Malouf introduces a servant who is the epitome of the Australian 'battler' or 'digger' into the story of King Priam and Troy in *Ransom* (2009), when Murnane focuses on obscure towns on the North Platte River in Nebraska to reground his metafictive vision of the Australian plains, it is not just to foreground a sort of Australian pride but to use their vantage-point to provide an alternative critique, a counter-sounding. What Australian studies in North America can do today is to call attention to this potential for the Australian perspective to broaden, and not just by ventilating the specifically Australian.

Today, writers such as Ouyang Yu, Brian Castro, Alexis Wright, and Kim Scott have redefined 'Australian literature'. Why not Australia, then? One might add, all the more, why not New Zealand? Just as Polynesian and South Pacific referents were important in the Cold War, the way Antipodean elements were not, for reasons described above, there could easily be a scenario where New Zealand, with its larger percentage of indigenous people and close links to the independent states of the South Pacific, was more glamorous than Australia, the floating island to Australia's stolid continent. But no, New Zealand is as 'behind' Australian defences in this respect as it was with respect to the Japanese in World War II or any other 'invasion from the north' scenario, in which New Zealand would have been invaded only *after* Australia had fallen.

This is less true before 1900; the work of Elizabeth DeLoughrey, Nicholas Thomas, Vanessa Smith, Bridget Orr, and the late Greg Dening has put the liminal encounters of islands and beaches on the postcolonial map; but the paradigmatic efficacy of this has, so far stopped at about Robert Louis Stevenson's death.[15] With some notable exceptions—such as Robert Dixon's work on Melanesia in *Prosthetic Gods*—comparable work does not extend into the twentieth century.[16] Indeed, when we reflect that, as Juniper Ellis has pointed out, the South Pacific as a whole is not a prominent area in postcolonial studies compared to India or Africa, one begins to wonder if postcolonialism stops east of the Wallace Line. In particular, is 'Oceania' or 'Australasia' still seen as more 'anthropological' than 'historical'? Despite the visibility of political strife in the area—and the extension of that aura of political contest to Australia, with 'the history wars', Sorry Day, the *Tampa* incident, the Bali bombing, and so on—the South Pacific still is underrated; in fact, as far as Polynesia and Melanesia are concerned, it has even less visibility than in the days of Mead and Michener. Indeed, the Pacific, with the rise of discourses of the 'black Atlantic' no longer seems the most excitingly polyvalent ocean. Part of that has to do with the greater visibility of African diaspora history than in the days when John Hope Franklin took his Fulbright. In that era, the Atlantic was seen as the ocean of the NATO alliance, the Pacific as the ocean where even the principal allies of the West were non-white. It is gratifying to see Atlantic identity made more multiracial; Arlin Turner, who was very brave to bring even white anti-racism into the picture in the 1950s, would have rejoiced to see the day. But one wonders where all this leaves the Pacific. A Patrick White of today would receive more global recognition than Helmericks was able to give him. But would he be any 'hotter' academically?

One reason for this shift from multiracial Pacific to multiracial Atlantic was that, in the Cold War, metropolitan thinkers thought in geostrategic terms: which alliance possessed or controlled what volume

15 See e.g. Nicholas Thomas, *Entangled Objects: Exchange, Material Culture and Colonialism in the Pacific* (Cambridge: Harvard University Press, 1991).

16 Robert Dixon, *Prosthetic Gods: Travel, Representation, and Colonial Governance* (St Lucia: University of Queensland Press, 2001).

of area? In the current era, people think more in demographic terms with respect to population flows, immigration to metropolitan countries, refugees, detainees, terrorist cells: it is people that matter more than places, 'biopower' in the Agambenian sense, more than land mass. In this calculation, Australia and Oceania, by far the least populous settled area of the world, is at a tremendous disadvantage. China, for instance, dwarfs Australia far more demographically than geographically, and this almost ensures any study from outside Australia about the Chinese diaspora within it will be more about China than about Australia. Just as Australia would have attracted more notice during the Cold War had it participated more in the milieu of anti-communist Asia, so would Australia loom larger if the White Australia policy had not kept down the population so much! This might explain the asymmetry: appointments with Australia are now being kept, but the resonance of what emerges from those appointments is still muffled. And this sense of the underpopulated, the demographically deprived, responding to the demographically surfeited may in turn be a frame in which Australia's contribution to making the rest of the world more knowledgeable about itself may be seen as distinctive.

Section 2

Poetry and Poetics

7

East–West Turnings: Australian and American Poetry in Light of Asia

Paul Kane

I want to suggest in this essay something unremarkable, in the sense that it has already been remarked upon quite a lot: that both American and Australian poetry engages with the East in significant ways. This is hardly a new idea. Ever since Edward Said's seminal study *Orientalism* and its later companion volume, *Culture and Imperialism*,[1] we have been attuned to issues of Western representations of the East. With the rise of postcolonial studies, we have learned a good deal about the intersections of history, culture, power and perception. This has become not so much a field of study as a veritable Outback of study, except it isn't outback at all: it's front and centre. But perhaps because the point is so obvious to us now we might gain something by looking at it afresh, or at least again.

My interest here, however, is not primarily in postcolonial perspectives or orientalism or subaltern studies or other similar undertakings, which typically analyse structures of dominance and resistance and illuminate ideological implications and mystifications. Indeed, the superabundance of such studies is already in excess of anything I could add. Nor am I considering the wealth of literary works that constitute Asian-American or Asian-Australian literature (which is also a burgeoning and exciting field of study). My perspective is more limited, and perhaps—as I've said—unremarkable. I simply

1 Edward W. Said, *Orientalism* (New York: Random House, 1978), and *Culture and Imperialism* (New York: Alfred A. Knopf, 1993.)

want to suggest that the East so-called (it is hardly monolithic) has also functioned as a generative force—whether as provocation or inspiration—for certain poets in Australia and America, beginning in the nineteenth century and especially recently, and that there are some unusual features to this phenomenon worthy of inspection. I am going to note several examples of such poets and then say something about possible conclusions we might draw as we look to the future.

I'm going to begin with Emerson—that originator *par excellence*. Emerson's engagement with Eastern philosophy is well known, as American transcendentalism has many filiations with it. Indeed, to some Indian commentators, Emerson looks like an error in reincarnation: he should have been born near the Ganges, not the Charles River in Boston; this is reinforced for them by the fact that some of Emerson's most 'Eastern' ideas were formulated prior to his extensive reading in Vedantic literature. Mid-century readers in America were quite aware of Emerson's interest in and debt to the East, which was fully laid out later by Frederic Ives Carpenter in his *Emerson and Asia*, which appeared in 1930.[2] Moreover, Emerson is largely responsible for Thoreau's intensive study of Indian and Chinese texts as well as Whitman's enthusiastic embrace of the East, as in his famous 'Passage to India.'[3] But I would like to pause briefly to note the importance of Persian poetry on Emerson, particularly the work of Hafiz, from the fourteenth-century.[4] Emerson translated, from German sources, over 150 poems and fragments of Hafiz, some of which he published but most of which he left in manuscript books. The more one reads Emerson, the more one realises how crucial Hafiz was to Emerson's imagination and practice. Lawrence Buell puts it best, when, in remarking upon Wai-Chee Dimock's work on Emerson's 'passion for classical Persian poetry,' he says: 'Typically this is

2 Frederic Ives Carpenter, *Emerson and Asia* (Cambridge: Harvard University Press, 1930).

3 Walt Whitman, 'Passage to India', in *Walt Whitman: Complete Poetry and Collected Prose* (New York: The Library of America, 1982), pp. 531–40.

4 See: Hafiz [Shams al-Dín Muhammad], *Diván-i-Háfiz*, Parvíz Nátíl Khánlari, ed. (Terhran: Khwarezmí, 1362AH/1983–84).

put at the edges of discussion of his work. It ought to be at the center.'[5] One of the features Emerson found most attractive in Hafiz was the poet's irreverence in the face of false piety and other forms of hypocrisy. Hafiz is constantly excoriating dervishes and clerics; he prefers wine and women and boys. Thus, an early *ghazal* Emerson translated begins:

> Secretly to love & to drink, what is it? tis a dissolute day's
> work.
> I side with the open drunkards, be it as it may,
> Loose the knots of the heart & cumber thee no farther for
> the lot
> No geometer has yet disentangled this confusion ...[6]

Many commentators claim that Hafiz is actually a thoroughgoing allegorist, such that his low-life references all have religious meanings firmly attached to them. Emerson refuses such bowlderising interpretations; as he says in his essay 'Persian Poetry':

> We do not wish to strew sugar on bottled spiders, or try to make mystical divinity out of the Song of Solomon, much less out of the erotic and bacchanalian songs of Hafiz. Hafiz himself is determined to defy all such hypocritical interpretation, and tears off his turban and throws it at the head of the meddling dervish, and throws his glass after the turban.[7]

At the same time, Emerson is aware that there is, in fact, a religious dimension to Hafiz, but it is one much more in line with Emerson's

---

5 Lawrence Buell, *Emerson* (Cambridge: Harvard University Press, 2003), p. 151. See also: Wai Chee Dimock, *Through Other Continents: American Literature Across Deep Time* (Princeton: Princeton University Press, 2006).

6 Ralph Waldo Emerson, *Ralph Waldo Emerson: Collected Poems and Translations,* Harold Bloom and Paul Kane, eds. (New York: The Library of America, 1994), p. 473.

7 Ralph Waldo Emerson, 'Persian Poetry', *Letters and Social Aims*, in *The Collected Works of Ralph Waldo Emerson,* Robert E. Spiller, et al., eds., vol. 8 (Cambridge: Harvard University Press, 1971), p. 249.

own post-Christian moral sentiment than with anything orthodox to Islam. That's the ground upon which Hafiz truly speaks to Emerson. As Emerson writes in 'Poetry and Imagination':

> Every correspondence we observe in mind and matter suggests a substance older and deeper than either of these old nobilities. We see the law gleaming through, like the sense of a half-translated ode of Hafiz.[8]

* * *

I want to turn now to a nineteenth-century Australian writer, Francis Adams (1862–1893). Adams isn't much read these days, but he stands in contrast to his more conventionally 'orientalising' contemporaries. Early Australian engagements with the East, in poetry at least, tend to be neither felicitous nor particularly edifying. A lot of this verse is to be found in the periodical literature, where references run the gamut from paranoid to patronising, reflecting an entrenched bigotry and racism stemming largely from the clutch of anti-Chinese sentiment from the goldfields. The same attitudes, of course, predominate in America during this period, but there are fewer exceptions in Australia, which is why Francis Adams stands out. Noel Rowe and Vivian Smith make this same point in the introduction to their anthology *Windchimes: Asia in Australian Poetry*, though they do not include any poems by Adams.[9] But before we look at Adams, it's worthwhile noting one interesting example Rowe and Smith do include, Henry Lawson's 'The Tracks that Lie by India.' Although it is a fanciful ballad, in which Lawson dreams of travelling to the East by way of London (where he will 'raise the wherewithal' for the trip), and during which he hopes to dally in France and Italy, courting 'some foreign girl with eyes of lustrous glow', the final stanza does articulate a desire—however stereotyped the

8 Ralph Waldo Emerson, 'Poetry and Imagination', in *The Complete Works of Ralph Waldo Emerson* (Centenary Edition), vol. 9 (Boston: Houghton Mifflin, 1903–04), pp. 9–10.

9 Noel Rowe and Vivian Smith, eds., *Windchimes: Asia in Australian Poetry* (Canberra: Pandanus Books, 2006).

expression—that should alert us to some underlying impulses that will emerge more forcefully in later poets:

> The tracks that run by India to China and Japan,
> The tracks where all the rovers go—the tracks that call a Man!
> I'm wearied of the formal lands of parson and of priest,
> Of dollars and of 'fashions,' and I'm drifting towards the East;
> I'm tired of cant and cackle, and of sordid jobbery—
> The misty ways of Asia are calling unto me.[10]

This is classic 'orientalism' in its exotic representation of the East, but it's also a critique of the West for its materialism and hypocrisy. That critique is more sharply delineated in Francis Adams. Here's an excerpt from his *Australian Essays* (1886):

> In India, whose climate is too extreme for us ever to make it a colony in the sense that America and Australia are colonies; in India, since we could neither make the aborigines give way, nor make them adapt themselves to us, we have simply let them alone. They do not understand us, nor we them. Of late, it is true, an interest in them, in their religion and literature, has been springing up, but what a strange aspect do we, the lords of India for some hundred and thirty years, present! 'In my own experience among Englishmen,' says an Indian scholar writing to the *Times* in 1874, 'I have found no general indifference to India, but I have found a Cimmerian darkness about the manners and habits of my countrymen, an almost poetical description of our customs and a conception no less wild and startling than the vagaries of Mandeville and Marco Polo concerning our religion.'[11]

While we might dispute a few of Adams' assertions here, it's quite telling that he would quote an Indian scholar to make his point about the

---

10 Rowe and Smith, *Windchimes*, p. 23.

11 Francis W.L. Adams, *Australian Essays* (Melbourne: William Inglis & Co., 1886), p. 9.

benighted conceptions of Englishmen (and by extension Australians) concerning the customs and religions of the East. It is in that light that Adams' sonnet, 'Dai Butsu', can be read, which describes the enormous statue of the Buddha in Kamakura, Japan:

> He sits. Upon the kingly head doth rest
> The round-balled wimple, and the heavy rings
> Touch on the shoulders where the shadow clings.
> The downward garment shows the ambiguous breast;
> The Face—that Face one scarce can look on, lest
> One learn the secret of unspeakable things;
> But the dread gaze descends with shudderings,
> To the veiled couched knees, the hands and thumbs close pressed.
> O lidded, downcast Eyes that bear the weight
> Of all our woes and terrible wrong's increase:
> Proud Nostrils, Lips proud-perfecter than these,
> With what a soul within you do you wait!
> Disdain and pity, love late-born of hate,
> Passion eternal, patience, pride and peace![12]

Adams seems fairly overcome with this vision of sacred character; it challenges the onlooker with superior knowledge, understanding, forbearance and love, while also exhibiting traces of spiritual pride and Olympian disdain. It is all born of suffering and its endurance or transcendence. In both senses of the word, there is something 'unspeakable' about it, he says. That fine doubleness is mirrored in the 'ambiguous breast' and the 'heavy rings' and 'wimple,' whereby the gender of the Buddha is uncertain or perhaps rendered hermaphroditic. There is otherness here, but it is an otherworldly otherness that exists in this world in some incommensurate way. Adams is no Buddhist, but his poem points us to twentieth-century poetry where the religious dimension of the East becomes prominent, if not, in some cases, pre-eminent.

---

12 Francis W.L. Adams, 'Dai Butsu', in *Songs of the Army of the Night* (London: William Reeves, 1894, originally published 1888), p. 83.

* * *

The history of Eastern religions in America is well known, with most historians pointing to the 1893 Columbian Exposition in Chicago, where the first World's Parliament of Religions was held, as the decisive event.[13] The so-called Yankee Hindoo movement of the transcendentalists paved the way for a national interest that, in turn, gave rise to the Parliament, where three representatives in particular had enormous impact: Swami Vivekananda (1863–1902), Anagārika Dharmapāla (1864–1933), and Shaku Sōen (1859–1919). Vivekananda was responsible for the founding of the Hindu Vedanta Societies; Dharmapāla founded the Buddhist Maha Bodhi Society; and Shaku brought Zen to America, particularly in the person of D.T. Suzuki. Suzuki's influence on Thomas Merton, Carl Jung, Martin Heidegger and other prominent thinkers is well documented, but his impact on the Beat writers Gary Snyder, Allen Ginsberg, and Jack Kerouac is of more concern here. They were an important bridge to the development of mid-century American interest in Eastern religions, and Buddhism in particular. Prior to that, though, the work of Ernest Fenolossa was brought to the attention of Ezra Pound and W.B. Yeats, who used it to bring Modernism (and imagism) into conversation with classic Japanese and Chinese literature. By the 1960s, it seemed everyone was reading R.H. Blyth's *Zen in English Literature and Oriental Classics*, which, according to the back cover, claimed that 'all that is good in European literature and culture is simply and solely that which is in accordance with the Spirit of Zen' (even if Blyth never actually says that in the book itself).[14] By the time of the centennial of the World's Parliament in 1993, Tibetan Buddhism and Islam had fully joined the pantheon of Eastern religions that directly affected American culture and its literature, to the point that already much of twenty-first century American poetry seems imbricated with it.

13 See for instance, Thomas A. Tweed and Stephen Prothero, eds, *Asian Religions in America: A Documentary History* (New York: Oxford University Press, 1999).

14 R.H. Blyth, *Zen in English Literature and Oriental Classics* (New York: E.P. Dutton, 1960, [1942]).

While there is still a good deal of 'orientalising' going on, and while not all poetry engaging with the East is necessarily religious, I do think that the turn to the East has had a profound impact on American poetry in the form of a religious displacement. Again, I am setting aside Asian-American poetry for the moment, though I will come to it later. Right now, I'm merely pointing out the obvious: American poetry, like American society, has always been rife with religiousness, and often in heterodox forms. Here, for instance, are the names of a few contemporary poets we might consider in this light, all of whom write, to some extent, under the auspices of Eastern religion: W.S. Merwin, Charles Wright, Olga Broumas, Sam Hamill, Jackson MacLow, Tess Gallagher, Jane Hirshfield, Chase Twichell and Eliot Weinberger. As far back as 1977, Kenneth Rexroth stated, proleptically, the point I'm trying to make here:

> Today, for a very large sector of American poets, the poetry of the Far East is more influential than 19th and 20th century French poetry, which has dominated the international idiom for so long, and certainly incomparably more influential than American or English poetry of the 19th century. The only rival is the slowly dying influence of 'metaphysical' verse of the English Renaissance. It would be possible to name over a hundred American poets deeply influenced by the poetry of the Far East and some who have difficulty in thinking poetry in any other idiom than Chinese or Japanese. Now, of course, there are a number of poets, by no means uninfluential, who read Chinese and Japanese and who are philosophically Buddhist or Taoist or both.[15]

Where Rexroth refers to Buddhism and Taoism as philosophies, I'm calling them religions, but I think our terms overlap to the degree that there are practices involved, including the practice of poetry. This, I take it, is the import of Charles Wright's conclusion to 'Portrait of the Artist with Li Po,' in *The World of the Ten Thousand Things*:

15 Kenneth Rexroth, 'Chinese Poetry and the American Imagination', in *The New Directions Anthology of Classical Chinese Poetry*, Eliot Weinberger, ed. (New York: New Directions, 2003), p. 210.

Over a thousand years later, I write out one of his lines in a
  notebook,
The peach blossom follows the moving water,
And watch the October darkness gather against the hills.
All night long the river of heaven will move westward while
  no one notices.
The distance between the dead and the living
                                    is more than a heartbeat and a breath.[16]

Though Wright is not a practising Buddhist, he has affinities with the religion, as he affirms in an interview in *Quarter Notes*.[17] Here, the sense of an almost cosmic distance is also a kind of second sense of a presence that connects overlapping lives.

Where contemporary American and Australian poetry tend to overlap is—increasingly, I think—in the area or arena of the East. This triple figure, if you will, of AAA—America, Australia and Asia—does not, however, constitute an equilateral triangle. While I doubt there is an Australian poet publishing today who has not been influenced by American poetry, the opposite cannot be said to be true. American awareness of Australian verse is generally casual or accidental. English and European poetry are shared inheritances, but—if what I'm suggesting is true—we may be entering a phase where both Australian and American poetry will have more in common than a family resemblance or a family romance. They may be talking to each other without realising it, in which case we ought to encourage them to meet more often.

* * *

In their anthology, *Windchimes*, Rowe and Smith include fifty or so contemporary poets, which is by no means exhaustive. Some of the

---

16 Charles Wright, 'Portrait of the Artist with Li Po', *The World of the Ten Thousand Things: Poems 1980–1990* (New York: Farrar, Straus & Giroux, 1990), p. 34.

17 See: Charles Wright, *Quarter Notes: Improvisations and Interviews* (Ann Arbor: University of Michigan Press, 1995), p. 124.

connections may seem attenuated, but there are still many well-known poets clearly associated with the East, and who are not Asian-Australian. Thus, the editors include Robert Gray, Jan Owen, Judith Beveridge and Caroline Caddy (though they leave out Barry Hill). Harold Stewart, from an earlier generation, is also a leading figure here. In Gray's recent memoir, *The Land I Came Through Last*, he gives an account of his early interest in Zen that likely resonates with the other poets. Having come across a couple of books by Alan Watts, Gray writes:

> These were about a 'critical' Buddhism that originated in China and was positive toward nature: its aim was to achieve absorption, like a craftsman or an artist, in all one's dealings with the world. It was about self-forgetfulness through intense involvement. I was at once an enthusiast for the austere aesthetics of Zen poetry, ink drawing, calligraphy, raku pottery, sliding screens, tatami matting.[18]

I've said nothing so far about the aesthetics of Asian art, which clearly appeal to so many. It is a topic unto itself, and one only need point to the popularity of such poetic forms as the haiku, renga, pantoum, ghazal and the like in English poetry to establish the ubiquity of Eastern poetic influence. Gray, though, makes an interesting point about the way his characteristic trope of metonomy or simile is related to Buddhism:

> The copious use of similes is all to do with the visual precision and clarity that Imagists want. But I've carried it further than the original exponents of the style. The more accurately you want to define a thing, the more you have to bring in aspects of other things. This points to the very interdependence of everything, of all qualities—a Buddhist idea. In fact it's the central one. This is what Buddhism means by 'There is no self-nature in anything'.
>
> A simile always involves two separate terms—there's no blurring two separate things together, as with symbols or

18 Robert Gray, *The Land I Came Through Last* (Sydney: Giramondo, 2008), pp. 218–19.

> metaphors. It's like keeping an outline around each one, and yet making them dependant on each other.[19]

We can see this eye for detail at work in the opening of Gray's poem, 'To The Master, Dõgen Zenji (1200–53 AD)', included in *Windchimes*:

> Dõgen came in and sat on the wood platform;
> all the people were gathered
> like birds upon the lake.
>
> After years, home from China,
> and he had brought no scriptures; he showed them
> empty hands.
>
> This in Kyoto,
> at someone-else's temple. He said, All that's important
> is the ordinary things.
>
> Making a fire
> to boil the bathwater, pounding rice, pulling weeds
> and knocking dirt from their roots,
>
> or pouring tea—those blown scarves,
> a moment, more beautiful than the drapery
> in paintings by a master.[20]

The metonymic moment, in which everything exists in and of itself, but is dependent upon everything else, turns metaphoric if we apply it to the engagement with the East. Once the other is joined, dogma gives way to dialogue; this entails a respect for the autonomy of the other and creates a learning situation, a new perception and new modes of appreciation. The ordinary replaces the exotic. This, I think, is the

---

19 Robert Gray, 'Robert Gray shows how the ordinary can be sublime: an interview with Don Anderson', May, 1986. Excerpts available at: www.duffyandsnellgrove.com.au/TeachersNotes/notes/Graytn.html [Accessed on 7 October 2009]

20 Robert Gray, 'To The Master, Dõgen Zenji (1200–53 AD)', in Rowe and Smith, eds, *Windchimes*, pp. 143–46.

future of our poetic triangulation of the East: America, Australia and Asia will connect in deeper ways. One of the driving forces behind this will be the growth of Asian-American and Asian-Australian writing, which will exert a pressure on each country to come to terms with a new reality. One key date, in the United States, will be two decades from now, when, according to the Census Bureau, there will be no majority race among children born in America. The norms of white America are already shifting and there will be much more hybridity, with an admixture of black, Hispanic, white and Asian identities. The numbers are quite different in Australia, where the white population is closer to ninety per cent, and the Aboriginal two and a half per cent. And yet there seems to be considerable awareness of multiculturalism in Australian literature, even if the raw numbers do not suggest it. It's partly a question of narrative: who gets to write the story of what's happening. As Alice Pung points out in her original introduction to the anthology *Growing Up Asian in Australia*:

> Many people continue to subscribe to a particular version of Australian history—one that spans only two centuries, and one that tries hard to cram everyone into a very rigid national narrative. Perhaps the reason Asian-Australians find it difficult to fit into this national narrative is that we rarely get to do the storytelling.[21]

As more and more Asian-Australians tell their stories, the context of Australian poetry will shift so that the turn to the East will also be an embrace of home. None of this will happen quickly or easily—the politics of it are complex and somewhat discouraging—but I expect the future will look quite different from what we imagine at present, and that goes for poetry too.

As I warned at the beginning, none of what I've said is especially new. But I hope I've identified a certain trajectory—or horizon, perhaps: one which we associate with light, both to the east and west in America, but mainly to the north in Australia.

21 Alice Pung, ed., *Growing Up Asian in Australia* (Melbourne: Black Inc., 2008), p. 3. Available at: www.alicepung.com/blog/ [Accessed on 7 October 2009].

8

Smooth and Troubled Passages Across the Pacific

Kevin Hart

Somewhere in the Library of Babel there is a multi-volume history of the reception of American literature in Australia: the section to do with Walt Whitman has been available for some years in other libraries, as has *The American Model*, and similar studies.[1] Somewhere, too, there is a history of the reception of Australian literature in America; and there, in a chapter entitled 'The Yale Years', one finds passages by Harold Bloom, Geoffrey Hartman, and John Hollander praising the poetry of A.D. Hope. There are many anthologies in this library, including some that are in general circulation, such as Thomas W. Shapcott's *Contemporary American and Australian Poetry* (1976), and there are many that are difficult to locate outside the Library, such as *The Norton Anthology of American Allusions to Australia*. There one finds lines such as Philip Marlowe's in Raymond Chandler's *The Long Goodbye* (1953):

> It's going to be a peach of a day. Light breeze. You can hear those tough old eucalyptus trees across the street whispering to each other. Talking about old times in Australia when the wallabies hopped about underneath the branches and the koala bears rode piggyback on each other.[2]

1 See A.L. McLeod, *Walt Whitman in Australia and New Zealand* (Sydney: Wentworth Press, 1964), and Joan Kirkby, *The American Model: Influence and Independence in Australian Poetry* (Sydney: Hale and Iremonger, 1982). Also see Jorge Luis Borges, 'The Library of Babel', in *Collected Fictions*, trans. Andrew Hurley (New York: Viking, 1998), pp. 112–18.

2 Raymond Chandler, 'The Long Goodbye', in *Later Novels and Other Writings*,

Australia in America; and of course it is not quite right. You may be assured that in another wing of the Library there is a volume entitled *Corrections to 'The Norton Anthology of American Allusions to Australia'* in which a scrupulous editor points out that a koala is *not* a bear but belongs to the *phascolaractidæ* family. Since the editor of that book is nothing if not meticulous, we are referred to Chandler writing in May, 1957, 'I am interested in Australia, in everything about it, what it looks like, what its houses are like, how many rooms they have, and what sort, what flowers grow there, what animals and birds are there, what the seasons are … '[3] This sentence comes from a letter that Chandler wrote to Deirdre Gartell, a young Australian girl, and he was to write in more intimate terms to her. She had first written to him, and her imagined existence, as well as her quite real vital statistics, helped to keep the novelist more or less on the rails in the late 1950s when he was going through a bad patch. 'In some mysterious way you have put me inside of you … a girl I have not even seen,' Chandler wrote in one letter to Gartell;[4] and so we see America in Australia. More generally, as we shall see, mystery and strangeness are pronounced themes in American poems about Australia.

Other books in the Library point us to how Australians have seen America. One is entitled *The Complete 'Over-Paid, Over-Sexed, and Over Here'*; it documents in withering detail how Australians saw American soldiers in World War II, and one chapter focuses on how young American men, from California to Maine and everywhere in between, quoted verses by Edna St Vincent Millay and e.e. cummings to win the hearts and bodies of Australian girls.[5] Is there a book that documents the poems that the Australian girls recited to their handsome, clean-cut farm boys and slick big city boys? There must be, for the Library

Frank MacShane, ed. (New York: The Library of America, 1995), p. 438.

3 Alan Close, *The Australian Love Letters of Raymond Chandler* (Melbourne: McPhee Gribble, 1995), p. 37.

4 Close, *The Australian Love Letters of Raymond Chandler*, p. 374.

5 This book is not to be confused with John Hammond Moore's *Over-Sexed, Over-Paid, and Over Here: Americans in Australia 1941–1945* (St Lucia: University of Queensland Press, 1981).

contains the books of all possible worlds in which Australia appears, and not merely the one in which we happen to live. How often boys from Iowa or Missouri must have swooned at hearing 'I Love a Sunburnt Country' intoned to them by girls walking beside Sydney Harbour on warm summer evenings! On my last visit to the Library, made possible by a very generous grant from the Ford Foundation, I managed, with the help of several research assistants, to gather a wealth of material. Some of it, drawing from an immense series of books, *Scandals Resulting from the Visits of American Poets to Australia*, is too rich to quote from here. Early volumes attend to Harry Roskolenko and Karl Shapiro, among others; later volumes, by far the thicker, dilate on the antipodean adventures of John Ashbery, Robert Bly, Robert Creeley, James Dickey, Robert Duncan, Allen Ginsberg, Galway Kinnell, August Kleinzahler, Kenneth Rexroth, Mark Strand, and several others. The Librarian has marked a few of the later volumes in the *Scandals* series as not to be read without written permission from a Department Chairman and only in the presence of the Cardinal Archbishop of Babel, for it is feared that some readers might find their moral compass in need of repair before they get very far in any of the stories.

Another volume, discovered only towards the end of my research leave, is *Peculiar Events in the Lives of Australian Poets in New York and Other Places*; it is a substantial tome on which I hope to report in detail on another occasion. How did Richard Howard entertain John Tranter when the Australian poet visited him in his apartment? What sort of trouble have the wives of Sydney poets had with revolving doors in New York? Which Melbourne poets can handle two martinis when dining with John Ashbery? Which Sydney poets can handle one? These and many other fascinating questions are explored in the volume. All I can say now, though, is that, in general, there is very little evidence that Australian poets see America in terms of mystery and strangeness. Quite other terms are used. As part of my research, I tracked down a collection of essays, which, it turned out, I was to write one day, and one of these essays, this one, is concerned less with empirical influences that cross the Pacific, or histories of *rapprochement*, or even anecdotes of poets behaving badly when overseas, than with how a few American poets have envisioned Australia in their poems and how several Australians have done the same with America.

* * *

There are poems by Americans who were visiting Australia at the time the poem was written. For example, Karl Shapiro's 'Christmas Eve: Australia', composed while stationed in the antipodes during World War II, remarks the 'foreign birds / And insects different as their fish' and notices the oppressive heat at a time when, back home, it would be snowing: 'A cloud burnt to a crisp at some great height / Sips at the dark condensing in deep pools'.[6] The strangeness of Australia here is limited to fauna and climate, and it is significant that Shapiro does not even say precisely where he is, as though the name 'Australia' gives quite enough geographical detail for the purposes of American readers. Liturgical time is more significant for him than place; and what interests Shapiro is being a Jew far from home on the eve of a major Christian holiday, a day of peace in the midst of a war. The same poem could be called 'Christmas Eve: South Africa', and the new title would not affect the meaning of the poem. There are other poems by Americans in which Australia features, but no more than as the vehicle of a tenor. So when Jane Hirshfield writes about the contemporary world's scant reaction to the threat of global warming being like the Aborigines' lack of interest in Cook's ship when it appeared on their shores —'Unable, it seems, to fear what was too large to be comprehended'—one feels that a similar story about Greenland or Japan, if there is one, would do just as well.[7] Of more interest, I think, is the set of poems in which American poets attend to Australia without visiting the country, or before or after they have done so, and without a general concern in mind that might be illustrated equally well by another place.

Herbert Morris, in 'Thinking of Darwin', provides us with a good point to begin, if only because Australia, or at least a part of it, is actually given to thought here. When we say we are 'thinking of' something it

6 Karl Shapiro, *Selected Poems* (New York: Vintage Books, 1973), p. 92.

7 Jane Hirshfield, 'Global Warming', in *After* (New York: Harper Collins, 2006), p. 62.

might mean that we have formed an intention with respect to it, or that we are contemplating it, or even, perhaps, that we are expressing concern for it. An element of distance, physical or temporal, is assumed. Yet for Morris another sense of 'thinking of' is primarily in play. He sees a photograph of Darwin after Cyclone Tracy devastated the city, a dark event that began on Christmas Eve 1974 and lasted throughout Christmas Day. The religious reference does not enter the poem, at least not in any overt way or any coded covert way. Morris sees a photograph of the smashed city, and were it not for the sight of 'matchbox houses coming down,' he says, 'we might never have thought of Darwin.'[8] The city is remote from the East Coast of the United States; it is neither deeply marked as aesthetically, culturally or historically significant for the American mind (as Havana is, for example, in another poem by Morris) nor labeled as a tourist destination. 'We,' presumably the American people (or maybe people anywhere), who open a paper or a magazine in late December, 1974 and see a photograph of a city in the 'final stages' of destruction, think of Darwin only because the image vividly brings a natural disaster to our minds, and we are all potential victims of natural disasters. It is this 'we' that makes the poem far easier to read in America than in Australia. For 'we' —we Australians —think of Darwin in all sorts of ways, in terms of what we learned in primary school about HMS *Beagle* passing near where the city was to be built, the construction of the overland telegraph, the defense of the national coastline in World War II, the city's dramatic climate in the wet season, and so on. There are problems of cultural translation as well as linguistic translation, and some of them are intractable even in the case of a little word like 'We.'

The thinking in question in Morris' poem is neither speculative nor calculative; it is an act of memory, for we must recall that, whether in Darwin or on Long Island, where Morris lived, there is 'nothing but desert at our backs.' This is the desert as metaphor of death, but what captures the reader's attention is less the commonplace than what Morris goes on to say,

8 Herbert Morris, 'Thinking of Darwin', in *Peru* (New York: Harper Collins, 1983), pp. 19–20.

the very texture of the air
evoking strangeness in us, distance,
deep water harbor on the rim
of an island whose aspirations,
despite itself, assume proportions
hemispheric, continental,
set adrift in uncharted waters
where a wind from the Timor Sea
smacks of Celebes, of Java,
celebrates archipelegoes
for which no names have been devised.

The visual representation of Darwin's air after the cyclone does not make the air strange; instead, the representation evokes 'strangeness *in us*' [my emphasis], the ones who see it from the safe distance of the United States. I take it that Morris is touching on the feeling of *Unheimlichkeit* that Martin Heidegger analyses in *Being and Time* (1927), the sense of not being at home on earth, which is all the more sharply registered when one's home can be suddenly swept away at night and when otherwise one might be thinking of the Holy Family or just having one's family over for Christmas dinner the following day.[9] The photograph evokes in us the uncanny sense that we are never truly at home in life, despite all that we do to ward off disaster. More than this is at issue, however. Australia is an island nation with a small population that has little or nothing that compels Americans to think of it. Despite its modesty as a player on the world stage, the country aspires to be 'hemispheric, continental,' like the United States. One day the influence of the culture may be comparable in significance to the size of the landmass, Morris surmises, though at the moment it is a long way from being so. Distant, Darwin is not only on the rim of a far flung continent but also on the very border of what has been named or can be named. Perhaps there are names for many of the little islands north of Darwin in the Banda Sea; but we have no names for what comes to us in death; and

9 See Martin Heidegger, *Being and Time*, trans. John Macquarrie and Edward Robinson (Oxford: Basil Blackwell, 1973), pp. 188–89.

Darwin gives Morris an image of what sweeps in from the unknown and unknowable.

Whether we live in Darwin or Long Island, all that we can do at night is lie in bed, naked, 'inventing / names for our nakedness,' being suspended 'between the wastes of self and weather.' The poem's rhythm is insistent, almost obsessive; it turns and turns again around its basic words: 'names', 'remember', 'forget'. Australia is a prime metaphor for the dark side of the human condition, Morris suggests, because thinking of it involves,

> Mapping what will not quite stay mapped,
> nothing but desert at our backs,
> nothing but darkness to advance on,
> night on the routes that enter strangeness
> more dangerously, in the evening,
> than we can bring ourselves to say,
> darkness and an interior
> for which, of course, there is no name
> except, unmapped, unknown, ourselves.

The proper noun 'Australia', especially the proper noun 'Darwin', helps us to name ourselves, that is, to realise that the names we use to identify ourselves are no more than catachreses: they try to name what in naked reality has no name. If Morris seems to be making a statement reminiscent of St Augustine, a judgment about our inner life, in which we cannot truly name what is deepest in ourselves because it is the unnameable God who is more intimate to me than I am to myself (*interior intimo meo*), he veers away from it to make a more Socratic or Freudian observation: we simply do not know ourselves.[10] When we think about Darwin from the perspective of the United States we do more than remind ourselves about our mortality and our fragility; we think of 'the routes that enter strangeness / more dangerously … than we can bring ourselves to say.' Australia leads Morris, through a chance photograph of one of its cities suffering a natural disaster, to an essential meditation on being human.

---

10 See Augustine, *Confessions*, II.vi.11.

* * *

Herbert Morris thought about Australia from afar, and never visited Darwin or any other part of the country. I turn now to John Ashbery, who did both. Now the New York School is not known for its range of allusions to the Antipodes, although there is of course John Perreault's zany and moving 'Boomerang' ('Why is everything I do in my life like a boomerang?').[11] Ashbery may not have mentioned the Murray River in his huge catalogue of rivers in 'Into the Dusk-Charged Air', but he evokes the country as a whole in a poem he wrote before visiting it.[12] 'Poem at the New Year' begins in Ashbery's characteristic high manner, as an echo of Hölderlin's odes. If the great German's influence is distanced, deflated, displaced, and even parodied, it also presses on the poem from afar:

> Once, out on the water in the clear, early nineteenth-century
> twilight,
> you asked time to suspend its flight. If wishes could beget
> more than sobs,
> that would be my wish for you, my darling, my angel. But
> other
> principles prevail in this glum haven, don't they? If that's
> what it is.
>
> Then the wind fell of its own accord.
> We went out and saw that it had actually happened.
> The season stood motionless, alert. How still the drop was
> on the burr I know not. I come all
> packaged and serene, yet I keep losing things.[13]

11 John Perreault, 'Boomerang', in *Camouflage* (New York: Lines, 1966), no pagination. One gauge of the differences between Australian poetry and the poetry of the New York School in the late 1950s and early 1960s would be to compare Perreault's poem with William Hart-Smith's poem 'Boomerang', in *Selected Poems 1936–1984* (Sydney: Angus and Robertson, 1985), p. 12.

12 See John Ashbery, 'Into the Dusk-Charged Air', in *Rivers and Mountains* (New York: Holt, Reinhart and Winston, 1966).

13 Ashbery, 'Poem at the New Year', in *Hotel Lautréamont* (New York: Knopf, 1992), p. 83.

Then, suddenly, in the middle of this love poem, there comes a completely unexpected turn to Australia. We should not be at all surprised by quixotic shifts of tone, manner, or subject in a poem by Ashbery. He learned one or two lessons very well from Ern Malley, after all.[14] The third verse paragraph begins with wishing to stop time having turned into wondering about Australia:

> I wonder about Australia. Is it anything like Canada?
> Do pigeons flutter? Is there a strangeness there, to complete
> the one in me? Or must I relearn my filing system?

'I *wonder* about Australia' [my emphasis]: that is, I am curious about the country, I desire to know more about it, I doubt a little about what I have heard about it, and also, more importantly, I admire something about it, and I marvel about it.

The wonder is fleshed out in four questions, none of which is answered and none of which is rhetorical. The first asks if Canada provides an adequate comparison with Australia (in size, in population, in culture, in language?). The second introduces the possibility of something utterly different from Canada: either there are no pigeons down under or they do not flutter, which would be very odd. The third carries this strangeness to a personal remark. Like Morris, Ashbery thinks of Australia in terms of strangeness: not an exterior strangeness (like the one that Karl Shapiro experienced) but an interior one (perhaps like the one that Herbert Morris has in mind). Yet where Australia enabled Morris to identify a strangeness in himself, in Americans and in all human beings—a sort of general ontological structure—Ashbery wonders if there is a strangeness in Australia that will '*complete* / the one *in me*' [my emphases]. No general remarks about the nature of human being are made. John Ashbery is *already* strange to himself, and he knows it, has come to terms with it already and even affirms it. Rather than seeking the ideal of self-knowledge that has been held aloft as an ideal in the West since Socrates' friend Chaerephon visited Delphi, he entertains the thought of being complete, of being whole, even of

14 See, for example, Ashbery's poems 'Potsdam' and 'Aenobarbus', in *Jacket* 17 (2002), a part of 'Nine Ern Malley Poems'.

achieving salvation, in terms of strangeness rather than in the clarity of self-knowledge.[15] The three questions have ascended in their interest to the reader, and the fourth question is perhaps the most intriguing of the set. 'Or must I relearn my filing system?' Ashbery asks. But what is actually being asked here?

The fourth question might be taken to be simply the fourth in a sequence. If so, it suggests that in Australia there is another way of thinking about order, one that will extend the range of subjects that he considers of importance. Perhaps Australia imaginatively presents Ashbery with a country so different that he has to extend his vocabulary, his concepts, and his images. Yet it is also possible that the question is not just one of a series but a reflection on the series, in which case he is faced with mastering another order of things, much as Borges does in his splendid piece, 'John Wilkins' Analytical Language'. As you will recall, Borges describes there 'a certain Chinese Encyclopedia', the *Celestial Emporium of Benevolent Knowledge*, in which all animals fall into one or another of fourteen categories. The reader is asked to consider animals 'that belong to the Emperor', 'embalmed ones', 'suckling pigs', 'those included in the present classification', 'those drawn with a very fine camelhair brush', among several other sorts; and of course one simply cannot think in that way.[16] Does 'Australia' offer itself as so different to the United States that it is not only unlike Canada but also—if pigeons do not *flutter* there—utterly unlike how we usually think about the world? That question would be disturbing, and may well make Ashbery ponder how strange apparently familiar categories are in the United States, just as it made Michel Foucault rethink the relations between words and things.[17] A third, and even odder possibility, is that Ashbery is asking if, faced the prospect of Australia, must he *relearn* his filing system. This would suggest that his filing system, used for negotiating daily life in the United States but presumably fallen into disuse by now

15 See Plato, *Apology*, 21a.

16 See Borges, 'John Wilkins' Analytical Language', in Eliot Weinberger, ed., Esther Allen et al., trans., *Selected Non-Fictions* (New York: Viking, 1999), p. 231.

17 See Michel Foucault, *The Order of Things: An Archeology of the Human Sciences* (New York: Random House, 1970), p. xv.

because it does not quite fit the realities (or perceived realities) there, must be consciously relearned since now, at long last, he is faced with a country whose sheer otherness fits his particular way of conceiving the world even if it is not quite *his* way of conceiving the world. In that case, there would surely be 'a strangeness there, *to complete* / the one *in me*' [my emphases]. So when Ashbery asks, in the fifth and final question, the one I have not quoted until now, 'Can we trust others to indict us / who see us only in the evening rush hour / and never stop to think?' the answer presumably would be 'No', at least for Ashbery. Only Australians and those who have been to Australia could be trusted to indict someone for being truly strange.

'I *wonder* about Australia', Ashbery writes, and what he wonders about is its possible 'strangeness'. 'Poem at the New Year' was written before he visited the country, and one can only wonder if he did indeed find a strangeness there to complete his own at the Melbourne Writers' Festival. So far as I can tell he has made no mention of the country in a poem since returning to New York in 1992. Exactly the opposite is the case with John Koethe, a poet who we might place in the line of Wallace Stevens and John Ashbery. He was a guest of Writers' Week of the Adelaide Festival in 2002, and never mentioned Australia in any poem before visiting. Yet, on returning home, he wrote a poem entitled 'Adelaide', which he dedicated to one of my favourite Australian poets:

It was a wonderful time, and we,
Its creators and subjects, were never more alive.
There were rumors in the bars and bookstores,
Reputations, giddy conversations
In the cabs, on the long walks home after the readings.
Some stood the test of time, some flourished
For a day, but all knew what the shouting was about
And who the heroes were. And then it was over —
Pessimists or optimists, we didn't *matter* anymore,
At least not in *that* way. There is this sense of place,
Though not of purpose, yet the place itself feels unfamiliar
As we rub our eyes and look around with but a hazy

Sense of what we stand for, who we are.
What *are* our mottos? Who is this *we*?

Meanwhile the gnome was at his spinning wheel,
Defying reason, defying even the defiance of reason,
Stranded in that dreamtime where the stream flows on forever
In cascading clauses sometimes spilling over on a page,
But mostly shadowing the darkness in the heart
Where the real poem begins, and ends.
What have *I* conceived? Some thin, bright clouds
Through which an airplane gradually descends
On the other side of the world? The crowds o'erflow the tents
In the February heat along the River Torrens
Where the tunes roll on all summer long,
Yet seem so local now, and too immediate to believe.
Why can't I just repeat the songs I learned in singing school?
But those seem futile, much too far removed
From what I feel here in the isolation of my room.
Come here to the window. Let me show you my street.[18]

This is not a poem 'about' Adelaide, not even in the sense in which 'Thinking of Darwin' is about Darwin. Rather, it is a poem that explores the nature and celebration of poetry, and that uses the Adelaide Festival as its point of entry.

Koethe does not wonder about Australia in the poem; he presents his time in Adelaide in late February and early March 2002 as 'wonderful': a week consecrated to artists of all kinds, people who were the 'creators and subjects' of the time he experienced. Local allusions—the River Torrens, the festival tents—are incidental; the essential matter of the poem loops through Australia in the linking of imagination and the 'dreamtime.' It is in dreaming, composing, musing, that one's 'filing system' is rethought or relearned. Adelaide may be 'unfamiliar' but it is not the basis for calling Australia 'strange'. There is no 'we', as in Morris' poem, for whom

18 John Koethe, 'Adelaide', in *Sally's Hair* (New York: Harper Collins, 2006), pp. 46–47.

Australia is suddenly brought into focus. Instead, the 'we'—the unity of the group of invited artists at the festival—is put into question. 'Who is this *we*?' What, if anything, links together, over a few days at a festival, a number of poets and novelists, musicians and visual artists? Is this a genuine community, or perhaps what Maurice Blanchot would call an 'unavowable community', an open set of relationships that no one can simply avow because no one has a substantial selfhood that could ground the avowal?[19] Or, again, we may question whether a community was formed in any sense at all for the opposite reason: artists are all, deep down, self-reliant Emersonian individuals. For his part, Koethe cannot 'just repeat the songs' that he 'learned in singing school' because poetry demands something unique as well as something memorable. Yeats' 'singing school' is important, but it is ultimately important for producing composers and soloists.[20] 'What have *I* conceived?' is always the most pressing question that an artist can ask of himself or herself.

'Adelaide' ends with Koethe pondering the difference between what a poet learns and enjoys, even at a literary festival, and how he or she can create once the learning and fun are over. What has been learned and celebrated now 'seems futile, much too far removed / From what I feel here in the isolation of my room', although even here one hears an echo of Wordsworth. In 'I wandered lonely as a cloud' (1804) Wordsworth contrasted the dancing golden daffodils that he had encountered with the time when he was 'In vacant or in pensive mood' in his room. Romantic though he surely is, and a keen observer of clouds as well, Koethe does not commend memories that 'flash upon that inward eye / Which is the bliss of solitude' but rather asks the dedicatee of the poem (and, more generally, the reader) to 'Come here to the window'.[21] He says, 'Let me show you my street'. It is in looking from his room at his street, being embedded in his locality, that he is able to write poems. It

19 See Maurice Blanchot, *The Unavowable Community*, Pierre Joris, trans. (Barrytown, New York: Station Hill Press, 1988).

20 See W.B. Yeats, 'Sailing to Byzantium', in *Collected Poems* (London: Macmillan, 1950), p. 217.

21 See Koethe, 'Clouds', in *Ninety-Fifth Street: Poems* (New York: Harper Collins, 2009), pp. 31–32.

is not in gaiety but 'in the darkness of the heart' that one finds 'Where the real poem begins'. If Adelaide is a figure of festivity, of elusive and perhaps illusory community, it is also a means by which the poet can begin to distil for himself a better understanding of his own locale and the relationship between locality and imagination.

* * *

How has America been envisaged in Australian poems? I have said something about how Australians began to see Americans in the early mid-1940s, and that was the time when America started to come into focus for Australians, including its poetry. One finds poems by Langston Hughes, Karl Shapiro, Robert Penn Warren, and William Carlos Williams appearing in little magazines in Australia.[22] I begin, though, much later on with Les Murray, a poet who is, by his own testimony, not 'at ease with this epoch', which has been and still is the American age.[23] Perhaps his strongest early poem, 'Driving Through Sawmill Towns', from *The Ilex Tree* (1965), lives and breathes in a world made possible by Robert Bly's *Silence in the Snowy Fields* (1962). Rural northern New South Wales resembles rural Minnesota in more than one way. Bly's poetry arrived in Australia many years before Bly himself visited the country, and in some respects Murray's poem is a naturalisation of a poem such as Bly's 'Driving toward the Lac Qui Parle River'.[24] Where Bly alternates deep images ('water kneeling in the moonlight') and plain speech ('In small towns the houses are built right on the ground'), Murray devotes himself wholly to plain speech:

---

22 See John Tregenza, *Australian Little Magazines 1923–1954: Their Role in Forming and Reflecting Literary Trends* (Adelaide: Libraries Board of South Australia, 1964). It should be noted that *Overland* published the correspondence of Walt Whitman and Bernard O'Dowd in the Autumn of 1962.

23 Les Murray, *Collected Poems* (Sydney: Angus and Robertson, 1991), p. 54.

24 See Robert Bly, 'Driving Toward the Lac Qui Parle River', in *Silence in the Snowy Fields* (Middletown: Wesleyan University Press, 1962), p. 20. It is worth noting that Bly also influenced Adamson in his early poems. The lyric 'There are fish that we never quite catch swimming' reveals a reading of the Bly in and around *The Light Around the Body* (New York: Harper and Row, 1967). See Adamson, *Swamp Riddles* (Sydney: Island Press, 1974), unpaginated.

You glide on through town,
your mudguards damp with cloud.
The houses there wear verandahs out of shyness,
all day in calendared kitchens, women listen
for cars on the road,
lost children in the bush,
a cry from the mill, a footstep—
nothing happens.

The half-heard radio sings
its song of sidewalks.

Sometimes a woman, sweeping her front step,
or a plain young wife at a tankstand fetching water
in a metal bucket will turn around and gaze
at the mountains in wonderment,
looking for a city.[25]

An attentive reader can hear something of the early Bly in the line 'The houses there wear verandahs out of shyness', although Murray's strong voice makes the line his own and America enters the poem more surely in another way.

Even in rural New South Wales the radio plays American pop music: 'The half-heard radio sings / its song of *sidewalks*' [my emphasis]. The women in the sawmill towns are introduced to another culture, one that is at once attractive and unsettling. Here there is no wondering, and nothing is wonderful; yet the women gaze 'in wonderment, / looking for a city'. How can the feel of the city's sidewalks be so present to them when there is no such city to be seen? Such is the subtle power of American popular culture. At the end of the poem we are given an intimate tableau: 'Men sit after tea / by the stove while their wives talk, rolling a dead match / between their fingers, / thinking of the future'.[26] The future may involve many things, although almost certainly it will include the culture evoked in the 'song of sidewalks.' America will edge

25 Murray, *Collected Poems*, p. 9.

26 Murray, *Collected Poems*, p. 10.

its imperious way into rural Australia, changing its social norms, the expectations and hopes of the young, and perhaps even extinguishing some of its cultural values (the image of the 'dead match' is far from idle), even though New York and Los Angeles stay just where they are, and no more soldiers, sailors and airmen come to Australia from the US. American popular culture is so powerful, so pervasive, that it comes, is seen, and conquers without any apparent effort by American individuals or agencies. Wonderment and fear converge in the distance in Murray's poem, even though it has been made possible in part by the very allure that the poem finds disquieting.

Exactly the opposite view of America, dizzy admiration, is to be found in John Forbes' lyric 'To the Bobbydazzlers'. A bobby-dazzler, in Lancashire slang, is a snappily dressed young person, and the word came to Australia with British migrants from the north of England, although it became popular in Australia only in 1977 with the broadcasting of 'Bobby Dazzler', a Channel 7 sitcom starring Johnnie Farnham. For Forbes, though, the real bobby-dazzlers are not fashionable English or Australian youth but American poets, and this introduces a new theme, how the poets of each country see the poets of the other. At the time he wrote the poem, Forbes had already imitated the Ashbery of *Rivers and Mountains* (1966), though he speaks more surely in his own voice here in an apparently slight lyric:

American poets!
you have saved
America from
its reputation
if not its fate
& you saved me
too, in 1970
when I first
breathed freely
in Ted Berrigan's
Sonnets, escaping
the talented earache of Modern
Poetry.

Sitting
on the beach I
look towards you
but the curve
of the Pacific
gets in the way
& I see stars
instead knocked
out by your poems
American poets,
the Great Dead
are smiling
in your faces.
I salute their
luminous hum![27]

The poet sits on a beach gazing across the Pacific but is unable to see the American poets as fully as he wishes. Note that he sharply distinguishes 'America' from 'American poets'; it is the latter who have 'saved' the former's 'reputation / if not its fate.' The politics of the Nixon era and the Vietnam War are one thing, it seems, and the pleasures of reading Ted Berrigan's *The Sonnets* (1964) another.

The Pacific is not a protection against unwanted cultural influence but instead 'gets in the way' of seeing American poets. From the opening line, all Australian and British poets (not to mention everyone else) are turned aside. It is only the American poets who are hailed, and only some of them: the New York School. Yet they cannot hear or see Forbes because of the distance between them. What happens in the following lines? It may be that Forbes is sitting on the beach in the evening as the stars come out; even they are 'knocked / out' by contemporary American poetry. Perhaps they are 'the Great Dead', the mighty poets of the past, now safely ensconced in the heavens. (They hum like the spheres, if one has ears to hear.) Equally, or more than equally, it may be that it is daylight, and Forbes is on a beach reading, say, *An Anthol-*

27 John Forbes, *Collected Poems: 1970–1998* (Sydney: Brandl and Schlesinger, 2001), p. 69. For an early exercise imitating Ashbery, see 'Topothesia', pp. 70–71.

ogy of New York Poets (1970) or *The East Side Scene: American Poetry, 1960–65* (1972), and is so knocked out by what he reads that he sees stars.[28] One thinks of American cartoon characters, like those in *The Katzenjammer Kids*, who 'see stars' when they are hit on the head. Contemporary American poets, the New York School in particular, are the living face of poetry at its finest. (The Great Dead hum in the bright light of their poems.) Where Murray might well think that American culture is 'in your face', posing a threat to rural values, for Forbes even the Great Dead are smiling in the faces of Ted Berrigan and all. Of course, Forbes cannot *see* the faces of any American poets—'the curve / of the Pacific / gets in the way'—so we must take 'faces' to be a metaphor for the individuality of each poem that he reads on the beach. They are smiling at him for as long as he is reading them.[29] If the poem begins by saluting contemporary American poets, it ends by saluting not them, at least not directly, but the Great Dead who, like Forbes, affirm the poetry of contemporary America: 'I salute *their* / luminous hum!' [my emphasis], he says, alluding to James Schuyler ('I salute / that various field').[30]Although Forbes could not breathe freely in the poetry of the Great Dead, no more so than in the talented formalism of Richard Wilbur, James Merrill, and Anthony Hecht, he can salute the poets of the past for their recognition of the poetry that enables him to be a poet. So here writing across the Pacific is not writing on water but is a way of having commerce with the great poets of the past.

28 See Ron Padgett and David Shapiro, ed., *An Anthology of New York Poets* (New York: Vintage Books, 1970) and Allen de Loach, ed., *The East Side Scene: American Poetry, 1960–65* (New York: Doubleday and Co., 1972). I note that homages to Forbes often go by way of an allusion to America. See Meaghan Morris, *Ecstasy and Economics: American Essays for John Forbes* (Sydney: EMPress, 1992), and Robert Adamson, 'American Sonnet: For John Forbes', in *Mulberry Leaves: New and Selected Poems, 1970–2001* (Sydney: Paper Bark Press, 2001), p. 176. It is also worth recalling John Ashbery's poem 'America' which begins 'Piling upward / the fact the stars', in *The Tennis Court Oath* (Middletown: Wesleyan University Press, 1962), p. 15.

29 The figure of poets from another culture smiling is one worth pursuing. See Aram Saroyan, 'French Poets', in *An Anthology of New York Poets*, p. 451.

30 See James Schuyler, 'Salute', in *Collected Poems* (New York: Farrar Straus Giroux, 1993), p. 44.

Berrigan's *The Sonnets* is, as Forbes says, at the origin of his poetry; it is also the *ductus* of this particular lyric: we have been led into the poem by a cultural reference; the book to which Forbes alludes is an anti-monument to which we must bow in order to gain entry and free access. (It has also been personally appropriated by him: he speaks of 'Ted Berrigan's / *Sonnets*' and does not give the full title: *The Sonnets*.) It is a heavily signposted path into the poem, and if one refuses the way offered to us, and mutters under one's breath, 'I wish it had been *Berryman's Sonnets* or Allen Tate's *Sonnets at Christmas* or Robert Lowell's *History*', then one may well stumble in reading the poem. For the poem is ultimately about space. Morris has indicated his view of Australia's aspirations; Forbes gives us an idea of recent inspirations, one of which is *The Sonnets*. It is the place where he 'first / breathed freely', without the Great Dead breathing down his neck. Of course, several of the Great Dead also appear in Berrigan's sonnets. Recall 'Sonnet 37':

> It is night. You are asleep. And beautiful tears
> Have blossomed in my eyes. Guillaume Apollinaire is dead.
> The big green day today is singing to itself
> A vast orange library of dreams, dreams
> Dressed in newspaper, wan as pale thighs
> Making vast apple strides towards "The Poems."
> "The Poems" is not a dream. It is night. You
> Are asleep. Vast orange libraries of dreams
> Stir inside "The Poems." On the dirt-covered ground
> Crystal tears drench the ground. Vast orange-dreams
> Are unclenched. It is night. Songs have blossomed
> In the pale crystal library of tears. You
> Are asleep. A lovely light is singing to itself,
> In "The Poems," in my eyes, in the line "Guillaume Apollinaire is dead."[31]

Somewhere in the Orange Library a poet sits and dreams of precisely this poem. Or perhaps he sits in a library in Sydney or Brisbane.

31 Ted Berrigan, *The Sonnets* (New York: Grove Press, Inc., 1964), p. 33.

* * *

The poet is John Tranter whose book *Crying in Early Infancy: 100 Sonnets* (1977) breathes in 'The Poems' of Berrigan and other New York poets, while adding a half-twist of irony. In reading Forbes and Tranter we realise that something else comes across the Pacific, the disease that Harold Bloom calls 'the anxiety of influence'.[32] It seems to come only in a westerly direction: no American poet seems to labour under the heavy weight of having read Christopher Brennan or James McAuley. If reading the New York School enables a certain kind of poetry to be written in Sydney, it also disables it unless the poet is especially strong. Many Australian poets, male and female, have been influenced by American poetry, although the turning of American poetry into a theme, sometimes even a poetics, is restricted to male poets. Gwen Harwood reads Robert Penn Warren and learns from him but does not hail him in any poem. Alison Croggan writes 'Ode to Walt Whitman' but her poetics are not at risk in the poem.[33] Murray overcomes Bly in the books that follow *The Ilex Tree* until his talent begins to wane in the 1980s; but the successes of Forbes and Tranter are more equivocal. Doubtless Forbes and Tranter, along with some others, felt that they were being addressed by particular poems they read. In reading *The Sonnets* a young man, John Forbes, becomes someone who will write several books of poems, becomes 'John Forbes', and lives for several years in a place as real as it is imaginary, an intersection of Sydney and New York. Forbes becomes himself in choosing to regard himself as the addressee of *The Sonnets*.[34] Of course, 'becoming himself', whether for Forbes or Tranter, is not simply receiving the letter from overseas—a poem by Ashbery, Berrigan, Schuyler, or O'Hara (though never Kenneth Koch)—but repeating

32 See Harold Bloom, *The Anxiety of Influence: A Theory of Poetry* (Oxford: Oxford University Press, 1973).

33 See Alison Croggan, 'Ode to Walt Whitman', in *Calyx: Thirty Contemporary Australian Poets*, Michael Brennan and Peter Minter, eds. (Sydney: Paper Bark Press, 2000), pp. 98–99.

34 See Jacques Derrida, 'Telepathy', in *Psyche: Inventions of the Other*, 2 vols (Stanford: Stanford University Press, 2007), vol. 1, p. 119.

it with a difference, one that has come from French Symbolism or Surrealism, and to which a half-twist of irony has been added.

Consider a poem from Tranter's *Crying in Early Infancy*. 'The Chicago "Manual of Style" is really neat', one sonnet begins, then veers into a messy night scene of teenage sex, before ending, 'Just about then, / on the edge of love and terror, the Chicago / "Manual of Style" appears and takes you home'.[35] If America opens up a 'library of dreams' it also presents us with a new set of conventions and rules, a filing system, if you like, that is 'neat' in the sense of being orderly rather than 'neat' in the sense of being wonderful. In order for the double meaning to work, Tranter has to adopt American slang: no Australian teenager says 'neat' in that way. Tranter may lament that it is 'my fault / not to be born Frank O'Hara' and may imagine a visiting American poet whose plane is refueling in Auckland airport and viewing Australia as 'the end of the line', and the reader may suspect that there is less irony in the voice than is needed for Tranter to protect himself from a debilitating politics of culture.[36] A ready defense mechanism is to attack that which one loves most, and *Crying in Early Infancy* includes an unrhymed sonnet, silently addressed to Robert Adamson, about an American poet returning to the States after visiting Sydney. Here, it's not so much a matter of talking up 'the Americans, baby', an expression coming from Rexroth's visit to Sydney in 1967, as it is of deflating everything to do with that attitude:

> FAMOUS POET JETS HOME TO USA!
> How lucky to live in America, where
> supermarkets stock up heavily on writers!
> Thinking of the famous poets floating home
> to that luxurious and splendid place
> inhabited by living legends like an old movie
> you blush with a sudden flush of Romanticism
> and your false teeth chatter and shake loose!

35 John Tranter, *Selected Poems* (Sydney: Hale and Iremonger, 1982), p. 102.

36 See Tranter, *Under Berlin: New Poems—1988* (St Lucia: University of Queensland Press, 1988), pp. 41, 43.

> How it spoils the magic! In America no writers
> have false teeth, they are too beautiful!
> Imagine meeting Duncan in your Laundromat—
> in America it happens all the time—you say
> Hi, Robert!—and your teeth fall out!
> And you can't write a poem about that![37]

Robert Adamson, author of 'Sonnets for Robert Duncan' and 'Black Water' ('I took Robert Duncan in my grandfather's skiff'), is lampooned here partly for his admiration of the American poet, his idealised view of the United States, and—is nothing sacred?—even for his false teeth.[38]

Adamson may mark an extreme in Australia in his clear signaling of his love of American poetry. Who else, after all, has a book title like *Waving to Hart Crane* or *Dark Water: Towards Zukofsky*? Not even Forbes. Who else would write a poem such as 'Elizabeth Bishop in Tasmania'?[39] Not even Gwen Harwood. A poem from *The Clean Dark* (1989), 'The Difference Looking Back', begins: 'Australia when I was a boy seemed like / a far outpost of Hollywood'. As Murray realised, American popular culture had arrived and was invincible because of its insouciance and its links to power though style. 'I moved from gangsters and Rocket Man / to James Dean / then from Blackboard Jungle / to rock'n'roll and Sandra Dee': the young Adamson embraces the same popular culture that worries Murray. Apart from the British film *Blackboard Jungle* (1955), the references are to American popular culture, and the poem approaches closure by focusing on the United States:

---

37 Tranter, *Selected Poems*, p. 125. Also see Frank Moorhouse, *The Americans, Baby: A Discontinuous Narrative* (Sydney: Angus and Robertson, 1972). Rexroth's visit to Sydney is documented briefly by Linda Hamalian in her *A Life of Kenneth Rexroth* (New York: W.W. Norton and Co., 1991), p. 324. Sydney is misspelled 'Sidney'.

38 See Adamson, 'Sonnets for Robert Duncan', in *Mulberry Leaves,* pp. 186–89, and 'Black Water', in *Black Water: Approaching Zukofsky* (Sydney: Brendl and Schlesinger, 1999), pp. 50–51. *Black Water* has an epigraph from Duncan. Of course, Adamson's poetry is equally marked by French Symbolist poetry and by Australian poetry, not to mention Bob Dylan. For his early influences, see *Inside Out: An Autobiography* (Melbourne: Text Publishing, 2004).

39 See Adamson, *Mulberry Leaves,* p. 23.

America
as limitless as electricity
as dangerous as the F.B.I.
and a world away from chooks
bats and rusty drainpipes America
every Saturday afternoon

There it is, the image we have been waiting for: 'America / as limitless as electricity'. The image gives at once an idea of how America disseminates itself and the power that is disseminated. 'America', Adamson concludes, 'my shiny dark and beckoning surreal / Eden'.[40] America as the new Eden is well known, for imaginative histories assure us that Eden moves forever west; it is shiny and dark, though, because it comes to us through the glittering darkened movie cinemas of the 1960s which in Australia were mostly foreign owned and which specialised in Hollywood films. More could be said about this line, but for me the most important word is 'my': '*my* shiny dark and surreal Eden' [my emphasis]. America, the land over the horizon, the land on which he has not yet set foot, is already *his*, and his in a highly particular way. It has come to him not so much through the radio (as in Murray's poem) as through the silver screen. The paradox of course is that America already belongs to Adamson and yet it beckons him. There is intimacy and there is closer intimacy, it seems. For all this, there is no cultural cringe in Adamson; and it is an irony that when reading some of Tranter's poems one feels that he really does wish that he could have been a character in John Koethe's long poem 'Ninety-Fifth Street', somewhere around the lines when the young Koethe, already in Ashbery's apartment, finds himself in exalted company: 'The doorbell rang and Frank O'Hara, fresh from the museum / And swelte in a houndstooth sports coat entered, followed shortly / By 'excitement-prone Kenneth Koch' in somber gray, / And I was one with my immortals'.[41]

As things stand, Tranter is a character in other poems to do with America. Adamson recalls scenes of reading Ashbery in his lyric 'The

40 Adamson, 'The Difference Looking Back', in *The Clean Dark* (Sydney: Paper Bark Press, 1989), pp. 43–44.

41 Koethe, 'Ninety-Fifth Street', in *Ninety-Fifth Street*, p. 74.

Flow-Through', which is 'for the Johns' (John Ashbery, John Forbes, and John Tranter). The poem ends with Adamson thinking of Ashbery's poems as a complex space where friendships can be nourished:

> These poems were places I made friends in.
> I remember Tranter standing in a classroom
>
> reading them, his laughter edged with
> irony and kindness. Ashbery days, when poets
> were drunk on code within code,
>
> when language cracked open and showed us
> the power of whimsy and a dark abyss
> that said "perhaps" as it echoed.[42]

Ashbery days or Ashbery daze? Either way, Ashbery's poetry does not come into sharp focus in terms of linguistic codes, or the distinction between code and message. There is no arbitrary filing system of signs, or a higher sign, not even 'Whitman' (the one that Bloom proposes), that can be used fully to decode *Rivers and Mountains* (1966) or *Flow-chart* (1991) or any of his books. Adamson's insight is that Australian poets of the age, the late sixties and seventies, were 'drunk' on cultural codes. If 'the professors' were able to decode the poems, the poets wished to re-encode them in new ways. How, though, to decode the cultural work that Ashbery's poems do and then encode that work in Australian poetry so that it works otherwise, in ways that serve voices other than Ashbery's? It is a question that was vaguely intuited rather than properly posed at the time, and it has not been satisfactorily answered in the poetry that welcomed the New York School. 'Perhaps' is an apt word, as Adamson sees very well, to modify 'whether / this was *the* way to go' [my emphasis] for Australian poetry. After all, why should Australian poetry all go in any one direction at all? Why, when all of literary history is available in English or in English translation, should just one contemporary American poet indicate 'the way' ahead? Octavio Paz was right when he observed that, 'Though it perpetually changes, poetry does not

42 Adamson, *The Golden Bird: New and Selected Poems* (Melbourne: Black Inc., 2008), pp. 223–24.

advance'.[43] The avant-garde loves the model of the labyrinth but must rely on a crude linear idea of literary history.

If Adamson is gentle with Tranter, August Kleinzahler pokes a little fun at him for his Newyorkophilia in his 'Tranter in America'. The estimable country boy from Moruya, New South Wales, finds himself on the West Coast, playing tenpin bowls, and, Kleinzahler leans over to him and says,

> You are drifting, drifting even further from Frank O'Hara's Lower East Side flat
> where you sit daydreaming: it is 1959 and you are staring out the window
> at a finny Bel Air scarred rather nicely by kids or sleet, parked
> on a billboard across the street kittycorner to a Nedick's,
> the orange drink tumbling and roiling in its smudged plastic tank
> a slow, piss-scented elevator ride up from the cavern
> Grendel in warpaint flashes and roars through
> and from which the frail sonneteer and critic of ballet
> will emerge in twenty-three minutes to knock ever so delicately
> just in time for a spot of Jim Beam to keep off the chill, the first
> of September, as Frank puts the final touch to *Poem*
> the one beginning "Kruschev is coming on the right day!"
> then kicks open the door to his study and, breathless as the young Rita Hayworth
> after a terrible fright, cries out—*We're on with de Kooning*
> *for a tequila sunrise at eight, then ... How is everyone? All right?*[44]

43 See Octavio Paz, 'Recapitulations', in *Alternating Current*, Helen R. Lane, trans. (London: Wildwood House, 1974), p. 67.

44 August Kleinzahler, 'Four Worthies: 1. Tranter in America', in *Earthquake Weather* (Mont Kisco, NY: Moyer Bell Ltd., 1989), p. 63.

Just imagine it: Tranter gets to live in the sort of scene that Koethe actually experienced! Here 'writing across the Pacific' has the effect of imaginatively giving an Australian poet another life, doubtless one of those new and better American lives that Australians heard of from US troops in the 1940s when Tranter was a child and that were played out in talk of 'the American dream' as it made vast strides towards Australia. Of course, by 1959, the time of the scene, Tranter would have been sixteen, about as good an age for hero worship as one could name, and 'Poem' ('Kruschev is coming on the right day!') would have been the epitome of camp style dangled before him, like water he could never quite drink from. Tranter as Tantalus! Even the 'orange drink' he has or sees in Kleinzahler's poem could be an 'orange library of dreams' *avant la lettre*, as the Francophile New York poets of that age would have said.

* * *

Koethe's and Kleinzahler's poems make New York in the 1960s seem an innocent time, although doubtless some of its edges were rough and others all too sharp. Australian poets were not thick on the ground there. A.D. Hope visited Amherst in 1958 and celebrated the fall there in his 'Ode on the Death of Pius the Twelfth', and he taught at Sweetbriar College in Virginia for a year in 1970. By and large, though, most Australian poets not in the academy went to America only in the late 1970s and 1980s when they could go on Literature Board junkets.[45] Some went in search of Big Friends who could help them; others went in search of publishers, even if Big Friends could not be found to serve as go betweens; and others simply went along for the ride. Many stories are contained in *Peculiar Events in the Lives of Australian Poets in New York and Other Places*, as I have said, and it is a book of misery and elation. Any volume that requires of the Librarian that a little shot of brandy be available to Australian readers on opening the book needs to be taken very seriously indeed.

So far as I know, Robert Gray has not yet visited the Library of Babel. His personal experience of the United States came somewhat after the

45 See A.D. Hope, 'Ode on the Death of Pius the Twelfth', in *Collected Poems 1930–1970* (Sydney: Angus and Robertson, 1972), p. 209.

heyday of enthusiasm for it. He had already learned what he needed from American poets—Reznikoff, Snyder and Williams—as well as from American prose writers, especially Raymond Chandler. Like other Australian poets, he had also learned from other cultures, principally from Chinese and Japanese poets: there is a north-south conversation as well as an east-west one, although, again, at the moment it goes mainly in one direction. The New York School was never to his taste; it was realism and not surrealism that attracted him from the very beginning.[46] Let us hear him talking of a visit to America long after the vanishing points of his imagination had been established:

> There is no more innocence here
> Than there's sincerity in all of that talk about you're welcome and
> having a nice day.
> Americans seem to believe that you may have to eat or be
> eaten, and therefore
> The complementary, frightened insistence on sociability.[47]

Nowhere else in his work does Gray sound more bad tempered than he does here. America is no Eden for him, unless it is Eden after the Fall: innocence lost. Gray has not made the ritual sacrifice, common to male poets of his generation, of writing about or to an American poet, and his view of the art world in the United States is no less acerbic than is his general estimate of American society, as is clear in 'Cows in Massachusetts'. We hear about this and that,

---

46 See, for example, the comments on some Sydney poets in *The Younger Australian Poets*, Robert Gray and Geoffrey Lehmann, eds. (Sydney: Hale and Iremonger, 1983). Of John Tranter the editors say, 'In many of his poems Tranter has adopted the role of having nothing to say, excluding all coherent subject matter, so that his writing resembles a series of deliberately unrelated movie stills' (p. 111). Forbes fares much better, though he too is given a rap over the knuckles: 'Some poems remain at the level of mere word games, and we have not represented these' p. 177.

47 Gray, 'Walking in an American Wood', in *New Selected Poems* (Sydney: Duffy and Snellgrove, 1998), p. 105.

And about

Jasper Johns, whom someone said that one could meet
in New York,

or Andy Warhol —'I can fix it for you.'
But I left there

and went on, and saw the cows pass,
who know what they like, and did not think Alas. (174)

Gray's poems about America are the very antithesis of 'To the Bobby-dazzlers' and related poems. The stout affirmation of knowing what one likes, as distinct from following mere fashion and worrying about 'the way to go', is appealing after reviewing some Sydney poetry of the seventies and eighties. Yet he too has a clear idea about the right way to go, and Williams is the main signpost. It is possible for an internal quarrel about American poetry to take place in Australian poems, a quarrel that sometimes occurs at the level of theme and at other times is indicated by form, mode and structure.

* * *

American poets have tended to see Australia as strange, by dint of its isolation, or as wonderful (because of what it can do to affirm or focus the self). Doubtless Australian poets have regarded America as sublime, as bringing forth wonderment, though reticence forbids them from making that judgment too directly or too often. It is one thing to rail against 'America', quite another to be published by Farrar Straus and Giroux. When Forbes hails American poets, and praises them for their cultural achievements, he does so by indicating a curious division between nature and culture. It is in reading *poems* that he first '*breathed* freely', although of course the statement also means that he was freely inspired by what he read. For him, nothing is strange about the New York School; rather, it offers him something entirely natural, the ability to breathe, which was presumably not available to him while growing up in Sydney. Needless to say, this something that is as 'natural' as breathing is style. When Adamson writes to Forbes in his 'American Sonnet' about his hat that is worn 'for style more than anything', we see that America gives itself as 'style' to some Australian poets.[48] The phenomenon 'America' may give itself in many other ways, of course, for after all 'America' is a concept as much as a name; but in Australia it is what is received that has been significant. Yet style is a gift of which one should be wary; it can be a weapon used on one's neighbours or even on oneself. It can offer one something exotic or encase one in alien conventions with universal claims (*The Chicago Manual of Style*). Can one accept 'style' without also accepting 'idiom'? It is doubtful: the danger is that the *stilus* one is offered may determine what one writes and how one writes.

As I read Australian poems, for some years now from the distance of the United States, what increasingly stands out to me are those poets whose idiom seems irreducible to anything I hear or read in America or elsewhere: poets such as David Campbell, Robert Adamson, Robert Gray, A.D. Hope, Kenneth Slessor, Francis Webb, Gwen Harwood, Rosemary Dobson, the early Les Murray and the early Judith Wright. The singularity of idiom is what makes poetry, or any writing, memorable.[49] The more singular it is, the more difficult it is to define, for it shrinks to the very edge of any genus, and resists being captured by any concept. At its limit, literary criticism of the best poetry becomes a displaced negative theology; and this is not because the finest poems place 'code within code', for even apparently transparent diction can have a highly distinctive idiom. To read a line, any line, by David Campbell is to know what idiom is. The rest of literary criticism is literary history, sociology, the politics of culture, and so on: displaced ecclesiology and dogmatics. The Library of Babel is full of it. In the end, perhaps the most important thing that the steady wave of American culture on Australian shores will have done is to have made it more difficult to write Australian poetry, to give capable poets an opportunity to assert their individuality; and

48 Adamson, 'American Sonnet', in *The Golden Bird*, p. 210.

49 On idiom, see Derrida, *The Ear of the Other: Otobiography, Transference, Translation*, Christie V. McDonald, ed., Peggy Kamuf, trans. (New York: Schocken Books, 1985), pp. 46, 84, 106, 110, 122, 148.

not only the wave that brings American poetry but also those that bring the poetry of the whole world. An idiom is only ever achieved by not following fashion, by finding vanishing points not given at large. It is that individuality that finally will make Australian poetry of interest to Americans, that will enable it to cross the Pacific from east to west, and give American poets not only something worthy of genuine wonder but also something to be worried about. Some of it is already there to be read, circulating outside the Library of Babel.

Section 3

Literature and Popular Culture

9

Transnational Connectivities of Whiteness: American Blackface in *Life in Sydney*

Benjamin Miller

During the nineteenth century Americans appear to have been ambivalent about Australians. In *Moby Dick* (1851), for example, Ishmael refers to Australia as '[t]hat great America on the other side of the sphere ... given to the enlightened world by the whaleman'; later he states that out of all 'race of mankind ... Sydney men' are the 'most distrusted by our whaling captains'.[1]

For Melville, it seems, there were positive similarities between these two emerging nations of the New World, even if questions remained—probably due to Australia's convict heritage and ongoing political ties to Britain—about the character of Sydneysiders. This chapter considers a form of entertainment popular during the nineteenth century in America and Australia—blackface entertainment—to investigate some connections between the two nations. This chapter suggests that blackface entertainment was one of an array of technologies that encoded transnational views about nation, class and race. During the 1830s and 1840s, in both America and Australia, discourses of otherness energised and united a transnational community of white workers who challenged the social and cultural authority of the upper classes at the same time as asserting their authority over racial minorities.

During the nineteenth century Australians embraced American technology and culture.[2] Tools that were developed or refined in America

1 Herman Melville, *Moby-Dick; or, The Whale*, (New York: Penguin, 2009 [1851]), pp. 121, 273.

2 See for example Clinton Hartley Gratton, *The United States in the Southwest*

for communication, travel, mining and agriculture were to be found in Australian cities, on farms and in mining settlements: telegraph wires, coaches, windmills, axes, shovels, ploughs, and so on. During the mid-nineteenth century, American popular entertainments such as circuses, Wild West shows and blackface entertainments also made their way across the Pacific. In 1838 the first official performance in Australia of an American blackface character was presented by Morris Phillips at Sydney's Royal Victoria Theatre; the eponymous character was Jim Crow, who had first been performed in America by T.D. Rice in 1830. Despite the fact that *The Herald* immediately denounced the routine as 'a mass of vulgar buffoonery and impiety' and expressed confidence that the management 'will not allow the ears of decent people to be annoyed by it anymore', American blackface characters such as Jim Crow, Zip Coon, and Jim Brown became favourites of theatre-goers in both Sydney and Melbourne.[3] But, as Richard Waterhouse makes clear in *From Minstrel Show to Vaudeville* (1990), blackface entertainment had reached Australia prior to 1838: crude blackface routines had been performed at race-meets and in hotel back-rooms, Australians had read stories and reviews about such characters in American and British newspapers, and both stories and song-sheets had traversed the Pacific with international travellers. Blackface entertainment, that is, very soon after its popular emergence in America, was one of a number of transnational connections linking America and Australia.

Studies of transnationalism can trace the complex ways in which transnational communities cohere around transmuted and adapted discourses that have travelled across national borders. For example, Inderpal Grewal's concept of 'transnational connectivities', coined in Transnational America (2005), recalls the term 'collectivities' to indicate that transnational networks 'produce groups, identities, [and]

Pacific (Melbourne: Oxford University Press, 1961), p. 101; Werner Levi, *American–Australian Relations* (Minneapolis: University of Minnesota Press, 1947), pp. 44–5; Neil McLachlan, '"The Future America": Some Bicentennial Reflections', *Australian Historical Studies* 17.68 (1977): 378.

3 Richard Waterhouse, *From Minstrel Show to Vaudeville: The Australian Popular Stage 1788–1914* (Kensington: UNSW Press, 1990), p. 27.

nationalisms' across borders.[4] For Grewal, diverse communities can be united to varying degrees, forming both 'strong and weak connectivities' around transnational discourses and artefacts:

> the power of many discourses to be understood, translated, and used in a variety of sites means that subjects become constituted and connected through these new technologies and rationalities.[5]

Communities are formed, regardless of national borders and tyrannies of distance, by the spread of cultural texts and discourses. The mediums that form the basis of transnational communities vary: from books, films, documentaries, costumes, uniforms, and clothing, to television, tools, machinery, radio, and actual people bringing or displaying, consciously or not, information from other places. Some technologies and rationalities are significantly altered as they are adapted, others require less adaptation.

It can be argued that blackface entertainment was a transnational technology that represents not simply shared fascination with a certain style of performance, but that it was a vital technology in the formation of a transpacific connectivity of whiteness. In *What White Looks Like* (2004), George Yancy describes whiteness as a 'white socio-ontological cartography'—a way of being in and seeing the world—shaped by

> a multitude of individual, collective, intentional, unintentional, isolated, systemic actions that synergistically work to sustain and constantly regenerate relationships of unequal power between whites and nonwhites.[6]

Yancy argues that the epistemological and ontological practices of whiteness are not always conscious, but that whiteness refers to individual, communal and institutional practices that normalise

4 Inderpal Grewal, *Transnational America: Feminisms, Diasporas, Neoliberalisms* (Durham: Duke University Press, 2005), p. 23.

5 Ibid, p. 23.

6 George Yancy, *What White Looks Like: African-American Philosophers on the Whiteness Question* (New York: Routledge, 2004), pp. 14–15.

relationships of inequality based on perceptions of race. For Yancy, whiteness is conscious and habitual, individual and institutional, localised and globalised.

Myths, caricatures and images of blackness disseminated through blackface entertainment, and their material effects, supported a transpacific connectivity of whiteness during the 1830s and 1840s. In each location—America and Australia—blackface was incorporated (and adapted) within specific national contexts and created frameworks and fantasies for the expression of alterity and ideas about what it means to be white in the modern world. The following sections of this chapter will contextualise the early Australian play *Life in Sydney; or, the Ran Dan Club* (1843), provide a close reading of the character of Jim Brown in the play and conclude with a brief discussion of what is arguably one of the earliest representations of Aboriginality directly influenced by American blackface entertainment.

From the 1830s through to the 1870s, Jim Crow consistently appears in Australian culture. In *Visual Ephemera* (2000), Anita Callaway reveals the figure of Jim Crow to have been a common character at Australian social functions. Isaac Solomon, perhaps an early larrikin, was arrested in 1839 for his attendance at a 'disreputable private fancy-dress party' disguised as 'the American Jim Crow'.[7] That this disguise might be punishable by imprisonment may seem harsh, but colonial culture and society (especially as regards anything that might be considered socially disruptive, like carnivalesque masquerades) was heavily censored and regulated. The first public masquerade ball advertised in Australia was proposed to take place at Barnett Levey's Theatre Royal on 31 January 1834. However, the Colonial Secretary banned the event, citing the fact that Levey's licence did not allow masquerades. Masquerades were even banned in England at this time, for fear of class infiltrations by, as the Colonial Secretary put it, 'adulteresses, concubines and prostitutes'.[8] While Callaway concedes there were many other disreputable masquerade balls, she has found no other evidence of the attendees and

7 Anita Callaway, *Visual Ephemera: Theatrical Art in Nineteenth-Century Australia* (Kensington: UNSW Press, 2000), p. 91.

8 Quoted in Callaway, p. 87.

costumes at such functions. This is not to say that such masquerades and performances did not exist, just that they were not advertised or officially sanctioned. Nevertheless, blackface performances continued, albeit off the record, despite colonial censorship.

While American critics have interrogated the meanings of blackface entertainment, this work has not been broadened to include global contexts. David Roediger—a labour historian—has described American blackface entertainment as a 'simple physical disguise'—black face paint and contorted, grotesque, physicality—that was used to create an 'elaborate cultural disguise'.[9] The elaborate cultural disguise, for Roediger, helped create a unified community of white workers that included identity groups previously considered 'nonwhite', such as Irish and Jewish migrants.[10] (In this sense we might consider what it meant for Isaac Solomon, if he was Jewish, to dress as Jim Crow—his Jewishness aligns with other brands of whiteness under the simple blackface mask). To this end, though it is not the focus of this chapter, there is much work to be done investigating how various communities of whiteness—Irish, Scottish, Jewish, Australian-born, and so on—were united in Australia through a shared engagement with blackface entertainment. Blackface entertainment has been credited with mobilising whiteness in order to unite a diverse working class against both blackness (and, as we will see, Aboriginality) and authoritarian ruling classes. Arguably, the unification of white working classes was crucial to the egalitarian (and racist) brand of nationalism that emerged in the ambivalently tethered nations of America and Australia during the nineteenth century.

American blackface was put to Australian uses in the early Australian play, *Life in Sydney; or, The Ran Dan Club*.[11] The play is based on an English play of the time, *Tom and Jerry* (1820–21). Both plays

9 David Roediger, *Wages of Whiteness: Race and the Making of the American Working Class* (London: Verso, 1991), p. 117.

10 See for example Karen Brodkin, *How Jews Became White and What That Says About Race in America* (New Brunswick: Rutgers University Press, 1998), p. 55; Noel Ignatiev, *How the Irish Became White* (New York: Routledge, 1995), p. 215.

11 A.B.C., *Life in Sydney; or, The Ran Dan Club* [1843], in Richard Fotheringham, ed., *Australian Plays for the Colonial Stage 1834–1899* (St Lucia: University of Queensland Press, 2006), pp. 39–94.

provide episodic skits set in various locations of a city; *Life in Sydney* is obviously set in Sydney, while *Tom and Jerry* is set in London. Both attempt to parody several of their city's personalities and celebrities. *Life in Sydney* is not merely derivative but transnational in the sense that, while it mimics an English play's structure, the material is adapted to local situations. However, there is a peripheral character that appears in *Life in Sydney*—Jim Brown, an African-American band leader—that broadens the transnational perspective of this play suggesting, at the very least, that both English and American theatrical trends resonated in the Australian context.

As the main characters of *Life in Sydney* move through settings such as Macquarie Place, near Circular Quay in Sydney, they arrive at the Shakespeare Tavern. This tavern was a real location on Pitt Street opposite the Royal Victoria Theatre. The setting—across the road from an actual theatre—immediately implies the existence of a counter-theatre in Australia, outside and across the road from the normal bounds of theatre. The scene is set in a room of the tavern where 'several parties' sit drinking and 'playing a game of cards' (68). The characters sit down, order drinks, begin to play cards and order from the barman (Dan) some entertainment in the form of Jim Brown:

> TOM. I say Dan, glasses round, cigars etc—by the bye where's Jim Brown—
>
> JERRY. Who's Jim Brown, Tom.
>
> TOM. Jim Brown, my boy, is a Celebrated Nigger,[12]came all the way from New York, to astonish the natives with his songs,—you have often seen and heard Rice I dare say, but

---

12 While I acknowledge that words such as 'nigger' can be confronting and hurtful, in quoting such terms I am following the argument of Jabari Asim in *The N Word*: 'the word "nigger" serves ... as a linguistic extension of white supremacy, the most potent part of a language of oppression that has changed over time from overt to coded'. Arguably, refusing to quote such terms can further repress contemporary legacies of racism. Jabiri Asim, *The N Word: Who Can Say It, Who Shouldn't and Why* (New York: Houghton, 2007), p. 4.

> this fellow is an original black and sings Jim Brown in a most successful manner, I say Dan send Jim in with the strings. (70)

The slippage in Tom's description, between Jim Brown as an 'original black' and Jim Brown as song/performance, suggests that any claims to authenticity are made speciously. The play on authenticity also suggests that audiences and performers could, consciously and otherwise, simultaneously consider certain elements of blackface performance factually while seeing other aspects of the performance as pure fabrication. In this way blackface could resonate in local contexts. For example, for many in the audience, the racial ideology embodied in the buffoonish figure of Jim Brown may have added support to racial ideologies already circulating in Australia about Aboriginal people. So, the performance of Jim Brown may well have helped to 'astonish the natives'. However, the reference to 'natives' in the above passage is to Australian-born white people, not Aboriginal people. In *The Native Born: the First White Australians* (2000), John Moloney describes a number of appellations referring to white people born in Australia: 'colonial youth', 'rising colonists', 'natives', 'cornstalkers', 'currency lads and lasses', and so on. According to Maloney, 'the use of "colonial" and its derivatives … [implied] provincialism, coarseness, vulgarity and implicit inferiority'; such terms were generally avoided after the 1840s.[13] In *Life in Sydney*, the use of 'native' instead of, for example, 'colonist' can be read as an Australian nationalist invocation, typical in its blindness of Aboriginal people. That is, *Life in Sydney* proudly endeavours to unite Australian-born nationalists: attempting to avoid derision as a lower class of colonial whiteness, and, at the same time, erasing actual 'natives'—Aboriginal people—from sight. In many ways the nationalist implications in Tom's description reads like an advert for white Australian nationalism.

In fact, Richard Fotheringham, the editor of a recent edition of *Life in Sydney*, reveals that Jim Brown was advertised at the Royal Victoria Theatre in 1841; the 'real' Jim Brown act was popular enough to last

13 John Moloney, *The Native Born: The First White Australians* (Carlton: Melbourne University Press, 2000), p. 24.

eighteen months in licensed Sydney theatres.[14] Tom's introduction of Jim Brown (above) as well as the ensuing remarks parodying a real classical violinist (not quoted here), emphasise that this is a play about actual Sydney personalities and events of the day. Yet this scene indicates something more about early Australian society. As the barman leaves to prepare the drinks and find Jim Brown, another man watches out the door ready to warn the publican if the police (or 'traps') are sighted. As Tom explains: 'this is Dans [sic] private room, and as the Big wigs are so devilish moral here [in Sydney], a game of cards is almost equal to High treason' (70). Thus, in many ways, the scene is set off the record—in an illegal gaming house where not only are card games played, but so are blackface songs, perhaps even more ribald than Rice's 'Jim Crow' or the published lyrics of 'Jim Brown'. *Life in Sydney* undermines the myth of Sydney's 'moral' theatre by presenting an alternate drama that occurs unofficially. The reference to Jim Brown is also, then, a reference to more than Jim Brown—that across the road from the theatre in which this play was to be performed there are to be found performances of similar libellous entertainments, including blackface entertainment. The collusion of an American blackface character with an Australian nationalist appellation ('native') and anti-authoritarian sentiments (mocking the 'devilish[ly] moral' big wigs) may indicate why working-class Australians took to blackface entertainment with fervour. Melville, that is, need not have worried about any strong allegiances with British ideals held by Sydney's working class; both Americans and Australians, it seems, had a healthy disrespect for authority and strictly enforced cultural regulations.

When he actually appears, Jim appears in a typical early blackface characterisation. He brings the main characters their drinks, bantering in the style of early American blackface entertainment:

> TOM. Well Jim my boy how are you, hows [sic] your windpipe to night, all right for a tune—
>
> JIM. Yes Massa him windpipe all right, cepting him rather dusty in the corners, but him wery soon wash him clean if massa give him leave.

14 Richard Fotheringham, ed., *Australian Plays*, p. 70.

JERRY. A devilish sensible fellow, oh fire way. I'll stand whatever you like to drink (70).

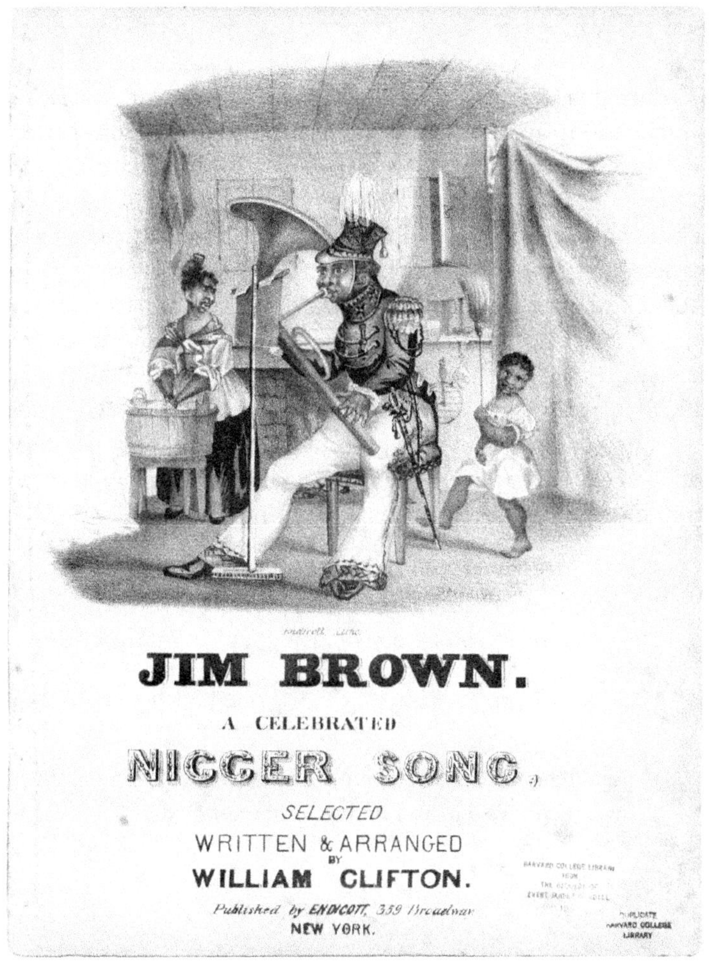

Fig. 1: 'Jim Brown', New York: Endicott, 1836. Image courtesy of Brown University Library.

The Jim Brown song that was to be sung in *Life in Sydney* would most likely have followed an existing version. The script lists the song performed by Jim Brown as 'Jim Brown No 2'. Fotheringham quotes from an early blackface tune entitled 'Jim Brown' as a suggestion as to what the tune may have been, resigned to the fact that 'the tune has not been located'.[15] 'Jim Brown' was indeed a popular blackface act in the United States during the mid to late 1830s and lyrics published in American versions of the song may give some indication as to the versions performed in Sydney in the early 1840s. Two cover pages of New York sheet music publications for 'Jim Brown' (1835–36) are reproduced in Fig. 1 and Fig. 2. It is highly likely that the Jim Brown character in *Life in Sydney* was to have been dressed as a bandleader, as in these publications.

As in lithographs of other blackface characters from the early American blackface period, the lithographs of Jim Brown are overtly sexualised. In Fig. 1 the trumpet is positioned in a phallic manner, while, as Eric Lott has observed in *Love and Theft* (1993), referring to the image reproduced in Fig. 2, the 'appendages' are strategically positioned to convey the threatening sexuality of the character.[16] This is mirrored in the song lyrics as Jim Brown sings:

> De gals in de city dey all run arter me,
> Because I am so hansome de like dey neber see:
> Dey coax me to choose one ob dem, but I don't know who
> shall be,
> Dey are such lubly creters, and dey all lubs me
> …
> O den I'll hab de encores, from all de lubly sex,
> An wen I choose one for my wife, O, de rest ob dem be vex.[17]

15 Fotheringham, ed., *Australian Plays*, p. 71.

16 Eric Lott, *Love and Theft: Blackface Minstrelsy and the American Working Class* (New York: Oxford University Press, 1993), p. 120.

17 'Jim Brown', 1836, n.p.

Fig. 2: Fig. 2: 'Jim Brown', New York: Hewitt, 1835. Image courtesy of Brown University Library.

Presumably, 'Jim Brown' appealed to Australian audiences in the early 1840s because of its trumpeting of both masculinity and whiteness. After all, the audience can enjoy Brown's overt sexual pursuits, while also being comforted by the assumption that an audibly illiterate and overly pretentious African-American man would 'naturally' fail in any attempt at wooing a civilised white woman. As was the case in America, it is possible that the ribald blackface entertainments—allowed because of myths about African-American hyper-sexuality—actually contributed to the softening of sexual taboos (codified as censorship policies in Australia) more generally during the mid- to late nineteenth century.[18] Arguably, however, the main reason Australian workingclasses would have enjoyed such entertainment was to enjoy the community of whiteness—manly, anti-authoritarian, working class—formed in opposition to a buffoonish black character. Blackface characters such as Jim Brown lampooned and deflated white working-class concerns about social, racial, sexual and cultural inferiority.

Life in Sydney provides a fascinating glimpse at blackface on the Australian stage in the early 1840s. How did audiences react? Quite simply, they didn't; or, rather, they weren't, officially at least, given the opportunity. At the time *Life in Sydney* was written, the Colonial Secretary had the authority to approve or censor all plays performed in Australia. The Colonial Secretary in 1843 was Edward Deas Thomson. He initially refused to approve the play as it had no author listed—just the pseudonym 'A.B.C.'. Shortly afterwards, H.C. O'Flaherty (not necessarily the author—the play may even have been co-authored according to Fotheringham)[19] sent a letter to the Colonial Secretary claiming to act on behalf of the author, and asking that the play now be considered. It was considered and, again, denied, Thomson noting on the play itself:

> Inform Mr O'Flaherty that I regret I cannot sanction the representation of this piece at the theatre as it contains matter of a libellous character independently of other objections.[20]

---

18 Seymour Stark suggests that '[p]rimitivism ... on stage permitted minstrels to break the puritan taboo against sexuality'. Seymour Stark, *Men in Blackface: True Stories of the Minstrel Show* (United States: Xlibris, 2000), p. 26.

19 Fotheringham, p. 46.

20 Quoted in Fotheringham, p. 42.

Just what 'matter' the Colonial Secretary found libellous is unclear. Presumably, the scene recounted above was among *Life in Sydney*'s more unsettling—revealing illegal gaming and 'low' entertainment, not to mention the simple immorality of displaying, even championing, 'improper' sexual pursuits, drinking and men at leisure. Despite the fact that it was never performed, it provides a glimpse of popular entertainment through the eyes of a contemporary playwright. In fact, the scene recounted above may even suggest that the censorship by the Colonial Secretary was not preventing certain entertainments (such as rowdy blackface songs), but simply forcing them into a different venue. Entertainments such as blackface performance were, it might be argued, part of an emerging counter-culture that was despised by many journalists and government officers—an emerging nationalism that resisted authority at the same time as enacting an authority over blackness. This ideological nationalist impulse is the strongest of links that can be found between American and Australian blackface performance. Blackface performance in the 1830s and 1840s was fostering a community of middle- and lower-class white people who found an entertainment technology that enabled them to align against authority (be it colonial or bourgeois) and against racial minorities (be they African-American or Aboriginal) at the same time.

By the 1840s portrayals of Aboriginality in Australia had begun to incorporate elements of the American blackface tradition. In 1845 John Rae wrote a poem about the first official fancy-dress (not masked) ball; one of the characters was an 'Australian Chief'. Both an official drawing of the ball and John Rae's poem reflect on the moment when:

> *An Australian Chief*, with his blanket, vaults,
> With hop, step, and jump, to the midst of the waltz;
> And, armed with a wommera, waddy, and lance,
> Exults in a wild Aboriginal dance![21]

Callaway notes that this is the first Aboriginal costume at an official fancy-dress ball. Certainly it is one of the earliest instances of an Aboriginal character influenced by American blackface entertainment. In the

21 Quoted in Callaway, p. 90.

lingo of Jim Crow and Zip Coon, this is Aboriginality 'hopping ober, dubble trubble'. There is more than a hint of Jim Crow to Rae's description of the Chief's interruption of a waltz (which itself is an action Jim Crow would have enjoyed—an invasion of upper-class entertainment). That the ball was an occasion for the upper echelons of colonial society to enjoy suggests that blackface entertainment was nebulous enough to be enjoyed by working classes and the upper classes. While working classes may have enjoyed the anti-authoritarian aspects of blackface entertainment, for example, both working classes and the bourgeois endorsed the overt caricaturing of racial minorities. Further, the fact that Aboriginal people are referred to as 'Chiefs' in Rae's description, and more widely in Australian culture as well, suggests that discursive connections were drawn not only between Aboriginal people and African American stereotypes but also between Aboriginal people and Native American people. In *Science, Sexuality, and Race in the United States and Australia* (2009), Gregory Smithers analyses the circulation of scientific discourses of whiteness and race between America and Australia, suggesting that discourses of whiteness and race worked to restrict 'the social mobility of African-Americans, Native Americans, and Australian Aborigines'.[22] Arguably Aboriginal people, Native American people and African-American people formed a transpacific triumvirate of minorities, each maligned and oppressed by discourses that centred whiteness as racially and culturally superior.[23] The 'Australian Chief'—an Aboriginal character with a Native American appellation and a stereotypical African-American dance style—represents one of the few cultural instances where this triumvirate is explicitly compressed into the single figure.

22 Gregory Smithers, *Science, Sexuality, and Race in the United States and Australia, 1780s–1890s* (New York: Routledge, 2009), p. 5.

23 Following the lead of Helen Gilbert and Jacqueline Lo, further studies of colonial representation should extend the set of colonial caricatures supporting discourses of whiteness to include characterisations of Pacific Islander, Chinese, Japanese and Indian people. Helen Gilbert and Jacqueline Lo, *Performance and Cosmopolitics: Cross-cultural Transactions in Australia* (Basingstoke: Palgrave, 2007).

In fact, there were two patrons dressed as Aboriginal characters at the 1844 ball: Rae mentions one of them dancing, and the other using entertaining 'lingo'.[24] Crude mimicries of black lingo were, of course, central to nineteenth-century representations of blackness, as evident in the lyrics of 'Jim Brown'. Given both Rae's description of blackface dancing and lingo, it is clear that the styles of American blackface entertainment were beginning to be adapted to representations of Aboriginality in Australian culture by the early 1840s. In his *Sydney Morning Herald* article covering the event, Rae prefigured his poem by mentioning the invasion of the waltz:

> One of these sable heroes, arrayed in a tattered blanket, enlivened the audience vastly on one occasion, by bursting into the centre of a circle of waltzers, and giving a ludicrous facsimile of an Aboriginal dance.[25]

It is highly likely that this facsimile was a mélange of crude imitation with a Jim Crow-style 'hop, step, and jump'. Rae's description of an Aboriginal character in 1844 highlights the fact that, at least as far as the few scarce pieces of evidence go, a change in the representation of Aboriginal people may have been occurring: a new 'ludicrous facsimile' of Aboriginality was developing. In both nations otherness had become, by 1844, a fantasy that allowed white performers and audiences to inhabit and domesticate alterity in order to resolve the anxieties of their local situations.

As American and Australian audiences embraced blackface entertainment, the actual consequences for racial minorities were numerous and dire. Blackface entertainment espoused views of intellectual and physical inferiority that confirmed in the minds of colonists the spurious notion that there was no use enabling education, social mobility or political agency for racial minorities and that nonwhite people were only suited to participation in unskilled labour. The privileges gained by those who invested in such myths came at the cost of generations of disadvantage for nonwhite people, while the

24 Callaway, p. 90.

25 Quoted in Callaway, p. 91.

social inequality that resulted from such cultural insensitivity is still only beginning to be addressed. The analysis in this chapter suggests that the cultural myths that helped clear the path into racial inequality developed transnationally; perhaps contemporary attempts to establish equality require both an awareness of racial discourses and their effects in local contexts and a critical interrogation of how local racial discourses garner support beyond national borders.

10

The *Novel Newspaper* and its Role in the Transmission of American Fiction to Australia

Elizabeth Webby

In a recent article, Emily B. Todd argues that the popularity of Scott's novels in America in the first half of the nineteenth century made them vitally important in building a readership for fiction, and hence in the development of a local publishing industry. Nationalist literary historians, she claims, have tended to downplay Scott's significance in helping establish an American literary marketplace in favour of a focus on a home-grown literary hero, James Fenimore Cooper. But, 'if we shift our gaze to the transatlantic literary field, we see Scott as an important figure in the American one'.[1] Following Todd, I want to argue that, when we look at the development of a readership for fiction in Australia during this same period, we need to widen our gaze from British authors like Scott to include American ones such as Cooper. We need to recognise a significant transpacific input into the reading culture of early Australia, even if it came via a transatlantic connection. Scott was, based on the number of advertisements of his works, their representation in public and private libraries and in records of reading, also the most popular author in Australia from 1820 through to 1850. In all three decades Shakespeare and Byron were the second and third most popular authors, but in the 1840s Fenimore Cooper came fourth,

1 Emily B. Todd, 'Establishing Routes for Fiction in the United States: Walter Scott's Novels and the Early Nineteenth-Century American Publishing Industry', *Book History* 12 (2009): 123.

with his novels appearing in more book advertisements than those by Charles Dickens.[2] The main reason for this was the wide circulation within Australia during this decade of cheap reprints that went under the name of the *Novel Newspaper*.

Over forty years ago, I embarked on a PhD thesis on the literary culture of Australia from the beginnings of settlement to 1850. As part of my investigation, I collected and analysed advertisements of book sales to see which authors were most frequently advertised. Since these advertisements usually just listed titles of books rather than authors' names, I then needed to spend hours going through such sources as *The English Catalogue of Books* to identify the authors of many now obscure though once popular works of fiction. There were, however, some titles that I could not identify, though they kept cropping up in many advertisements, especially during the 1840s. And they were not only advertised by auctioneers and booksellers operating in the capital cities, but by store-keepers in country towns. Eventually, and I am not sure now how this came about, I discovered that all the titles I could not identify were by American authors whom I had then never heard of, such as Robert Montgomery Bird and William Gilmore Simms. And so I became aware of the remarkable, but still little known, example of cheap publishing and literary piracy that was the *Novel Newspaper.*

Most literary scholars today are aware that there was little respect for copyright in the first half of the nineteenth century. It is especially well known that popular English authors like Charles Dickens, to their great chagrin, had their novels reprinted in America with no thought of payment to the author. Indeed, many of Dickens' novels were also serialised in Australian newspapers from the 1830s and a pirated edition of *The Pickwick Papers*, complete with illustrations, was published in Hobart in 1838, all again with no payment to the author. Few people, however, as I have discovered, are aware that English publishers were just as prepared to ignore copyright or that some of them decided to get their own back on the Americans by including American novels in their cheap reprint series. Scholarly work on the *Novel Newspaper*

2 See Elizabeth Webby, 'Literature and the Reading Public in Australia 1800–1850', PhD Thesis, University of Sydney, 1971, IV:10.

still, it seems, amounts to only the few pages of description in Michael Sadleir's *XIXth Century Fiction: A Bibliographical Record* (1951). Sadleir records that twelve volumes of the *Novel Newspaper* were published between 1839 and 1842, though he was able to sight and describe only ten of these. Volumes I and II carry the imprint 'T.L. Holt, 266 Strand'; later ones that of 'J. Cunningham, Crown Court, Fleet Street'.[3] But it seems clear that Cunningham was involved as printer of the series from the beginning since his imprint appears on the title pages of all but one of the ten individual novels included in the first two volumes. Perhaps the idea for the series came from Holt, a journalist and something of a bohemian literary entrepreneur, who was involved with various radical and unstamped presses during the 1830s. John Cunningham had been in business in London since at least 1820, mainly as a printer of cheap scientific and trade journals; he died in 1841, volume XI of the *Novel Newspaper* carrying the imprint 'Published at the Office of the late John Cunningham', and Volume XII that of 'N. Bruce, Peterborough Court, Fleet Street'.[4] Sadleir raises the possibility of further volumes having been published; evidence from Australian advertisements suggested that this certainly was the case. And a Google search led me to Robert Temple, a London bookseller, who was offering Volume XVII of the *Novel Newspaper*, dated 1845, and carrying the imprint of Bruce and Wyld, 84 Farringdon Street, for sale for GB£170.00.[5]

The original proprietors of the series had claimed in the Preface to Volume VIII that American novels were morally superior to English ones:

> The plots of their dramas do not turn upon adulteries or robberies; they do not seek their heroes in the prison or on the road, nor is every woman a Lucrece Borgia, modernised with sentiment and fashionable virtue. If the reasons given

3 Michael Sadleir, *XIXth Century Fiction: A Bibliographical Record* (Cambridge: Cambridge University Press, 1951), vol. II, p. 142.

4 Sadleir, vol. II, p. 142.

5 Robert Temple, Home Page. Reference no CRT 800415, available at www.telinco.co.uk/RobertTemple/ [Accessed on 25 March 2010].

> serve to excuse our preference for American novel-writers over English romancists, they will avail us with double force as regards the French novelists of the days of Victor Hugo, Madame Sand and Paul de Kock, for the total exclusion of whose works from *The Novel Newspaper* we are proud to acknowledge having received the thanks of the heads of many families.[6]

Bruce and Wyld evidently had no such qualms, happily extending their piracies from American to European titles, though at least some of these also came via the US. Volume XVII of the *Novel Newspaper* included recent novels translated from Swedish and German as well as Eugene Sue's *The Salamander*, translated by Henry William Herbert and originally published in New York in 1844.

In contrast, Volume I of the *Novel Newspaper* had been made up of five of Fenimore Cooper's novels: *The Pilot*, *The Spy*, *The Pioneers, The Last of the Mohicans* and *Lionel Lincoln*. It carried the following preface, as quoted by Sadleir:

> It has been said that … it is unfair to issue Mr Cooper's novels at such a price. To this we reply that Mr Cooper suffers in common with Sir Edward Bulwer, Captain Marryatt [sic] and other English writers, whose new works are successively reprinted in America without one farthing being paid for copyright. Nor will Mr Cooper regret the wide circulation throughout England of the five novels contained in the present volume; since, being mainly on subjects of American history, they will tend to diffuse a better knowledge of his country amongst a class of persons whose national prejudices are even yet stronger than their reason.[7]

Further titles by Cooper appeared in volumes III and IV, and the series also featured many novels by other American writers, including Robert Montgomery Bird, John Pendleton Kennedy, William Gilmore

6 Sadleir, vol. II, p. 145.

7 Sadleir, vol. II, p. 145.

Simms and James Kirke Paulding. Volume VIII, for example, included Longfellow's *Hyperion* (1839) and Caroline Kirkland's equally recent *A New Home: Who'll Follow: or, Glimpses of Western Life* (1839), a work of particular interest for Australian readers. Later volumes were padded out by older, out-of-copyright works by English authors, mainly in the Gothic vein, such as William Godwin's *Caleb Williams* (1794), Charlotte Smith's *The Old Manor House* (1793), and Mary Anne Radcliffe's *Manfrone or the One Handed Monk* (1809).

As well as being sold in the volume form, individual titles were also issued separately. Sadleir describes a copy of Bird's *The Hawks of Hawk Hollow* (1835) in 'a buff wrapper lettered in black and imprinted E. Elliot, 14 Holywell Street, Strand, and undated', an indication that Cunningham sold individual titles in sheets to other retailers.[8] The London bookseller mentioned above was also offering Anna Maria Porter's *Don Sebastian* (1809), an English work out of copyright by 1839, and one of the five novels in Volume II of the *Novel Newspaper*, for GB£22.00.[9] Several years ago I managed to acquire a *Novel Newspaper* copy of Cooper's *The Water Witch* for A$35.00. It has now been nicely rebound but presumably was also originally issued in paper wrappers. As my copy makes clear, the low cost of these novels necessitated the use of cheap paper and very small print, in addition to the economy of not having to pay royalties to authors.

The earliest Australian advertisement for *Novel Newspaper* titles appears to be one by auctioneer William Yates in the Sydney *Free Press* for 13 January 1841, offering 'twenty-nine of the most popular novels of the day, each complete in one volume, for £2.2.0'. The list of titles indicates that these were *Novel Newspaper* reprints, twenty-nine novels having been included in the first six volumes, published between 1839 and 1840. Despite their cheapness, Yates evidently was unable to attract purchasers, perhaps because the type of persons to whom these cheap books appealed did not have two guineas to spare. He had apparently expected Sydney bookstall owners and general storekeepers to be his

8 Sadleir, vol. II, p. 144.

9 Robert Temple, Home Page. Reference no CRT 800415, available at www.telinco.co.uk/RobertTemple/ [Accessed on 25 March 2010].

main customers since a note at the end of the advertisement stated 'Five per cent allowed where ten copies are taken'. On 30 June, the same sets were advertised at a much reduced price of £1.12s.6d., and one assumes Yates was then able to sell them. It is noticeable that other booksellers later offered the *Novel Newspaper* reprints as individual titles priced at one to two shillings each, depending on number of pages. A few days after Yates' first advertisement, Hobart auctioneer W.T. Macmichael advertised *Novel Newspaper* reprints in the *Hobart Town Courier* for 15 January 1841. They continued to be featured in auction sales in Sydney, Hobart and Launceston during the remainder of the 1840s. Towards the end of 1843 they had reached Melbourne and Adelaide, with Melbourne auctioneers Carfrae and Bland including *Novel Newspaper* titles in a sale advertised in the *Port Phillip Patriot* for 3 November, and William Bulpitt, Broker and General Dealer, offering fifty-eight *Novel Newspaper* titles in the *Adelaide Observer* for 16 December. While the financial difficulties which beset the first settlements in Western Australia meant that very few books were advertised in Perth before 1850, by 1848 Brisbane was able to boast a circulating library run by Ann Dowse, who also offered books for sale. Many of the titles she listed in an advertisement in the *Moreton Bay Courier* for 10 June 1848 were *Novel Newspaper* reprints.

The spread of newspapers outside the capital cities during the 1840s allows us to trace the growth of bookselling in larger country towns as well. Again, advertisements demonstrate that copies of *Novel Newspaper* reprints circulated widely throughout the then settled parts of Australia. In many cases, books were offered for sale by those responsible for editing and printing local newspapers, a combination of roles also found earlier in Sydney, Hobart, Melbourne and Launceston. William Lipscomb of West Maitland, in the NSW Hunter Valley, however, managed to stay afloat as a country bookseller all through the 1840s, commencing in business in 1839 in association with the Sydney bookseller James Tegg and continuing to sell books, along with stationery and many other items, after Tegg ceased trading in 1844. Initially, Lipscomb had to advertise his wares in Sydney papers such as the *Australian*, but after 1843 his advertisements frequently appeared in the *Maitland Mercury*.

By 1845, he was regularly offering copies of the *Novel Newspaper*, 'the cheapest Edition hitherto published'. On 8 May 1848, he announced that he had just received a further 1300 copies of *Novel Newspaper* reprints, which he sold for one shilling and threepence each. On 21 June, he garnished another advertisement headed 'Newspaper Novels' with a little tale illustrative of the advantages of buying cheap books when living in the bush:

> 'These cheap works are just the sort I want,' said a bush gentleman residing in a cottage of the primitive style of architecture, and covered with nature's own titles, as he was paying me £1 17s. 9d. for a lot he had just purchased. 'They will just do to lend to one's friends, who never return them, or, for a friend who walks into the cottage during my absence on the run, and walks off with a book, my ebony short pipe, a fig of tobacco, my pocket knife, my flint and steel, or any other trifle I may have inconsiderately left on my solid circular table, which a matter of fact fellow who called one day styled a good big round stump.'

Among the works being offered in this advertisement was Longfellow's *Hyperion* for a shilling; Walter Scott's *Lay of the Last Minstrel* was even cheaper, at tenpence.

Another to offer cheap fiction to those in the bush was William Jones, proprietor and editor of the *Goulburn Herald*, where on 24 March 1849 he advertised 'Cheap Reading for the Bush', which included copies of Fenimore Cooper's *Lionel Lincoln* priced at one-and-threepence. It is possible that he obtained these books from the major Sydney booksellers Colman and Piddington, who in the same issue of the *Goulburn Herald* advertised *Lionel Lincoln*, along with Cooper's *The Water Witch*, and other titles, for sale at one shilling each, with a discount for large purchases, 'Storekeepers and others purchasing the above by the dozen charged 9s'. If so, Jones was making a fair profit on each copy of a *Novel Newspaper* reprint sold to bush readers. New novels were, of course, considerably more expensive, with Jones advertising on 15 September 1849 R.S. Surtees' *Hawbuck Grange* (1847) for twelve-and-six. This was, however, only a little more than the English price listed in the *English Catalogue of Books.*

In Victoria during the 1840s, James Harrison ran the *Geelong Advertiser* and the Geelong Stationery Warehouse, as well as, for a time, a circulating library. On 31 December 1847, the following unsigned advertisement appeared in the *Advertiser*:

> NOVEL NEWSPAPER
>
> -----------
>
> NOW PUBLISHING,
>
> In Parts, Octavo, Each Part Containing One or More Complete Novels, STANDARD LIBRARY EDITION of the following Popular Novels and Tales, printed from their Original Texts, without the slightest Abridgement, thus giving for EIGHTEEN PENCE, works originally publishd at a GUINEA AND A HALF!

The inclusion of novels by Eugene Sue alongside those by Cooper, Bird, Simms and the other American, English and European authors represented in earlier volumes of the *Novel Newspaper* again indicates that the series continued well into the 1840s. Harrison had advertised many of these same titles on 3 August 1847, and continued to do so during 1848 and 1849, often specifically referring to the *Novel Newspaper*, and indicating that the books were 'just unpacked'.

Works by American authors were, of course, available in Australia before the *Novel Newspaper* began publishing in 1839. Two titles by Fenimore Cooper were advertised during the 1820s, followed by forty-seven listings in the 1830s. Thanks to the wide advertising of the *Novel Newspaper* reprints, however, works by Cooper were listed 512 times in the 1840s, only slightly less than works by Byron and, as mentioned earlier, slightly more than works by Dickens. In comparison, Washington Irving, another popular American author whose works were not featured in the *Novel Newspaper*, had six listings in the 1820s, sixteen in the 1830s and 167 in the 1840s.[10] Both Cooper and Irving had

10 Figures taken from Webby, PhD Thesis, IV:10–11.

their Australian imitators, with James Martin, for example, publishing his *Australian Sketch Book* in 1838. Charles Rowcroft drew heavily on *The Last of the Mohicans* for his *The Bushranger of Van Diemen's Land* (1846), where the heroine is abducted by a tribe of Aborigines rather than Native Americans.

The influence of American literature on conceptions of the possibility of an Australian literature should also not be underrated. An interesting piece in Sydney's *Colonial Literary Journal* of 27 February 1845 takes the form of a conversation between two men supposedly overheard by the narrator as he strolls on the Circular Quay Wharf. Interested in their discussion, he follows the men to the Domain where they continue to debate the likelihood of a 'Colonial Literature'. One of them strongly objects to the use of the word 'colonial' with respect to literature, arguing instead for either 'Australian' or 'National': 'Depend upon it that Australia will never be more than a cipher among the nations, until her sons assume to themselves national characteristics, and proudly stamp them by the pen to be acknowledged and admired by the world!'

To the objection that there are no 'materials from which a literature purely colonial could be raised', he responds:

> whence the material of American literature? In the woods, and prairies, on the rivers, and lakes. Among the red Indians and snowy mountains, ay, and in the city too, in the drawing room, in the counting house, in the cottage, and in the hall! If anything be wanted here, it is the men and not the matter, nor do I believe that even *they* are absent, but that if Australians as a nation, would cherish and be proud of literature as of national and not of European character and interest—a Fenimore Cooper, a Washington Irving, a Channing, a Franklin, and a Willis, would soon spring up in our midst to spread a halo over Australia, by seizing each in his own manner on the materials presented in the town, in the bush, among sheep stations, homesteads, squatters, blackfellows, kangaroos or parrots; among seaman or landsmen, nativeborn or emigrant, military, naval or civilian!

11

Elvis Down Under: Simulations of a US Pop Icon in Australian Fiction

Paul Genoni

> Elvis will not leave the building because his image remains, if anything, *overflowing* with meaning and historicity.
>
> Thomas C. Carlson [1]

> Elvis is such a packed cultural symbol.
>
> Shady Cosgrove[2]

During a late-career concert in Atlanta, Elvis Presley proclaimed from the stage—probably to the puzzlement of his audience—'Watch the feedback Bruce or I'll send you back to Australia in a kangaroo pouch'.[3] The comment was directed at his sound engineer, Australian Bruce Jackson. It marks, to my knowledge, the only public expression by Presley that he was aware that Australia existed. Needless to say, however, when this comment was made in late 1976, Australia had been very aware of Elvis Presley for over two decades.

Presley died in the year following the Atlanta concert, and his death was followed by the public mourning, career reappraisals, reissuing

1 Thomas C. Carlson, 'Bit Parts: Dismembering Elvis in Recent Hollywood Films', *Film Criticism* 24.1 (1999): 75.

2 Shady Cosgrove, *She Played Elvis* (Crows Nest: Allan & Unwin, 2009), p. 29.

3 Presley's Atlanta concert took place on 30 December 1976. Film and sound are available at www.youtube.com/watch?v=S8ydbsxu2dQ [Accessed 15 January 2010]. The comment regarding Australia can be heard at six minutes and 45 seconds.

of product, and massive upturn in sales, that have been witnessed subsequently with the demise of pop-culture figures of similar stature, such as John Lennon and Michael Jackson. In the wake of that predictable short-term response to Presley's death, however, something more interesting began to take place—something with little precedent in terms of its scale and global reach.

That is, while the physical Elvis had certainly passed away, Elvis-the-icon embarked on a posthumous career that was every bit as lucrative, nearly as influential, and that is by now, more long lasting than the one that sustained him in life. Both in America and elsewhere there was a collective reluctance to let Elvis go, as if his sudden passing had left many with a need to cling to the vestiges of his life and glittering career.

One of the most obvious manifestations of Presley's healthy afterlife were the continued rumours and belief that his death was a hoax and a conspiracy, and that somehow, somewhere and for some reason, he was awaiting the right moment for his greatest comeback. For years the occasional Elvis 'sighting' titillated the international press and gave his demise an unsettled afterglow.

Presley's death also gave impetus to another phenomenon, the Elvis impersonator. The practitioners of this zombie artform crossed ages, ethnicities and genders, seemingly united by the belief that they were passing on the memory of Presley's presence in a barely diminished form. If Elvis had indeed left the building, his spirit could nonetheless be found hard at work every Friday night at the local bar or juke-joint or RSL club.

Beyond these very apparent indications of the desire to retain Elvis, there also developed further, and perhaps more interesting layers of representation of the deceased star. Presley's image and various fragments of 'style' that informed it (snatches of clothing, language, mannerisms) began to be consciously borrowed, referenced, or re-invented as part of a bewildering array of cultural production that allowed 'Elvis Presley' to survive and proliferate as part of social, political, cultural and intellectual discourses from which he had been largely excluded in life. Elvis art, Elvis cartoons, Elvis comics, Elvis films, Elvis songs, Elvis poetry, Elvis fiction, all shaped up as genres, or sub-genres, or subversive genres, that gave form to what Greil Marcus described as a massive communal art project. As Marcus wrote:

> When he died, the event was a kind of explosion that went off silently, in minds and hearts; out of that explosion came many fragments, … No one, I think, could have predicted the ubiquity, the playfulness, the perversity, the terror, and the fun of this, of Elvis Presley's second life: a great common … conversation between spectres and fans, made out of songs, art works, books, movies, dreams; sometimes more than anything cultural noise, the glossolalia of money, advertisements, tabloid headlines, bestsellers, urban legends, nightclub japes. [It] was—is—a story that needed no authoritative voice, no narrator, a story that flourishes precisely because it is free of any such thing, a story that told itself.[4]

While accepting the spirit of what Marcus wrote, the purpose of this paper is to consider one element of Presley's 'second life' where there *is* an authoritative voice, or at least an authorial voice, in the form of literary fiction that is in some way 'about' Elvis Presley. Moreover the texts I will focus on are written by Australians, inevitably raising questions as to why it is that Australian authors elect to participate in this spectacle of the Elvis-who-refuses-to-die.

The Simulated Elvis

Marcus' *Dead Elvis* (1991)—from which the above quote was taken—was one of a number of scholarly texts that appeared from the early 1990s onwards recording how, and explaining why, Presley had retained such an unprecedented presence for a deceased star. Others included John Strausbaugh's *E: Reflections on the Birth of the Elvis Faith* (1995);[5]

---

4 Greil Marcus, *Dead Elvis: A Chronicle of a Cultural Obsession* (New York: Doubleday, 1991), 'Introduction' [n.p.].

5 John Strausbaugh, *E: Reflections on the Birth of the Elvis Faith* (New York: Blast Books, 1995).

Gilbert Rodman's *Elvis After Elvis* (1996);[6] George Plasketes' *Images of Elvis Presley in American Culture, 1977–1997* (1997);[7] and Gregory Reece's *Elvis Religion* (2006).[8]

It is not the purpose of this paper to join the discussion about exactly why Presley has generated so many persistent signifiers in the cultural landscape, although it is perhaps relevant to note Rodman's assertion that, 'Elvis' posthumous career is to too large, too scattered, and too diverse to be easily circumscribed or explained by any one meta-narrative'.[9] It is also worth noting that in so far as these books had a precursor in exploring Presley's cultural persistence, it was Australian McKenzie Wark's article, 'Elvis: Listen to the Loss', which appeared in a 1989 number of the Australian journal *Art & Text*.[10] Wark wrote of Presley's rise to fame on the back of his genius for discovering and amalgamating the fragments of disembodied musical culture that made their way via radio to the cultural melting-pot of Memphis. Elvis, claims Wark, represented 'Talent in a brand new bag', with the ambitious young singer possessing an 'openness, [his] antennae tuned into the minutiae of immaterial culture'.[11] According to Wark, Presley was the first performer who instinctively understood what it meant to make music in an immaterial world, wherein his physical presence was secondary to his massively and mechanically reproduced voice. This account of Presley's artistic origins allows Wark to explain—or explain away—the persistence of Elvis in the post-mortem phase of his career, because his physical presence was never intrinsic to his celebrity. Wark writes that following Presley's death, we are left with,

6 Gilbert Rodman, *Elvis After Elvis: The Posthumous Career of a Living Legend* (London: Routledge, 1996).

7 George Plasketes, *Images of Elvis Presley in American Culture, 1977–1997: The Mystery Terrain* (New York: Harrington, 1997).

8 Gregory L. Reece, *Elvis Religion: The Cult of the King* (New York: Macmillan, 2006).

9 Rodman, p. 24.

10 McKenzie Wark, 'Elvis: Listen to the Loss', *Art & Text* 31: 24–28.

11 Wark, p. 26.

> the sacrifice of the presence of life to its endlessly ululating echo. Graceland stands as a monument to the moment in the passage of G.I. Elvis, to the moment the body is doomed to recorded culture, to the cult of the dead. The universal tributes to Elvis are no accident, but a way of preserving this signal moment, the day his regal robes and commanding stutter became the recorded ghost that still walks, the lifeless flesh that returns forever to Memphis in a long black limousine ... [12]

Wark's analysis situates Presley's initial impact and lingering presence within a framework of the technologies of modernity that allowed his voice and image to proliferate globally.[13] Another twenty years on, however, and Wark's 'endlessly ululating echo' is heard even further from its source, as we are faced with a Presley who evolves ceaselessly through a process of (re)invention that constantly imbues his image with layers of signification that are increasingly remote from their origin. Presley's abundant semiotic afterlife has transformed his image into a postmodern phenomenon—a prime example of what Jean Baudrillard described as simulations, the shallow but seductive images, divorced from the reality and circumstances that are their genesis, and that mask rather than reveal the essence of the thing they represent. As Baudrillard noted simulations are not a matter of imitation or parody, but rather 'of substituting signs of the real for the real itself',[14] to the point where they forge their own reality. That is, simulations assume a capacity to generate subsidiary images that are primarily informed by those previous simulations rather than by the reality that was originally signified. In the case of Presley, the extraordinary multiplicity

12 Wark, p. 28.

13 Wark's analysis was supported by fellow Australian John Frow, who agreed that the 'real person of Elvis is always and from the beginning a copied person, the authenticity of which derives from the fact and the extent of copying, of representation'. John Frow, 'Is Elvis a god? Cult, culture, questions of method' *International Journal of Cultural Studies* 1.2 (1998): 203.

14 Jean Baudrillard, 'Simulacra and simulations', *Jean Baudrillard: Selected Writings*, ed. Mark Poster (Stanford: Stanford University Press, 1988), p. 167.

and richness of the subordinate, corrupted images that now 'sign' Elvis Presley flourish to the extent that they have become the principal means by which the deceased star is recognised and known.

Elvis Fiction

One of the many forms of cultural production where the dead Elvis has left his trace is fiction. As Reece writes in *Elvis Religion*:

> I was completely shocked … to discover that Elvis had such an important place in contemporary literature. Much to my surprise, it seems that Elvis stands among the ranks of recurring literary characters such as James Bond, Sherlock Holmes, Tarzan and Conan the Barbarian. Like these characters the character of Elvis has featured in countless works of fiction. Unlike his companions, however, who ended up trapped in one particular genre or another, the character of Elvis appears in a diverse set of literary genres and has been brought to life, or back to life as it were, by a diverse set of authors. Elvis has made appearances in mystery novels, in science fiction stories, in historical fiction and in parodies … Out of all the places that I found Elvis in my studies, the world of fiction remains the most surprising … [15]

It isn't possible to account accurately for the amount of Elvis fiction. An online site 'Elvis Presley: A Life in Books',[16] currently lists some ninety titles, but it is very incomplete. It does not, for example, include any of the Australian novels discussed in this paper. Two things about Elvis fiction are, however, apparent from scanning this or similar bibliographies. Firstly, as Presley bibliographer Mary Hancock Hinds has noted, before his death 'there was no such thing … as Elvis fiction'.[17] It is a body of fiction shaped by both the unremarkable reality of Presley's

---

15 Reece, p. 71.

16 Available at: www.xs4all.nl/~vnhouten/ [Accessed 8 December 2010].

17 Mary H. Hinds, *Infinite Elvis: An Annotated Bibliography* (Chicago: A Cappella, 2001), p. 271.

physical death, and his quite remarkable symbolic persistence through various post-mortem manifestations. It is notable that very little Elvis fiction—particularly with literary pretensions—features Elvis Presley as a character, but instead dwells on Presley in simulated forms. This is achieved most commonly through the figure of an Elvis impersonator who manifests Presley's spirit in scenarios where the King himself never trod. There are also novels that re-imagine Presley's life as it might have transpired had he not expired in August 1977; those that feature fans dealing with the implications of his death for their own lives; appearances by the spirit or ghost of Elvis as it continues to move people and shape lives; accounts of Presley's fictional bastard children as they deal with the legacy of the superstar-father they never knew; and even novels that resurrect the character of Jesse, the twin that Elvis lost at birth.[18]

A second notable feature of Elvis fiction is that although titles from the United States are the most prevalent, it is an international phenomenon. There are numerous titles from the United Kingdom, plus contributions from South Africa (Christopher Hope's *Me the Moon and Elvis Presley*)[19] Nigeria (Chris Abani's *Graceland*)[20] India (Ivar Tabrizi's *The Avatar*)[21] New Zealand (Nigel Cox's *Tarzan Presley*)[22] France (Laure

18 Into this final category might be placed Australian musician-cum-novelist Nick Cave's, *And the Ass Saw the Angel* (London: Black Springs, 1989). Although the novel makes no direct mention of either Elvis or Jesse, it has been argued by Nathan Wiseman-Trowse ('Oedipus Wrecks: Cave and the Presley Myth', in *Cultural Seeds: Essays on the Work of Nick Cave*, Karen Welberry and Tanya Dalziell, eds. [Farnham: Ashgate, 2009], pp. 153–66) that this story constitutes one of a number of occasions on which Cave has explored the Presley myth. Wiseman-Trowse examines the novel's central character, Euchrid Eucrow, as a corrupted version of the classic Presley myth. In Cave's version, the 'good son' dies at birth and the malevolent Euchrid, representing 'an inversion of the mythical, archetypal Elvis' (163) lives on. The notion of the lost twin is also an important element in Gail Jones's 'Heartbreak Hotel'.

19 Christopher Hope, *Me, the Moon and Elvis Presley* (London: Macmillan, 1997).

20 Chris Albani, *Gracleand* (New York: Picador, 2004).

21 Ivar Tabrizi, *The Avatar* (Victoria: Trafford, 2004).

22 Nigel Cox, *Tarzan Presley* (Wellington: Victoria University Press, 2004).

Limongi's *Fonction Elvis*)[23] Canada (Andre Major's *La Folle d'Elvis*)[24] and Australia.

This international manifestation of Elvis-in-fiction begs the questions as to 'why', as Presley was in many ways an intrinsically American phenomenon. Not only was his musical repertoire the product of American traditions, but his impact and notoriety were built upon transgressions across boundaries that were essentially American; white vs black; city vs rural; north vs south; Perry Como vs Robert Johnson. And in Elvis' case his global popularity wasn't the result of in-person exposure to his famed backbeat, as he never performed outside of the United States other than for a handful of Canadian concerts in 1957. If, however, as Wark argued, Presley's triumph represented a potent manifestation of modernity whereby the immaterial prevailed over the material, then it also coincided with the point at which the products of American popular culture became irresistibly global.

Elvis' global triumph as it was manifested in Australia is recalled in Barry Donnelly's novel, *Boys by the Sea* (1989), a coming-of-age story set on the central NSW coast in the 1950s. The restless young Hermann, wrestling with his years of thwarted teenage ambition, appeals to the precedent set by Presley:

> Take, for instance, the new singing sensation that is sweeping the world. Take Elvis Presley, for instance! Do you think he was born with a silver spoon in his mouth? No siree! Elvis came from Memphis, Tennessee, out of a little weatherboard house no better than yours. Nobody ever heard of him! Do you think it worried Elvis Presley that he didn't have a piece of paper from some fancy university to wave around? No, siree! Elvis didn't sit around moping. He didn't stop to think about the world being fixed. It all started because he wanted to make a record for his mother. And what did they find? Talent! Real, natural talent—and Elvis let the world have it, straight between the eyes![25]

23 Laure Limongi, *Fonction Elvis* (Paris: Leo Scheer, 2006).

24 Andre Major, *La Folle d'Elvis* (Montreal: Amerique, 1981).

25 Barry Donnelly, *Boys by the Sea* (Sydney: Collins, 1989), p. 178.

These words draw upon classic elements of the Presley myth; the humble birth; the innate talent and ambition; the disdain for convention; the mother love; the meteoric rise from backwoods obscurity. But Donnelly also take the myth forward from its origins to its consequences—'Elvis let the world have it, straight between the eyes!' Indeed although the term 'globalisation' may have had little currency in Presley's lifetime, it could be argued that the youth music culture that he kick-started in the 1950s was one of the first and most pervasive globalised social movements, constituted at a time before pop-culture began to fragment under the ubiquity and immensity of its immateriality. As rock critic Lester Bangs wrote, 'I can guarantee you one thing: we will never again agree on anything as we agreed on Elvis'.[26]

But despite his global appeal Presley developed and retained his symbolic function as a representative American. To both Americans and non-Americans it is his status as an icon of certain American experience and values that can make his symbolic presence so compelling. As American Thomas Carlson wrote in an analysis of Presley's ubiquity in recent Hollywood films:

> Elvis is our national Rorschach, our virtual cultural referent by means of which we are able to engage in a complex ideological discourse on issues of collective importance to us.[27]

But representative Americans must live—and in Presley's case die—with the consequences of their iconic status, and one response in Elvis fiction is to have the singer serve as a symbol of American cultural and military imperialism. This is most apparent in novels set outside of the developed west, such as Chris Albani's *Graceland.* Set in Albani's homeland of Nigeria, *Graceland* follows the adventures of teenage Elvis. Named by his mother for her love of the singer, Elvis ekes out a living impersonating his namesake on the beachfronts of Lagos for tips from foreign tourists. Elvis' dream is to escape to the US and earn a living as a

26 Lester Bangs, *Psychotic Reactions and Carburettor Dung* (London: Heinemann, 1988), p. 216.

27 Carlson, p. 73.

dancer, but in the meantime he is caught in desperate circumstances of poverty, petty crime, and military brutality. He is also caught between the myriad products of US pop cultures that sow the seeds of unquenchable desire, and the subterranean tug of the diminished culture of his homeland. The military power of the US is interrogated in P.F. Kluge's *Biggest Elvis*,[28] wherein a trio of Elvis impersonators, each representing Presley at a different stage of his career, ply their trade around the US military bases in the Philippines, with each 'Elvis' starkly symbolising a different aspect of American imperial power. Australian novelists have similarly linked Presley to American military influence in south-east Asia. In Christopher Koch's *Highways to a War* (1995) one of the correspondents covering the Vietnam War repeatedly plays or sing's Presley's 'Can't Help Falling in Love';[29] and in John Donnelly's *Magic Garage* (2002) an Indonesian General moonlights as an Elvis impersonator. When he is attacked and badly mauled by a tiger that serves as the defender of a squatter settlement on the verge of redevelopment, his white Elvis-jumpsuit is left in tatters.[30]

Elvis in Australian Fiction

Australian fiction writers have not, however, always needed to go offshore to find a place for Presley in their narratives. The singer's re-invention as a global, postmodern omnipresence is the subject of Gail Jones' 'Heartbreak Hotel' (1997),[31] a story grounded in Presley's status as both iconic American and postmodern phenomenon, and containing one of the carefully constructed accounts of the formulations of modernity and/or postmodernity that are the hallmark of Jones' fiction.

The story commences in suburban Australia of the late 1970s, in the aftermath of Presley's death. The unnamed teenage female narrator grows up infused with desire for the neighbourhood Elvis impersonator.

---

28 P.F. Kluge, *Biggest Elvis* (London: Vintage, 1996).

29 Christopher J. Koch, *Highways to a War* (Port Melbourne: Heinemann, 1995).

30 John Donnelly, *Magic Garage* (Canberra: Pandanus, 2002).

31 Gail Jones, 'Heartbreak Hotel', in *Fetish Lives* (Fremantle: Fremantle Arts Centre Press, 1997), pp. 114–25.

> Every Elvis was an avatar. God had dreamt up Elvis but one was simply not enough. Thus Teresa Papadopolous, Elvis-next-door, was another irrefutable sign of the one true faith, another undead performer to contest all those mendacious rumours. (115)

By being Greek, female, and given to impersonating the younger rebellious Elvis rather than the mature Vegas-crooner, Teresa both honours and subverts Elvis. And something else sets Teresa apart. When not being Elvis and dreaming of attending the 'Annual Elvis Presley Impersonators' Convention in downtown, limo-lined glassy LA' (122), she is a student of existentialism, given to discussing Sartre, Heidegger and Kierkegaard as part of a conversation about the Hollywood career of her idol. As a precocious existentialist, Teresa is able to calculate the equation between existence and essence in such a way that it explains the ongoing presence of Elvis in the world, believing that his spirit, his 'accumulated essence, *aka* star quality' has 'rent the fabric of space-time' (120). For Teresa, it is this manifestation of an 'Astral Elvis' that explains continued sightings of the supposedly dead singer.

Teresa eventually leaves the neighbourhood and the narrator follows her progress at second hand. The stories she hears are inconclusive, confirming only that Teresa has moved to the US, leaving the narrator in little doubt that she has made it to the Elvis Presley Impersonators' Convention. Here, she imagines that Teresa becomes lost in a Baudrillardian extravaganza of semiotic excess:

> in every vision, astral in its profundity, she was there performing. There were rows of sparkly dancers, Viva-Las-Vegas-style, Elvises of every confirming configuration, and the theatrical ecstasy of excess replication: miles of black hair symmetrically duck-tailed, lip-curls agogo, forests of pumping legs, pelvic gyrations of pornographic proportions. (125)

There are echoes of Teresa's ethnic-Elvis in the character of Akmed Joseph Allam ('Joe'), in Dorian Mode's *A Café in Venice* (2001).[32] Joe

32 Dorian Mode, *A Café in Venice* (Ringwood: Penguin, 2001).

is a Palestinian Christian of mixed Christian-Muslim heritage, with a Lebanese Christian wife. They live in Gaza where Joe earns his living as an Elvis impersonator, worshipping the man he describes as the 'Best there ever was, best there will ever be' (119). Joe dreams of emigrating to the United States, where he plans to make a living as a professional Elvis Impersonator. The incentive to turn this dream into reality is provided when Gaza is occupied by the Israeli army. When Joe attempts to escape to the US by fleeing firstly to Lebanon, his wife and child are shot and killed at the border by Israeli soldiers.

Unable to migrate to the US Joe eventually settles in Australia, and by mischance ends up owning and managing a roadside pizza café in inland South Australia. Here he continues to ply his trade as an impersonator, entertaining customers with appalling renditions of Presley classics and conducting full-scale 'concerts' in his café. All the while he continues to dream about pursuing his career as an impersonator in the US.

Despite having suffered a profound personal tragedy as the result of transnational warfare, Joe is a man devoid of national or political identity. Indeed many of his customers think he is Italian, an illusion he perpetuates in order to sell pizzas. Joe is seemingly a post-national man, his identity grounded not in national sentiment or ethnic allegiance, but rather on his lifelong commitment to that most global of personalities, Elvis Presley.

> Quite often, when he was down, Joe actually thought he was Elvis. I mean, *really* thought he was Elvis. He'd talk about missing Priscilla. And how difficult it was filming *Blue Hawaii.* On those dark days, it was hard for him to distinguish fantasy from fact. Sometimes I had to point out that Elvis wasn't actually born in the Middle East. (149)

Indeed Joe's only identity marker with regard to nationality or ethnicity is a profound anti-Semitism resulting from the killing of his family. But even in this his identity is eventually destabilised when he forms a new romantic attachment with Ruth, a New York Jew. Joe woos Ruth with his version of 'Love me Tender', the same song with which he had impressed his wife-to-be over twenty years previously, and soon she is dressing as Priscilla to his Elvis.

Joe's story is but one in a complex novel that deals with issues of identity, personal attachment, and the inevitable tensions that arise between personal desire and community obligations. For several characters their dreams are expressed as a desire to travel to the US, a dream that is embodied in an open air-ticket to New York that is traded between them as their circumstances fluctuate. At the novel's conclusion the ticket is passed to Joe, offering him—as with Teresa—the chance to fulfil his dream of earning a living by taking his version of Elvis to America.

Elvis is represented in a form other than an impersonator in Julie Capaldo's *Weather* (2001).[33] The novel features Ruby Seabourne, a woman possessed of extra-sensory powers. Ruby is described as an 'angel' who is 'not totally of this world' (42), and she works from her house as a fortune teller. Her otherworldly powers and natural wisdom are called upon to deal with her very worldly son, Cosmos, who works as a manager at The World Mega Supermarket. The World—as the shopping centre is commonly known—is described as a 'world unto itself, a religious experience, a Shrine to Consumption … [where] People were told what to buy, where to buy, what to eat and how to live' (2–3). In order to provide for further expansion of this symbol of global consumerism it is necessary for Cosmos to acquire Ruby's house, and he becomes engaged in a plan to have his mother moved to a facility for the aged.

Ruby's special powers are more pervasive than her ability to see the future; she is deeply sensitive to both her spiritual environment and is in contact with the deceased. To help her in her troubles she is visited by none other than the spirit of the King himself, who has troubles of his own. Although dead for over twenty years Elvis has been unable to find peace by fully passing over to the other side. His spirit has been restlessly travelling the world for these years, traceable by the occasional sightings and bizarre weather events that follow in his wake—apparently the result of his extraordinary magnetism—in places as far apart as Alaska,

---

33 Julie Capaldo, *Weather* (Milsons Point: Random House, 2001).

Peru, Fiji and Japan. Elvis declares to Ruby that he is 'sort of stuck' (72) and realises that 'surely there is more to [the afterlife] than becoming the weatherman or being glimpsed in McDonalds?' (73).

Together Ruby and Elvis are able to help each other to solve their various problems. Elvis almost destroys The World Mega Supermarket by hurling lightning at it, and then suddenly realising that his true purpose was 'to *save* the World' (253) he calms the flames with his singing. In the process he learns the lessons necessary to complete what he refers to as his 'map', the knowledge he needs in order to finally accomplish a transition to death.

The most recent Australian novel to use simulations of Presley as a symbol of cultural persistence is Debra Adelaide's *The Household Guide to Dying* (2008).[34] Adelaide's novel is narrated by Delia Bennet, a woman with a terminal disease, and tells the tale of her attempt to settle some business from her past surrounding the death of her seven-year-old son ('Sonny') many years previously, and her relationship with Pearl, a woman whom Sonny had befriended. Pearl's main commitment in life is to Elvis Presley and keeping his memory alive. She is President of the Amethyst and District Elvis Fan Club, for which she organises quasi-religious gatherings for an eclectic group of fellow devotees. As Delia muses, 'in a secular age, it was probably as valid a religion as anything else' (233).

Pearl recognises that young Sonny is a talented singer, and she introduces him to the songs of Elvis. Sonny takes to the music immediately and delights in both singing and performing as Elvis. Abetted by Pearl he is soon dressed up in satin suits and embarked on a career as one of the youngest of Elvis impersonators, performing at gatherings of the fan club and at local fetes and parties. But the fact of a six- or seven-year-old Elvis impersonator doesn't seem particularly odd or unusual. As Delia notes, the act of simulation required little grounding in reality:

> the impersonators … existed in every possible shape, size and dimension, so that the world abounded in short, grossly

34 Debra Adelaide, *The Household Guide to Dying* (Sydney: Picador, 2008).

> fat, bald, bearded, female, disabled, bespectacled, black and blind Elvis impersonators. There were Elvis impersonators who couldn't sing. (234)

Sonny's career as an impersonator is, however, cut short when he is killed in a road accident. Delia gives permission for his heart to be donated for use in a transplant patient. As the boy's heart is removed his favourite Elvis songs are played in the operating theatre, and afterwards he is dressed for burial in the 'costume of pale blue satin and silver foil rhinestones which was his current favourite' (280).

Towards the novel's conclusion, as her own death nears, Delia sets out to find the person—a young girl, Amber—who had received Sonny's heart. She is eventually located and the two have an emotional meeting. They discover that Amber has inherited, through 'cellular memory' many of Sonny's personality traits and his likes and dislikes. This includes, not surprisingly, a love for the music of Elvis Presley. As Amber explains:

> I also developed a taste for more adult music, hated all the kiddy stuff I used to listen to. I remember hearing Elvis singing 'Burning Love' on the radio one day and just started singing along. Somehow I knew the words. (372)

So again Elvis proves indestructible in his simulated forms—firstly kept alive by the devotion of a quasi-hippie in regional Queensland; then reborn through the enthusiasm of her child protégé; and when the child dies, transported intact into a new host in the form of Amber.

Conclusion

Gilbert Rodman commented that, 'Elvis' current ubiquity is particularly noteworthy, not just because he refuses to go away, but because he keeps showing up in places where he seemingly doesn't belong'.[35] One of those places where Presley might be thought not to belong, is Australian fiction. Even if we accept that celebrity culture is ubiquitous and global, and national fiction is a redundant concept, these phenomena

35 Rodman, p. 1.

do not by themselves explain Presley's appeal to writers of fiction in Australia or elsewhere outside the US. We have not for example, seen a similar response in either fiction or other forms of cultural production, to the demise of other massively popular but deceased stars of stage or screen.[36]

As noted earlier, in most of the literary fiction that refers to Presley the singer in some way survives his death. This is certainly the case with these Australian novels, whereby Elvis 'lives' in the acts of impersonation, in the devotion of fans, or in a spiritual/ghostly form. Greil Marcus offers one explanation as to why this might be the case, claiming that: 'Elvis was too big, too complex—too much—for any of us to quite take in, to see all at once … Like Medusa, you can't look at him head on. So we look sideways'.[37]

And looking sideways in Presley's case means looking at what he has become in death, at the various simulated forms by which his legacy is now manifested. In literary fiction this provides a version of Elvis Presley in which the singer is largely drained of his personal potency and reduced to his symbolic functions. This is not to argue that authors are necessarily disinterested in the achievements of the *real* Elvis, but rather they find his value to their fiction lies in his extraordinary evolving symbolic richness.

In part that symbolic richness is grounded in the transgressive reality of Presley's lived experience: the God-fearing white boy who sang the blues; the dirt-poor sharecropper's son who made it to the mansion; the rebel who served without complaint; the jailhouse rocker who became a staple of Hollywood beach movies; the 'hillbilly' who reached his apotheosis in Las Vegas. In the course of his life these contradictions were consumed by the global scale of his audience and the trajectory of a career-in-progress, but in death they have become the source of the bewildering multiplicity of symbols that feed the simulated forms in which Presley is now encountered. 'Elvis Presley'

---

36 It is worth noting that Anson Cameron's *Stealing Picasso* (2009) includes an unemployed gay Michael Jackson impersonator. It is apparent that this was written prior to Jackson's death.

37 Marcus, p. 28.

provides a signifier that is seemingly capable of absorbing any number of contradictory, anarchic or inverted signifieds. Indeed it is intrinsic to the symbolic role, and therefore the literary function, fulfilled by Presley in the post-mortem phase of his career that transgression and inversion have become the norm. As a result the image of Elvis Presley is now so rich, and yet so destabilised, that it appears to demand expression in forms that challenge our knowledge of the *thing* itself, and in consuming these images we are constantly required to re-imagine Presley, or—more accurately perhaps—what he has become in death. And what he has become is a paramount example of a reality subsumed by simulation, where every encounter with 'Elvis Presley' is burdened by the accretion of decades of (re)presentation that serves, in Baudrillard's terms, to denature the thing that is represented. In the words of music critic Robert Christgau: 'Elvis Presley ... has become a literary hero, his meaning defined at least as much by the texts he's inspired as by those he created'.[38]

It is in this multi-textual, simulated form, that we find the source of Presley's fascination for writers of contemporary, postmodern fiction, irrespective of their nationality. For whereas Wark declared the young Elvis to be an avatar for a new kind of modernism, in death he has become *the* poster-boy for postmodernism. As Jones, Mode, Capaldo and Adelaide indicate in their fictions, Presley fascinates in death as he did in life, but the particular point of fascination is the *process* of simulation by which the dead Elvis is constantly given new life in ways that mask the original.

38 Robert Christgau, 'The King and I', *Village Voice*, 10 June 1997, available at www.robertchristgau.com/xg/bkrev/elvis-97.php [Accessed on 12 February 2010].

12

Cold Dreams: National Efforts and Global Visions in Antarctic Arts Programs

John Scheckter

Pity the penguins.[1] They have too much to do. For more than a century, they have been the public relations face of the entire Antarctic continent, the webfooted projection of human hopes and fears. Recently, they won an Oscar for *March of the Penguins* (2005): 'In the harshest place on Earth, love finds a way'.[2] They won another for *Happy Feet* (2006): 'Into the world of the Emperor Penguins, who find their soul mates through song, a penguin is born who cannot sing. But he can tap dance something fierce!'[3] Nor has their attraction escaped official attention: according to a photo caption on the website of the Australian Antarctic Division, they are simply 'too cute'.[4]

Cuteness produces backlash, of course, so that serious commentators on Antarctica feel compelled to issue a penguin disclaimer.[5] Werner

---

1 *Happy Feet*, Dir. George Miller and Warren Coleman. Movie still, 2006. Available at: antonmarquez.wordpress.com/2009/04/26/our-baby-has-happy-feet/ [Accessed on 27 December 2009].

2 *March of the Penguins*, orig. title *La marche de l'empereur*. Dir. Luc Jaquet. 2005. Internet Movie Data Base, available at: www.imdb.com/title/tt0428803/ [Accessed on 27 December 2009].

3 *Happy Feet*, Internet Movie Data Base, available at: www.imdb.com/title/tt0366548/ [Accessed on 27 December 2009].

4 David Waterhouse, 'We're too cute', photograph, n.d., available at: www.aad.gov.au/default.asp?casid=3892 [Accessed on 27 December 2009].

5 'Scott and Shackleton Penquin Sketches Found in Cambridge', available at:

Herzog marvels that his film received US government funding despite a flat statement that it would not include penguins; Paul D. Martin, a media artist also known as DJ Spooky, delivers most of an hour-long presentation on Antarctica before observing the absence of penguins; and the Australian painter Stephen Eastaugh wonders in the *Sydney Morning Herald* whether he will 'turn into some sort of wacky penguin portrait artist'.[6] Disclaimer notwithstanding, the cuteness of penguins isolates and emphasises a characteristic factor of Antarctic narration: that is, the necessary and self-conscious construction of an anthropomorphic story. Concerning Antarctica, such factors as physical scale, chronological scale, contrast, causality, and expectation of outcome are typically and obviously manipulated in order to produce a speculation about survival by humans or their penguin surrogates. To repeat: the story of Antarctica has no indigenous human level, and while narrative manipulation occurs everywhere, the physical environment there sharply interferes with the mechanisms of social analogy and cultural relativity that elsewhere provide more comfort in the relationship between the text and its audience.

The science-fiction writer Kim Stanley Robinson, whose visit to Antarctica resulted in a near-future novel, uses the term 'physical aesthetics' to describe the circumstances of experience, particularly the massiveness and extremity of the environment and the isolation and vulnerability of the observer.[7] The physicality of travel in strange sunlight and great cold affects any observation, and therefore shapes any insight gathered amid ice formations 'so spectacular everywhere,

---

www.wildlifeextra.com.au/go/news/shackleton-drawings647.html#cr [Accessed on 27 December 2009].

6 Andrew Darby, 'Pack Lots of White Paint: Antarctic Artist Ready for a Winter of Content, *Sydney Morning Herald*, 19 Jan. 2009, available at: www.smh.com.au/news/entertainment/arts/pack-lots-of-white-paint/2009/01/18/1232213446729.html [Accessed on 27 December 2009].

7 Kim Stanley Robinson, *Antarctica* (New York: Bantam, 1998), p. 239; Frank Hurley, 'Launching the James Caird', photograph, 1915, available at: commons.wikimedia.org/wiki/File:LaunchingTheJamesCaird2.jpg [Accessed on 27 December 2009].

but in a fractal way, self-similar at all scales, so that one lost perspective'.[8] Robinson's onsite observations presuppose high levels of physical strength, simply in order to survive the experience and carry it back out as story or artifact.His character Val, leading an expedition group, rappels into a glacial crevasse to recover their sled; a hundred feet down the wall, literally at the end of her rope, she enters an ice chamber:

> This new space within the ice was really big, and a much deeper blue than what she had come through so far, the Rayleigh scattering of sunlight so far advanced that only the very bluest light made it down here, glowing from out of the ice in an intense creamy translucent turquoise, or actually an unnamed blue unlike any she had seen. The interior of the space was a magnificent shambles. Entire columns of pale blue ice had peeled off the walls and fallen across the chamber intact, like broken pillars of a shattered temple.[9]

Part of this description recalls a tradition of the polar sublime that goes back at least two centuries, in which the meritorious individual attains a rare, mighty view of nature through risk-taking and endurance.[10] Another part, however, is more basic than sublime privilege: as Francis Spufford puts it 'you cannot die in a story; you have to die in your body'.[11] When Val clambers out of the crevasse, she tells her group that the sled, with their tents, sleeping bags, and food, is down there for good. Her vision of extreme beauty takes place within a wider possibility of calamitous loss, to be survived not by means of privileged

---

8 Robinson, p. 239.

9 Ibid., p. 341. Erika Blumenfeld, 'Untitled', photograph, 2009, available at: www.levygallery.com/artists/erika_blumenfeld/9487.html [Accessed on 27 December 2009].

10 Francis Spufford, *I May Be Some Time: Ice and the English Imagination* (New York: Picador, 1997), pp. 22–25; 'Paleocrystic Ice in Robeson Channel', Point Barrow, Alaska, The First International Polar Year, photograph, 1882–1883, available at: www.arctic.noaa.gov/aro/ipy-1/images/G1V1-246.jpg [Accessed on 27 December 2009].

11 Spufford, p. 334.

sensitivity but through an emergency trek of a hundred kilometres just to come back with the story.

Adding to Robinson's discussion, I want to locate his physical aesthetics within a notion of physical hermeneutics.[12] That is, the physically determined narration of the Antarctic is structured elsewhere, before and after the event, by the narrator's travel to and within Antarctica at least, along with the transportation there of every component of logistics, performance, and production. Stories of material supply are anchored in manufacture in the warmer world, and sponsorship—often a combination of government and corporate support—is a given factor. Because long distances and transportation costs discourage redundancy, scientific and artistic projects alike require detailed justification. In similar ways, theoretical structures, which condition experimental and creative possibilities, are determined beforehand, always, again, within the structure of encountering an unforgiving environment and returning to tell the story: well-detailed procedural models increase a project's chances of survival, not just in the circuses of bureaucratic funding, but also on the ground. The newspaper article on Stephen Eastaugh, for example, is headed 'Pack Lots of White Paint'; the joke, presumably, is the colour, but the real story is in the packing, the need to provide all materials in advance, and, further, in questioning how that preparation will determine the artist's on-site observation and production.[13] Similarly, DJ Spooky recognised that his physical presence in Antarctica was ordered around carrying a backpack filled with high-definition sound gear and a terabyte hard drive. Spooky's project was to record the deterioration of glaciers, and he found in Antarctica both a metaphor and a direct confirmation of the city he says he carried in his head: the city referent is only slightly ironic if we follow Bruce Mau's suggestion that cosmopolitan space is marked by an urge to co-ordinate all aspects of structure and

12 Lisa Roberts, 'Drawing', n.d., available at: www.aad.gov.au/default.asp?casid=12549 [Accessed on 27 December 2009].

13 Stephen Eastaugh, 'My Icy Sickness', painting, n.d., available at: www.smh.com.au/news/entertainment/arts/pack-lots-of-white-paint/2009/01/18/1232213446729.html 12549 [Accessed on 27 December 2009].

infrastructure.[14] In Antarctica, there can be no experience outside the sustaining infrastructure, no travel off the beaten track. The place of the arts in such a space—by now, a globalised environment—is to provide a variety and quantity of feedback that produces better work within closed systems, reducing inefficiency and potential error. Everywhere, deliberation now counts more than improvisation, and Antarctica again is the type and model of this redefined competence.

It is remarkable that the protocols of international co-operation, the Antarctic Treaty System, emerged fifty years ago in the depths of the Cold War, by way of the International Geophysical Year of 1957–58; IGY itself, however, followed the earlier International Polar Years of 1882–83 and 1932–33, which produced gratifying cooperation within traditions of imperial adventure.[15] Signatories to the Antarctic Treaty, including Australia and the United States, famously suspend claims of national territory, placing the Southern Hemisphere in distinct historical contrast to the Northern. With commercial and military development banned, nations have found alternative validations of their presence in Articles 2 and 3, specifying freedom of scientific investigation and exchange of information; by extension, Antarctic arts programs functionally support these principles by explaining the scientific mission to a home audience and by producing an accessible—and beautiful—presentation of both the extreme environment and the human presence there. The American Artists and Writers Program began in 1958, and reached its greatest expansion in the 1990s and 2000s under the Office of Polar Programs of the National Science Foundation.[16] The program, funding up to four visitors a year, follows OPP's general practice of subcontracting both scientific projects and support services. Significantly, it is administered within OPP: unlike the British program, run by the British Antarctic

14 Bruce Mau, *Massive Change* (London: Phaidon, 2004), p. 45.

15 Australian Antarctic Territory, commemorative stamp cover, 1959, available at: en.wikipedia.org/wiki/File:Australian_Antarctic_Territory_postal_cover1959.jpg 12549 [Accessed on 27 December 2009].

16 *Encounters at the End of the World*, Dir. Werner Herzog, movie still, 2007, available at: www.collider.com/uploads/imagegallery/encounters_at_the_end_of_world/encounters_at_the_end_of_the_world_movie_image_werner_herzog__5_.jpg [Accessed on 27 December 2009].

Survey but funded by the Arts Council of England, budgetary considerations for the American program are entirely independent of the National Endowment for the Arts or other agencies.[17] 'The purpose of the Antarctic Artists and Writers Program', officially stated, 'is to enable serious writings and works of art that exemplify the Antarctic heritage of humankind. In particular', that is, following Articles 2 and 3, 'the program seeks to increase public understanding of the Antarctic region ... as well as the associated research and education endeavors'.[18] This last purpose, to bring back the story of the scientists who work there, confronts a long-standing American suspicion of basic research, a cultural habit that found political strength during the Bush administration. How welcome, then, that instead of cute penguins, Werner Herzog's 2007 film *Encounters at the End of the World* focuses on human nobility.

One of the funny scenes in *Encounters* shows Herzog and other newcomers attending survival school at McMurdo Base—physical aesthetics again prefacing any field observation. To simulate whiteout conditions, the visitors try to move coherently with plastic buckets on their heads. Herzog notes that the buckets have been decorated with faces, and the surprising thing is his deep appreciation of this humanising gesture. Herzog has always focused upon human obsession and physical extremity, but recognises at last in Antarctica that extremity is a universal given, and obsession, therefore, is a prelude to love: that is, an immersion into self-awareness deep enough to produce a comprehensive individual ethic in an overwhelming world. Love, then, motivates both skill and dedication. It is why divers go under the ice to study tiny invertebrates, why mechanics take pride in fixing machinery at –60°, and why the cafeteria crowds line up for ice cream in Antarctica. By the time Herzog asks an expert 'is there such a thing as

17 'Press Release—Arts and Science Work Together in Antarctica—British Antarctic Survey and Arts Council of England Fellowships', British Antarctic Survey, 6 February 2003, available at: www.antarctica.ac.uk/press/press_releases/press_release.php?id=20 [Accessed on 1 January 2010].

18 'Antarctic Artists and Writers Program', Office of Polar Programs, National Science Foundation, available at: www.nsf.gov/funding/pgm_summ.jsp?pims_id=12783&org=ANT&from=home [Accessed on 31 December 2009].

madness among penguins?' we know that the answer will be harrowing, and that we need it more than we need cuteness.[19]

The Australian Antarctic Arts Fellowship program began in 1984, and has expanded, like the American, to include a variety of media. The program is similarly administered internally by the Australian Antarctic Division, with outside consultants for the selection of one or two fellows per year, again both established artists and those early in their careers. The official program goals are slightly more prescriptive than the American, or at least more emotive, proposing such considerations as 'the extraordinary and beautiful natural environment' and 'the small human communities forged on a vast continent of extreme climate and terrain'.[20] From the outset, primary concerns clearly include the shaping of the story, and the ability to address 'a significant audience' counts for thirty per cent in the application scoring.[21] One direction of this dedicated outreach is an interest in school-age audiences. Hazel Edwards, for example, a fellow in 2001, went on to write *Antarctic Dad* (2006) for children in lower grades, dealing with family issues such as absent parents and online friendship, and with site-generated considerations of ecology, wildlife studies, and 'BIG vehicles'.[22] In *Antarctica's Frozen Chosen* (2004), for readers twelve and up, Edwards' adolescent protagonist 'faces questions of mateship' and early romance, while scientists question the political use of research data, and environmental activists confront illegal fishing and eco-terrorism. Another childhood specialist, Alison Lester, hosted an Antarctic

---

19 *Encounters at the End of the World*, Dir. Werner Herzog, 2007, movie still, (disoriented penguin walking 'to certain death'), available at: www.youtube.com/watch?v=x7kdDeGXUjI [Accessed on 31 December 2009].

20 'Objectives of the Program', Australian Antarctic Division, Antarctic Arts Fellowship, available at: www.antarctica.gov.au/about-antarctica/antarctic-arts-fellowship [Accessed on 1 January 2010].

21 'Assessment Criteria', Australian Antarctic Division, Antarctic Arts Fellowship, available at: www.antarctica.gov.au/about-antarctica/antarctic-arts-fellowship/how-and-when-to-apply/assessment-criteria [Accessed on 1 January 2010].

22 'Hazel Edwards: An Australian Author', available at: www.hazeledwards.com; cover illustration of *Antarctic Dad*, 2006, available at: www.hazeledwards.com/page/antarctic_dad.html [Accessed on 1 January 2010].

blog in 2005.[23] As 'thousands of children' in Australia followed her experience, Lester asked them to draw their impressions, and collected their drawings on her return. 'Alison has since used these illustrations to complete an exhibition of work which combines the children's line drawings with her design and colour'; the resulting compilations are delightful, and at the same time emphasise important aspects of co-operation, inclusion, and mutual responsibility.[24]

Antarctica for Paul D. Miller 'isn't a place: it's a location'.[25] Citing the physical hermeneutic rather than denying the effects of rock and ice, Miller's returned 'urban' story, a live performance piece for piano quartet and electronics, places Antarctica among other co-ordinates on a single, coherent globe. Likewise, the production flow chart by the Australian multimedia artist Lisa Roberts looks very much like a southern polar projection map, and the resulting animated videos make great use of moving spirals—signifying ocean currents, wind patterns, and the circulation of ideas—to propel its ecological message: 'Antarctica is melting', says one caption, and with it goes the conceptual centre of the entire system.[26] Roberts' two-dimensional pieces, made during and after her visit in 2001–02, overprint location data in the manner of scientific or forensic evidence; as with medieval painting, the use of text

---

23 'Alison Lester', Australian Antarctic Division, Antarctic Arts Fellowship, available at: www.antarctica.gov.au/about-antarctica/antarctic-arts-fellowship/previous-participants/authors-writers-journalists/alison-lester-04-05 [Accessed on 1 January 2010].

24 Alison Lester, 'Alison Lester's Kids Antarctic Arts Project', available at: www.alisonlester.citymax.com/page/page/1781659.htm [Accessed on 1 January 2010]. Alison Lester and unnamed children, 'Kids Antarctic Art Exhibition', 2007, available at: www.alisonlester.citymax.com/page/page/4809677.htm [Accessed on 1 January 2010].

25 Elena Glasberg, 'An Interview with Paul D. Miller on … *Terra Nova*', *Networked Performance*, 27 October 2008, available at: turbulence.org/blog/2008/10/27/an-interview-with-paul-d-miller-on-terra-nova/ [Accessed on 1 January 2010].

26 Lisa Roberts, 'Thesis', drawing, nd., in 'Antarctic Animation: Gestures and Lines Describe a Changing Environment', PhD Thesis, University of New South Wales, October 2010, available at:www.antarcticanimation.com/content/thesis/thesis.php [Accessed on 1 January 2010].

in the frame suggests continuities of intellectual activities rather than a separation by discipline or medium.[27] Roberts' three-dimensional works in engraved perspex and glass are modelled on the ice-core samples that currently present some of the surest evidence of global climate change; like Kim Stanley Robinson's description of the glowing blue ice-room, their beauty emphasises the fragility of the moment and the location.[28]

The mathematical unity of location, again, rather than the singularity of the place, took Xavier Cortada from Miami, Florida, to the South Pole in 2006–07. Cortada's work there is completely site-specific but, therefore, completely globalised, as he uses the 360° of available longitude to emphasise worldwide problems of overdevelopment and rapid change.[29] Planting twenty-four flags at the pole, fifteen degrees apart, he uses acrylic paint mixed with melted seawater to label each with the Latin name of an endangered species—using the site to ironise emblems of imperial conquest, the old universal language, new media, the wine dark sea. References to older visions of global unity undermine our current confidence in theory and application, just as Robinson reminds us that our having better parkas than Scott and Amundsen does not necessarily give us better knowledge or make us better people.[30] Still at the Pole, Cortada used frangible scales of time and movement to bring Sir Ernest Shackleton home. His portrait combines pre-arranged supplies with materials acquired nearby: 'canvas, acrylic paint, crushed Mt Erebus crystals, soil samples from the Dry Valleys, soil samples from Ross Island, McMurdo Sound seawater, GIS maps of the Antarctic continent, copies of historic photographs'.[31] The result is a unification of

---

27 Lisa Roberts, *2002–21feb–02–69s75e*, detail of triptych, oil on canvas, 2003, available at: www.lisaroberts.com.au/content/artworks/2d/2d2003/2d2003.php [Accessed on 1 January 2010].

28 Lisa Roberts, *Ice Cores and Spirals*, engraved perspex, 2008, available at: www.lisaroberts.com.au/content/artworks/3d/3d2008/3d2008.php [Accessed on 1 January 2010].

29 Xavier Cortada, *Endangered World*, site-specific flags and mixed media, 2007, available at: www.cortada.com/antarctica/endangered/ [Accessed on 1 January 2010].

30 Robinson, p. 537; Xavier Cortada, Ibid.

31 Xavier Cortada, *Shackleton in the South Pole*, mixed media, 2007, available at:

diverse and fragmented contributions, brought to the convergent point that Shackleton himself never reached; Cortada's work thus emphasises the possibilities of art to respect historical continuity even as it demands revision and redress.[32]

The physical aesthetic of Antarctic visitation has always pushed the physical hermeneutic toward the state of the art; extreme circumstances produce tight feedback loops that result in rapid revisions of equipment and technique, but also of critical concept.[33] Peter Morse had an Australian fellowship in 2005–06 to link photography with satellite and aerial surveys 'to create an interactive 3D virtual-reality representation of Antarctica'. He returned to Antarctica with the Mawson's Huts Expedition, which on New Year's Day, 2010, discovered the remnants of the first aircraft in Antarctica.[34] In keeping with the expedition's goal of re-situating historical evidence, Morse envisions using the huts' site as the floor of a fulldome video survey—that is, a high-definition 3-D video designed for projection within a planetarium. At the same time, his project includes re-contextualising photographs taken by Frank Hurley on the original Mawson expedition, 1911–14.[35] As it was in the past, so it will be: as Hurley attempted, with the most advanced technology of the time, so Morse intends to produce a visual experience approaching an Antarctic virtual reality, and thus to justify the ways of cold to man.

At their peak, the national Antarctic programs placed a dozen writers and artists at a time.[36] As with such institutions everywhere,

---

www.Cortada.Com/antarctica/mural/ [Accessed on 1 January 2010].

32 Ibid.

33 'Peter Morse', Australian Antarctic Division, Antarctic Arts Fellowship, 3 January 2010; Peter Morse, 'The Ice Museum', photograph, 2009, available at: www.petermorse.com.au/2009/11/the-ice-museum-2010/ [Accessed on 1 January 2010].

34 Peter Morse, 'Mawson's Huts 209–2010 Expedition', photograph, 2009, available at: www.petermorse.com.au/2009/11/mawsons-huts-2009-2010-expedition/ [Accessed on 1 January 2010].

35 Frank Hurley, 'Mawson's Hut, Cape Denison Station, Commonwealth Bay, Antarctica 1911–1914', photograph, available at: www.petespolarplace.com/images/5-Mawson%27s-Hut-lg.jpg [Accessed on 1 January 2010].

36 Erika Blumenfeld, photograph, 2009, 'Antarctica Volume 3', available at: www.

they have suffered in the current economy. The American program has suspended applications for the 2010–11 season, while expressing hopes to resume later.[37] Arts Council England has not renewed its grant to the British Antarctic Survey; the amount at stake is only £17,000, but the entire arrangement is in danger.[38] The New Zealand program, after ten years of considering open applications, has reverted to invitation-only support. Among national programs, then, only Australia's retains full strength. These losses are real, but some exciting compensation may arise: artists such as the American photographer Erika Blumenfeld have found space in the Interpolar Transnational Art Science Constellation, a consortium of governments, NGOs, and universities organised by South Africa in 2005; describing itself as 'lichen-like' in its uncentred coordination and exchange, ITASC seeks to redress the exclusivity of national efforts in all senses. In 2009, for example, the group deployed a wind- and solar-powered station at 71° South to coincide with a multi-continent exhibition focused on climate. Whether travel to Antarctica occurs in the traditional national models or in the newer transnational co-operatives, we are greatly aided by artists and writers who return with the story. We need them to continue going there.[39] The penguins are waiting.

---

levygallery.com/artists/erika_blumenfeld/9484.6.html [Accessed on 1 January 2010].

37 National Science Foundation, 'Antarctic Artists and Writers Program', available at: www.nsf.gov/publications/pub_summ.jsp?ods_key=nsf08552 [Accessed on 1 January 2010].

38 Andy Broadhead (Arts Council England), email to the author, 6 January 2010; John R. Shears (British Antarctic Survey), email to the author, 4 January 2010.

39 Frank Hurley, 'Eric Douglas Playing Music to Unappreciative Adelie Penguins', photograph, c. 1929–31, available at: www.aad.gov.au/default.asp?casid=34784 [Accessed on 1 January 2010].

Section 4

The Cold War

13

Troubled Waters: Australian Spies in the Pacific—Glimpses from the Early Twentieth Century

Bruce Bennett

The national story of Australian spies and spying begins in the Pacific during the political machinations and manoeuvring that led to an Australian Commonwealth in 1901. Although political agitation and unrest in the region were peripheral to the imperial ambitions of Britain, France or Germany, such events seemed more pressing from the Australian continent. From a British imperial (but not yet an American) perspective, Australia offered a vantage point for keeping an eye on British interests in the Pacific and threats to them; and Australia's emergent national interest coincided for a time with this approach.

An Australian perspective on the South Pacific is offered in the stories and novels of Louis Becke who sailed these seas from the 1870s to the 1890s as an adventurer and trader. Becke's adventures included signing on as supercargo for the legendary American pirate 'Bully' Hayes, but Becke was himself acquitted of piracy charges.[1] The overriding impression left by Becke's *Pacific Tales* and other books is of the primacy of trading—of goods and chattels, of impressions and ideas, information and maps, and sometimes of people. In the background are larger rivalries and enmities between the European empires that vied for authority and control in the Pacific—especially the British, French, German and Dutch. Intelligence gathering and espionage were usually commercially motivated; and although images of a paradisiacal Pacific

1 A. Grove Day, *Louis Becke* (Melbourne: Hill of Content, 1966), p. 112.

recur in Becke's writings and prefigure Margaret Mead's popularisation of notions of 'free love' in the South Pacific a generation later (vigorously contested by Australian anthropologist Derek Freeman), Becke's 'trader's eye' is more attuned to the exchanges of beliefs, stories and values that occur in these islands at a time of international unrest.[2] The trader in impressions, information and ideas who is also a writer has much in common with the spy and may be seen as a natural precursor, though the piratical buccaneer figure of Bully Hayes fits more readily than does Becke into a James Bond stereotype.

While apparently peripheral to European power-plays, Australia by the 1890s was moving towards separate nationhood within broader notions of empire—'a new Britannia' in these southern seas. In this context of political currents and cross-currents, Australia quietly commenced its history as an international spying nation.

Bridges in the Pacific

In 1898, William Bridges, Australia's first military spy was sent at the age of thirty-seven to Samoa to 'assess the situation' in this German possession in the Pacific where 'trouble had been developing ... and finally erupted into open warfare' between factions backed by Germany versus Britain and the US.[3] During his spying assignment, Bridges showed his cross-cultural adaptability with a visit to the rebel King Tamasese.

Several years later, Major Bridges was on another spying mission in the Pacific, this time in New Caledonia. Under cover as 'Mr Bridges', a commercial agent for Dalgetys Ltd, he was tasked with mapping and marking the position of gun batteries around the harbour at Noumea which could provide anchorage for French warships. Between May and July 1902, Bridges obtained valuable information and photographs for Australia's new Director-General of Military Intelligence and Mobilisation in an espionage mission described by General Hutton

---

2 See Bruce Bennett, 'The Traveller's Eye—Louis Becke's South Pacific', in *Homing in: Essays on Australian Literature and Selfhood* (Perth: API Network, 2006), pp. 147–55.

3 See C.D. Coulthard-Clark, *A Heritage of Spirit: A Biography of Major-General Sir William Throsby Bridges* (Carlton: Melbourne University Press, 1979), p. 27.

as 'secret and somewhat dangerous'.[4] Bridges' reports were forwarded to the War Office in London. These early experiences in intelligence-gathering and reporting were influential in Bridges' illustrious career in the Australian Army and later benefited students at Australia's first military college, Duntroon, in Canberra, where General Bridges was the highly praised foundation Commandant.[5]

Australia's early international spying efforts were inevitably small-scale missions carried out by 'lone rangers'. In 1901, the new Australian government sent scholar Wilson Le Couteur as a secret agent to the New Hebrides for three months to gather information on French activity in New Caledonia.[6] Le Couteur's civilian mission fits an imperial pattern of the educated 'gentleman spy' whose knowledge of the history, language and geography of a place or region informs and gives substance to their reportage.[7] Their underlying purpose was the strengthening of empire.

Changing Focus in Australian Intelligence Towards Japan

While much information-gathering and covert surveillance by residents of Australia in the early years of the Commonwealth of Australia concerned Pacific 'areas of darkness' or possible sources of threat such as New Guinea, German Samoa or French possessions in the Pacific, a larger and more persistent threat was perceived in Japan. As Australian Prime Minister Alfred Deakin wrote, 'Japan, or her head-quarters is, so to speak, next door, while the Mother Country is many streets away'.[8] International relations with Japan vacillated during Australia's first decade as a nation but Japan's military victory over Russia in 1905

4 Coulthard-Clark, p. 43.

5 Coulthard-Clark, p. 112.

6 C.D. Coulthard-Clark, *The Citizen-General Staff: The Australian Intelligence Corps 1907–1914* (Canberra: Military Historical Society of Australia, 1976), p. 112. See also R.C. Thompson, 'Australian Imperialism and the New Hebrides, 1862–1922', PhD Thesis, Australian National University, 1970, pp. 413–15.

7 See John Fisher, *Gentleman Spies: Intelligence Agents in the British Empire and Beyond* (Stroud, UK: Sutton, 2002).

8 N. Meaney, *Towards a New Vision: Australia and Japan Across Time* (Sydney: UNSW Press, 2006), p. 4.

re-established the island nation as a potential threat to British imperial interests and hence Australia. A change in attitude towards Japan can be discerned during 1907–08 with reports in Queensland newspapers of Japanese 'pseudo-fishermen' making surveys of the Great Barrier Reef and others allegedly mapping stock-routes. Lieutenant-Colonel Bridges, now in charge of the Australian Intelligence Corps, investigated these reports through state police forces and declared them unfounded. Nevertheless, increasing fear and suspicion of Japan became a significant stimulus to activities of the Australian Intelligence Corps.[9]

Literary accounts contributed to apprehension, and sometimes a deeper knowledge of international intrigues. A.G. Hales' novel *Little Blue Pigeon: A Story of Japan* (1904), for example, presents Tokyo during the build-up to the Russo-Japanese war as a hotbed of international espionage. The Adelaide-born Hales was a war-correspondent, miner, international adventurer and prolific author. After covering the South African war where he was wounded and captured by the Boers, Hales reported for the London *Daily News* on the Macedonian rebellion against the Turks and was at some of the major Russo-Japanese battles in 1905.[10] He was an acute observer and analyst of British, Chinese and Japanese imperial ambitions, from his independent Australian standpoint.

Hales incorporated these concerns into his entertaining novel about the romance of Clifford, an agent in the service of the British Empire, and Blue Pigeon, a geisha girl of Samurai family background who has learnt English during an unexplained stint of two years in Sydney. Pursued also by Quong Foy, a Chinese-born agent for the Russians, Blue Pigeon is the centrepiece of competing claims by Britain, Russia and China for the heart and soul of Japan. In an interesting twist, some key Russian spies in this novel pose as American missionaries. Fortunately, the seductive but trustworthy Blue Pigeon can tell the difference between

9 Coulthard-Clark, p. 26. See also D.C. Sissons, 'Australia's Attitudes to Japan and Defence 1890–1923', MA Thesis, University of Melbourne, 1956.

10 See Donald Grant, 'Hales, Alfred Arthur Greenwood (1860–1936)', in *Australian Dictionary of Biography*, 9 (Carlton: Melbourne University Press, 1983), pp. 159–60.

Russians and Americans and remains a true asset of the red-bearded Clifford who has won her heart and her loyalty.

From a secret service perspective, Hales' novel is interesting for its depiction of the way agents of Czarist Russia attempt to involve Australia in their attempted destruction of British imperial interests. Their agent in place, Chinese-born Quong Foy, presents a persuasive scenario to fellow Russian agent Boris Metchkin. When the Japan-Russia war is on, he says, the combined 'yellow races' of Japan and China will demand that the embargo on 'Asiatics' in Australia be removed. This will be a direct blow to Australia and the rest of the Empire, for the Australians 'hate the yellow man worse than the Americans hate the black man.'[11] Quong Foy believes—and so does Boris Metchkin who has worked in Britain—that the rich British aristocrats who run that country will not ultimately defend Australia against Japanese attacks because they have no real interest in supporting the ideals of the democracies. However, the success of this scenario which predicts the dissolution of the British empire depends on the 'Yellow Bond' of Japan and China—of which Quong Foy believes he has solid evidence through Chinese secret societies. These hypothetical scenarios based on partial evidence and contemporary prejudice contain some shrewd insights and premonitions of arguments later presented to the Paris Peace Conference in 1919 by Australia's Prime Minister Hughes. While not knowing of any secret 'Yellow Bond' (until he is told of it by Blue Pigeon) Clifford agrees with the Russian view that a Japanese attack on Australia would be catastrophic—it would break 'the backbone of the British empire.'[12]

Another interesting insight provided by Hales' novel is the role that women can play in secret intelligence. Because official reports are usually written by senior (male) officials, the roles of junior or unofficial agents or assets (often female) are diminished or ignored. Yet, as *Blue Pigeon* shows, a whole plot can hinge on the motives, intuitions and intelligence of women. While the melodrama, violence and stereotypes

---

11 A.G. Hales, *Little Blue Pigeon: A Story of Japan* (London: Hutchinson, 1905), p. 173.

12 Hales, p. 198.

make *Little Blue Pigeon* in some respects 'an archetypal James Bond story',[13] the courage and perseverance of the Japanese geisha girl of Samurai background give her an enhanced symbolic value in the world of international intelligence.

A shift in Australian intelligence gathering towards somewhat more sophisticated forms of inquiry was discernible by the end of Australia's first decade as a nation. Lord Kitchener's visit to Australia in January 1910 and his recommendation to strengthen intelligence partly through area officers to be drawn from the military college which he had recommended was a start.[14] The Royal Military College at Duntroon, modelled on West Point, Sandhurst and Kingston, Ontario, opened in 1911. Recruitment of well-educated and capable army officers into the Australian Intelligence Corps became more feasible. In 1909, the AIC numbered sixty officers and included Edmund Leolin Piesse from Tasmania who was to figure prominently in intelligence circles during World War I and the postwar years. While internal surveillance of German interests in Australia necessarily dominated the energies of the Counter Espionage Bureau (forerunner of ASIO) headed by Major George Steward, Piesse and others also looked further afield and to longer-term international strategic concerns in the Pacific in an organisation foreshadowing the Australian Secret Intelligence Service (ASIS) half a century later.

George Steward served as private secretary of Australia's Governor-General—indeed he served five governors general—and was ironically dubbed by Munro Ferguson, his fifth, as 'Pickle the Spy' after a popular fictional character,[15] because of the unsavoury individuals who were said to lurk around Government House to meet with Steward.[16] A

13 Megumi Kato, *Narrating the Other: Australian Literary Perceptions of Japan* (Clayton: Monash University Press, 2008), p. 23.

14 See Coulthard-Clark, pp. 32, 53.

15 See Andrew Lang, *Pickle the Spy; Or, the Incognito of Prince Charles* (London: Longman Greens, 1897).

16 Chris Cunneen, 'Steward, Sir George Charles Thomas (1865–1920)', in *Australian Dictionary of Biography*, 12 (Carlton: Melbourne University Press, 1990), pp. 81–82.

former boxer and sculler of humble origins from London's East End, Steward was suspicious of intellectuals and critical of Australian censors during the war years; they were, he said, 'for the most part University Professors [and] show a great want of that degree of imagination which is necessary in work of this character'.[17] This apparently damning criticism of university professors (what did their imagination deficit actually amount to?) raises questions about alliances between academe and intelligence work and the uses of imagination in these two professions. Reliable and efficient in administrative matters, Steward himself could be brusque in manner but appears to have been a reliable guardian and transmitter of secret ciphers between Australia and Britain; and he could be astute in his dealings with men ranging from prime ministers and governors-general to spies and informers. But his comments about 'imagination' and its appropriate applications in the spying game have continued to reverberate (with various interpretations of 'imagination', and its uses and abuses) through the history of Australian intelligence.

Scholar Spies and Strategic Intelligence: James Murdoch and Edmund Piesse

Edmund Piesse became friendly with James Murdoch—university academic, linguist and historian of Japan—in the early years of World War I and thus commenced a remarkable collaborative engagement with great potential benefit for Australian intelligence. Such intelligence gathering and analysis arose from a deep knowledge base in history, literature, language, religion, the arts and science. When applied to more immediate operational goals such as military tactics or political decision-making, such intelligence could seem complex and sometimes contradictory to its users—as 'real' (as opposed to 'raw') intelligence often does. In such circumstances, the basis for conflict between politicians and their intelligence advisors is ever present.

Piesse first met Murdoch in 1915 when he was thirty-five and Murdoch was fifty-nine. The spymaster Piesse recognised that he could benefit personally and professionally from the older man's knowledge and understanding of Japan, which he soon discovered was far from

17 Cunneen, pp. 81–82. See also Coulthard-Clark, p. 56.

superficial. The Scottish-born Murdoch had taught in Queensland schools after his arrival in Australia in 1881 with his English wife, Lucy; it was an unhappy marriage that produced one son. Murdoch worked on the radical nationalist journal the *Boomerang* and visited southeast and northeast Asia. He later returned to Japan with his eight-year-old son, taught in schools and entered Tokyo Imperial University in 1889 where for four years he studied and engaged in literary activities, wrote poetry, short stories and a novel, and edited a magazine.

A number of Murdoch's stories in *From Australia and Japan* (1892) reveal a young radical socialist of working-class Scottish origins encountering the radically different societies of Australia and Japan. (One of Murdoch's personae in these stories is 'Felix Holt Secundus', a Scottish version of George Eliot's idealistic radical.) As Megumi Kato notes, Murdoch's young narrator differs from many other Western commentators on Japan by participating in what he sees and hears, introducing cultural differences and acting at times as 'a mediator between East and West'.[18] With this kind of outlook, and his inquisitive intelligence, Murdoch was less likely than certain Australian nationalist authors, such as Randolph Bedford or C.H. Kirmess, to see the Japanese *en masse* in stereotypical terms or to share easily aroused Australian fears of a foreign invader. As he demonstrated in his *History of Japan*, Murdoch's knowledge of Japanese culture became deep and extensive. But Murdoch's imaginative romantic adventurers in *From Australia to Japan* also reveal similarities to characters in fiction by John Buchan, the writer of spy stories; in an interesting coincidence, Buchan was commissioned by Murdoch's publisher the following year.[19] The chief difference between the two writers is that Murdoch's alter ego is that of a working-class hero who asserts himself energetically but he lacks the aristocratic panache of Buchan's Richard Hannay. Nevertheless, the combination of spy/investigator/writer continued to interact in Murdoch's persona and career.

18 Kato, p. 26.

19 D.C.S. Sissons, 'James Murdoch (1856–1921): Historian, Teacher and Much Else Besides', in *Transactions of the Asiatic Society of Japan*, vol. 2, 1987, pp. 1–57. Mention of Buchan 1987 is on p. 23.

In further study at the British Museum, Murdoch made translations of sixteenth century Japanese texts, and returned and taught economic history at the Higher Commercial College (later Hitotsubashi University) in Tokyo, where in 1899 he married Takeko Okada. They bought an orchard near Tokyo. Thanks to Piesse and the Defence Department, Murdoch returned with his Japanese wife to Australia in 1917 to teach Japanese at the Royal Military College, Duntroon; he was subsequently appointed Professor of Oriental Studies at the University of Sydney.[20]

Despite his relative youthfulness, Piesse was a policy 'wonk' who brought much to the collaboration. A science graduate of the University of Tasmania in 1900, he had studied mathematics at King's College, Cambridge, but was obliged to return home when his father died in 1902; he graduated in law in 1905. Piesse retained a strong interest in the natural sciences thoughout his life and was honorary secretary of the local Royal Society in 1912–14. He was a scientist, humanist and lawyer who became a practical policy-maker with a strong belief in evidence-based policy. Having joined the newly established Australian Intelligence Corps in 1909, Piesse produced the first military survey of Tasmania before he transferred to Melbourne in 1916 and was promoted to major and director of military intelligence at the Directorate of Military Operations. Piesse's special talent and his most satisfying work was in the collation and analysis of strategic intelligence.[21]

Under Murdoch's guidance, Piesse learnt Japanese. When the Australian government created a Pacific branch of the Prime Minister's Department in 1919 to study 'the affairs of the countries of the Far East and the Pacific' and desirable Australian policy it did so on Piesse's advice and he was appointed its director.[22] Together, their efforts introduced a small nucleus of Australians to Japanese language and culture with a view to better intelligence in the region.[23] One such beneficiary was

20 D.C.S. Sissons, 'James Murdoch (1856–1921)', in *Australian Dictionary of Biography*, 10 (Carlton: Melbourne University Press, 1986), p. 619.

21 N.K. Meaney, 'Piesse, Edmund Leolin (1880–1947)', in *Australian Dictionary of Biography*, 11 (Carlton: Melbourne University Press, 1988), pp. 227–29.

22 Meaney, p. 228.

23 Sissons, *Australian Dictionary of Biography*, pp. 46–48.

Eric Longfield Lloyd who had taken part in the landing at Gallipoli on 25 April 1915 and when wounded served in the Intelligence Section of the General Staff. He joined Piesse's Pacific Branch and began learning Japanese. He held a number of senior roles in intelligence both before and during World War II.

A remarkable set of conversations opened up between Piesse and Murdoch, and intensified during and after World War I. These discussions and their ensuing correspondence contained secret and confidential as well as 'public domain' material. They played a strong part in advice given to the Australian prime minister and government. Murdoch's regular and often extended visits to Japan provided much useful information and food for thought for Piesse as he grappled with Australian–Asian relations, especially with Japan. Some of Murdoch's observations were provocative challenges to Australian military authorities as when he remarked that: 'The best brains in Japan are in the Army and Navy and often to be found in the Intelligence Service'.[24] At a more general, reflective level, Murdoch had come to reject theories of innate racial differences as 'pestiferous explosive poppy-cock'. As he pointed out to Piesse in 1918, 'If we really want war, all we've got to do is to keep harping upon our pseudo-scientific racial "biology" '.[25]

Murdoch's sources in Tokyo included journalists, academics and high-level government officials ranging from the Japanese Head of the Ministry of Foreign Affairs, Shidehara, to the American Ambassador, Roland Morris, whose knowledge and insight impressed Murdoch greatly. When writing to Piesse, Murdoch addressed his correspondence to a code name at Piesse's residential address—'Mr MacRae'. He knew he had to be careful because, 'the Japanese were watching all correspondence very carefully'.[26]

Information to which Murdoch was given access, or extracted from sources, included Japanese troop movements and numbers. He learnt,

24 Royal Military College of Australia, *Annual Report*, 1918.

25 Letter of Murdoch to Piesse, National Library of Australia, in E.L. Piesse, MS. 882/5/16.

26 Murdoch to Piesse, National Library of Australia, in E.L. Piesse, MS. 882/5/7, 14/3/1919.

for instance, of Japan's 'complete plan for the military annexation of Eastern Siberia'.[27] But he also believed in an older form of intelligence that he described as 'swapping wisdom', as when he distilled the results of a discussion with journalist friends:

> The collapse of Germany has at last had its effect;—German militarism is now being held up as a terrible example and able editors are everywhere preaching to their public the advisability of taking warning and turning over a new leaf … and on the whole, the country has become reasonable, very reasonable. In short, things are much more hopeful than they have ever been since 1914.[28]

Yet racial discrimination in Australia, as an historical consequence of the White Australia policy, continued to bedevil Australia's relations with Japan and other countries of what was later called the Asia–Pacific region in Australia or the Pacific Rim in the USA. Murdoch, who earlier in life had depicted the Chinese in racial terms, became a voice of calm reason as he tried to moderate Australian fears of Japan during and after World War I. In this process, we can see an interplay of politics, prejudice and international rivalry as different nations vied for advantage at the Paris Peace conference and at the subsequent Washington Conference of 1921–22.

Murdoch's advice to Piesse was presented in reasonable and temperate terms and he also sought to influence Japanese opinion through his contacts there. For example, through Murdoch's connections with Japanese journalists and editors he managed to persuade influential newspapers in Japan to present the view that the 'White Australia' policy was mainly a labour problem and not directed against the Japanese or Chinese as a race.[29] As a result of Murdoch's advice and his own investigations, Piesse became convinced in the early post-World War I

27 Murdoch to Piesse,National Library of Australia, MS. 822/5/7, 14/3/1919.

28 Murdoch to Piesse,National Library of Australia, MS. 822/5/7, 25/1/1919.

29 D.C.S. Sissons, Papers and Manuscripts, National Library of Australia, MS. 3092, pp 79–80.

years that 'Japan had no designs on Australia and that Australia should remove its discriminatory barriers against Japanese immigration and trade'.[30] Australian Prime Minister Hughes, who was presented with these views in a memo from Piesse, responded with one word, 'Rot'.[31] Piesse would not be the first or last respected senior intelligence advisor to the Australian government to be disparaged and his case summarily dismissed by a prime minister determined to defend Australia's borders against real or imagined invaders. Another senior intelligence advisor during the term of the Howard government who met this fate was Andrew Wilkie, who resigned in March 2003 in protest over Australia's impending entry into the Iraq war.[32]

Prime Minister Hughes' attitudes and approach at the Paris Peace conference were attacked in the Japanese press. The Tokyo *Nichi Nichi Shimbun* offered a neat admonishment of Australia's prime minister while also exposing Japan's continuing southward ambitions in the Pacific:

> If Mr Hughes understands the spirit of the Anglo-Japanese alliance and realises how much Japan contributed militarily and economically to the Allies' victory, he ought to be the first to welcome both the abandonment of racial discrimination, which must precede the formation of the League of Nations, and also the Southward development of Japan, and by falling in with the policy of Japan contributing to the establishment of a permanent peace—the primary motive of the recent war. He on the contrary, in opposition to the policy of the Mother Country, persists in his anti-Japanese attitude, clings to his principles of racial prejudice and, much to our surprise, is entirely devoid of the characteristic magnanimity of a great Empire.

30 Meaney, p. 228.

31 Australian Archives, Canberra, CP447/2, item SC, 42; cited in Sissons, National Library of Australia, MS. 3092, p. 87.

32 See Andrew Wilkie, *Axis of Deceit* (Melbourne: Black Inc. Agenda, 2004).

> The permanent occupation of the South Sea Islands and the abolition of racial discrimination are to be Japan's chief claims at the Peace Conference. These are not only Japan's reward but are guarantees for the future peace of the world ...[33]

Prime Minister Hughes continued to see Japan as a threat and publicly declared that the next war was likely to be in the Pacific.[34] In these circumstances, it is not surprising that Australian foreign policy in the aftermath of World War I was seen largely as a civilian extension of defence intelligence and that suspicion of Japan was at its heart.[35] Denigrated by his prime minister and flying in the face of public opinion, the intelligence expert Piesse and his key advisor Murdoch were hereafter firmly excluded from any influential role in Australian foreign policy. Thus, Piesse's influence on Australian policy towards Japan diminished after World War I and he was not invited by Hughes to the Imperial Conference in London in 1921. Two years after Murdoch's death in 1921, Piesse resigned from the Pacific Branch and joined a Melbourne law firm. He continued to take an interest in defence and foreign policy issues with special reference to Japan. In the mid-1920s he discounted the dangers from Japan, including espionage, but by the early 1930s he saw renewed danger from that quarter and used his influence to ensure greater public spending on defence in the later 1930s.

Afterthoughts: The Divided Pacific

The Pacific Islands Forum, held in Cairns in 2009 and chaired by Australian Prime Minister Kevin Rudd was a reminder of the manifold divided interests of inhabitants of those islands. A major topic was climate change underscored by fears of rising seas and—for some

33 *Nichi Nichi Shimbun* (Tokyo), 27 January 1919, cited in Sissons, National Library of Australia, MS. 3092, p. 81.

34 See N. Meaney, *Towards a New Vision: Australia and Japan Across Time* (Sydney: UNSW Press, 2006), p. 117.

35 See P.G. Edwards, *Prime Ministers and Diplomats: The Making of Australian Foreign Policy* (Melbourne: Oxford University Press, 1983).

islanders—the prospect of obliteration. Politics and power issues, as well as economic concerns were to the fore. Many critical words were spoken about coup-prone Fiji but doors were left open for further negotiation. It is pertinent that the US is not a member of this forum but an Under Secretary of State was present and Secretary of State Hillary Clinton has expressed a strong interest in Asian and Pacific (or what used to be called Pacific Rim) affairs.

Within these oceanographic limits, Japan and northeast Asia are of more urgent concern to the great powers than are Australia's neighbouring islands in the Pacific. Because of our strong economy as a middle-ranking power and our continuing strong links with Britain and more especially with the US, Australia's intelligence interests in the region are now more firmly fixed than they were a century ago on Japan, China and Indonesia. This follows the regional argument for an Australian Secret Intelligence Service in 1950 by Prime Minister Menzies who stressed that ASIS would operate in 'South East Asia and in Pacific areas adjacent to Australia'[36]. At that time, under Menzies, the British Commonwealth role remained paramount: the new secret service, it was hoped, 'would in some small measure reduce the onerous worldwide commitments of the United Kingdom ... and enhance the security of the British Commonwealth in the Pacific'.[37] By 1966, however, Australian Prime Minister Harold Holt made the first of many professions of undying love for the USA when he charmed President Lyndon Johnson (though not necessarily the Australian public) with his 'All the way with LBJ' statement.

A conservative political culture had lagged behind cultural developments. Even before World War II, seasoned observers of the Pacific and its region were raising questions about American–Australian relations. Closer relations would inevitably involve questions of national intelligence and its sharing. Would the intelligence culture change from the scattered kinds of 'lone ranger' exercises described in this paper and carried out in the interests of the British empire and

36 Brian Toohey and William Pinwill, *Oyster: The Story of the Australian Secret Intelligence Service* (Port Melbourne: Heinemann, 1989), p. 27.

37 Toohey and Pinwill, p. 29.

self defence? One experienced observer, Hartley Grattan, saw these issues in cultural terms. In his article 'An Australian–American Axis?' published eighteen months before Pearl Harbour, Grattan wrote, 'the hard realities of Pacific politics are drawing the Australians into the American sphere'.[38] But this would happen only if 'the spell of Britain was exorcised'.[39] In Grattan's view, only an independent Australia—one which acted 'for itself and apart from Britain'—would be of real use to either country.[40] From these precepts, Grattan praised the development of an independent Australian literature and closer literary and cultural relations between Australia and America.

As Australia-US relations strengthened during the last half of the twentieth and the first decade of the twenty-first century, Australian intelligence involvement in the Pacific and Asian countries has varied widely. From the Cold War to Vietnam and 9/11, new crises have brought different kinds and levels of interaction between Australia and the US. When I interviewed former CIA chief George Tenet in Washington DC in 2006, he spoke warmly of Australian intelligence officers and his interaction with them and how much he respected especially their knowledge and understanding of Indonesia. The contrast in scale and sophistication of operations between the present situation and Australian intelligence operations in Asia and the Pacific a century ago is enormous. Yet we can find points of connection and commonality across this historical span too. From William Bridges' spying on military installations in New Caledonia at the beginning of the century to Edmund Piesse and James Murdoch's investigation and analysis of Japan's strategic intentions during and after World War I, we can see in embryonic form some of the major concerns of the spying game today. These rapid glimpses emphasise the need for more sustained comparative studies of Australian and US intelligence engagements and their cultural implications in the Asia–Pacific region.

38 See Laurie Hergenhan, *No Casual Traveller: Hartley Grattan and Australia* (St Lucia: University of Queensland Press, 1995), pp 147–48.

39 Hergenhan, p. 135.

40 Hergenhan, p. 140.

14

'A Skyrocket Waiting to Be Let Off', but to Where? Christina Stead's First Impressions of the United States and Her Postwar Literary Rehabilitation

Michael Ackland

Christina Stead was, as Jose Yglesias rightly highlighted in 1965, a product of the 1930s—its controversies and epochal events had indelibly shaped her novels and diverse pronouncements. The occasion was a review of the recently reissued *The Man Who Loved Children*, about which he made a number of crucial, dissenting points. Whereas others focused on the book's extraordinary human insights or, like Jarrell in his highly influential prefatory essay, praised it as an unforgettable, rarely equalled portrayal of family life, Yglesias insisted that 'Marxist ideas ... are inseparable from Stead's literary vision'.[1] They are 'what organizes her emotions and talent, what lends tension and drive to her creative process', and what ultimately 'has delayed her recognition'. Speaking of the novel itself he observed that, 'although it may be possible to ignore this now, as Jarrell does in his essay, it was, consciously or unconsciously, impossible in 1941'. Finally, he remarked presciently that, given the antipathy of 'our present establishment ... to Stead's ideology', it may be 'possible, as it happened with Brecht, to extract many important subsidiary virtues from her novels'. Current feminist interpretations would figure highly among these, as would autobiographical

1 . Quotations are from his 'Marx as Muse', in *Nation* 100 (1965): 368–70.

readings.[2] And Stead, in fascinating ways, confirmed the keenness of Yglesias' commentary. An unremarked, expanded version of it, marked 'Rough Galley', exists among her collection of reviews,[3] so that she was presumably consulted about its contents before it went to press. After its appearance, she disingenuously feigned surprise at Yglesias' remarks to one correspondent ('I have just been proclaimed a "Marxian muse" to everyone's astonishment, my own not least'), whereas to Stanley Burnshaw, with whom she had long exchanged private, at times heretical opinions, she was more candid: 'I do like the Jose Yglesias review very much, it is pertinent and canny'.[4] This comment amounts to acknowledgement of the centrality of Marxist ideology in her writing, and is further strengthened by the fact that she had apparently vetted the review; however, the Marxist dimension of her work has generally been overlooked, and nowhere received the detailed treatment it merits.[5]

---

2 See, for example, Joan Lidoff, *Christina Stead* (New York: Ungar, 1982); Judith Kegan Gardiner, 'Male Narcissism, Capitalism and the Daughter of *The Man Who Loved Children*' in Lynda E. Brose and Betty S. Flowers, eds, *Daughters and Fathers* (Baltimore: John Hopkins University Press, 1989), rpt. in Margaret Harris, ed., *The Magic Phrase: Critical Essays on Christina Stead* (St. Lucia: University of Queensland Press, 2000), pp. 145–62; Diana Brydon, *Christina Stead* (Totowa: Barnes & Noble, 1987); Susan Sheridan, *Christina Stead* (Bloomington: Indiana University Press, 1988); Hazel Rowley, *Christina Stead* (Melbourne: Heinemann, 1993); and Louise Yelin, *From the Margins of Empire: Christina Stead, Doris Lessing and Nadine Gordimer* (Ithaca: Cornell University Press, 1998).

3 National Library of Australia, MS. 4967, folder 80.

4 Quoted in Rowley, *Christina Stead*, p. 612. I have chosen throughout to quote from Rowley's original version of the biography rather than the most recent 'new edition', published by Melbourne University Press in 2007. It alone contains this information, for the alleged newness of the later edition rests not on further insights, nor on the incorporation of a decade and a half of Stead scholarship, but mainly on the deletion of approximately twenty per cent of the original text to create a tighter, more reader-friendly narrative. As Rowley observed at the time of the relaunch: 'I like to think I've become a sharper storyteller through the years and more economical with words' ('The Mocking Country', *Weekend Australian*, 25–26 August 2007, p. 9).

5 Sporadic calls for revising the place of Marxism in her work do, however, occur. See, for instance, Michael Ackland, 'Realigning Christina Stead', *Overland*, 192 (2008): 49–53 and 'Literary Politics and the Cold War: The Case of Christina

Instead commentary intent on her literary rehabilitation has tended to downplay the extent of her ideological commitment. According to the Australian's principal biographer, for instance, Stead was an author passionately driven to write and create characters, her 'commitment was to her writing, not politics',[6] as if the two were discreet, rather than mutually nourishing spheres, while Rowley and others have treated Stead's political interests as being largely a reflection of passion for male Marxist intellectuals, such as Ralph Fox and William J. Blake. Thus commentary has failed to take at face value her occasionally outspoken radicalism, as in her report on the 1935 Writers' Congress in Paris which she attended as a member of the British delegation. Doctrinaire passages, readers are told, 'sound like Bill Blech [Blake]; he probably helped her with the article',[7] and palliating reasons are urged for the work's political bias: 'her impassioned rhetoric probably appealed to her communist readers rather than reflecting deeply felt convictions'.[8] Such assertions not only amount to special pleading and wishful thinking, they are also curiously disempowering of Stead. They imply that after seven years in Europe and massive international crises she had yet to form firm opinions of her own. Her account of the congress suggests otherwise. There she reiterates the need for writers to 'study politics', acknowledges 'the frightful insistence of the economic question',[9] and adds her voice to the chorus urging commitment—to such good effect that in 1936 she could credibly be 'invited to spend six months in Moscow to work on International Literature'.[10]

This depoliticising tendency is discernible as well in the editing of selected manuscript works. The most important of these published

---

Stead', *Pacific and American Studies* 10 (2010): 50–65; Stephen Cowden, 'Christina Stead and the 'Marxist Imaginary', *Southerly* 63 (2003): 63–75; and Brigid Rooney, 'Loving the Revolutionary: Re-reading Christina Stead's Encounter with Men, Marxism and the Popular Front in 1930s Paris', *Southerly* 58 (1998): 84–102.

6 Rowley, p. 254.

7 Rowley, p. 173.

8 Rowley, p. 172.

9 'The Writer Takes Sides', *Left Review* 1.2 (1935): 453.

10 Letter to Gilbert Stead, dated 25 January 1937, in Christina Stead, *A Web of Friendship: Selected Letters (1928–1973)*, R.G. Geering, ed. (Sydney: Angus & Robertson, 1992), p. 71.

to date is undoubtedly *I'm Dying Laughing* which, according to Anne Pender, 'uses only a fraction of Stead's drafts'.[11] In particular, 'extended passages dramatising the politics of the protagonists' have been omitted, as well as 'much of the political material that Stead had worked so hard to provide'.[12] Repeatedly Pender hesitates to attribute motives to the editor, R.G. Geering, one of Stead's major postwar proselytisers and later her literary executor. She notes only that such omissions accorded well with his stated belief that 'novel is "concerned primarily with character and morality"', although more sweepingly (and correctly) Pender observes: 'In all his critical writing on Stead's novels, Geering downplayed the political content, and rejected any notion of a determinist element in the relationship between character and society'.[13]Similar observations hold true for his editing of the manuscript headed 'America'.[14] This describes Stead's first impressions of the US, when she lived there from approximately July 1935 to May 1936. The manuscript, consisting of

11 '"Scorched Earth": Washington and the Missing Manuscript of *I'm Dying Laughing*', *Australian Literary Studies* 21 (2004): 235.

12 Pender, pp. 241, 234.

13 Pender, p. 241.

14 The United States holds a crucial but often neglected place in Stead's intellectual formation. Apart from living four decades with an intellectual from that country in Blake, Stead visited it initially for almost a year midway through the decade, then again in August 1936, for what became a decade-long sojourn till her return to Europe in December 1946. Presumably, too, its economic and political turmoil in the wake of the Wall Street Crash has ensured it of a prominent place in her thinking long before she disembarked in Boston. Baruch Mendelssohn, one of her most impressive socialist protagonists, sets off for its shore to complete his political education at the end of her first novel, *Seven Poor Men of Sydney* (1934), while her Parisian speculators in *House of All Nations* (1938), set in the early 1930s, keep a sharp weather-eye on the American share market and mounting signs of democracy's failure there. Her two stays in America have, of course, been treated at considerable length in two major biographies: Rowley pp. 181–206, pp. 236–340 and Williams, pp. 115–16, pp. 123–69. Yet even the more detailed account of the two has major shortcomings. Although it describes the main stations in Stead's ideological pilgrimage, and acknowledges her communist affiliations and friendships, this is done in a piece-meal fashion, rather than as a coherent examination of Stead's lifelong intellectual interests. These are secondary to probing the effects of authorial traumas and passionate relationships, to speculating on what was happening in Stead's heart rather than in her head.

seven single-spaced, typed pages and more than 3900 words, was obviously a work in progress. Clearly, too, it was formulated during a period of pronounced political engagement, midway between the Paris Writers' Congress and an enthusiastic trip later in 1936 to Spain, where republican and communist forces were in the ascendancy.[15] This ardour permeates the original—but not a shorter, tidier version of these notes, totalling about 1450 words, which appeared nearly half a century later under the heading: 'It is all a scramble for boodle: Christina Stead sums up America'.[16] The posthumously supplied title is highly revelatory not of Stead's, but of the editor's putative intentions. At a stroke it recasts ideologically tendentious material as a familiar diatribe against American materialism. Certainly the Geering-edited version gives a fair sampling of scenes from the original, but selective omissions downplay its political orientation, and specifically Stead's preoccupation with evidence of smouldering class warfare, which accorded well with the official Comintern line that 'class struggle in America' must assume 'an extremely tense and revolutionary character'.[17] In addition, Geering's text disrupts the argumentative structure and implicit polemic of the original, thereby adding to the apparent innocuousness of Stead's comments, while it obscures a wealth of information about where Stead stood intellectually midway through the 1930s—shortfalls which the ensuing discussion of her original manuscript, the first to date, is intended to redress.

As usual Stead's ideological position and reading of social history are orthodoxly Marxist, though, with her customary flair, she presents her material as a dawning revelation, rather than as a polemical platform. Her uncut text is concerned with ways of seeing or knowing the United States. It distinguishes sharply between the image of the country disseminated popularly, through musicals and especially the cinema,

15 See her MS. account of this sojourn, rpt. in R.G. Geering, 'From the Personal Papers of Christina Stead', *Southerly* 50 (1990): 399–400.

16 *Australian Book Review* 141 (June 1992): 22–24.

17 Third Congress report, qtd. in Fernando Claudin, *The Communist Movement: From Comintern to Cominform*, Brian Pearce, trans. (Harmondsworth: Penguin, 1975), p. 66.

and impressions made by direct contact with American society: at first superficially, then with greater insight. In its posthumously published form, however, the third and often highly judgmental phase of Stead's encounter is largely omitted, thereby rendering many of her remarks, like those in the following passage, banal, inconsequential and politically low key or neutral:

> I come from a commonwealth which loves America, regards it as the rising English-speaking nation, which imitates its fads, whistles its way down every crotchet of tinpan alley and whose constitution is founded on your own, whose labour movement is as strong, whose love of liberty still lingers as fresh and whose schoolchildren dream more of ninepins in the Catskills than of the arrows of Robin Hood. I visited the memorials of your war of liberation with a sort of patriotic fervour.[18]

Why be concerned with Robin Hood in realms so abundant that the people whistle and can indulge in pleasant pastimes? What need of arrows if there is neither oppressive nobility nor social injustice? Moreover, with law-enforcers and blue-collar workers addressing each other as 'buddy' in ensuing scenes, with 'officials of all sorts, amiable and not obsequious', the newly arrived observer is most favourably struck by the contrast with 'the brass hats and brass buttons of Europe'. There hierarchical structures and aristocratic influence predominate, dispensing lessons in fortitude and the iniquity of lucre 'to prevent the workers from wanting food, clothing and warmth'. In contemporary Boston, though perhaps not yet Bellamy's utopian city, all seem to partake of material wellbeing, so that 'the first day … I thought I was in a sort of socialist commonwealth'. Admittedly, the edited text ends this lengthy peroration with a vivid image of poverty: 'Under the beautiful sky of Boston, under its bright lights, beside its fine bay is the rottenest slum in my experience'. But it leaves unanswered the crucial question implicitly raised by the original text: what need has such a land today of the 'love of liberty', that still exists as fresh as in 'stirring times'?

18 *Australian Book Review*, p. 23.

The unedited narrative turns on her realisation of the true state of affairs in this dazzlingly affluent nation. Its opening line evokes Hollywood's glamorous, compelling visions, only to destabilise them in the next breath, foreshadowing the ambivalence and binaries that will shape her account: 'After an extensive night-course on American society under C.B. DeMille and Sam Goldwyn we sailed for the land of boundless importunity'.[19] On arrival the signs are propitious. Instead of racial conflict, she observes African-Americans lunching at ease with whites in a coffee shop, food is plentiful and cheap, public libraries as opulent as palaces, skyscrapers more awesome and beautiful than imagined. As well there are numerous indices of untapped, prodigious energy that makes her think of 'a skyrocket waiting to be let off' or, in the reassuring rhetoric of settler societies holding out the promise of material betterment: 'This is the land of riches, I thought, the only place in the world to bring up children' (23). But celluloid projections and superficial bonhomie deflect attention from a darker side, which is omitted from the published text:

> Later I am to have the impression that a guerrilla civil war is [going] on: cops wear obvious guns, strange vehicles, armoured cars with meurtieres [loop-holes] run through the streets, fighting is going on in the mills at [Salem?][20] and men and women are shot, they are marching to commemorate the anniversary of the death of Sacco and Vanzetti, pickets are everywhere, policemen watch the pickets with detestation.

Then follow vignettes of visits to Lexington, venerated for its fallen patriots ('Americans shed tears at the sight'), to Concord, 'where we meet farmers from the far west' come 'to look at the monument to the

19 Unless otherwise noted, her judgements on America are quoted from National Library of Australia, MS. 4967 folder 79. A rough working text entitled 'AMERICA', it contains occasional typographical and other errors which I have silently corrected in the interests of readability.

20 The text at this point is rendered indecipherable by a Stead deletion. Later in the MS., however, she mentions similar disturbances in Salem, hence my conjectural reading here.

"embattled farmers"', and finally to Walden, ever-linked with memories 'of the famous anarchist Thoreau'. Stead visited the same memorials, she confesses, 'with a sort of patriotic fervour', inspired no doubt by inklings of what she later signals: that Americans will not eternally abide tyranny, that they too have a proud tradition of revolution, and that even the most disadvantaged groups, such as impoverished small farmers, may like herself awaken one day to grim reality, and rise again in a second, and much needed, 'war of liberation'. This was Stead's mindset in 1935.

Undoubtedly Stead is critical of American materialism, of the country's obsession with 'boodle', but as part of a larger analysis of local class structures, and the power of money to create and dissipate tensions in the midst of a worldwide crisis. Although her later novels would convincingly dramatise the pitiless, sordid peaks of this social pyramid, her early jottings scarcely rise above clichés: 'the upper classes moneyseeking, hard, corrupt, cruel, and careless of Maecenas bounties'—with so much wealth a little can be offered to placate opinion and recast oneself as an enlightened philanthropist—as well as 'ruthless, wideawake and class-conscious; self-satisified and determined that everyone will go down before them'. In spite of bank failures, currency depreciation and accumulated losses, the moneyed classes were still 'fooling themselves with hope of an upturn'. Socialism was 'distrusted', while alarmingly the bourgeoisie, in America as in Europe, was determined to maintain its possessions and privileges, if need be, by the most desperate political means, or in the leftist shorthand of the day that flowed glibly from Stead's pen: 'Babbittry and its works are certain foci of fascist infection here'. According to ideologues, such as Stead, this predictable recourse to fascism was the last act of a doomed social order, and a sure sign that 'the universality of the crisis' of advanced capitalism was reaching its climax.[21] Its overthrow was only a matter of time—unless democracy could reinvent itself. And America, which had long led the world in economic and political innovation, had once again become a key laboratory for social experimentation, and the Roosevelt presidency its acid test.

---

21 Letter to Gwen Walker-Smith, dated 24 November 1930, in *A Web of Friendship*, p. 36.

By the time of Stead's arrival in 1935, the Roosevelt administration was nearing the end of its first term in office, the New Deal remained as contentious as ever, but her notes are silent on these matters.[22] Their concern, after all, is with initial impressions, not already-held political convictions; however, they do focus on a closely related subject, American self-imaging, or the popularly disseminated projection versus mundane actuality. 'We do not make pictures', she quotes the local film director Zukor as saying 'with any idea of depicting real life but only as fiction and entertainment'. Her notes of 1935 highlight this gap. They begin with her reportedly expecting 'that Americans are incurably tough, cruel wisecrackers, snipers of the gibe that kills, machine-gunners of quickfire backchat, muckrakers of private potholes and broadcasters of human shame'. Instead she finds her interlocutors surprisingly slow, genial and dull.

> Far from spitting fire, only after going off the deep-end into a pool of thought and coming up and breathing and shaking their ears would they drag into the conversation some half-drowned pun or dead tale, squat-footed, faithful through the years, strangely dumb.

There is little sign of investigative, much less revolutionary, spark here, or of those word-plays, 'rising to fusion-point', which she contends can be 'symptomatic of social earth-tremors'. Rather her description suggests total, loyal immersion in one's environment, as well as blinkered adherence to conventional patterns of thought: in short, a habitual complacency that might explain the failure of the local Communist Party to make greater inroads into the electorate. Such a dumbly trusting people, too, might be taken in by the noisy, self-promoting Roosevelt regime. Nevertheless, Stead is hopeful. The passage concludes with her

22 Elsewhere Stead showed little patience with the president and his New Deal policies, and spoke contemptuously of Roosevelt as 'God's Gift to The Americas', who spoke 'with a lot of fumbling, blundering, anxiety and crossness: he is no longer the guy who jumped cheerfully to power on the hopes of the forgotten man, that's certain', letter to William Blake, dated 28 May 1942, rpt. in Margaret Harris, ed., *Dearest Munx: The Letters of Christina Stead and William J. Blake* (Melbourne: Miegunyah, 2005), p. 142.

treasured image of the country's potential maintained in spite of contradictory impressions: 'But I still think that America, like other raw youths, likes to spar up to [the] bathroom mirror with bristling teeth and gory propositions to get into shape for the business of the day'. The nation she envisages is young, loud and bellicose, but presumably hardly knows either its own strength or where its real interests lie, and has yet to be moulded into its mature shape.

This lack of self-awareness, together with the pressing issues of the day, potentially assured the committed writer of an invigorating, but danger-fraught role, which emerges in a section of her 1935 notes headed 'American Art'. It is immediately characterised as 'the stage the most living outside of Russia'—high praise indeed from a Marxist-Leninist, but anathema during the Cold War and omitted by Geering. The accolade is earned by the way American artists are allegedly responding to the current crisis. Unable to take pride in the nation's consuming quest for wealth, its 'blatant money-religion', liberals are driven 'further and further left', while middle-class artists are left 'without a decent theme but that of the working classes in revolt'. Predictably, too, the working-classes are to be the source of 'American new literature' and, with 'their sympathisers', of 'all fresh intellectual life'. This glib analysis sounds reassuringly doctrinaire; however, it contains Stead's usual caveats. The proletariat as crucial theme is confirmed, but it is not the sole predestined maker of the art of the future, a role which Stead ascribes confrontationally to autocratic, middle-class intellectuals like herself: 'art is dependent on great individuals and artists should learn from each of the peculiar visions of these great [creators]'. The approach to proletarian literature, affirmed here, is refreshingly heterodox, and likely to be driven more by the dictates of individual genius and subject matter than strict adherence to the party line.[23] Stead, however, stops well short of embracing bourgeois subjectivity, or its fallacious aspirations. Instead she ticks off the fata morganas that have failed it:

23 On Stead's own early treatment of the proletariat in fiction see Michael Ackland, '"What a history is that? What an enigma ... ?", Imagination, Destiny and Socialist Imperatives in Christina Stead's *Seven Poor Men of Sydney*', *Southerly* 68 (2008): 189–212.

'the dream of endless wealth (stock market) and of the presidency (old families coming in)', as well as the risible pap of Hollywood ('so foolish that directors admit they do not try to portray contemporary life'). Only the promise of the proletariat remains undiminished: 'the working-classes offer an ideology, a hope, a dream, you offer nonesuch and the middle-classes cannot live by a savings-bank account alone'. Perhaps in 1935, caught up in the rush of epochal events and surrounded by communist comrades, the fragility of this dream may not have been self-evident. But who was to say that it had any more substance than former, 'slowly fading' ones? And who could guarantee that American society might not yet offer other, and more inspiring, narratives to its people than the foreordained dictatorship of the proletariat?

Asserting artistic independence did not of course preclude dramatising and projecting a thoroughly orthodox viewpoint. Her notes offer, she claimed, local life in the raw: 'these reverses and obverses met me in the first week in Boston'. Nonetheless, the depiction of glaring social contrasts is too consistent to be purely random. A glittering military pageant is played off against furtive figures from the invisible, but swelling army of destitute African-Americans, 'buying tainted meat secretly at dusk from unpainted wagon', gleaming 'Wall-Street ranges, miles of vertical glass' are juxtaposed with drab lines of 'workers waiting for morning-call', and the vaulting, technological brilliance of Brooklyn Bridge, together with 'endless viaducts', soaring, purposeful, joining lives and dreams, set like 'ribs against the sky', yields to a climactic image of human misery and alienation 'at the foot of the uptown buildings, a whiteskinned youthful suicide in blue shirt and grey pants, a working-boy'. Far removed from Hollywood's hollow fables, this is as much the art of honest indignation as Stead's earlier exclamation: 'how is it possible to have unrest poverty and misery in such a rich country', followed by a vignette which contrasts the entrancing beauty of Boston with 'the rottenest slum in my experience'. With heavy brush-strokes, too, she paints the well-to-do as increasingly uneasy in their affluence: 'They are a very tall, fat and muscular, sanguine race but they look troubled. Perhaps the welter of working-races underneath them give them anxious nights'. A universal glumness, she insists, pervades 'the faces of all middle and upper class America'. As does dread of the proletariat. 'Your successful middle-classes display a great hatred of the workers, a strange burning bitterness … They have a feeling that this country is shackled by economic mishaps, as I have'. The signs spelling out a failed, as well as doomed, social order are in the streets and on the faces for anyone to see. Class conflict seems bound to erupt with great violence after long suppression; there is more than 'just a little steam coming out' of the deep fissures of this nation which she twice likens deterministically to Vesuvius.

Yet all Stead's views were not neatly formatted to meet the party line. Though decrying the 'acute worship of Mammon' as 'horrible, revolting', she could nevertheless claim it partook of 'something marvellous, incredible as the gold halls of Babylon'—the artist fascinated with superabundant manifestations of great wealth, who gave posterity 'A Day at the Redshields' and 'A Stuffed Carp', was not to be denied.[24] More disconcerting from an orthodox point of view was the potential contradiction that exists between her highly critical descriptions of America's social disparities, and her scarcely concealed admiration for the almost boundless possibilities of the land and its people. 'If this country ever gets its foot on the starter, what speed there will be: for strangely enough one has the impression that all this production, organisation, machinery is preparation for a long and great journey'. This was unseemly admiration for 'a democracy created by capitalism' on the bedrock of imperial colonies. It recurs, however, and at times even more outspokenly, for there was something intrinsically appealing about the new country that did not conform easily to doctrinaire clichés. Moreover, despite Lincoln Steffens' famous claim that in the Soviet Union he had seen the future and it worked, his own native land, as usual, seemed to hold the key to humanity's further unfolding, so that even a cynically inclined Stead, moved by America's riches and technology, could write:

> One wishes for eternal youth in this land (Central Park West lined with giant apartment houses) to see what will happen

24 These incidents are recounted in respectively *The Salzburg Tales* (1934) and *The House of All Nations* (1938).

> next. It makes one feel that life has only just started and that the normal span of human life should be about 200 years.

Then, as if to counterbalance this heretical enthusiasm, not dampened by the conspicuous fortunes abutting Central Park, Stead offers a self-placatory afterthought, jammed in between single-spaced lines: 'art should flourish here when labour or socialist party gains ground. Corruption cannot produce good literature'. But neither could socialist dogma, or tamely adhering to the party line. The tension is obvious in Stead's prose, to herself as well as posterity, and her experiences with the American Communist Party would do nothing to lessen it.[25]

America, as Stead rightly intuited in 1935, was likely to mark a turning point in her own life and the history of mankind, though much still needed to change. Unabashedly she wished for social dislocation and hardship, with the certitude born of Marxist-Leninist dogma: 'no labour party will emerge till your middle-classes are poorer still till great general strikes have shaken the country'. Also her unfolding reflections mirror, and thereby offer mute homage to, the greater dialectical process thought to impel world history. The thesis of naïve first impressions is answered by an antithetical vision of social rupture and impending eruption:

> Vulgar civil war for money between boodle-barons and two-gun poachers and bitter class-war with usual cruel fratricidal struggles between workers, union and non-union, lay and police not to mention ever-present terror of black-white struggle: trembled in Harlem to see citadel of the oppressed, early Americans herded together to whom uptown seems faraway.

A reader will search in vain for such savagely forthright verdicts in Geering's version of 'America'. Fittingly, in the original, the ensuing synthesis appropriates Americans' abiding addiction with, their 'heart-dream' of,

25 On the ideological dilemmas encountered there, and their literary consequences, see Michael Ackland, 'Christina Stead and the Politics of Covert Statement', *Mosaic* 43 (2010): 127–42.

'people who "get away" with it'. So, too, may the United States—if the proletariat gains control.

> What will this country be like if it ever gets away with it: what will the working classes of this country be like if they ever sweep to power: one almost fears to think of this country free and with everyone rich and no race distinction.

This is what it would take for America to 'get its foot on the starter', to undertake the 'long and great journey', for which it has long been preparing, towards a socialist utopia.

Gazing as a new arrival in the mid-1930s on what she adjudged 'the finest modern country in the world', Stead's excitement, hope and curiosity were almost palpable. Here perhaps she would witness the birth of the socialist homeland of her dreams, most likely she thought 'from south, middle west, Pacific seaboard'. Her heady anticipation had been shared by many, including Friedrich Engels forty years earlier, and she would almost certainly have been familiar with his sentiments:

> In such a country, continually renewed waves of advance followed by equally certain set-backs are inevitable. Only the advancing waves are always becoming more powerful, the set-backs less paralysing, and on the whole the thing moves forward all the same. But this I consider certain: the purely bourgeois basis, with no pre-bourgeois swindle behind it, the corresponding colossal energy of the development … will one day bring about a change which will astonish the whole world. Once the Americans get started it will be with an energy and violence compared with which we in Europe shall be mere children.[26]

Engels had been right about the qualified advances, about the land's capacity for stunningly energetic development; however, the outcome was by no means certain. Capitalist democracy would not exit

26 Quoted without source in John Strachey, 'The American Scene', *Left Review* 1 (June 1935): 358.

peacefully, and America's citizens were still haunted, according to Stead, by 'the dream of material wealth and social standing'. Even she, though clad in Marxist armour, felt its spell. Staid Boston recalled too vividly English class divisions, with 'poor workers very much underneath'. But in New York she felt the 'mystic might of Rockefeller Centre', and Radio City appeared to her 'like Jacobs ladder'. In 1935 she took stock of the known facts and asked herself candidly: 'What will be the end? Here, as elsewhere I a pilgrim and patriot of your country's patriotism, see that liberty will have to be fought for all over again'. The pilgrim would see her share of fights, but never her version of the Celestial City, and very soon would find herself in a deep Slough of Despond. Decades later her first impressions and revisions would be bequeathed to a nation out of sympathy with her ideology, and edited to suit the times. Stead's political engagement was once again obscured, as well as a crucial phase in her intellectual development, while a manuscript was temporarily assigned to archival oblivion which could have helped explain why the aging author, looking back on American in the 1930s, could exclaim with more than a trace of her former eagerness: 'the whole of society was in ferment, nobody really knew which way the society was going. Oh it was a terrific epoch, very thrilling'.[27]

27 Ann Whitehead, 'Christina Stead: An Interview', *Australian Literary Studies* 6 (1974): 244.

15

The 'American Dilemma': Christina Stead's Cold War Anatomy

Fiona Morrison

In previous work on Christina Stead's posthumously published novel, *I'm Dying Laughing*, I have been concerned with the notion of 'legibility' with respect to the effects of expatriate production and reception and the related matters of gender, genre and figure. This work has been organised around the figure of the female renegade and her outlaw texts, and grounded in readings of Marxist political history and terminology as well as feminist readings of genre, specifically Menippean satire. My interest in the category of the 'readable' or 'legible' acknowledges the rhetorical, spatial and temporal complexities which are the cause *and* the effect of a mobile authorship, in Stead's case a mobile authorship attendant on not just one transpacific expatriate relocation, but a lifetime of constant mobility between Australia, England, Europe and America. This paper seeks to think more specifically about how Stead's work hails or addresses the question of America, and the effect therefore of the interaction between nation, genre, figure and mode in *I'm Dying Laughing*. The nature of Stead's speaking position as a commentator and critic of America and radical Americans is crucial to this focus, as is a further consideration of satire as a genre and mode with a particularly American trajectory and meaning, and its place in a larger history of revolutionary writing. Emerging from this consideration of America and Menippean satire, Stead's dialogue with Dreiser's *An American Tragedy* also becomes newly suggestive, especially in light of her dialogue with American political commitment, literary genealogy and textual practice.

Many contemporary categories that describe transnational experience are extremely useful in allowing us to consider Stead's body of work as a whole: the 'cosmopolitan' and the 'nomad' are both figures that prompt productive engagement with the complexity of her work. However, I am concerned that these kinds of conceptualisations of the 'trans' experience fail to fully register one significant fact: Christina Stead, with her partner Bill Blake (formerly Blech), had wrought a mobile home out of their consistent and persistent identification as socialist 'fellow travellers'.[1] For Stead and Blake, classical Marxist theory (economic theory properly read, well-understood and endlessly discussed) provided a mobile discursive and political home. It was the international system of ideas that supported Stead and Blake and kept them ideologically afloat and properly affiliated through the Hitler–Stalin pact and during an increasingly marginalised and seemingly homeless movement through England and Europe after 1946 and 1956. The very tenacity of Stead and Blake's political loyalty speaks volumes about the importance of Marxist theory as the fundamental identificatory set of co-ordinates which could not be repealed, even in the context of a restless and increasingly difficult search for congenial peers, readers, raw materials and publishing markets during the Cold War. Betrayal was seen as the road to bohemia, and this was not an option for Stead and Blake—this way anarchy and disorientation—the cold, dark and meaningless outside of theory and proper affiliation.[2]

1 'Fellow traveller' is a term used by Trotsky in *Literature and Revolution* (1924) to identify those in the Soviet Union who did not actively support its Bolshevik Revolution of 1917, but who were not against it either. In the Soviet 1920s, the term recognised the artist's need for freedom and his importance of links with cultural traditions. The increasing political importance of socialist realism meant that by the end of the 1920s, 'fellow travellers' were seen as almost counter-revolutionary. Outside the Soviet Union the term was widely used in the Cold War era as a political label to refer to any person who, while not thought to be an actual member of the party, was sympathetic to their aims.

2 Kate Webb provides a provocative reading of 'bohemia' in Stead's work. Kate Webb, 'Nothing is Lost', available at: katewebb.wordpress.com/out-of-obscurity-christina-stead [Accessed 14 January 2010].

As she claimed in her later interviews, Stead was a leftist, but not of the 'joining variety.'[3] In the mid-thirties she used the phrase 'not in, but alongside' to describe Stanley Burnshaw's relationship to the CPUSA. This phrase describes her own position very well, since Stead was also inclined to use the rhetoric of 'sides' when it came to both politics and writing—'taking sides', 'alongside' and 'sidelong' all appear as descriptions of affiliation and rhetorical position.[4] To sustain the degree of observation required for authorship, Stead claimed that the writer must be able to 'see both sides',[5] and the option of 'alignment' over full membership allowed her to move opportunistically between the inside and outside of the Communist Party and other left-wing circles in America and elsewhere.[6] 'Alongside' is an elaboration of a marginal position that allows for imaginative mobility, and it is also a term that indicates a *strategic* knowledge of classificatory boundary or limit. As an Australian expatriate who had come to America via England and Europe, Stead's location on both political and national margins (inside and outside the nation and the party) enabled her to scrutinise the hypocrites, the renegades and the 'radical chic' of American radical politics, as well as pursue her enduring naturalist's interest in exploitation, tyranny and monomania and the energetic individuals

---

3 Joan Lidoff, 'Interview with Christina Stead', in *Christina Stead* (New York: Ungar, 1982), p. 220.

4 Letter to Stanley Burnshaw, 29 September 1938, Burnshaw Collection, Harry Ransom Humanities Research Centre, University of Texas, Austin, Folder 1. Stead uses this phrase to describe Burnshaw, who was also not a member of the CPUSA, and her humourous repetition of the phrase may refer to the fact that, in 1938, Bill Blake was momentarily a member of the party.

5 This phrase is from 'Uses of the Many-Charactered Novel', a paper Stead gave at the Third National Writers' Conference for the League of American Writers, 1939. Stead, Christina, 'Uses of the Many Charactered Novel', in *Christina Stead: Selected Fiction and Nonfiction*, R.G. Geering and A. Segerberg eds (St Lucia: University of Queensland Press, 1994), p. 198.

6 In a footnote to information about Bill's short stint as a member of the party (January 1938–August 1939) Rowley includes a diary note from Stead: 'Myself: at a loss. Can't join branch for status reasons: where to go to get social background. No one cares! Will have to 'join something' v. soon'. 4 January 1938, Hazel Rowley, *Christina Stead: A Biography* (Melbourne: Heinemann, 1993), p. 590.

who exemplified these things. From her mobile home in theoretically sound and eminently rational Marxism, Stead could and did produce an anatomy (a term that Northrop Frye prefers to the alternative Menippean satire) of the behaviour of American radicals both inside and outside the Party (or 'the besieged fortress') and inside and outside the nation, after 1945 for the most part.

After a year in New York in 1935–36, Christina Stead had commented in a letter to Stanley Burnshaw that 'the whole spirit of New York is opposed to the creative mind'[7], yet it was New York, (Bill Blake's birthplace) that became the obvious place for a retreat from Europe as World War II closed in, and it was the place in which she found congenial publishers and produced an enormous amount of work from the late Popular Front years until the end of World War II (1937–45). In the years after the publication of *The House of All Nations* (1938), America and Americans became the central matter and source of productive inspiration (or indeed irritation) for five of her subsequent major novels. *I'm Dying Laughing*, the last American novel, was begun in the late 1940s, worked on throughout the 1950s and a little in the 1960s, abandoned as an unfinished *magnum opus* in the 1970s and heroically assembled from drafts and published posthumously in 1986. It is a work that displays the material complexities of the multiple locations of production and reception consistent with Stead's expatriate career and political affiliations, as well as the deracination and disorientation of the expatriate left-wing writer during the Cold War.

In 1935–36, Blake and Stead had made firm connections with Bill's friends and associates from the Lower East Side, including the *New Masses* editors, many of whom were also 'fellow travellers'. From 1937, on their return, they became involved with another CPUSA front, the League of American Writers, which they continued to support faithfully until its demise in 1942. The League was inaugurated during the Popular Front period in 1935 and although it looked to the international scene and was aware of the Soviet recommendations about socialist realism,

7 C.S. to Stanley Burnshaw, 2 October 1936, in Christina Stead, *Web of Friendship: Selected Letters, 1928–1973*, R.G. Geering ed. (Pymble: Angus and Robertson, 1992), p. 67

the League was focused on building a native (read anti-modernist) American literary tradition, with Popular Front heroes like Mark Twain in mind. It is interesting that Stead was proximate to this work, and was herself turning toward both satire and an obsession with accurately recording American idiom.[8] Stead's idiosyncratic brand of naturalistic satire began to emerge in 1938 with *The House of All Nations*, and in 1940 with *The Man Who Loved Children*. This move increases in focus and direction with the satirical anatomisation of America during the later war years and early Cold War: *Letty Fox* (1944), *A Little Tea, A Little Chat* (1948) and *I'm Dying Laughing* (begun 1949, published posthumously 1986).

Stead's development of the kind of satiric anatomy that characterises the mode of her American novels occurred against a backdrop of discussions about the responsibility of the revolutionary artist. While still in France in June 1935, Stead had written a report of the First International Writer's Congress for the Defense of Culture, which was published as 'The Writer's Take Sides' in *Left Review* in July of that year. Here she claimed that the role of the author in Popular Front struggle was to 'enter the political arena, take lessons from workmen and use their pen as the scalpel lifting the living tissues, cutting through the morbid tissues, of the social anatomy.'[9] In 1937, she became very influenced by Ralph Fox's *The Novel and the People*, which supported the radical possibilities of Rabelais, Cervantes and satire for revolutionary writers.[10] Fox was

---

8 Christina Stead, 'Uses of the Many-Charactered Novel', in Geering and Segerberg, eds, *Christina Stead: Selected Fiction and Nonfiction*, p. 198. The position on the array of characters speaks most tellingly about *The House of All Nations* (1938), written two years before. Stead, interested in the drama of conflict and the vicissitudes of the survival instinct, understood and valued disorientation and strangeness, as well as attack and contradiction: 'this form of novel is all a sidelong critique, and mostly ironic ... Here, it is not easy to take sides: the reader must draw his own conclusions from the diverse material, as from life itself'. Stead's analysis uncannily resembles a description of Menippean satire ('causes for laughter, anger, action') and heteroglossic textuality.

9 Christina Stead, 'The Writers' Take Sides', *Left Review* 1.2 (1935): 454.

10 Ralph Fox, *The Novel and the People* (London: Lawrence and Wishart, 1937), p. 95; Hazel Rowley, 'Christina Stead: Politics and Literature in the Radical Years, 1935–1942', *Meridian* 8.2 (1989): 149–59; Hazel Rowley, *Christina Stead: A*

particularly (and unusually for his *milieu*) interested in the importance of the presence of an energetic villain in revolutionary narrative, and in *The House of All Nations* (1937–38) Stead experimented with this energetic gangster figure (e.g. Jules Bertillion, the 'glorious swindler'). It was carrying the manuscript for *The House of All Nations*, and in flight from the collapse of The Travellers' Bank at the hands of the 'real-life' model for the 'glorious swindler' that Stead and Blake returned to American in 1937. The combination of firsthand experience of unstable capital and larger Popular Front issues of national identity, writing and class politics were certainly on Stead's mind when she sailed into Boston. 'Uses of the Many-Charactered Novel', a paper Stead gave for the League of American Writers two years later in June 1939, demonstrates the ways in which she drew these 1930s threads together in preparation for tackling the vexing and fascinating question of America.[11]

In an unpublished document titled 'America', presumably written soon after arriving in Boston (and later published in 1992 in *Australian Book Review* as 'A Scramble for Boodle'), Stead produced a reading of America and Americans that culminates in an argument for an independent American literary tradition. This document is a very strange one, bearing the disorienting marks of hasty writing and idiosyncratic editing. Stead's speaking position switches rather abruptly from an explicitly first-person account of arrival in a strange new land to the creation of an explicit external subject of address 'you'. This 'you' seems to be a generalised address to the American middle-class and excludes the working class, artists or liberals. The article is also one in which Stead erases entirely her own expatriate choices with respect to Australia and artistic production, and this reads as a rather dizzying combination of autobiographical self-assertion and equivalent self-

---

Biography, (Melbourne: Heinemann, 1993), pp. 224–25. Rowley tells us that Ralph Fox liked Rabelais and Cervantes and that he thought 'the satirical novella is a powerful instrument in political struggle, like the figure of the pen as scalpel'.

11 In 1939 the League of American Writers had 750 members. They held the Third National Writers' congress in New York in June, 1939. It was here Stead gave her paper about the importance of 'the novel of strife'.

effacement.[12] Stead initially acknowledges her Australian origins through a series of positive colonial parallels with America, but it is her experience of European politics, especially French, that forms the basis of political analysis.[13] Stead's speaking position indicates that she comes to America from Australia via England and France, so although her autobiographical opening stresses her Australianness, her analysis of America derives from international experience. The European-Marxist perspective on America is that it has resources, energy and idealism but that a long-term political program or system is lacking. Without a system or any political theoretical support, American new world energy is focused on survival and money in the crudest terms: 'it is all a scramble for boodle and nothing else'.[14] Marxist theory would offer the necessary revolutionary program for the American middle-classes, and the instabilities and crudity (*the scramble*) of New World capitalism *(boodle*—the gangster obsession with money) would be appropriately controlled and directed.[15] Stead argues (and the argument is as disjointed and peculiar as this published version of the text) that the scramble for boodle and the worship of Mammon had meant that the American artists, 'robbed ... of their natural right—worship of their own country' (24),[16] had fled abroad and its liberals had stepped to the Left. This meant that the middle-classes were rudderless and the

---

12 Christina Stead, 'It is all a Scramble for Boodle: Christina Stead Sums up America', *Australian Book Review* 141.6 (1992): 22–24.

13 These parallels find an extension but also a counterpoint in Stead's 1973 interview with Anne Whitehead, where differences between Australia and America are stressed. Anne Whitehead, 'Interview with Christina Stead', *Australian Literary Studies* 6 (1974): 230–48.

14 Stead, 'It is all a Scramble', p. 23.

15 Although a colonial politics of Australian–American primitive socialism might seem an interesting contrast also, Stead does not deploy it. She cites America's great natural wealth, beauty and energy where, by contrast, Australia was built on a radical legend and an emphasis on colonial survival, it was also avowedly a labour commonwealth in Stead's eyes, and a killing continent—the Australian outback is described by Stead as littered with corpses of brave explorers. Anne Whitehead, pp. 230–48.

16 Stead, 'It is all a Scramble', p. 24.

only interesting 'theme' or story belonged to the troublesome working classes, whose political work was quite clear. Stead concludes that the American middle-class artists, possessed of this rich and fertile land, should ignore European art and 'write and think *in American*, think in the vulgate of valours'.[17] It is in this context that Stead references Sinclair Lewis' portrait of Babbitry, which satirically represented as a kind of 'fascist infection' in America. Her reference indicates her early awareness of this well-known American humourist of the 1920s; in 1937, Stead was already thinking in broad terms about the homegrown American tradition in terms of the importance of American idiom, and the critical and satirical reach of the American humourist.[18]

I'm Dying Laughing particularly engages the American drive for money and success (so 'brutally outspoken and crassly advertised', 23) as a crucial component of national identity AND as the most significant problem for radical activism. The desire for success, even notoriety, and fear of failure and its attendant unthinkable obscurity, is thematised as the central contradiction of the left-wing 'American dilemma.' In 1973, Stead offered these historical co-ordinates for *I'm Dying Laughing*:

> It was all about the passion—I use passion in almost the religious sense—of two people, two Americans, New Yorkers, in the thirties. They were politically minded. They went to Hollywood. They came to Europe to avoid the McCarthy trouble. Of course, they were deeply involved. And then, they lived around Europe, oh, in a wild and exciting extravagant style. *But there was nothing to support it.* At the same time

17 Stead, 'It is all a Scramble', p. 24. One of the characteristics that grants the Vulgate its 'valour' is that it is translated from the original languages and not just a translation of a translation. The Vulgate Old Testament is the first Latin version translated directly from the Hebrew rather than from the Greek. The phrase indicates the importance of using a national idiom close to its source. Stead demonstrates her naturalistic commitment to a 'direct translation' of American idiomatic speech in *The Man Who Loved Children,* and it is very evident also in *Letty Fox, A Little Tea, A Little Chat* and *I'm Dying Laughing.*

18 *Babbitt* is a novel by Sinclair Lewis first published in 1922. It is a famous satire of American middle-class society in the 1920s.

> they wanted to be on the side of angels, good Communists, good people, and also to be very rich. Well, of course … they came to a bad end.[19]

Although *I'm Dying Laughing* satirises the contradictory desire to be 'on the side of angels … and also very rich', Stead's use of passion 'in almost the religious sense' indicates a tragic key. The lack of ideological strength or system to support the pressures of the American radical dilemma required a Menippean combination of satiric and tragic treatment indicated in the phrase: 'of course … they came to a bad end', Emily Wilkes, the central character of *I'm Dying Laughing*, is the representative American: a radical, a writer, a mid-Westerner, an idiomatic humourist, a passionate rebel—full of energy, genius and potential but lacking discipline. In body, in speech and in text she is as large, generative, greedy and heterodox as America itself. And although *I'm Dying Laughing* engages the Menippean and carnival potential of the heterodox, the loquacious, the grotesque and the improperly combined, Stead's is, in the final analysis, a tragic portrait of the disintegration, in exile, of the Emily's heterodox and contradictory self, in fatal need of an orthodox theoretical structure and 'hold' that might stabilise her anywhere.

When Emily Wilkes first sees her future husband, Stephen Howard, they are both on their way to the Writers' Congress in Paris in 1935, and she is talking (and what talking it is), busily explaining the contradictions at the heart of her country:

> It's sickening for Americans to be living on handouts, when we're the richest country and believe in the survival of the fittest. None of it makes sense, and that's our dilemma. We won and we won and we've lost and there's no reason for it. The American dilemma is the essence of America.[20]

And while the American dilemma is the essence of America, she says, American humour is the quintessential American reaction to the

19 Lidoff, 'An Interview with Christina Stead', , p. 181. My emphasis.

20 Christina Stead, *I'm Dying Laughing* (London: Virago, 1986), p. 17.

contradictions of their national situation. In the following extract, Emily Wilkes defines this specifically American humour as founded in hypocrisy and irony, and against the British and French comic traditions:

> Well, that's the bitter truth, the savagery of life which staggers you, keeps you rooted to the spot and your outcries stop your breath; and yet it is wildly out of line with all our ideals, humanity, peace, brotherly love, do unto others, until you laugh, shout, you understand your own simplicity and wickedness and denseness and greed—that's American humour. It's better than Daumier with lumpen-proletariat gargoyles gaping. You listen to any Hollywood dialogue in a modern film and you'll hear such a mash of good sense, brashness, earthy wit, impudence—that's American wisdom, that's our humour. It's not *les bon mots* and *le raffine,'* she said (with a strong home accent), 'it's not hissing the double entendre through thin lips, it's not like Punch, hitting a flour-filled sock, no hit no mark; it bites to the bone; its not like satire which is just needling someone you're afraid to touch; American humour is another way of seeing the truth; and what a vision! It isn't giggles or smut, it isn't anecdotes about baby-sitters and chars and Uncle Brown's habits; it is homespun godlike truth stalking in from the plains and the tall timber, coonskin and deerhide, with a gun to disturb our little home comforts. (20)

Emily's states early in her career that 'I'm a humourist: humourists are always pessimists. They're reactionaries: because they see that every golden cloud has a black lining; so why get a stomach ulcer' (17). Here Emily acknowledges the Marxist concern about comedy and comic genres—that they have great energy and commercial power, but that they leave the political *status quo* untouched. Early in their Parisian exile, Stephen Howard, now Emily's husband, responds to her struggle with the choice between serious revolutionary writing and humourous commercial work in this way: 'You see things otherwise. You say your say in your own humane way and luckily for us it's a selling way and we don't have to starve in a shanty, while you're revolving the novel of the century' (116). He later says of her serious plans that 'tragedies belong to the bad old world, which was black. You're a real American, the new world' (212)—comedy sells, and it is naturally American, says the loyal party man and patriotic American. The 'novel of the century' that communist Emily wants to write is not, however, comic, it is tragic:

> I've got an idea. I'm going to write a horror book, about the most dreaded figure in American society, a failure ... and the terrible aching poignancy of knowing, in a way, for they know, it's all a mistake, and these hectic drab lives are living for nothing, because the country's mindless, and life here is without a system; and it could be better ... We're all pressed down on every side, like fish at the bottom of the ocean, as Mike Gold says, with dollars, dollars ... (149)

Emily's book of horror will satirise American commitment to the cult of the wealthy and successful individual to the detriment of any equitable social system, and in this sense Emily's book is an outline of the Menippean satire that satirises her; a satire that launches a critique of the contradictions at the heart of American political, national and gender identity, and the way in which the left-wing America, 'pressed down on every side' by the demands of capital, is vulnerable to corruption. Instead of writing commercially successful 'Toonerville Tales' (her 'humourist' stories of her family and small town American life) Emily wants to use satire as the power of rational superiority gesturing at declining, corrupted others and produce a sustained critique of the American radical movement, 'the way I see it and what's wrong with it', a political ambition outside the traditional orbit of female authorship:

> I'd try to put a finger on essential human weaknesses; the ignorance and self-indulgence that has led us into Bohemia ... I ought to say how everything becomes its opposite not only outside the besieged fortress but within (71–72).

Emily declares that: 'It would be for the real rebels, the real labour movement, against all vampires who take all that's best in the world, even the name of the most sacred causes and use them for promotion; shepherds killing and eating the lambs' (72). This is, in fact, the Howards' story—they become the vampires and traitorous shepherds.

While Emily aspires to write this satiric-tragic text of radical revolutionary proportions (113) in the style of Dreiser's *An American Tragedy* (350 ff.) her addiction to luxury requires her to continue with her humourist pieces, linking gender, genre and pecuniary motive in her commodification of her own regional origins and class position. When Emily arrives in Paris in the early Cold War years, in flight from party expulsion and McCarthyism at home, one of her many ideas for a new book concerns an autobiographical sketch of herself—'Emily Wilkes, in *Double or Nothing*.' She is encouraged to make this choice because of her 'fame, however decayed, shot through and mistaken' (191), and she sees increasing satiric and textual capital in her own grotesque notoriety. Emily suggests to Stephen that she has an idea about something in her 'best style' that would *sell*. In her lengthy synopsis of another project—'The Sorrows of a Really Fat Person Like Me' (301)—Emily's relentless commodification of her political and personal life slides schizophrenically and incoherently between 'she' and 'me', between subject and object and between public and private. That Emily takes her own monstrosity (of text, body size, region and gender) as a subject for a humorous allegory of American dilemmas ('A typical Middle-Western Mamma, with a beer-barrel waist, overstuffed dewlaps, panting about looking for an ice-cream soda' (310) is an outright reification of herself and a literary move that signals her most serious Cold War alienation and disorientation. Her narcissistic and masochistic textual self-framing is a desperate bid (or gamble—*double or nothing*) to keep earning, and it has drawn her away from all functioning collectivity and filiation—personal, national or political.

The figure of Emily as an isolated figure, laughing wildly on the steps of the Forum Romanum as the pages of her great work scatter to the wind concludes Stead's cautionary tale about loyalty, limit and the breaking of filiation. The laughter is tragic but takes the reader back to the early American humourist, and reminds us that *I'm Dying Laughing* is also a deeply desiring portrait of creativity and individuality. *I'm Dying*

Laughing delights in the tremendous life force—the sheer linguistic force—that is the ungovernable American, Emily Wilkes—her excesses, her transgressions of order, of size and speech, her disrespect for the law and her overproduction are as much desired as they are censured. It follows that Stead also had this position on America, and the difference is that she was never in the party, and was tied to larger codes of belonging than the merely national to which she remained loyal. Her relentless serio-comic portrait of corrupt American socialists, written from the 'alongside' position of theoretical stability and strategic alignment was for 'the real rebels' and 'the real labour movement', who were also to be found both inside and outside America.

16

An Imperishable Spring? Stow's *Tourmaline*, the Cold War and the Phenomenon of the Star

Kerry Leves

Randolph Stow's *Tourmaline* begins with the death of one of the town's inhabitants, Billy Bogada. Billy's relatives go to Tom Spring's store and bring back a packing case to serve as a coffin. There are two words on the packing case: 'SPRING—it said. PERISHABLE.'[1] This detail miniaturises the thematic if not the narrative arc, but in reverse. It is not the 'perishable spring' of mortality that the Tourmaliners desire (who does?) but the imperishable spring of youth and beauty that the novel concentrates in the figure of Michael Random—in a time that appeared to be all about perishability.

Like *A Canticle for Leibovitz* (1959) by the American Walter Miller, and *On The Beach* (1957) by the Australian Nevil Shute, Stow's *Tourmaline* (1963) addresses its times. These novels share a historical provenance that is framed by Cold War anxieties: about science; about the earth's being rendered unliveable by nuclear war; about biological morphing as an effect of nuclear radiation. In the 1950s and 1960s, the latter was usually called 'mutation', as in the later popular graffito: 'Mutate now and avoid the rush.'

Stow, who says that in National Service in the 1950s he 'first collided with the facts of life in the atomic age',[2] peppers the text of *Tourma-*

1 Randolph Stow, *Tourmaline* (St Lucia: University of Queensland Press, 2002 [1963]), p. 3. All quotations from *Tourmaline* are from this edition.

2 John Hetherington, 'Randolph Stow: Young Man In No Hurry', in *Forty-Two*

line with allusions to apocalyptic events that have already happened in the world from which the former goldmining town is cut off by desert; where a monthly visit from a supply truck provides the only connection to anywhere else. *Tourmaline*'s Conradian narrator, The Law (i.e. the town's policeman, or former policeman) writes of 'the terrible danger' outside Tourmaline that 'fills [his] sleep with images of wind and annihilation' (38). When the supply truck delivers an envoy from the world outside—the dehydrated, grossly sunburnt water diviner, Michael—to the townspeople's care, some of Michael's first words to his carers are about the world 'out there': he describes it as 'hell', as 'chaos', and when pressed for details, says, 'Wild beasts are loose on the world' (39)—this character's first echo of the prophetic language of the King James' Bible. The young part-Aboriginal woman Deborah, asked why Michael doesn't want her home-baked bread, replies: 'The wheat's sick … Like everything out there' (108). When Deborah's lover and, possibly, father, Kestrel, returns to town after a trip away, he brings three henchmen recruited 'out there', one of whom is described as having 'no nose or mouth; only teeth' (197). Thus through the accumulation of tiny but telling details, Stow builds a picture of a world in which both civilisation and nature have gone, as Michael might have said, to hell. And the road to hell in the early 1960s was that of nuclear war and nuclear fallout. The total absence of rain in Tourmaline indicates climatic modification, even 'climatological destruction', which appeared, in 1959, on the American Protestant Evangelist Dr Billy Graham's list of 'absolute weapons' that threatened humanity: also on Dr Graham's list were 'biological' and 'chemical' weapons, along with 'the hydrogen bomb'.[3]

In a revivalist meeting that allegedly drew a crowd of '125 000 persons' to Times Square, New York, in 1957, Graham gave a reason why the times were so perilous: 'sin … a thousand moral and social sins … we have broken the ten commandments … we have broken the

---

Faces (London: Angus & Robertson, 1963), p. 245.

3 Billy Graham, *Sun-Herald*, 2 February 1959, cited in Judith Smart, 'The Evangelist as Star: The Billy Graham Crusade in Australia, 1959', *Journal of Popular Culture* 33.1 (Summer 1999): 165.

laws of God … that's why we have wars in the world'. The evangelist exhorted his audience not only to 'tell the world tonight that our trust is not in our stockpile of atomic bombs and hydrogen bombs but in almighty God', but also to 'frankly admit that we have sinned'. [4] In 1959, Graham led a 'crusade' in Australia that drew three million people to his revivalist meetings, in various cities, over a fifteen-week period. The aim of Dr Graham's 'crusade' was to induce people to 'receive God in their hearts' by making 'a decision for Christ',[5] a redemptive project for the individual and the world. Graham's diagnosis and treatment might be read productively against the water diviner Michael's diagnosis of Tourmaline's ills—'Get rid of the grog, and so on. A—a Utopia we could have, with the water … I could save this place' (67)—and his cure, which starts with the prayer: 'Take charge of my life, father, I am close to breaking' (186).

Graham was a brilliant orator, with a wide vocal and emotional range and a compelling delivery. The Law describes Michael's as: 'A voice like an incantation. A shaman's voice' (157). Elsewhere the text negotiates similarities between Michael's and Graham's techniques for eliciting acknowledgment of 'sin'. In Chapter 11 Michael calls Deborah, who has earlier flirted with him and been rejected, an 'animal', as well as by the Biblical epithet, 'harlot'. The text describes Michael as 'burn[ing] in zeal and exaltation', as he breaks down Deborah's resistance, in order to 'win [her] for God'. When she lies, 'weakly sobbing, at his feet' (147–49), he exacts affirmations from her that resemble a little the 'decision for Christ' that Graham routinely asked his audiences to make, towards the close of his meetings, after his fiery yet highly structured sermons:

> 'Will you come to God?' he asked her.
> She could not speak.
> 'Do you confess you've been a sinner?'
> 'Yes,' she whispered. 'Yes.'
> 'Will you come to God?'
> 'Yes.' (149)

4 Graham, *Times Square Story*, Dir. David J. Cazalet. Chancel Films, 1957.

5 Graham, *Sydney Morning Herald,* 25 April 1959, cited in Smart, p. 166.

Stow's text ensures that Deborah's conversion experience does not go unchallenged. The Law writes, 'although I could see he had brought her happiness in the end, it was difficult not to feel that she had been brutally humiliated' (172).

Readers may note that eighteen-year-old Deborah's main offences have been (a) that she has some sexual experience and (b) that she has told Michael that she loves him. Historian Judith Smart points out that, in a time when 'married women began to contest their positions as wives and mothers, and young people came to be represented as teenage rebels', Graham 'made no concessions';[6] Smart quotes Graham from a Brisbane rally attended by 50,000 people, of whom 35,000 were under twenty-five: 'sex is something you were built for, but it was made to be controlled … if you have lost the sex battle you have lost the battle of life.'[7]

Tourmaline activates, then complicates and intensifies a reader's sense of 'sex battle[s]' that are in process of being 'lost', in part through the passionate, violent, probably incestuous love affair between Deborah and Kestrel, of which we note that when Deborah announces she's pregnant to him, the blood drains from Kestrel's face, unseen by Deborah (200); in part through the tacitly homoerotic, sadomasochistic relationship between Kestrel and Byrnie, the latter being also the first explicitly homosexual character to appear in Stow's fiction. Alcoholic, with a cratered face, the result of severe teenage acne, and a 'masturbation problem' (176), Byrnie declares his unrequited passion for Michael Random—perhaps a less oedipally challenging alternative to Kestrel, who brought Byrnie up—only at novel's end: '"I reckon I love you, mate." And he waited, with his terrible secret (he thought it a secret) at last confessed, to be struck by lightning' (205).

But earlier dialogue has indicated why the relationship could never take the turn that Byrnie might be supposed to desire:

> 'Do you care?' said the diviner, surprised by a new thought.
> 'What about?'

6 Smart, pp. 168, 171.

7 Graham, *Sunday Mail*, 31 May 1959, cited in Smart, p. 171.

> 'The way you look.'
> 'No, I don't care,' said Byrne, with a happy laugh. 'Far as anyone knows, I'm the ugliest bloke in the world. It's an honour.'

The pitch and tone of Michael's response suggest not only the degree of his personal vanity, but also fastidious, even precious, disdain: '"I couldn't live," said the diviner' (203).

But the novel indicates that Michael has something to be narcissistic about. The Law declares him 'personable', and admires 'his profile' as the diviner gazes out over the town: 'The nostrils of his fine straight nose were dilated, his mouth was tense. A sullen blue light smouldered in his eyes, under the fair lashes' (67). The Law later declares that, 'There was so much hope in the look of him'; and again: 'when he laughed, I could see nothing in him but a charming and candid boy, to whom my soft old heart warmed in an instant' (68). In the Law's fascination with Michael, some readers may infer an intertext with the narrator Marlow's obsessive interest in the tall, blond, blue-eyed Lord Jim, in Conrad's eponymous novel (Stow commenced a thesis on Conrad at the University of Western Australia in 1961, but did not complete it).[8]

Yet Michael fascinates everyone. 'This bloke's something special', says Horse Carson. 'You only got to look at him' (48). Long before her conversion, Deborah touches the diviner 'as if touching him meant something' (23). The Law writes of himself and the townspeople that, 'we had fawned upon him like eager and loving dogs' (27). Graham experienced something similar. At a 'special meeting … for "teenagers" held in Sydney in 1959, people 'surged against a flimsy rope fence … Teenage girls pushed forward to try to touch Dr Graham as he mounted the steps to the dais'.[9] Likewise in Melbourne, 'women reached out to touch his raincoat as he walked smiling through the dense crowd'.[10] Contemporaneous accounts testify to Graham's star quality and *Tour-*

---

8 Anthony J. Hassall, 'Chronology', in *Strange Country: A Study of Randolph Stow*, rev. ed. (St Lucia: University of Queensland Press, 1990), p. xv.

9 *Sydney Morning Herald*, 4 May 1959, cited in Smart, p. 169.

10 *Sydney Morning Herald*, 2 February 1959, cited in Smart, p. 170.

maline creates an aura of stardom around Michael. The text iterates and reiterates Michael's 'blue and golden' good looks, as well as evoking the fans'—the Tourmaliners'—receptivity. In the passages of communal worship, Michael enters 'in a nimbus of fiery gold' and walks 'through the breaking waves of our need and adoration ... He was the focus, the awakener of all this feeling, but not its source' (163, 164). The Law testifies:

> On those nights, I believed in him. Because he was no longer himself. On those nights we created him, dedicating him to the glory of God. If he had been an image, an anthem, a cathedral, he could not have been less his own. (185)

As Edgar Morin writes, 'The star is indeed a myth: not only a daydream but an idea-force.' Morin identifies stars as '*patterns of culture* in the literal sense of the term, giv[ing] shape to the total human process which has produced them'.[11]

But for some readers, Michael's movie-star-like stardom may reach its apogee in the scene of his confrontation with Kestrel. Kestrel, the town publican, throws a free-grog street party to spite the 'witch doctor' (95) Michael. A number of the guests start brawling around a bonfire. Michael appears like the hero of a Western movie, striding into the flames to stamp them to embers. Having done so, 'he stood there, ringed with the dying fire, all blue and golden, but cold as ice, and silent' (137). Kestrel, defeated, goes to bed. What is arresting is not only the suggestion of an intertext with the 1953 western *Shane* (with golden-blond Alan Ladd as the chivalrous hero, and dark, devilish-looking Jack Palance as the villain),[12] but also the apparent correlation between *Tourmaline*'s descriptions of Michael's looks, and representations of Dr Graham in the Australian media of 1959.

Smart writes that 'journalistic description represented [Graham] as young, sexually attractive and intensely masculine',[13] citing the

11 Edgar Morin, *The Stars*, Richard Howard, trans., (New York: Grove Press, 1960), p. 183.

12 *Shane*, Dir. George Stevens, Paramount, 1953.

13 Smart, p. 170.

Sydney newspaper *Truth*: 'He has long legs, long arms, profuse and wavy hair, and a very direct blue gaze which smoulders',[14] along with the Melbourne *Age*'s 'enthus[ings]' about 'the youthful stride of [Dr Graham's] long muscular body.' 'He is', the *Age* concluded, 'fantastically handsome, Hollywood style'.[15] Graham himself, in a sermon, spoke about Jesus Christ's rugged masculine beauty, in terms that evoke Billy Graham's own good looks, especially in the detail of the jawline. 'Christ was probably the strongest man physically that ever lived. He could have been a star athlete on any team. He was a real man with His strong shoulders [and] squarish jaw.'[16]

Is *Tourmaline* having a go at Dr Graham? The answer, I think, is a qualified 'yes', on several counts. First, transgressively, through the homoerotic-oedipal-narcissistic nexus that the novel creates for the Byrnie-Kestrel-Michael relationship; second, obliquely, through Tom Spring's summation of Michael, and his vulgar imitator Kestrel, as 'incurable' self-haters, 'two sides of the same coin' (177); third, socio-politically, through the responses of some Tourmaliners to Michael's brand of uplift. When Michael announces: 'I'm here to wake you up, to tell you what you mean' (157), even the Law protests: 'What makes you so hard? … This isn't the way we are in Tourmaline' (156). Dave Speed, too, objects to Michael's 'certainty' (155), in more markedly Australian idiom: 'But do we like strangers blowing in and sending the word round they got special powers to change the place?' (79).

But Dave—like the novel's other exponent of scepticism or logical positivism, Kestrel—misses something.

Mark Duffett schematises the star phenomenon as having a vertical and a horizontal axis. Duffett's vertical axis enables iteration of the publicly observed wattage or voltage of the star, the crowd-pulling capacity, the power; whereas on Duffett's horizontal axis, the iteration

---

14 *Truth,* 21 February 1959, cited in Smart, p. 170.

15 *Age,* 13 February 1959, cited in Smart, p. 170.

16 Graham, 'Sermon No. 13', *Charlotte Observer,* 5 October 1958; Eric R. Crouse, 'Popular Cold Warriors: Conservative Protestants, Communism, and Culture in Early Cold War America', *Journal of Religion and Popular Culture* II (Fall 2002), available at: www.usask.ca/relst/jrpc/popcoldwarprint.html [Accessed 23 July 2009]

of the star's contradictions, the inconsistencies that make the star appear human, perhaps even more like ourselves than the selves we imagine ourselves to be, can be explored with regard to a dynamics of receptivity that, ultimately, makes a star a star.[17] *Tourmaline* invites its readers to negotiate both these axes, through its nuanced presentation of Michael as both authoritarian demagogue and crazy mixed-up kid, decisive social leader and tormented spiritual aspirant; and through the contrastive presentation of the incredulous Dave; the cynical and 'theor[etical]' (199) Kestrel; and the ineffectual intellectual Tom Spring. By the end of the novel, neither Dave, nor Kestrel, nor Tom has actually learned anything, though Kestrel, as imitative as any Girardian hyper-mimetic personality, plans to turn himself into 'the pope of Tourmaline' and, ludicrously in the small-town context, thinks not of 'the single soul' but 'in thousands … and tens of thousands' (207). On the other hand the Law, the tergiversating 'old fool'—Stow's extra-textual expression for this character[18]—who succumbs, though with grave reservations, to Michael's project of social and personal redemption, has, by novel's end, learned something:

> There is no sin but cruelty. Only one. And that original sin, that began when a man first cried to another, in his matted hair: Take charge of my life, I am close to breaking. (210)

While this is, of course, a refutation of Michael's teaching, of Christian doctrine, and, perhaps especially, of Dr Billy Graham's dogmatic assertions, it is also the novel's hard-won nugget of Truth, with a capital 'T'. And the text vouchsafes it to the Law—who is also 'the memory and conscience of Tourmaline'—and who, as he writes his testament, can be read as 'working through', to use the Freudian expression, something

17 Mark Duffett, 'Understanding Star Appeal: The Power of Elvis', conference on the History of Stardom Reconsidered, University of Turku, Finland. Available at: www.markduffett.com/pdfs/understanding%20elvis%20conference.pdf [Accessed 11 November 2006].

18 Xavier Pons, and Neil Keeble, 'A Colonist With Words' (interview with Stow), in Anthony J. Hassall, ed., *Randolph Stow: Visitants, Episodes from Other Novels, Poems, Stories, Interviews, And Essays* (St. Lucia: University of Queensland Press, 1990), p. 365.

like a psychoanalytic transference on the diviner. Slavoj Žižek writes: 'Transference … is an illusion, but the point is that we cannot bypass it and reach directly for the Truth: the Truth itself is constituted through the illusion proper to the transference'. Žižek quotes Lacan: 'the Truth arises from misrecognition'. [19]

More than a satirical account of a particular Australian–American historical moment, *Tourmaline* is a parable of religious sociality. If, as a character, Michael is written to connote Billy Graham, Michael's story also evokes that of Jesus, and the text, troping on Michael's frailities—his vanity and anger, along with his on-again-off-again charm—provides a rough map of the Gospel Jesus' irreducible, and, arguably, irresistible human traits. *Tourmaline* anticipates celebrity culture, yet, Janus-faced, looks backward also; it offers us an imagining of the quotidian beginnings of the Christian hermeneutic through mid-twentieth-century eschatological lenses.

19 Slavoj Žižek, *The Sublime Object of Ideology*, 1989 (London: Verso, 2008), pp. 59–60.

17

'Turning a Place into a Field': Shirley Hazzard's *The Great Fire* and Cold War Area Studies

Robert Dixon

'It has been one of the enduring ironies of the study of Asia', writes Harry Harootunian, 'that Asia itself, as an object, simply doesn't exist'.[1] In *Learning Places: The Afterlives of Area Studies* (2002), Harootunian and Masao Miyoshi observe that 'Historically, area studies programs … originated in the immediate post-World War II era and sought to meet the necessity of gathering and providing information about the enemy'.[2] This was made possible by large infusions of money from a range of institutions, including private corporations, scholarly organisations and government agencies. Assisted by US military occupation, 'places' like Japan were turned into social laboratories where specialists from Europe, the US and Australia came to do fieldwork. 'Turning a place into a field' was symptomatic of the orientalism endemic to Cold War area studies.[3]

1 H.D. Harootunian, 'Tracking the Dinosaur: Area Studies in a Time of "Globalism"', in *History's Disquiet: Modernity, Cultural Practice, and the Question of Everyday Life* (New York: Columbia University Press, 2000), p. 25.

2 H.D. Harootunian and Masao Miyoshi, 'Introduction: The "After Life" of Area Studies', in Masao Miyoshi and H.D. Harootunian, eds, *Learning Places: The Afterlives of Area Studies* (Durham and London: Duke, 2002), pp. 1–18 (this quotation from p. 2); for an earlier version, see also Harootunian, 'Tracking the Dinosaur'.

3 Harootunian, 'Tracking the Dinosaur', p. 39.

In this chapter I examine expatriate Australian writer Shirley Hazzard's novel *The Great Fire* (2003) in the context of Cold War orientalism.[4] In its main characters and events, *The Great Fire* depicts area studies' formation in the immediate postwar period in US-occupied Japan and British Hong Kong. Hazzard insists that her protagonists, Aldred Leith and Peter Exley, are set apart from the military and intelligence apparatus by their commitment to humanist values and the ideals of European high culture, but *The Great Fire* is marred by its strikingly orientalist depictions of 'Asia' and 'the East'. Hazzard was writing about the historical origins of area studies from the time of its 'afterlife'. With the benefit of hindsight, does she grasp what Harootunian calls the 'everydayness' of life in Hong Kong and Japan,[5] or does she, in the manner of Cold War orientalism, reconstitute them as totalised cultures outside the time of the West?

Area Studies and Cold War Orientalism

Today's area studies disciplines have their origin in what Bruce Cumings, drawing on the work of Sigmund Diamond, calls 'the intelligence-university nexus': that is, a working collaboration between scholars, university administrators, agencies of the military and state intelligence communities, and private and corporate sponsors.[6] The original laboratory for this nexus was the Washington-based United States Office of Strategic Services (OSS), especially its Research and Analysis Branch, which gathered information from personnel in the field and actively recruited academic informants. In 1941, its director, William Donovan, enunciated the rationale for employing the nation's best expertise 'to collect and analyse all information and data which may bear upon

4 Shirley Hazzard, *The Great Fire* (London: Virago, 2003). All subsequent references are to this edition.

5 Harootunian, 'Tracking the Dinosaur', pp. 14–15, 19.

6 Bruce Cumings, 'Boundary Displacement: The State, the Foundations, and Area Studies During and After the Cold War, in Miyoshi and Harootunian, eds, *Learning Places*, pp. 261–302; Sigmund Diamond, *Compromised Campus: The Collaboration of Universities with the Intelligence Community* (New York: Oxford University Press, 1992).

national security'. Donovan was assisted by members of the American Council of Learned Societies in drawing up 'a slate of [academic] advisors'.[7] The wartime OSS and the early postwar CIA were largely staffed by university personnel: the military were outnumbered by professors in such disciplines as history, political science, economics, geography, anthropology, archaeology and art history, and from universities including Harvard, Yale, Berkeley, Michigan, and Duke. The purpose of the OSS was to mobilise American scholarship for military intelligence purposes, and from 1942 the Research and Analysis Branch contracted out research projects to specialised institutes at various universities. This was the model for postwar collaboration between the intelligence and academic communities, including the projects of interdisciplinary research that soon thereafter came to be called 'area studies'.[8]

In 1964, McGeorge Bundy, who was then Dean of Arts and Sciences at Harvard University, gave a lecture at the School of Advanced International Studies at Johns Hopkins University, in which he described the formative relationship between the intelligence community and area studies. His lecture was titled, 'The Battlefields of Power and the Searchlights of the Academy':

> It is a curious fact of academic history that the first great centre of area studies was not located in any university, but in Washington, during the Second World War, in the Office of Strategic Services ... It is still true today, and I hope it always will be, that there is a high measure of interpenetration between universities with area programs and the information-gathering agencies of government of the United States.[9]

For a generation after World War II, this 'interpenetration' defined the form and shaped the preoccupations of area studies programs.

---

7 Quoted in Cumings, p. 264.

8 Cumings, p. 264.

9 McGeorge Bundy, 'The Battlefields of Power and the Searchlights of the Academy', in E.A.J. Johnson, ed., *The Dimensions of Diplomacy* (Johns Hopkins: Baltimore, 1964), Bundy, quoted in Diamond, p. 10.

Briefly, what kinds of knowledge did area studies disciplines produce, and what have been the main criticisms developed in their 'afterlife', which Harootonian dates from the publication of Edward Said's *Orientalism* in 1978?

1. Their *complicity with the state and intelligence apparatus* both during and after the Cold War: documents from the 1950s, for example, indicate that the Centre for International Studies at MIT was established 'almost as a subsidiary enterprise' of the CIA, and that then CIA director, Allen Dulles, had personal direction in the hiring of senior staff.[10]

2. Their *totalisation of knowledge* around orientalism's cultural binaries and essentialisms: Harootunian speaks of 'the still axiomatic duality between an essentialized, totalized, but completed Western self and an equally essentialized, totalized but incomplete East'.[11]

3. A typically *'instrumental' approach to knowledge* as a 'service to the state and business': in a 1970 report on Japanese studies for the SSRC, John W. Hall, formerly of Yale, described Japanese area studies programs and their personnel as 'a national resource'.[12]

4. Area studies' embrace of functionalist social science led to *an emphasis on the present and future*, and 'the elimination of the long duration of history'.[13]

5. The *treatment of places outside the West as sites of fieldwork*. For Harootunian, 'This differentiation between field and country suggested both distance, physical and figural, and the existence of different temporalities marking the boundary between modern and premodern'.[14]

---

10 Diamond, p. 278.

11 Harootunian, p. 27.

12 Harootunian, p. 31.

13 Harootunian, p. 33.

14 Harootunian, p. 39.

6. A *hermeneutic of 'empathetic immediacy'* and *'identification'* with the field and its people that was strongly gendered: Harootunian notes that 'trainees in Japanese studies since the end of the war have regularly acquired wives who could double as native informants ... [and] this rite of passage ... was usually one way, with men acquiring Japanese wives'.[15]

According to Harootunian, area studies missed the opportunity represented by the publication of Said's *Orientalism* to become more methodologically self-aware, to examine the extent to which their knowledge was mediated by the relation to power.[16] What comparisons, then, can be made between these criticisms of area studies by scholars such as Cumings, Diamond, Harootunian, and Miyoshi, and Hazzard's fictionalised account of their formation in *The Great Fire*? What are *her* views on the relation between area studies and the military-intelligence apparatus? Do her characters display the orientalist perspectives typical of Japanese studies at this time? If they do, is this because she sought deliberately to recreate attitudes appropriate to 1947? Does Hazzard's humanist perspective provide a view of Japan and Hong Kong that is distinct from area studies' Cold War orientalism?

Aldred Leith in Japan

The Great Fire begins in Japan in the spring of 1947. Aldred Leith, a Major in the British Army, boards a train in Tokyo and passes through scenes of devastation caused by the American bombing. But as the train moves out of the station into the 'real' Japan, his mind is drawn to the book in his hand, a travelogue about Greece, and by that medium his European sensibility is separated from his physical presence in the Japanese train (5). When he again registers his location, the narrative, focalised through his perspective, is flooded with orientalist discourse:

> He had the shabby little compartment to himself ... It was clean, and the window had been washed. Other sections of

15 Harootunian, p. 39.

16 Harootunian, pp. 47–48.

> the train were crammed with famished, threadbare Japanese. But the victors travelled at their ease, inviolable in their alien uniforms. Ahead and behind, the vanquished overflowed hard benches and soiled corridors: men, women, infants, in the miasma of endurance. In the steam of humanity and the stench from an appalling latrine. Deploring, Aldred Leith was nevertheless grateful for solitude … Having looked a while at Asia from his window, he brought out a different, heavier book from his canvas bag. (5)

In this opening description of Japan, partly focalised through Leith's point of view, there is a narrative irony at work that establishes Leith's sense of his own distinction: although one of the 'victors' and dressed in their 'alien uniform', he deplores the victory and its consequences for the Japanese. Yet Hazzard also employs the classic orientalist tropes of Cold War orientalism: fieldwork's binary divisions between subject and object, the modern and the pre-modern, and the transformation of place into space, as Japan becomes 'Asia'.

Leith is going to visit the Japanese Naval Academy at Kure. A travel writer and oriental scholar, he has come to meet Professor Gardiner, an elderly orientalist of the old school, and to stay at a facility set up by the Americans to accommodate the influx of area studies scholars since the occupation. Taken together, Gardiner and Leith correspond to the main tradition of Western scholarship on Japan represented by the careers of Basil Hall Chamberlain, George B. Sansom and Edwin O. Reischauer, which span the period from the Russo-Japanese War to World War I, through the worsening relations of the 1930s to the Pacific War, and on to the American occupation and the Cold War.[17] In a survey of this tradition for *The Journal of Asian Studies*, published in 1980 in response to Said's *Orientalism*, Richard H. Minear found orientalist thinking to be more or less unchanged and unchallenged until the 1960s when, in Reischauer's late work, there was finally some modification.[18]

---

17 Richard H. Minear, 'Orientalism and the Study of Japan', *The Journal of Asian Studies* 39.3 (May 1980): 507–17 (513).

18 Minear, p. 512.

Hazzard's Professor Gardiner is a British scholar whose parents, themselves orientalists, had settled in Japan. Like scholars of Chamberlain and Sansom's generation, Gardiner looks back to an originary Japanese civilisation destroyed by the 'great fire' of war and military occupation. This cultural essence is symbolised by a traditional Japanese house and garden that survive in the wooded interior of the island which Garinder describes as architecturally 'pure':

> The central house is pure, you know, not like this … There's a small valley … with a falling stream and temple. The property was a retreat for an admiral when the academy, this building here, was created in the thirties … They've flung up a lot of prefabs, Nissen huts, that sort of thing. (16).

Leith is one of a stream of scholars come to do fieldwork in Japan: 'scientists, historians, journalists. It's Hiroshima that draws them' (17). In the background is the shadowy presence of British and US military intelligence. In 1940, Gardiner had wanted to return to Britain, but he tells Leith that 'a secret chap from London came to see me, said I'd be more use to them here' (18). Like others of his generation, Gardiner has passed through 'the rite of passage': marriage to a Japanese woman. During the war she was denounced as a traitor by her parents for marrying an Englishman, and committed suicide in 1943 (20). It is the first of the novel's several echoes of the Madame Butterfly motif, an orientalist trope that invokes classic notions of a feminised, pre-modern oriental civilisation.

The American facility at Kure is administered by the Australian Brigadier Barry Driscoll and his wife, Melba. The Driscolls, as Gardiner had warned, are 'disquieting as a symptom of new power' (29), and Hazzard works to create a sense of distinction between the Brigadier's 'drilled belligerence' and the opinions of what his wife disparagingly calls 'the university lot' (28). Leith here meets other scholars doing fieldwork, including Hugh Calder, a Renaissance historian (278), who feel an undergraduate sense of bonding in opposition to the Driscoll's regime (28). The Driscolls resist adopting Japanese customs at table, and treat their household staff with distant authority, feminising and infantilising them: 'Two women in kimonos, possibly a mother and daughter, slipped about, providing and removing. The girl was extremely slight, in body nearly a child' (29). Leith senses a distinction between those in the occupation force who are sensitive to the 'humanity' of the Japanese and those who are not. While being driven into the hills, he is aware of the island's rural poor: 'Labourers passed them in pairs and foursomes, all moving downhill, all bearing burdens; each falling silent as the car approaches, not meeting glances from these invulnerable strangers in their well-fed uniforms' (24). Leith's driver, Talbot, shares this insight, expressed as a niggling doubt about his own 'invulnerability': 'He hadn't expected this contest, continual, between a decreed strength and the nagging humanity of things. Any show of softness would bring, from his companions, the good laugh, to shut him up' (24).

The word 'humanity' recurs in Hazzard's novel as the mark of those who can transcend the brute functionality of power. In an important article on Hazzard's humanism, Brigitta Olubas argues that 'her work generates a distinctive form of "cosmopolitan cultural mobility" grounded in what she calls, after Emily Apter, a 'Saidian humanism'.[19] Central to Said's and Hazzard's ethical stance, as Apter and Olubas see it, is a capacity to identify beyond the self, beyond the ideologies of nationalism and colonialism, that derives from what Apter calls an 'emancipatory humanism'. While drawing on the positive strengths of Renaissance Europe's humanist traditions, this 'Saidian humanism' has the capacity to produce 'an anti-imperialist understanding of world culture', even to generate 'a politics of utopia'.[20] These are strong claims that must be tested by a close reading of the novel. Does Leith's 'humanity' allow him to move beyond the orientalist thinking of the military apparatus and the generation of scholars complicit with it?

In their thinking about the past, Chamberlain, Sansom and Reischauer aestheticised 'the old Japan' while ranking it lower in their estimation than the European heritage. At the same time they valued

19 Brigitta Olubas, 'Shirley Hazzard's Australia: belated reading and cultural mobility', a paper delivered at ASAL 2009, forthcoming in *JASAL*; Emily Apter, 'Saidian Humanism', *Boundary 2* 31.2 (2004): 35–53.

20 Apter, pp. 35, 52.

modernisation and generally endorsed the changes introduced by Westernisation. Sansom praises the aesthetic achievements of 'the old Japan' while comparing them unfavourably with 'the great victories of heart and brain that culminated in the splendours of the Renaissance … the intellectual treasures of Europe'.[21] Japan's feudal past is eulogised for producing the 'arts and graces of a dying civilization'. As Chamberlain put it in *Things Japanese* (1891), 'All the causes which produced the Old Japan of our dreams have vanished … In the place of chivalry there is industrialism … Old Japan is dead, and the only decent thing to do with the corpse is to bury it'.[22]

In Hazzard's novel, the character who epitomises occupied Japan is a young boy, educated in England and the son of an ambassador, brought to serve as an interpreter and *maggiordomo* to Brigadier Driscoll, who treats him with contempt. As he is walking to the 'pure' house, Leith discovers Driscoll screaming hysterically at the boy for a minor misdemeanour, and Leith and the boy exchange eye contact. Leith's reflection, 'God knows what he thinks of us' (37), is meant as a sign of humanist sympathy across the relation of power but oddly invokes ideas of oriental inscrutability. As witness to the scene of shaming, and despite the apparent differences between the military and 'the university lot', Leith is implicated in the boy's impending suicide: 'He himself felt secretly culpable—as if, with that look of acknowledgement, he'd conspired in the act' (41–42).

Leith finds the boy's disembowelled body next morning in the centre of a glade near the 'pure' Japanese house:

> The track appeared to peter out … The stream, or its cataract, became audible and there was a suggestion of ancient roofing; tiled, glinting farther down … The body lay in the centre of the glade in a welter of blood and innards partly contained by a coloured robe and loosened obi. The slippered feet projected, inviolate. (40)

21 Cited in Minear, 'Orientalism and the Study of Japan', p. 511.

22 Cited in Minear, 'Orientalism and the Study of Japan', p. 509.

Leith sees on the dead face, 'Eyes that had exchanged with him, hours since, their pained humanity' (40–41). Despite his capacity to empathise with the Japanese across the lines of military occupation, the boy's suicide suggests that Leith's scholarly interest in 'Asian' civilisations is complicit with the West's fatal impact: 'he had set himself to render consequences of war within an ancient and vanishing society … His theme was loss and disruption' (34). When Driscoll's son Ben suggests, 'there might have been mass suicides in Japan, with the surrender', the boy's body becomes an epitome: it is what Chamberlain might have described as the indecently exposed corpse of 'the Old Japan'. Leith replies, 'There may have been more suicides than we imagine, in the days of the defeat … I thought I might learn about this, travelling the country. Instead, here, at once, it reveals itself' (45).

When Leith returns to Kure after a visit to Hong Kong, he finds that an American intelligence officer named Slater has come from Washington to interview him, accompanied by a young soldier, Thaddeus Hill. Slater is barking orders into a phone, and Leith notes his 'fleshed and nearly featureless face that paradoxically represented a type … this was the man from Washington, come to find him' (152). The reference to Washington suggests that Slater may be with either the Office of Strategic Services or the FBI—or both. He is superficially polite but there is menace in his words: 'We think the world of your record … We have the greatest interest in your work' (153). Hill later warns Leith that Slater may conspire with Driscoll to use his interest in Driscoll's daughter, Helen, against him to force his co-operation with US intelligence: 'It would be their way to fault you. She's under age' (161).

These passages are typical of the way Hazzard alludes to the institutional affiliations of the military, intelligence and scholarly personnel in the novel, and also of her characterisation of Leith's values as transcending them. Leith's work is facilitated by the American military occupation of Japan but fundamentally at odds with it, and potentially subversive of US authority. Shortly after arriving at Kure, he writes to his Australian friend, Peter Exley:

> The role of the conqueror remains alien and distasteful. There is something equivocal about having prevailed so completely

> over one's fellow man—I don't speak of systems or regimes, but of individuals … I continue to be, as in China, a *franc tireur*, assisted not at all by official sources. (47)

Hazzard insists on Leith's ethical distinction from the US military, personified by Slater and his 'type' (152). She stresses his distaste for Driscoll's blunt exercise of power. Yet Leith's 'humanist' identification with a few individual Japanese does not prevent him from becoming entangled in their subjectification, while his own more general responses to Japanese places and people are often entangled with classic forms of Cold War orientalism. A similar pattern holds for Hazzard's account of Exley's experiences in Hong Kong.

Peter Exley in Hong Kong

Exley has come to Hong Kong in 1947 on secondment to the British Army's Far East Land Forces to investigate war crimes. When everyday life in Hong Kong is described from his point of view, it is reified and orientalised:

> Filth was in fact on Peter Exley's mind in those first weeks: the accretion filming the Orient, the shimmer of sweat or excrement. A railing or handle one's fingers would not willingly grasp … Ammoniac reek, or worse, in paved alleys and under stuccoed arcades … And the great clots and blobs of tubercular spittle shot with blood, unavoidable underfoot. In such uncleanness, nothing could appear innocent … He longed for a measure of cleanliness with which he had somehow associated peace. (70–71)

Judith Shulevitz suggests that in such passages, Hazzard 'writes of Hong Kong as seen by Exley'.[23] While the narrative is sometimes focalised through his point of view, Exley seems to lack Leith's sense of internal distantiation from the attitudes of the 'victors', and the orientalism is

23 Judith Shulevitz, 'Old-World Style: Shirley Hazzard's Long-Awaited Novel', *Slate*, 30 October 2003, available at: www.slate.com/id/2090516/ [Accessed on 17 October 2010].

not confined to passages of focalised narration: it bleeds out into the general narrative voice and Hazzard's overall conception of this subplot.

In Hong Kong, Exley is faced with the classic colonialist's dilemma: 'the absence of women, of pink-and-white women' (79). His coming to terms with Hong Kong is partly expressed through his reluctant flirtation with Rita Xavier, a typist in his office who is 'Eurasian, of Portuguese decent' (69). Repulsed by the 'filth' of Chinese women, he is initially reluctant to be drawn into a relationship with her on racial grounds. In Leith's case, the possibility of miscegenation is displaced by his love for Helen Driscoll: they meet in Japan, and their relationship is associated with the traditional house on Kure, and therefore with 'the old Japan'. As another victim of her father's violence, Helen is even associated with the dead Japanese boy. These elements of the plot suggest the 'hermeneutics of identification' that Harootunian argues is fundamental to area studies, especially its fieldwork phase. While Leith's identification with Asia is safely displaced on to Helen, Exley's finds a middle ground in this 'Eurasian, of Portuguese decent'.

After attending several weddings with Rita, Exley realises that he is gradually being drawn to her and to Hong Kong itself (195). But at this moment of accommodation, the 'real' Hong Kong—that is, the orientalised Kong Kong—strikes him down. When he offers to help a Chinese child stricken by poliomyelitis, Exley contracts the disease himself. In hospital, 'lying inert in the Asian afternoon' (223), he finds himself trapped by his tentative relationship with Rita. Reflecting on their possible future together if he were to be medically evacuated to Australia, he remembers the White Australia policy: 'Such a venture might be possible with high passion. [But h]e and Rita were dealing … with a proposal of shared resignation' (222). For all the novel's literary pretentions, Exley is Hazzard's version of that standby of middlebrow fiction, the white man in the tropics, rendered inert by the Orient's filth and miasma, and trapped in a miscegenous relationship. At the end of the novel, Leith receives news from Audrey Fellowes, a mutual friend, that Exley has tried to end his life by taking an overdose of pills, and that he has been saved by 'the Portuguese lady' (308). Audrey asks Leith to help her disabuse Exley of his sense of obligation to Rita, and there is no sign that Leith disagrees with her point of view.

Return from 'the East'

When he leaves Japan, Leith returns to England to wait for Helen Driscoll, who is now living in New Zealand, to come of age. He informs her that Thaddeus Hill is now studying at the University of California, Berkeley, 'a university, highly regarded, where they have a school of Japanese studies' (276). Leith's own book on China and Japan is finished but plays no part in the novel's romantic conclusion. But there is a final, significant reference to the 'interpenetration' of area studies with the intelligence community through Calder, the historian Leith had met at Kure:

> It emerges that Calder, when not a don, is a government agent—to put it plainly, a spy. He began this in the war, but has continued, less commendably, in peacetime. He offered to enlist me in the same business. Out of the question … I don't intend to live, or die, by such means. (278)

Ironically, Calder is a scholar of the very Renaissance humanism (278) upheld throughout the novel as a bulwark against the West's instrumental disregard for other cultures. Yet at the end of the novel Leith is drawn to return, Ulysses-like (241), from his wanderings in 'Asia' (227) and 'the East' (247), to London, which remains the Greenwich meridian of the idea of civilisation destroyed by the great fires of the twentieth century. His greatest wish is to be 'extracted' from the 'context of occupation' (278), to return from 'the far end of earth' to 'the heart of the world' (254). In New Zealand, at the edge of the British world, Helen imagines him 'on the other, centuried side of the earth' (293). Finally, then, Leith and Helen's romance represents not an overcoming of orientalist epistemologies, but an affirmation of high European culture, which alone possesses deep time. When Leith returns to London, the city built by Christopher Wren lies in ruins. He recalls climbing the monument to the Great Fire of London as a child, and 'emerging on a parapet topped by gilded flames, to the panorama of all their confident world: towers, domes, temples, and elastic river' (229). This paradoxical idea that the 'Great Fire' of the title represents the world-historical events of the mid-twentieth century, including the American bombing and occupation of Japan, but is best exemplified by the postwar decline of Great Britain is reflected in the choice of image for the cover of the novel, a detail from J.M.W. Turner's *Burning of the Houses of Parliament*—an image that is at once Eurocentric and belated in relation to the novel's setting and events in British Hong Kong and US-occupied Japan in 1947.

In its principal characters and events, *The Great Fire* accurately presents the broad outline of postwar area studies' formation in complicity with the US military and intelligence apparatus. Hazzard asserts that her protagonists hold themselves aloof from that apparatus through their commitment to humanism and the ideals of European culture. In Leith's case, this is ultimately expressed through the romance plot, which displaces the orientalist 'hermeneutics of identification' from Asia on to Helen Driscoll. Exley is less successful in avoiding the lure of the East and is emasculated by the encounter. While wanting to set itself off from the Cold War orientalism endemic to area studies in the 1940s and 1950s, Hazzard's novel therefore fails to develop a new perspective appropriate to the later moment of 2003—the 'afterlife' of area studies. This may be one reason why some reviewers initially found the novel belated and anachronistic.[24] This failure grasp what Harootunian calls the 'everydayness' of life[25] in other places is seen, formally, in the novel's lack of a clear and sustained distinction between its general narrative perspective and the orientalist depictions of Japan and Hong Kong that are only partially focalised through Leith and Exley in the late 1940s: the rural labourers at Kure, the Driscoll's household servants, the prostitutes in Hong Kong, and Exley's Chinese tailor, from whose child he contracts polio—these figures appear fleetingly in the background of the Europeans' consciousness like extras in a Hollywood film of the 1940s. The novel's ethical and epistemological dilemmas resemble those of Said's own humanist critique of area studies in *Orientalism*. As Harootunian argues,

---

24 See for example Brenda Niall, 'The Contingent Life: Review of Shirley Hazzard, *The Great Fire*', *Australian Book Review* (February 2004): 32–33.

25 Harootunian, 'Tracking the Dinosaur', pp. 14–15.

> If … *Orientalism* sensitized us to the practices of Europeans who were in a position to construct knowledges and identities of non-Europeans, invariably the colonized, and spoke for them as master ventriloquists, it did not, at the same time, propose the establishment of a new epistemology … promising a different way of looking at the world.[26]

26 Harootunian, 'Postcoloniality's Unconscious', p. 152.

Section 5

Publishing History and Transpacific Print Cultures

18

Literary Appreciation, American-Style: Channels of Influence in Early Twentieth-Century Australia

Patrick Buckridge

The study of something as vague as 'American influence' upon something as nebulous as 'literary appreciation' would seem likely to produce broad generalities at best. But it may just be possible to give specificity and substance to the topic by circumscribing the period of special focus—in this case to the first half of the twentieth century—and by identifying some of the specific channels through which American ideas, dispositions and methods in relation to the study of literature might have impinged on certain components of an Australian context which was, for historical reasons, mainly shaped by British models and practices.

I am regarding 'literary appreciation' here, very simply, as 'the liking of literature'.[1] Its slight awkwardness notwithstanding, this is a more useful definition for my present purposes than its more conceptually elaborated alternatives (as, for example, 'the ability to read literature with pleasure, understanding and discrimination'). The simpler definition

1 The word 'enjoyment' is an attractive (and idiomatic) alternative to 'liking', especially as it conveys something of the robust 'fun' quality that was often felt to be appealing in recommending literature to wider, less educated readerships in the early twentieth century; and indeed there are many books with titles like *The Enjoyment of Literature* published in Britain and America in this period that use the term in an uncomplicated way. But the term has recently acquired added complexity, especially through the work of Slavoj Žižek, and I have reluctantly decided not to use it.

more clearly highlights what I take to be its core characteristic—the experience of pleasure—and points to the obstacles to that experience, and to strategies for removing them, even if it does so without giving an account of the *kind* of pleasure that might be involved, or of other elements that might also be present.[2] 'Appreciation', thus conceived, is a less intellectually elaborated, articulated and integrative form of response than either 'interpretation' or 'criticism'; and because of this, the claim can plausibly be made (*pace* the Althusserian dogmatism of 'critical literacy') that appreciation has no inherent ideological affiliations—though, like many other politically neutral relations and practices, it has sometimes been roped into broader ideological projects.[3] Appreciation seems to become an issue—never for everyone, but sometimes, interestingly, for governments—at times when a perception is current among key political elites that for a significant part of the population literature simply does not figure (or, as often, 'no longer figures') as a main source of enjoyment and satisfaction. Whether we are at such a moment in Australia in 2010 is not clear: there would be differing views on the question, and any answer would depend, in part, on how broadly 'literature' was conceived.[4] But there was certainly a widespread conviction in the early decades of the twentieth century, throughout much of the English-speaking world, that just such a crisis existed. Leaving aside those for whom literature was (as it were) a closed book, there was a fear among progressive intellectuals (Walter

---

2 These and other issues of definition and meaning are explored in my 'Taste, Appreciation and the Study of Literature: F.D. Maurice, R.G. Moulton and the Extramural Effect', *Australasian Journal of Victorian Studies*, 13.1 (2009): 21–34.

3 It is instructive to note Terry Eagleton's virtual *volte-face* on this question in *How To Read a Poem* (London: Blackwell, 2007), pp. 1–8, some eighteen years after Robert Alter had arrived at substantially the same view in *The Pleasures of Reading in an Ideological Age* (New York: Simon and Schuster, 1989).

4 The fact that 'appreciation' is named in the new National English Curriculum papers as a desirable learning outcome that has been absent from recent state-based English curricula and needs to be restored, suggests that at least for the framers of the NEC and their political masters, the absence was a troubling one. For the NEC Draft Consultation version, see www.australiancurriculum.edu.au/Documents/English%20curriculum.pdf [Accessed on 12 January 2010].

Murdoch in Australia, for example[5])—that even those people who were fiercely determined, for whatever reasons, to *read* the great writers—the Leonard Basts and Mr Pollys of the prewar world—were finding it increasingly difficult to *enjoy* them.[6] The nameless addressee, the embattled and belaboured 'you', of that utterly seminal text for this phase of British cultural life, Arnold Bennett's *Literary Taste, and How To Form It* (1909), is the real-life counterpart to Messrs Bast and Polly.[7]

Responses to the crisis took many forms on both sides of the Atlantic as well as in Australia: reforms in school curriculum and pedagogy, expanded adult education schemes, a growth in the number of literary and part-literary societies, and a surge of 'reader-oriented' forms of publication such as reading-advice books, histories of readership, and a rash of anthologies, sets, and series interlarded with 'reader-friendly' mediating commentary and annotations. Many of these responses were not so much new initiatives as intensified continuations of late nineteenth-century developments, but some—like the large, cheap anthologies of literary classics and classic extracts—were new to the twentieth century.[8] Their general aim, simply stated, was to get people (including children, but not only children) to read and enjoy the works of the great writers.

For various historical reasons, America responded to the perceived crisis of 'literature-liking' at this time more directly and prolifically than

5 See, 'A Bookless World' and 'Superfluous Books', in Walter Murdoch, *Collected Essays of Walter Murdoch* (Sydney: Angus & Robertson, 1938), pp. 339–44, 355–58.

6 The references are to Leonard Bast, the self-educating office clerk in E.M. Forster's novel *Howard's End* (1910) and the eponymous hero of H.G. Wells' novel *The History of Mr Polly* (1910), both of whom experience this difficulty.

7 This is no doubt speculative, but it is difficult to overlook the almost exact simultaneity of the three books, all convergent on that year when, according to Virginia Woolf's whimsical assertion, 'human character changed'.

8 For a non-exhaustive account of classics anthologies in Australia, see P. Buckridge, 'Reading the Classics in Australia: Great Books Anthologies, 1900–1960', *Bibliographical Society of Australia and New Zealand Bulletin* 23.1 (1999): 38–48.

Britain did.[9] One concrete index of this is the larger number and greater popularity of reading-advice books published in America from the 1910s through the 1930s.[10] But this was just a small part of the response, which formed up over a wide cultural and educational front, and made its presence felt in Australia through a variety of publishing and educational avenues. I shall be looking at two such avenues—publishing and personal influence—using a single case study for each.

A British Conduit for American Influence: Harraps in Australia

The purpose of this section is to illustrate some of the ways in which international publishing networks were able, despite legal and informal obstacles to the direct importation of American books, to maintain a steady supply of American-authored books to Australia, mainly under British imprints. The British publishing firm of George G. Harrap & Co. provides a useful model of the triangular arrangement which made it possible for originally American works, including works of, and on, literary appreciation, to be marketed through the Australian retail book trade—over and above the relatively small number of American imprints entering the country by individual mail orders, and by Australian booksellers and American publishers flouting conventional preferences and contractual restrictions.

The firm of Harraps was founded in 1901 as a mainly educational publisher with a small but growing general list. By the 1920s they had established co-publishing arrangements with a large number of American educational publishers, notably D.C. Heath, Thomas Crowell, Frederick Stokes, Houghton Mifflin, J.B. Lippincott, David McKay, and the American Publishing Company. But it seems likely—and was

9 See, for example, Joan Shelley Rubin, *The Making of Middlebrow Culture* (Chapel Hill, N.C.: University of North Carolina Press, 1992), *passim*; Janice Radway, *A Feeling for Books: The Book-of-the-Month Club, Literary Taste, and Middle Class Desire* (Chapel Hill, N.C.: University of North Carolina Press, 1997), Chapter 3; Gerald Graff, *Professing Literature: An Institutional History* (Chicago: University of Chicago Press, 1987).

10 P. Buckridge, 'How to Read Books: Reading-Advice Books in Britain and North America, 1870–1960', *Bibliographical Society of Australia and New Zealand Bulletin* 26.2 (2002): 67–80.

certainly the proud boast of the founder of the firm, George G. Harrap in his 1935 memoir—that few other British firms entered into as many, or as robust American collaborations as Harraps did, or published as many titles in tandem with American publishers, in the first three decades of the century. In fact, though it was never more than a middle-sized company, Harraps punched well above their weight in the introduction, particularly, of American educational books, authors and ideas into Britain during these years. (To a lesser extent, they were also managing to sell British titles to some of the same American publishers.)[11]

Harraps' contribution to the transpacific publishing relationship between Australia and America was therefore at one remove: as a British publisher marketing their books in Australia, they were able, because of their own strong transatlantic list, to source a lot of American as well as British educational content, and to supply it to Australian booksellers under the Harrap imprint. Their English subject lists in the first quarter of the twentieth century included graded readers and anthologies, several series of school and college editions, classic reprints, books of literary history and biography, and guides to the study of literature and literary appreciation. (They were even better-positioned in the Australian market as suppliers of educational resources in European languages and literature, especially French and German.)[12]

Within the same time frame, Harraps also produced several literary series in a more broadly taste-forming mode—books and booklets designed to stimulate, increase and consolidate a love of literature by insinuating it into the fabric of people's everyday lives: such things as literary calendars, diaries, commonplace books, birthday books, and other types of what might, at a pinch, be called 'habitus-forming' -books, that is, that sought to make people's whole lives a little more 'bookish'.[13] These were not targeted principally at schools or children,

11 George G. Harrap, *Some Memories 1901–1935: A Publisher's Contribution to the History of Publishing* (London: Harrap, 1935), pp. 15–19, 143–49.

12 *Some Memories*, pp. 79–82, 97–100.

13 The Bourdieu-derived term 'habitus-forming' is intended to suggest a more holistic influence on people's lives than 'habit-forming' which tends to apply to the activity of book-reading is isolation from the rest of life. For an exploration

but they were certainly intended be available to them, and teachers were urged to adopt them as 'supplemental resources' to the main textbooks. Their primary target was the general public, and they were designed to contribute to the formation of a general environment of attitudes and activities within which formal literary education was just one part of a whole 'book-loving' way of life.

Harraps were not the only British publisher to produce books in this 'para-literary' genre, though they may have come up with more distinct subgenres than other, bigger British publishers like Oxford and Macmillan. But Harraps did not originate most of their 'habitus-forming' publishing initiatives; the ideas for nearly all of them were adopted from American publishers, some of whom had made a feature of such books since the 1890s or earlier. Thanks to their co-publishing arrangements, Harraps were able, for example, to build their Sesame Booklets, a series of 'Wayside Thoughts' from the great writers, to over fifty volumes in three years by acquiring as many as a third of them from the Boston publisher Thomas Y. Crowell, and either replacing the title page or, in a few cases, simply pasting over the Crowell imprint, a procedure that could result in Harrap imprints appearing five years before the firm came into being! (Or so it can seem.)

'Habitus-forming' books were one of several notional categories of publication by Harraps that were closely based on American exemplars, and contributed directly or indirectly to the study of literature in schools and universities in Britain and the many other countries in Europe, Asia, Africa and Australasia in which their books were marketed. Another important category comprised books that aimed at sensitising students and general readers to the aesthetic dimension of books-as-objects. Thus Harraps employed world-class illustrators—Willy Pogány, Harry Clarke, Arthur Rackham—to work on school poetry anthologies as well as fine collectors' editions of British and European literary classics.[14]

---

of 'bookishness' in its positive and negative senses in Australian history and literature, see P. Buckridge, 'Bookishness and Australian Literature', *Script & Print* 30.4 (2007): 223–36.

14 Examples include M.G. Edgar, ed., *A Treasury of Verses for Little Children* (illus. Pogány), 1923; Hans Christian Andersen, *Fairytales* (illus. Clarke), 1916; Washington Irving, *The Legend of Sleepy Hollow* (illus. Rackham), 1928.

One of the remarkable things about Harraps 'beautiful' books is the range of prices: even for the larger quartos, a range from 10/6 to 42s. was common in the late 1920s; and the illustrated anthologies went as low as 3/6. George G. Harrap meant it when he claimed, in 1935, that his intention was 'to produce educational books that looked as little like text-books as possible'; but books for school prizes—sometimes custom-bound for the individual school—also constituted an important part of their list.[15]

Once again, the chief models for affordable beauty in books—whether for schools, colleges, or the general reader—were American. George Harrap acknowledges this in general terms in his memoirs without naming specific publishers, but it is clear that his principal model for a smaller format series such as the 'King's Treasury' was the Maine publisher and book-designer Thomas Bird Mosher, in particular his long-running Bibelot series (1895–1925), which achieved similar remarkable economies, and worked within the same 'Arts and Crafts' aesthetic as Harraps and their early illustrators.[16]

What I am suggesting is that Anglo-American co-publishing arrangements of the kind I have just instanced produced a stronger presence for American educational and general literary publications in the British and Australian book trade in the early twentieth century than might have been expected, given the restrictions on American publishers supplying books direct to the Empire. The restriction applied only to parallel American editions in any case, and before World War II it was a matter of contractual agreement, rather than legislation, as between British and American publishers; and such agreements were themselves not always treated with great seriousness by the Americans. For example, the manager of the American Book Company, in signing

15 Harrap, *Some Memories*, pp. 22–24.

16 Mosher in Maine and Elbert Hubbard at the Roycroft Press in New York epitomise the two extremes of the Arts and Crafts (or Craftsman) Style in American book design in the early twentieth century. George Harrap and his partner George Oliver Anderson were clearly drawn to the simpler, less flamboyant style of Mosher. See William E. Fredeman, 'Thomas Bird Mosher and the Literature of Rapture', in Philip R. Bishop, *Thomas Bird Mosher, Pirate Prince of Publishers* (London: Oak Knoll Press and the British Library, 1998), pp. 6–7.

off on a Memorandum of Agreement with George Harrap for the co-publication of a French textbook in 1902, remarked on the clause prohibiting sales of the American edition in England or the Colonies, that 'it may be difficult to keep, because we cannot follow every little transaction that goes through our merchandising accounts, and our own edition may get over there in spite of us. But we suppose your own intention is that we should protect you as far as possible, and that we will do with pleasure.'[17]

Just how many American-published books—let alone how many Anglo-American co-publications—found their way into Australia in this period would be quite difficult to establish: the otherwise invaluable *Australian National Bibliography, 1901–1950* (predecessor to *Australian Books in Print*) can provide little or no assistance, as it lists only books published in Australia. Other sources, such as individual publishers', wholesalers' and booksellers' sales catalogues and invoices, are of course valuable, but the archive is notoriously patchy and incomplete.

It does seem clear, however, that significant numbers of American books on the study of literature were available in Australia, since they appear on Australian textbook lists. Even under the more strictly enforced Traditional Market Agreement of the 1950s and 60s, some American publications made their way onto Australian university booklists (as anyone who studied English at an Australian university in the 1960s can attest). Under the more relaxed protocols of the earlier period, one suspects that for all the Anglophilia of the ambient culture, the American presence may have been even stronger in the earlier period. Indeed, there may well have been more interest in American textbooks for literary study in Australia than there was in Britain at the same time. For example, F.H. Pritchard's *Training in Literary Appreciation* (a British book widely used in Australian schools, and reprinted nine times from 1922 to 1946) recommends only a handful of American books as 'Further Reading', whereas the Australian teacher-educator George Mackaness' *Inspirational Teaching* (1927) recommends as many

17 Covering letter (unsigned) from American Book Company, attached to Harrap Memorandum of Agreement with George G. Harrap, 1902, in respect of H.A.Guerber, *Contes et légendes*, Book 1. Chambers-Harrap Archive, Edinburgh (under C).

American as British books: among the American publishers he refers to are Houghton Mifflin, Little Brown, Harcourt Brace, Henry Holt, E.P. Dutton, Putnam's and Scribner's.[18]

In the end, though, there are limits to what the perspective of publishing history can tell us about the real impact in Australia of American assumptions, values and methods as regards the study of literature. At best, it can only tell us which American sources were *probably available* at a given time to Australian teachers, students and general readers. This is useful enough as far as it goes, but it cannot tell us much about the 'uptake' of those sources, how (or indeed if) they were communicated, disseminated, put into practice in classrooms, lecture theatres, libraries and private studies. To get a little closer to those processes and experiences, I shall try to complement the publishing perspective with a biographical perspective—a 'case study', in effect—of a man who acted as an interpreter and advocate for American-style appreciation and who, for a number of reasons, may have exercised a somewhat greater influence in Australia (at least in Sydney, and later in Brisbane) than one might expect a single individual to have done.

Ernest G. Moll: Appreciation and the Sydney Context

One of several American books on appreciation published during the 1920s and 1930s was *The Appreciation of Poetry* (F.S. Crofts, 1933) by Ernest G. Moll, then a youngish Professor of English at the University of Oregon in Eugene. He was also, as it happens, an Australian. Moll was born in country Victoria, went to school in Adelaide, and moved to America in his twentieth year, where he graduated from Lawrence College, took his Masters at Harvard, married, and got an Assistant Professorship in English literature at the University of Oregon in 1928. He retired to California in 1966 where he died many years later, at the age of ninety-seven.

One of the publisher's pre-readers for Moll's book, the eminent Yale critic and poet Mark Van Doren, found the book 'surprisingly interesting'; another, Warner Taylor (English Professor at the University

18 F.H. Pritchard, *A Training in Literary Appreciation* (London: Harrap, 1922); George Mackaness, *Inspirational Teaching* (London: Dent, 1928).

of Wisconsin)—compared it with a swag of eight books of similar type and pronounced it more interesting and effective than most, striking a better balance between arousing enthusiasm and conveying information, making it all seem 'natural and obvious', while 'meeting the student on his own ignorant ground'.[19] In an age of 'student-centred learning' Taylor's phrase can hardly fail to offend, but it does recognise and reflect the specificity of Moll's target audience. In his Preface he makes it plain that the book is aimed not at literature specialists, but at students taking just a few literature electives, who need to be introduced to the basic essentials of literary study. These essentials he defines not as a canon of indispensable authors or works but as the acquisition of a technique of close and imaginative observation, a growing capacity for noticing and taking pleasure in the sensuous dynamics of expression and in subtle nuances of thought and emotion.[20]

This technique is clearly not quite the same thing as the 'close reading' that the New Critics began to practise and proselytise a few years later. There is not the same drive to an intellectual resolution of the ironies and ambiguities revealed by critical analysis; there is rather a 'bringing to life' of the experiential content of the poem, a savouring of the sensuous pleasures of patterned sound, and an 'unpacking' of meanings and implications. This technique or process could hardly be called 'interpretation' at all, or the product 'literary criticism'; it is more in the nature of an appreciative and descriptive commentary on a series of poems, using a fairly large technical vocabulary, and invoking, but not exhaustively demonstrating, their formal coherence. 'The reader of poetry', Moll says, 'should appropriate for himself what the poet put into the poem';[21] and that seems to mean the poet's life experience and the poet's technical virtuosity in communicating it. In fact, Joseph Conrad's famous statement of his intended effect on the reader—which Moll quotes several times—also serves to define Moll's intended effect on *his* reader:

19 Warner Taylor, 'Report', in Ernest G. Moll Papers, National Library of Australia, MS928, Box 2 (Publishing Correspondence).

20 Ernest, G. Moll, *The Appreciation of Poetry* (New York: F.S. Crofts & Co., 1933), pp. viii–ix.

21 Moll, p. viii.

> My task which I am trying to achieve is, by the power of the written word to make you hear, to make you feel—it is, before all, to make you see. That—and no more, and it is everything.[22]

To this end, Moll makes considerable use of everyday analogies and personal anecdotes; at times the book reads like a series of rather engaging lectures; and indeed it originally was that, written up for publication as a monograph on a Carnegie Corporation fellowship in 1933, and framed in a wider scholarly context. Most of Moll's secondary references are, not surprisingly, American: books roughly similar to his own, by older professors of English like Bliss Perry, Arthur H. Fairchild, Frederick C. Prescott, and John Livingston Lowes[23]—but also by the radical Marxist Max Eastman, whose first book, *The Enjoyment of Poetry,* Moll quotes at some length.[24] There are also a few British references: books on poetry by Stephen J. Brown, T.E. Hulme, John Middleton Murry and Lascelles Abercrombie,[25] and one by another Australian, the Melbourne educational psychologist D.C. Griffiths, whose study *The Psychology of Literary Appreciation*—an eclectic blend of Coleridge,

---

22 Moll, p. ix. Qtd. from Joseph Conrad, *The Nigger of the Narcissus* (New York: Doubleday Doran, 1897), Preface.

23 Bliss Perry, *A Study of Poetry* (Boston: Houghton Mifflin, 1920); Frederick C. Prescott, *The Poetic Mind* (New York: Macmillan, 1922); Arthur H. Fairchild, *The Making of Poetry* (New York: Putnam's, 1912); John Livingston Lowes, *Convention and Revolt in Poetry* (Boston: Houghton Mifflin, 1919); Charles M. Gayley and Benjamin P. Kurtz, *Methods and Materials of Literary Criticism* (Boston: Ginn, 1920).

24 Max Eastman, *The Enjoyment of Poetry* (New York: Scribner's, 1913). The inclusion of Eastman, a fascinating figure in his own right, underlines the genuinely apolitical character of appreciation: on this subject a radical Trotskyist like Eastman could agree, in substance, with a genteel New England conservative like Bliss Perry.

25 Stephen J. Brown, *The World of Imagery* (London: Kegan Paul, 1927); T.E. Hulme, *Speculations* (London: Kegan Paul, 1924); John Middleton Murry, *The Problem of Style* (Oxford: Oxford University Press, 1922); Lascelles Abercrombie, *The Theory of Poetry* (London: Secker, 1924).

Freud, Jung and Croce—had only just appeared. Like Moll, Griffiths also draws on Abercrombie and Prescott.[26]

It is an interesting constellation of names, partly because—with one or two obvious exceptions—they are now so unfamiliar. In some local reviews of his book, however, a more familiar name appears, that of the great English critic and theorist I.A. Richards. Here it is reported that Moll has been requested by the education board of the Rockefeller Foundation to confer with Richards on a companion volume to be called 'The Appreciation of Prose'. It appears nothing came of this, since Richards never published a book of that name (and it would indeed have been a slightly odd collaboration).[27]

Moll and Richards did have something in common, though, and that was an interest in empirical research on student competence. The following year, 1934, Moll published a report on the experimental course on poetry appreciation that he had conducted two years earlier. In the report, which appeared in a volume of essays on 'Appreciation and the Arts', he explained the program of carefully graduated exposure to the sensory, emotional and intellectual dimensions of poetry that he had administered to two groups of fifteen students, mostly non-English majors. He describes some of their individual backgrounds and abilities, and quotes their own verbatim testimonies as to their initial hostility or indifference to poetry, and their partial conversions at his hands. Some of the testimonies are very much in the Puritan tradition of public repentance. The following is an example:

> My attitude towards poetry was one of extreme indifference. It made no impression at all upon me, and in fact I disliked the mere sound of it. I considered poetry a world outside of

26 D.C. Griffiths, *The Psychology of Literary Appreciation* (Melbourne: Melbourne University Press, 1932), Melbourne Educational Research Series 13.

27 Ernest G. Moll Papers, National Library of Australia, MS9283, Box 2 Folder 6. It is possible that Richards's hefty theoretical tome *Interpretation in Teaching* (London: Kegan Paul, 1937) was the belated by-product of an earlier intention to write such a book. His later, more popular monograph, *How to Read a Page* (London: Kegan Paul, 1943) may be another such by-product. Neither book looks much like a prose counterpart to Moll's book on poetry.

> my sphere and something so foreign and undesirable that I did not even try to like it, nor did it occur to me that I might try to do so at some future time. I imagined that only very intelligent people and those who were ethereal and poetic in nature were attracted by poetry, and this increased my dislike for it. It didn't seem a thing for a normal person to like and I wouldn't even try. [Tagged 'Freshman—English major—average ability'][28]

Jerry Moll visited Australia many times, thus maintaining close ties with his extended family throughout his seventy-five years of expatriation; and during all this time he declined (at some financial disadvantage to himself) to surrender his Australian citizenship. He was also a poet of some repute, and published seventeen volumes of poetry, mostly on Australian themes, including *Collected Poems* with Angus and Robertson in 1957. His most extended Australian visit was a year-long academic exchange in 1939–40 with the Sydney Teachers' College, arranged by George Mackaness, literary editor, scholar and bibliophile, who was then Head of English at the College, and a long-time champion of progressive literary education.

International exchanges were not common in the 1930s, and Moll's nationality may have played a part in bringing this one to fruition, since Mackaness had first contacted Moll some years before, at John Le Gay Brereton's suggestion, to ask for some of his poems for an Australian poetry anthology. But a major additional factor is likely to have been a genuine hope on the part of the college that his approach to the teaching of literature might help to reinvigorate that area of teacher-education at a time when the energies of the 'New Education', brought to the college by its founding Principal, Alexander Mackie in 1912, were in retreat after years of conflict with reactionary ministers and hostile department Heads. Percival Cole, Acting Principal of the STC at the time, and a close ally of Mackie's, expressed his hope that 'your presence and the fresh work which you will bring into our academic community will

28 E.G. Moll, 'Appreciation of Poetry', in John H. Mueller, E.G. Moll, N.B. Zane, Kate Hevner, eds, *Studies in Appreciation of Art*, (Eugene, Oregon: University of Oregon, 1934). Studies in College Teaching, vol. 1.3, pp. 41–42.

be of the greatest value, and may lead to an extension of international exchanges in the near future.'[29]

Central to the thinking of both Mackie and Cole, and also to that of Peter Board, the extraordinarily able and imaginative Director of Education whose forced resignation in 1922 slowed the pace of schooling reform in New South Wales, was a 'Neo-Herbartian' philosophy of education. The term denotes the vigorous revival of interest in the late nineteenth and early twentieth century in the work of the German educational philosopher and psychologist Johann Friedrich Herbart (1776–1841), whose emphasis on the formation of moral character carried important implications for curriculum and pedagogy.

Learning, for Herbart and his followers, was understood not as a training of separate mental faculties, but rather as an activation of the receptive powers of the mind by stimulating pupils' curiosity and empathy concerning the social, physical and intellectual worlds around them. History, literature, natural science and mathematics were seen as the key components of a broad but integrated curriculum, and pedagogy was focused on techniques (e.g. the 'Five Formal Steps'—preparation, presentation, association, generalisation and application) designed to arouse interest and to promote 'apperception', the process by which new knowledge was assimilated, by association, to bodies of ideas already present in the student's mind. Literature was seen as a key part of the modern curriculum by Herbart himself, and also by his disciples in Germany, the United States and Britain where the revival was strongest, because the study of it combined the affective, experiential, moral and cognitive components of the learning process.[30] For that reason, literary appreciation had an esteemed place in the 'New Education'—the British educationist Frank Hayward even wrote a book *The Lesson in Appreciation* (1915), which exemplified the teaching of literary and musical

29 Moll Papers, National Library of Australia, MS9283, Box 1, Folder 1.

30 The leaders of the movement in Germany were Wilhelm Rein and Tuiskon Ziller, both of whom had studied with Herbart himself. In America, where the movement was particularly strong, its earliest advocates were Charles A. McMurray and Charles De Garmo, and in Britain John Adams and Frank Hayward.

appreciation on programmatically Herbartian lines[31]—and before World War I, both Mackie and Cole, Principal and Vice-Principal of the Sydney Teachers' College, paid visits to the Pedagogical Seminary at Jena in Germany, the centre of the revival, to see the Herbartian system in action; as did Peter Board, and also John Smyth, the Principal of the Melbourne Teachers' College.[32]

This, then, was the context into which Moll was invited in 1939—one in which a top-down effort was being made to revive the skills of literary appreciation in the New South Wales classrooms by teaching student-teachers how it was done. During his eighteen-month stay in Sydney on this occasion, Moll and his wife made, and kept, a number of literary friendships, especially with Hugh McCrae, Mary Gilmore and A.D. Hope, all of whom admired his poetry. But above and beyond this circle of literary contacts, he was unusually well placed to exert a real influence on at least one annual cohort, perhaps two, of New South Wales English student-teachers. Their ability to convince Australian children in their own classrooms of the possibility of enjoying great literature, and of the value of studying it, may well have been strengthened and sharpened by the strategies for teaching literary appreciation Moll had developed and tested six years earlier in the United States. Judging by the large number of unsolicited and enthusiastic testimonials he received from past students at the University of Oregon, he probably made a memorable impact in the lecture rooms of the Sydney Teachers' College.[33]

Such personal influences may take years, even generations, to work their way through the system. After World War II, Cecil Hadgraft, lecturer and later Reader in English at the University of Queensland, became a close friend of Moll's and visited him in Oregon several times, where he attended some of his classes. In a letter written to him in 1966, the year of Moll's retirement, Hadgraft recalled 'your comment to an unresponsive class with whom you were reading "My Last Duchess"—

---

31 Frank H. Hayward, *The Lesson in Appreciation: An Essay in the Pedagogics of Beauty* (London & New York: Macmillan, 1915).

32 Alan Barcan, *A History of Australian Education* (Melbourne: Oxford University Press, 1980), pp. 223ff.

33 Moll Papers, National Library of Australia, MS9283, Box 1, Folder 4.

Well, would you like the fellow for a friend? You didn't know your lightest word made an impression that would last for four years.'[34] The anecdote is significant because what Hadgraft remembered as epitomising Moll's style of teaching is precisely that move towards appreciation by way of the student's life experience that Moll had described, tested, and reported on decades earlier, in the book he wrote, and the project he conducted, in the early 1930s.

It is worth reiterating that this kind of 'experiential' teaching, which we tend to associate with the sudden relaxation of social proprieties and academic hierarchies that occurred in Australia, as elsewhere, in the late 1960s and early 1970s, and with the ascendancy of the 'personal growth' model of English-teaching in Australian schools, actually has a longer history than this, though not an uninterrupted one. Moll's contribution in 1939–40, minuscule as it must seem in the larger scheme of things, was made at a moment when it *could* have had a disproportionate impact; though whether it actually *did* or not is a question I lack the evidence to answer.

I would like to close on a personal note. I never met Jerry Moll, but I was taught by both Cecil Hadgraft and the poet and academic Val Vallis at the University of Queensland in the late 1960s. Unusually for that time, they often worked as a team, and it was apparent that they shared a number of poetic 'touchstones'—no more than a dozen or so—to which they frequently had recourse as illustrations of particular poetic qualities and effects: the last stanza of Rossetti's 'The Woodspurge', Rupert Brooke's 'These I have loved … ', Keats' 'ardent marigolds' and several others. It was arresting to find that as many, if not most, of these (to me) very familiar, yet somewhat out-of-the-way touchstones are used in Moll's 1933 book on appreciation (which was praised by Mark Van Doren for its fresh illustrations).[35] No doubt he had continued to use them in *his* lectures and tutorials, in Sydney and Oregon, during the intervening three decades. Of such small threads, at times, is the fabric of influence woven.

34 Moll Papers, National Library of Australia, MS9283, Box 1, Folder 3.

35 Moll Papers, National Library of Australia, MS9283, Box 1, Folder 1.

19

New York City Limits: Australian Novels and American Print Culture[1]

Roger Osborne

In the 1974 Winter Book Number of the *New York Review of Books*, a review of Patrick White's *The Eye of the Storm* was placed beneath the headline, 'Patrick *Who*? From *Where*?' The US publication of *The Eye of the Storm* closely followed White's acceptance of the 1973 Nobel Prize for Literature, but reviewer Peter Wolfe could still say that White 'was probably the most unread and unsung major living novelist.'[2] Despite a long publishing history in the United States of America and positive reception whenever a new novel was published, White was never able to penetrate the core of America's literary culture. Patrick White was not alone in this situation which might cause one to ask, 'Why has Australia received so little attention in US literary circles?' This paper aims to propose one answer to that question by identifying American editions of Australian novels and by surveying reviews of these novels in journals and newspapers throughout the twentieth century. This survey will rely on searches conducted via the online version of the *Book Review Digest* and will be informed by Richard Ohmann's 'The Shaping of a Canon: U.S. Fiction, 1960–75'.[3] Drawing on several sociological studies

---

1 Research for this chapter was supported by Professor David Carter's ARC-funded project, 'America Publishes Australia: Australian Books and American Publishers, 1890–2005'.

2 Peter Wolfe, 'Patrick *Who?* From *Where?*' *New Republic* (January 5 & 12, 1974): 17–18.

3 Richard Ohmann, 'The Shaping of a Canon: U.S. Fiction, 1960–1975', *Critical Inquiry* 10.1 (Sep 1983): 199–223.

and other empirical data, Ohmann argues that canonisation in the US has relied on a small group of professional readers and a similarly small number of magazines and newspapers in which these books were discussed, most of which were based within New York City limits. While Australian novels might not have been considered for canonisation as such, the established print culture networks through which they moved ultimately influenced their critical and commercial success. Ultimately, the limited and irregular inclusion of Australia in the 'book talk' of a small number of New York intellectuals and periodicals goes a long way to explaining why Australia has received so little attention in US literary circles.

We are not the first to wonder why Australian novels find it hard to be first published and then receive critical attention in the US. Just as many have wondered what can be done about it. C. Hartley Grattan spent a lot of his life promoting Australian literature and writing about it in the *New York Times*, the *New Republic* and the *Saturday Review of Literature*. In the late 1940s he wrote about the difficulty of getting Australian books into the American marketplace:

> Australian writers have long thought that London was a bottleneck as far as 'dinkum' Australian books are concerned and have looked to New York with hope. Now that New York is opening up, it seems that only what gets through the London barricade can get here.[4]

During the 1940s there was a great effort by publishers, agents and the Australian government to raise awareness of Australian literature. In November 1948 the Australian Government Trade Commissioner devoted the entire Australian Display Centre at the Rockefeller Centre to Australian books, highlighting those available at nearby New York City book stores. More recently the Australia Council contracted the public relations manager Selma Shapiro to maintain the profile of Australian books.[5] Scholars like Bruce Sutherland and Henry Albinski at

4 In Laurie Hergenhan, *No Casual Traveller: Hartley Grattan and Australia–US Connections* (St Lucia: University of Queensland Press, 1995), p. 191.

5 Robyn Sheehan-Bright and Craig Munro, 'Writers', in *Paper Empires: A History*

Penn State and members of AAALS have also attempted to raise the profile of Australian literature in American universities in order to get more Australian books onto the syllabus. But, as John Wells concluded in 2004, except for the 10,000 odd students returning from their study abroad trip to Australia, there is little possibility for Australian studies to expand beyond small pockets of interest.[6] Wells' identification of study abroad students sounds a lot like the hope of many in the publishing industry who saw servicemen returning from the Pacific campaign of World War II as *the* group most certain to bring Australia to the attention of more American readers. Awareness might have been raised, but this did not translate into a substantial and enduring increase in sales. For the most part, Australian books seemed to find their own way to the American market.

Australian books have a long history in American print culture, reaching back to the first half of the nineteenth century, but this history has been dominated by the colonial influence of the British book trade. For many Australian writers London has been seen as the best place to publish their work and for most Australian booksellers London has been seen as the best place from which to get books for an enthusiastic reading public. Due to barriers imposed by national and international copyright law and the restrictions of the Traditional Markets Agreement the British (and colonial) market has been effectively closed to books produced in the US and the American book market has been effectively closed to books produced in Britain. British publisher Stanley Unwin estimated that less than five per cent of books published in Britain were also published in a distinct American edition.[7] Those that did relied

of the Book in Australia, 1946–2005 (St Lucia: University of Queensland Press, 2006), p. 141.

6 John Wells, 'Teaching Australian Studies in the United States: An Overview', in David Carter, Kate Darian-Smith and Gus Worby, eds, *Thinking Australian Studies* (St Lucia: University of Queensland Press, 2004), pp. 190–96.

7 For more detail on the Australian penetration of American publishing see Roger Osborne, 'Australian Literature in a World of Books: A Transnational History of Kylie Tennant's *The Battlers*', in Katherine Bode and Robert Dixon, eds, *Resourceful Reading: The New Empiricism, eResearch and Australian Literary Culture* (Sydney: Sydney University Press, 2009), pp. 105–18.

on transatlantic agreements between publishers or the enthusiasm of a literary agent based in either London or New York. With only a small percentage of exceptions in a 150-year history most American editions of Australian novels followed a British edition, and so even before an Australian book was seriously considered as a possibility for publication in the US it had already passed a rigorous process of assessment and planning for another market.

Without significant and wide-ranging archival evidence it is very difficult to make confident statements about the reasons why Australian novels, in general, were accepted by American publishers and why some were successful and others were utter failures. Some Australian novels sold only a few hundred copies of the standard 2000–5000 copy first print run, some sold that amount and no more and some reached sales figures that placed them in the status of the bestseller, but I think that it's safe to say that most Australian novels in this history produced only modest sales. It is also safe to say that New York was (and is) the dominant centre of the North American publishing world with most major publishers and literary agents having an office in that city within easy reach of long-established literary networks that had (and have) a significant influence on the initial and ongoing reputation of poets and novelists. Australian novels became American books in the process of their publication in the United States, susceptible to all of the influences that might entail. If we are to ask 'Why has Australia received so little attention in US literary circles?' we need to begin by asking how you get the attention of US literary circles in the first place.

To approach that question, I'm relying on Richard Ohmann's 'The Shaping of a Canon: US Fiction, 1960–1975'. Ohmann's research into the institutions that have influenced the taste of American readers in the twentieth century places significant attention on periodicals and this study is no exception, identifying a small group of prominent newspapers and magazines. Drawing on Charles Kadushin's research into the identification of an American intellectual elite, Ohmann argues that for a book to be taken seriously among a wide range of readers and subsequently approach or reach a canonical status it had first to be 'approved' by a small number of distinguished journals. Kadushin's surveys of cultural leaders in the 1960s and 1970s indicated that just eight journals had the power to provide such approval: the *New York Review of Books*, the *New Republic*, the *New York Times Book Review*, the *New Yorker*, *Commentary*, *Saturday Review*, *Partisan Review* and *Harper's Magazine*—with the first on this list having the greatest impact.[8] Kadushin concluded that these 'top intellectual journals constitute the American equivalent of an Oxbridge establishment, and have served as one of the main gatekeepers for new talent and new ideas.'[9] Such a role also came with commercial influence in the publishing world as seen by Jason Epstein's position as vice-president of Random House. (Epstein was the founding editor of the *New York Review of Books*.) Ohmann's survey of reviews in 1968 revealed that Random House books and Random House authors dominated that journal's pages, suggesting that 'it sometimes deployed that strength in ways consistent with the financial interest of Random House.'[10] But, despite such commercial nuances, the elevation of a novel to 'canonical status' relied on this mixture of culture and commerce:

> If a novel was certified in the court of prestigious journals, it was likely to draw the attention of academic critics in more specialized and academic journals ... and by this route make its way into college curricula, where the very context—course title, academic setting, methodology—gave it de facto recognition as literature.[11]

Going into detail about the origins and readers of these journals is beyond the scope of this paper, but some mapping of the literary field in which they circulated is required before I introduce Australian books to the discussion. First of all, it should be noted that less than fifteen per cent of books published in the US get the benefit of a review.[12] For instance, in 1985 it was estimated that of the 15,000 to 20,000 books sent

8 Charles Kadushin et al., 'How and Where to Find Intellectual Elite in the United States', *Public Opinion Quarterly* 35.1 (Spring 1971): 6.

9 Kadushin, p. 17

10 Ohmann, p. 205

11 Ohmann, pp. 205–06.

12 Kadushin, p. 308

to the *New York Times* for review only 2000 could possibly be reviewed. The practical necessity of this situation then has an effect on the attention paid to books in other newspapers and magazines because many harried editors look to the major newspaper for guidance about what should be reviewed—that is if the newspaper or magazine in question does more than just syndicate a *New York Times* review. The dominance of the *New York Times* review is consolidated by the 'near monopoly of early review' enjoyed by the paper.[13] Ultimately, a book's chance of wide discussion is limited by the taste and motivations of one person: the *New York Times* book review editor. It is debatable whether attention in the *New York Times* has a direct effect on sales figures, but as far as the accumulation of symbolic capital goes, the *New York Times* makes a substantial contribution.

Since 1960 the acquisition of symbolic capital in American print culture has been greatly influenced by the *New York Review of Books*. Whereas the *New York Times* is scanned by booksellers, librarians, editors, critics and general readers, the *New York Review of Books* has addressed the relatively new public 'that has largely come into existence as a result of the expansion of mass university education after the Second World War'.[14] More selective than the *New York Times*, the possibility of review in the *New York Review of Books* is even less likely, but the cultural reward of selection is widely sought by publishers and authors. Even if the review does not boost sales, 'a favourable one raises an author's standing and so makes him or her able to bargain for more money when negotiating a new contract'.[15] To have a single book reviewed in both the *New York Times* and the *New York Review of Books* is a privilege experienced by very few authors, but as those interviewed in Kadushin's studies suggest, that has to occur in order to have any chance of proceeding towards a canonical status in American literary culture.

The acquisition of symbolic capital subsequent to review in the *New York Times* or the *New York Review of Books* is consolidated by

13 Kadushin, p. 319.

14 Kadushin, p. 326.

15 Kadushin, p. 326.

reviews in the other periodical identified by Kadushin and discussed by Ohmann. The daily and fortnightly appearance of these two periodicals is punctuated by weekly and monthly appearances of other contributors of symbolic capital. Of the weeklies, the *New Republic* and the *New Yorker* have maintained a significant position in the field, the former possibly increasing its stature in the 1980s when the magazine's literary, cultural and arts pages were refashioned along the lines of the *New York Review of Books*, providing greater space for critical essays rather than standard book reviews. Even though book reviews in the *New Yorker* are frequently limited to book talk, the weekly magazine has an enduring reputation for sophistication that elevates any book's level of symbolic value. Journals such as *Harper's Magazine* and the *Saturday Review* have been considered significant contributors of symbolic capital in the past, but by the 1980s their 'middle-of-the-road' and 'middlebrow' reading publics probably limited their ability to be 'major arbiters of taste and culture' in competition with those journals mentioned above. So, too, the greatest influence of *Partisan Review* and *Commentary* might be restricted to the 1940s and 1950s and the lingering reputation of the 'New York Intellectuals' as a cultural group, but an appearance in their pages continued to have an effect on public opinion. Reviews in any one of these periodicals might have drawn significant attention to a book throughout the twentieth century, but as Kadushin and Ohmann have shown, a review of a single book in all of these magazines could clearly influence that book's elevation to a 'canonical' status in American literary culture. But where do we find Australian books in this well-structured network of literary influence?

To approach this question I have conducted searches on the *Book Review Digest* to determine how widely a selection of Australian novelists were reviewed in the periodicals I have mentioned. I acknowledge the limits of such a selection and survey, but I suggest that it is a good indicator for future contemplation. My selection ranges from Henry Handel Richardson's *Ultima Thule* (1929) and concludes with Peter Carey's *True History of the Kelly Gang* (2000). Of course, *Commentary, Partisan Review* and the *New York Review of Books* do not range across this entire period, but there is still room for discussion on the fringes.

Filling out the survey are Eleanor Dark, Patrick White, Christina Stead, Jon Cleary, Thomas Keneally, Colleen McCullough and David Malouf, providing a serviceable cross-section of Australian authors for this occasion.

First of all, I can declare that no Australian managed to hit all periodical targets with one book. Henry Handel Richardson and Eleanor Dark had no chance because of their temporal location, but the majority of my selection had at least some chance. The appearance of these two early novelists as the authors of main selections for the Book-of-the-Month Club in 1929 and 1941 brought them wide exposure, but not the symbolic capital necessary to maintain the attention of the literary establishment. *Ultima Thule* was reviewed in the *New Republic, New York Times* and *Saturday Review of Literature. The Timeless Land* added the *New Yorker* to that list, but without the added clout of *Partisan Review* and *Commentary* the books could not extend to regions of the New York literary field that might have increased the possibility of a greater profile in American literary circles.

Of any of the Australian authors of the last one hundred years, one might expect Patrick White or Christina Stead to have a presence across the field under discussion. White's novels were regularly reviewed in the *New York Times*, the *New Yorker* and occasionally the *Saturday Review of Literature*. The *New York Review of Books* began to review White's novels from the appearance of *The Solid Mandala* in 1966, providing a very high level of symbolic capital, but he was ignored by *Partisan Review* and *Commentary*, leaving him out of the public conversations of the New York Intellectuals. A Nobel Prize, notice in *Harper's Magazine, New Republic, New York Review of Books, New York Times* and the *New Yorker* by critics such as Christopher Ricks, Shirley Hazzard and George Steiner certainly added to White's position in New York, enough to keep him there for more than a moment. Perhaps the *New York Review of Books* consolidated White's position in New York literary culture by publishing *Riders in the Chariot* in its *New York Review of Books* Classics series in 2002. This followed the publication of Christina Stead's *Letty Fox* the previous year, making them the only two Australians with this distinction. Christina Stead had a similar profile to White's in New

York after she rose to prominence in the 1960s with the re-issue of *The Man Who Loved Children* and Randal Jarrell's introduction (which also appeared, perhaps unfortunately, in the *Atlantic Monthly*). But she was ignored by *Partisan Review* and *Commentary* restricting her profile in New York (even though Saul Bellow reportedly suggested her as a good Nobel Prize nomination after he won in 1976).[16] Nevertheless, according to the map of the literary field plotted by Ohmann and Kadushin, she and Patrick White represent Australian literature at its strongest position in the New York literary field.

Of the remaining novelists in this all too brief survey, none have achieved the breadth of exposure of White and Stead. Jon Cleary and Colleen McCullough hit only a few targets, most frequently the *New York Times*. Thomas Keneally and David Malouf both received notice a bit more broadly, but not to the extent of White and Stead. Perhaps of most interest, Peter Carey's current status as a New Yorker and regular prizewinner draws attention and a profile across the *New York Times*, *New York Review of Books* and the *New Yorker* (where he has been reviewed at length by John Updike). Carey is also one of the few Australians to have been noticed by the *Partisan Review*.

If, as Ohmann and others have argued, that to be accepted by America's literary establishment, a work must be noticed by the dominant periodicals of the day, then one answer to the question that prompted this paper becomes a bit clearer. No amount of individual promotion or government intervention will make America's literary establishment acknowledge Australian novelists on a regular basis unless the most dominant institutions (read periodicals) can be identified, infiltrated, and coerced to include Australian novels in the conversations of their most prominent spokespeople. As the history of Australian books shows that is not an easy task. If that is the answer, what is the significance of the question? Australian novels will continue to find their way to American publishers, booksellers and readers. They will be purchased and read, contributing to the economies that support the lives of writers, publishers and literary agents. Most of them will receive no attention in American literary circles but some of them will.

16 Hazel Rowley, *Christina Stead* (Port Melbourne: Heinemann, 1993), p. 535.

Some of these will hold the attention of literary culture for a short time. Very few of these will attain a position strong enough to make a lasting impact on American literary culture and very few will be found on university syllabi. That they receive so little attention in literary circles should not detract from this presence but prompt us to ask different questions about the types of American readers that Australian novels do serve. The answer to that lies beyond these New York City limits.

20

Rejected by America? Some Tensions in Australian–American Literary Relations

Louise Poland and Ivor Indyk

This chapter focuses on the period from the mid-1970s to the late 1980s, a watershed period in Australia–US literary relations, which saw the publication in the US of Australian novelists Peter Carey, David Malouf, Jessica Anderson, Thea Astley, Elizabeth Jolley, Helen Garner, Tim Winton and Beverley Farmer among others, but which was also crossed by tensions and contradictions which led to confusion, disappointment, lost opportunities, and sometimes the outright rejection of important Australian authors and their books.[1] Among these tensions, we look at three in particular: the promising but limited role played by the multinational publisher (in this case Penguin Books) offering Australian titles through its US affiliate (Viking Penguin); the intervention by literary agents in Australia–US literary publishing relations; and the difference in values between the two cultures, which served to hinder the appreciation of important works of Australian writing.

Prior to the 1980s, hardback and paperback publishers were usually different identities. More often than not, especially in the US, books were first published in hardback before being released in paperback by a second publisher. During the 1980s, Australian publishers began to adopt a mix of strategies to promote their books in the American market. These included: exporting finished books to an American

1 Other authors published in the US include: Carmel Bird (New Directions), Elsie Roughsey Labumore (Viking), Chester Eagle (Viking), Jill Neville (Viking), and Morris Lurie (Viking). Ed Iwanicki to Brian Johns, 24 October 1984, Penguin Books Archive.

associate or distributor; selling US rights to an American (hardback) publisher; co-publishing with an American publisher (a strategy adopted by independent Australian publishers such as University of Queensland Press [UQP]).

Some Australian publishers, such as McPhee Gribble and Outback Press, were also attempting to buy rights from American publishers for the Australian market. In this way, they sought to institute a reciprocity which they hoped—often in vain—would lead to those same US publishers buying Australian titles. As Hilary McPhee has since remarked, breaking new ground in rights trading in the 1980s was gruelling work:

> What we were proposing was good for authors, good for readers, good for publishing. We argued the case at every turn to agents, on public platforms, in the press … Now I can see we were chipping away, from our tiny base, at the coalface of postcolonial publishing relationships, with our bare hands.[2]

During the early 1980s, under the leadership of its new publishing director, Brian Johns, Penguin Books Australia concentrated on expanding the company's already successful Australian list by, firstly, extending its list of original Australian fiction and, secondly, supplementing this with 'takeover' paperbacks, that is to say paperback editions of hardbacks previously released by another publisher (such as Nelson or UQP). In addition, books published by Penguin Australia were offered to its overseas associates, including Viking Penguin in the US, who could decide to publish the books in their own right, but more often chose to take run-on copies from the Australian print run. This habit of sending finished books to Penguin in the US reduced the unit cost of the book in Australia, and meant that Viking US could offer Australian books (albeit in quite small numbers) to the American market without the production costs incurred by originating a book, and without a separate advance to the author.[3]

2 Hilary McPhee, *Other People's Words* (Sydney: Pan Macmillan, 2001), p. 178.

3 Between 1000 to 3000 copies.

However, Penguin's associated overseas companies did not automatically take copies of Australian books, and Viking US did not often find the books released by Penguin Australia of interest for the American market. According to Bruce Sims, former fiction publisher at Penguin, when Viking US considered Australian books, the typical response could be summarised as follows:

> [This author] is not without talent, but I think this is the wrong book with which to try to introduce him to an American audience—especially with our constricted market. There are a large number of strictly Australian references and a lot of strictly Australian vocabulary. Unless I misread this, the ultimate theme of the book is what being an Australian means, and that's an extremely difficult theme for us to sell. It's by no means impossible to market an Australian voice here, but it's almost impossible when that voice is so relentlessly Australian.[4]

Moreover, when Penguin Australia secured an order from Viking US for finished books, the arrangement did not always work out as hoped, or it resulted in unanticipated complications. For example, in 1982, an order for 4000 copies of Penguin Australia's new print run of Jessica Anderson's *Tirra Lirra by the River* was placed by someone in Penguin US who subsequently left the company. When *Publisher's Weekly* published a rave review, nobody at Viking Penguin US had read the novel, but when they did they figured they were on a winner, gave 2000 of the Australian copies away as promotion, returned the rest, and printed their own edition, which they then marketed as if they had originated the title. They sold around 27,000 copies from their own print runs, all under the original Australian contract, so that Anderson got no additional advance, and royalties diminished by the twenty-five per cent deduction paid to Macmillan as the original holder of the rights. There were similar confusions with novels by Helen Garner and Thea Astley, where copies ordered in from Australia were returned or held up, while

4 Bruce Sims, 'The Penguin Publishing Machine', unpublished paper, copy in authors' possession; quotation from letter to Bruce Sims, Penguin Books Archive.

alternative arrangements were sought for publication in hardback by another publisher.

In effect, Viking US was generally acting as a distributor for Penguin Australia's titles rather than publishing them in its own right, although the distinction wouldn't have been obvious to the layperson—including many of Penguin's authors. Because they didn't originate these titles themselves, Viking US didn't give them marketing support, and because the books were paperbacks and not hardbacks, they often didn't receive reviews. As a result, Viking US sold only small quantities of Australian books—less than 2000 copies per title if sales figures for 'front-rank' author, Thea Astley, are taken as a guide[5]—and Australian writers might be denied the opportunity to be published in America simply because Australian copies of their titles were already sitting in Penguin US's warehouse.

In defending the Penguin–Viking arrangement in 1988, Viking publisher, Ed Iwanicki, predicted a gloomy future for Australia's literary writers seeking to break into the American market:

> While we have been able to make major authors of Jessica Anderson, Elizabeth Jolley, etc, in the US, and other publishers have done the same with other Australian authors, it is more delusions of grandeur than anything that prompts most Australian writers of fiction to believe that the same thing can happen—even should happen—with them. Because it's happened with some does not mean it will happen with all—even with those some of us think it ought to happen to. I have been trying for years to do this with David Foster, to no avail whatsoever. I publish more Australian fiction than any other publisher in the US and the main reason for that is that I can do so without a separate US contract. If I had to contract separately for these books, we would not publish them at all; the economies involved with separate advances would not permit it. I had predicted to Brian [Johns] long

5 Ed Iwanicki, letter to Bruce Sims, 22 January 1988, Penguin Books Archive: *An Item from the Late News*—1,823; *Boat Load of Home Folk*—1,579; *Girl with a Monkey*—762. Note that Astley's *Beachmasters* was released as a Viking hardback.

> ago that his authors would increasingly be unwilling to give you US rights on your contracts. And I also predicted then, and I do so now, that most of these authors will not find US publishers willing to sign them up. They certainly have every right to try. But it will be their gamble. Most of them will end up not being published here at all. The agents have begun to descend like a plague of locusts. I wish them all the best, but after about five years of this, I believe the end result will be miniscule.[6]

Following the collapse in 1976 of the British Publishers' Traditional Market Agreement (also known as the British Commonwealth Market Agreement), which had previously led US publishers to view Australia as 'Britain's patch', and confined Australian publishers to 'original works emanating from Australia for the Australian market', the role of the American literary agent had grown in importance.[7] This growth was especially marked during the 1980s (and early 1990s) as the publishing industry became more concentrated, with American literary agents in some cases supplementing the traditional role of the Australian editor as the principal point of contact and continuity for an author. It was in the interests of the literary agents to split rights and operate territory-by-territory to maximise their returns, but this was in direct opposition to the interests of multinational publishers like Penguin who sought world rights, the better to work with their affiliates in other territories and to economise on production costs and royalties.

---

6 Ed Iwanicki, letter to Bruce Sims, 22 January 1988, Penguin Books Archive.

7 Kath McLean, 'Culture, Commerce and Ambivalence: Federal Government Intervention in Australian Book Publishing', PhD thesis, National Centre for Australian Studies, Monash University, 2003, p. 68. Literary agents' livelihoods depend on their capacity to persuade authors that they can achieve better terms for them in negotiating with publishers than the authors could themselves, and on their capacity to persuade publishers to accept terms which are sufficiently high to generate a reasonable stream of income from the commission on an author's earnings; John B. Thompson, *Books in the Digital Age: The Transformation of Academic and Higher Education Publishing in Britain and the United States* (Cambridge: Polity Press, 2005), p. 22.

Editors, too, have completely different agendas to literary agents. When the rights to Thea Astley's *It's Raining in Mango* were sold to the American publisher, Putnam, the complications of Australian spelling and usage troubled the editors at both Penguin in Melbourne and Putnam in New York. Even when the publishers involved in a co-production were Penguin affiliates, there could be conflict between editors. When Penguin Australia's senior fiction editor, Jackie Yowell, proposed a particular editorial arrangement to her counterpart at Putnam, her priority was not only to ensure that the project should be economically viable, but also to preserve Penguin's close editorial relationship with one of its most important authors. On a more prosaic level, Yowell was keen to clarify the extent to which Astley's 'Australianisms' might be at risk of change. She acknowledged her anxiety to Astley: 'I am anxious because we are not sure where all this splitting of rights leaves the editing situation. Of course we'd feel happier if we could edit it here.'[8] For Astley, too, the co-production of *It's Raining in Mango* became 'all so COMPLICATED'. In a letter to Penguin's rights manager, Astley noted:

> I would really prefer the book to be edited *here*. I have told Elise [Elise Goodman, her New York agent] that in letter written today ... Kiddo, I'm tired of hitting the typer. I had a vague idea an agent would free me from all this.[9]

The 'descent of the literary agents' as Viking publisher Ed Iwanicki later described it,[10] caused a number of other complications; not only did agents split markets or territories, and separate off the subsidiary rights, their interventions also complicated relations between publishers, and between authors and their publishers, and on occasion resulted in the pulping of significant numbers of finished books.

When Australian author Jessica Anderson appointed Elaine Markson as her American agent in 1985, significant author/publisher

8 Jackie Yowell, letter to Thea Astley, 25 February 1987, Penguin Books Archive.

9 Thea Astley, letter to Peg McColl, 10 March 1987, Penguin Books Archive.

10 Ed Iwanicki, fax to Bob Sessions, copied Peter Field, M. Lilien, Dawn Sefarian, 29 November 1988, Penguin Books Archive.

tensions emerged, as the following exchange reveals. Anderson wrote to Brian Johns on 30 May:

> I told you at the Miles Franklin that I now have an agent in New York. You made no comment at all … I repeated in my letter of 15 May that in any dealings with the US, my agreement with Elaine Markson … ha[s] to be taken into account. Again you do not comment. Why not? How do we stand on this? I have never had an overseas agent before, and I thought perhaps it may be possible for you to deal with her instead of my dealing with her directly.

Johns replied on 4 June:

> You are quite right … the reason I didn't go into it was that I didn't see Elaine Markson coming into the picture unless we failed to interest our overseas associates … I would naturally be inclined to try them first from here. Nevertheless it might well be that Elaine Markson, being on the spot, might both make her more effective and be more reassuring to you. I would be happy to let her handle it particularly if it removed any abrasiveness between us.

Anderson's reply, on 9 June, reveals the tension inherent in the situation:

> I do believe that if I am to continue to publish in the US without going slightly mad, I need an agent on the spot … I hope that an agent will be able to get me figures, and get my advances paid at the agreed time …[11]

Thea Astley also dismayed publisher Brian Johns at Penguin when she appointed American agent, Elise Goodman, who subsequently intervened in Penguin's inter-company arrangements to ask Viking US to remove Astley's *Hunting the Wild Pineapple and Other Stories* from its list.

11 Jessica Anderson, letters to Brian Johns, 30 May and 9 June 1985, Penguin Books Archive; Brian Johns, letter to Jessica Anderson, 4 June 1985, Penguin Books Archive.

Penguin Australia had supplied Viking in the US with 4000 run-on copies of *Hunting the Wild Pineapple* at the same time as Elise Goodman was attempting to secure its publication in hardback by another US publisher, Putnam.[12] The tension and anxiety that arose from this intervention become apparent in Ed Iwanicki's fax to Penguin publisher Bob Sessions:

> I came to the conclusion that no further fiction titles could be ordered from Australia without the explicit assurance from Australia that we could indeed have the title. We've ordered world titles, [then] … cannot have them after all, because the agent and/or the author wants to sell US rights separately. Then we've had to cancel publication … If Elise [Goodman], in particular, and others believe that US rights should or must be sub-licensed … Penguin Australia *must* tell us this or change their territory *before* we spin wheels …[13]

* * *

The difficulties of Australian–US literary relations, in regards to publishing, are even more forcefully represented by those books, important to Australian culture, which were not published at all in the US during the period we are considering. Though significant, such books are mute witnesses—because they were not published, there is no empirical evidence which would allow us to measure or to analyse the response to them. There was no response.

There are two works of fiction which, perhaps more powerfully than others, give a compelling insight into Australia's developing metropolitan culture during the formative period of the 1970s and

12 *Hunting the Wild Pineapple* was first published by Nelson in 1979. In a letter to Bob Sessions, 12 June 1989, Elise Goodman advised acceptance of an offer from Putnam for hardcover rights on *Hunting the Wild Pineapple and Other Stories*, Penguin Books Archive.

13 Ed Iwanicki, fax to Bob Sessions, copied to Peter Field, M Lilien, Dawn Sefarian, 29 November 1988, Penguin Books Archive.

1980s, but which were largely ignored in America—Helen Garner's *The Children's Bach* and Frank Moorhouse's *The Americans, Baby*. Hilary McPhee made strenuous efforts in the US on Garner's behalf, as for all her authors, and the extensive account she gives in her memoir *Other People's Words* is generally upbeat. But her portrait of Garner reading to a tiny audience in the New York Public Library, which quotes the author herself—'*of course we are basically a non-event*, we are from the void, as far as most of the people are concerned. I develop a policy of expecting no one to turn up so that even seven people look like a big house'—does convey something of the reality of it all.[14] Garner's *Monkey Grip* and *Honour and Other People's Children* had been published in the US by Seaview in the early 1980s 'with limited success'.[15] Seaview was a small press owned by *Playboy*, and disappeared after three years. Despite the efforts of McPhee Gribble's agent Ginger Barber, who also represented Virago authors in the US, both *The Children's Bach* and *Postcards from Surfers* ended up in the default position for Penguin's Australian titles: distributed rather than published by Viking Penguin in the US, using imported copies from the McPhee Gribble/Penguin editions in Australia. The US affiliate appears to have been resistant even to the idea of combining the two books in one volume as Bloomsbury had done in the UK. According to Hilary McPhee, Viking US didn't feel that Garner had sufficient appeal to warrant a US edition.[16]

The neglect of Moorhouse is all the more remarkable, given the preoccupation with America shown in both *The Americans, Baby* and *The Electrical Experience*. It is hard to imagine a more penetrating representation of what America meant to Australia in the last decades of the twentieth century than that given in those two books. *The Americans, Baby* was published in 1972 by John Abernethy at Angus & Robertson (A&R), who had worked as a publisher in the US, and had high hopes for its success there. He pitched the book and its author to

14 *Other People's Words*, p. 183.

15 Diana Gribble, letter to Brenda Lyons, n.d., Box 22, McPhee Gribble Archive, University of Melbourne Archives.

16 Hilary McPhee, letter to Selma Shapiro, 27 March 1986, Box 21, McPhee Gribble Archive, University of Melbourne Archives.

Viking, Norton, Holt Rinehart, a literary agent, and a contact with the *New Yorker*:

> I'm taking the liberty of sending you an Australian whom I think you'll find interesting. His name's Frank Moorhouse, and A. & R. will shortly be publishing a collection of his stories, many of which are tolerably dirty. I'd be more grateful to you than I am already if you'd spread him around writers and such. He's an able newspaperman, sweats freely, and performs impressively with knife, fork, bottle and glass. I commend him to your attention. He'll probably hit N. Y. towards the end of this month.[17]

Despite his contacts and his enthusiasm for the book, Abernethy was unable to place it. Nor was Richard Walsh, who was the publisher at A&R from 1974. A&R was not an international company: it had offices in the UK, from where its overseas rights were managed, but so little penetration in the US, that Walsh several times considered the purchase of a US publisher as a way of introducing A&R titles there. *The Americans, Baby* was personally represented by Walsh on his trips to the US in the late 1970s, and placed with a US agent, but again with no success. A&R also provided financial support for Moorhouse's visit to New York in September 1976, 'to promote … *The Americans, Baby*, to explore the possibilities of the sale of film rights in this book and to develop a script for such a proposed film'.[18] When finally the film *The Coca-Cola Kid*, based on stories from *The Americans, Baby* and *The Electrical Experience*, directed by Dusan Makavejev, with a screenplay by Moorhouse, was released in 1985, A&R published a selection of stories as a movie tie-in, under the same title. Moorhouse's Australian agent Rose Creswell, believing that the film would pave the way for his publication in the US, lobbied Walsh to bring out a 'Moorhouse compendium', and had a manuscript of 170,000 words typed up, 'so that it can be looked at

17 Letter to Merrill Pollack, 4 January 1972, A&R Third Archive, Mitchell Library, Box 215, Frank Moorhouse 1971–1977 (folder 1).

18 David Harris, letter to Frank Moorhouse, 20 September 1976, A&R Third Archive, Mitchell Library, Box 215, Frank Moorhouse 1971–1977 (folder 1).

freshly to see how it works'.[19] In the event, A&R's tie-in was a paperback reprint of the *Selected Stories* it had published three years earlier as a hardback in its Australian Classics series. The movie made little impact in the US—the selection even less.

The Americans, Baby is necessarily mute about its lack of impact on Australian–American literary relations, at least in the terms favoured by book historians, because it was never published there. How then to explain this indifference, or is it resistance, on the part of America?

The book itself is by no means mute on this subject, or innocent. The second story in the collection, 'The American, Paul Johnson', opens with:

> They'd met the American Paul Johnson in the bar of a hotel near the university.
> He'd offered to buy them beers and they'd let him, amused by the chance to bait an American.
> I graduated AB from New York City College,' he told them.
> And they went at him about the standard of American universities.
> And then they went at him about the Negroes …
> And then about Vietnam.[20]

In this story, and several times through the collection, Americans are referred to as 'the enemy'. Australian readers might find this unexceptionable—it is to their point of view that the stories play—in America it could be fatal.

But what is really provocative about 'The American, Paul Johnson' is the fact that it portrays the Australian–American relationship as a homosexual relationship, one which acknowledges sameness in difference, and more importantly, expresses the mixed feelings of animosity and attraction which come from sleeping with an enemy whom one really desires. This combination of antagonism on the one

19 Letter to Richard Walsh, 30 August 1984, A&R Third Archive, Mitchell Library, Box 215, Frank Moorhouse 1978–1988 (second folder).

20 Frank Moorhouse, *The Americans, Baby* (Sydney: Random House, 2008 [1972]), p. 13.

hand, and the yearning to be acknowledged by the American on the other, is seen by Carl, the half-reluctant Australian lover, as sado-masochistic: 'In some ways he was whipping Johnson too and he thought Johnson liked that. And when Johnson lashed back the sting of it wasn't a bad feeling.' After they've been to bed together, there is guilt, puzzlement and recrimination to deal with as well. 'I think we are basically different', the Australian tells the American. 'I guess this is the way it is with us', the American tells the Australian.[21]

This same mixture of feelings is expressed in the other stories featuring Americans in the collection, particularly 'The American Poet's Visit', and 'The Coca-Cola Kid'—in the former the aggression stems explicitly from a sense of cultural inferiority on the Australian side, in the latter from the suspicion of economic exploitation, embodied in the ubiquity of Coca-Cola as an object of desire. In both stories what you feel most is the anxiety of the provincial—the fear of counting for nothing, of going unregarded, of being overlooked. It's particularly acute in 'The Coca-Cola Kid': here the Australian, Kim, already feels himself to be inferior and ignored as a rural left-wing school teacher at a party dominated by well-healed Liberals. He needs to be disagreeable with them in order 'to demonstrate where he stood, who he was. He wasn't one of them.' When he encounters the American, Becker, his contrariness suddenly escalates to a feverish intensity. 'He desparately wanted to be pleased with himself ... He wanted to assert himself with Becker. With Becker especially. Because he was an American.'[22]

Accusation and desire, determination and self-consciousness, guilt, embarrassment, puzzlement and recrimination, are the habitual responses of Moorhouse's feeling characters—the encounters with Americans only brings out what is in them already. They are provincials, either explicitly so, because like Moorhouse, they have come to the city from the country, or implicitly, because they find themselves having to negotiate social, political and sexual mores, with which they have little experience. Two other well-known stories which make this provincial perspective explicit are 'The Girl Who Met Simone de Beauvoir in

21 *The Americans, Baby*, pp. 15, 29, 33.

22 *The Americans, Baby*, pp. 185, 193.

Paris' and the infamous 'Letters to Twiggy', in both of which a defensive narrator, all too conscious of his inferiority, lashes out at those who have basked in fame, or brushed with it. 'Letters to Twiggy' was infamous for its escalation into pornography, as an extension of the provincial desire to shock, to magnify, to draw attention to itself, refusing to recognise any limit, least of all the sexual. In another story, a country girl from the Riverina plains wards off the looming perils of fellatio from a perspective down by the hairy calves of her lover. 'There they were, upside down talking to each other. She felt ridiculous. As well as angry. And embarrassed.'[23]

The sexual provocations in *The Americans, Baby* are likely to have been a factor in its rejection by US publishers and their readers, when it got that far. But it is not the provocations alone, either anti-American or sexual, that would have been disconcerting in Moorhouse's work, it is the whole ungainly combination of emotions through which his characters travel in their negotiations with each other. It makes them seem awkward, clumsy, self-conscious, comical. The smallest things become huge with complication, distorting the familiar orders of reality. Their expression of the feelings which buffet them is necessarily contradictory, and therefore hard to read. In 'The American Poet's Visit' Moorhouse uses the phrase 'nonchalantly ill at ease' to describe the attitude which looks to be relaxed but is ready to strike at the slightest hint of judgement or embarrassment. Angela Carter, reviewing *Forty-Seventeen* for the *New York Times*, referred approvingly to Moorhouse's own paradoxical formulation 'the discipline of indiscipline' before coining her own phrase, 'dishevelled elegance', to describe the appeal of his work. 'The effect is unexpected, exhilarating, disorienting, sometimes hilarious.'[24] This was in 1989, seventeen years after the publication of *The Americans, Baby*. Carter of course was an English writer. *Forty-Seventeen* was the first Moorhouse title to be published independently in the US, by Harcourt Brace Jovanovich, after Faber took it up in the UK and Canada. It was followed by *Grand Days*, as

23 'Anti-Bureaucratisation and the *Apparatchiki*', in *The Americans, Baby*, p. 271.

24 Angela Carter, '40 Means You Cry Over Spilt Love', *New York Times*, 13 August 1989, p. 30.

one might expect, given that its setting was the League of Nations. But not by the second volume in Moorhouse's trilogy, *Dark Palace*, which remains unpublished in the US.

You can't blame the Americans for being offended, or put off, by *The Americans, Baby*. The book gave as good as it got. No book is innocent of the reception it is given. Some of Australia's most significant books exhibit a resistance to American (or English) appreciation, which compromises their publication prospects, no matter how vigorously these prospects are promoted.

21

American Dreams and the University of Queensland Press

Deborah Jordan

The University of Queensland Press (UQP) was the first and most significant independent Australian press to develop the North American market for Australian books. Through the agency of the US-born publisher, Frank Thompson, who was employed at the press from 1961 to 1983, UQP was transformed from the merely scholarly into a creative, engaged, independent Australian publishing house with an international market. In the explosive days of the late 1960s and early 1970s, Thompson embodied the democratic challenge to the old Britain-dominated regime both in publishing circles and on campus, and forged new networks of exchange. UQP's innovative publishing lists laid the basis for the renaissance in Australian poetry, fiction and scholarship. Through joint publishing with several American publishers, sale and purchase of rights, and direct marketing and distribution in the United States of America, UQP created the largest American presence of all Australian publishers during this period. Australian novels were no longer 'the most unmarketable of all fiction', as Alex Abernathy had announced returning from New York in the 1960s, that was apart from South American novels.[1]

Thomas Shapcott foreshadowed a transpacific approach to the history of the book in Australia in *Contemporary American and Australian Poetry*. The benefits in juxtaposing two late-twentieth-century English-

1 Quoted in Thomas Shapcott, *Biting the Bullet: A Literary Memoir* (NSW: Simon and Schuster, New Endeavour Press, 1990), p. 211.

language cultures included 'looking freshly at one's own poetry from a new, and possibly unexpected, angle'.[2] American readers could be offered a voyage of discovery. Even more than this, Shapcott believed, was the possibility of discovering 'not only each other, but oneself, and the neighbourhood of our cultures'. The notion of the 'neighbourhood of our cultures' challenges us to think about nations, that is Australia and the US, not as single-cell entities, but as a 'ganglier, operating through exchanges, networks, juxtapositions and interrelationship'.[3] In the fields of literature and publishing there are 'intricate interdependencies',[4] and intertextual dialogues and exchanges. Across the Pacific, more than just in the realm of discourse, there is and was the movement of people and books, both confined and enabled by the entrenched economic, legal and political structures.

To address some of the ongoing negotiations on the circumferences and the transformations of literary production in Australia, this essay starts to map the transpacific relationships generated by UQP. 'How best to fashion a domain of inquiry not replicating the terms of territorial sovereignty?' asks the American Wai-Chee Dimock.[5] Given the disparities in population and market power and the rarely challenged primacy of the US compared to Australia, the usual conflation of literary field and nation can be interrogated. How best to fashion a domain of inquiry interrogating the infrastructures of the nation states that inhibit or facilitate transnational flows? In this context of the history of the book, the focus needs to be not only on the literary field and *mentalités* but territorial copyright and the legal and economic structures of international trade. At a critical transition in the expansion of publishing in Australia, Thompson was appointed manager of UQP. His involvement, that is the 'cross-fertilisation' of

2 Thomas Shapcott, ed., *Contemporary American & Australian Poetry* (St Lucia: University of Queensland Press, 1976), p. xxxiii.

3 Elleke Boehmer, S*tories of Women, Gender and Narrative in the Postcolonial Nation* (Manchester and New York: Manchester University Press, 2005), p. 209.

4 Wai Chee Dimock and Lawrence Buell, *Shades of the Planet American Literature as World Literature* (Princeton and Oxford, Princeton University Press, 2007), p. 3.

5 Wai Chee Dimock in Dimock and Buell, *Shades of the Planet*, p. 56.

the 'imported' American publisher's values and determinations, was of 'strategic significance' contributing an extra dynamic.[6] UQP can be theorised as a creative industry, in biographical, administrative and legal frames, that is as a hub building cultural alliances and networks of trust transnationally.

Frank Thompson was born in Long Beach and grew up in Los Angeles. He was educated at Michigan State University, where he also worked at the University Press (MSUP). Employed by the Australian, G. Lyle Blair, it was a 'hard-edged' four years and 'so intense, so frustrating and so fraught'.[7] Blair, described as extraordinarily competent, aggressive and even 'swashbuckling',[8] had had his own training through Jonathan Cape in London and was in the process of launching MSUP with an 'unusually strong and distinguished list of books in literature and the humanities'.[9] Blair republished Henry Lawson and invited United Nations officials to the launch of R.G. Casey's memoirs. He advised Thompson to go to Sydney, not London nor New York, to pursue a career in publishing. Thompson, like his mentor, was to combine 'the instincts and values of a scholar' with the 'pragmatic skills of the businessman' as well as a sensitivity to those obscured by the British establishment.[10] In Australia, from 1958, Thompson taught and worked in the book trade for Angus and Robertson. Beatrice Davies, the distinguished editor, gave him a pile of Australian fiction to read one time he had the mumps. Thompson became Prentice-Hall's first Australasian tertiary

---

6 Anne Galligan, 'The Culture of the Publishing House: Structure and Strategies in the Australian Publishing Industry', in David Carter and Anne Galligan (eds.), *Making Books Contemporary Australian Publishing* (St Lucia, University of Queensland Press, 2007), p. 41.

7 Frank W. Thompson, 'Creating a Press of National Value' in Craig Munro (ed.), *UQP: The Writer's Press 1948–1998* (St Lucia, University of Queensland Press, 1998), p. 40.

8 Maurice Hungiville, *From a Single Window Michigan State University and Its Press, 1947–1997* (East Lansing: Michigan State University Press, 1998), p. 23.

9 Russel Nye quoted in Hungiville, *From a Single Window*, p. 53.

10 Hungiville, *From a Single Window*, p. 53; see also Pearl Bowman, 'Frank Thompson: An American's Career in Australian Publishing', *Antipodes* 3.2 (Winter 1989): 116.

marketing representative with a terrain which included New Zealand and Indonesia.

In 1961 Thompson became manager of UQP. He was twenty-eight. His initial brief was to reorganise the University bookshop. It is important in this context to see Thompson as an agent, as an 'organic intellectual' in the Gramscian sense, attentive, visionary, bringing his experiences in the US to what became his self-conceived task of 'creating a press of national value' in an international context. Publishing houses are strongly dependent on networks of personal relationships.[11] One of Thompson's strategies, in building up the press, was to draw on the under recognised expertise of less senior academics at the University of Queensland (UQ), and publish their work. Similarly he utilised another undervalued resource—the intellect of women, in their case often as UQP employees. As initially the sole employee of UQP, Thompson managed to arrange secretarial assistance by writing repeatedly to the Register with his handwriting deteriorating until the only word readable was secretary. The press' first secretary, Ann Lahey, Thompson trained as an editor. Shirley Hocking joined her as an academic editor and Penny Rogers became 'their editorial protégé'.[12] As the number of staff employed grew, women outnumbered men substantially. Merril Yule was appointed assistant to the manager and later became Head of Editorial, (and she like Thompson had family ties with the US). Books could be and were edited to high standards so that they were saleable overseas.[13]

Complex changes were taking place economically, socially and culturally, creating a different space for writers, readers and listeners. The 1960s marks an important time of transformation in Australian politics and intellectual consciousness. Historically there was a new generation of men and women testing their powers, a generation less entangled, less regimented by the experiences of World War II and its Cold War aftermath. John O'Grady's very popular *They're a Weird Mob*,

11 Galligan, 'The Culture of the Publishing House', p. 35.

12 Roger McDonald, 'Imbibing Culture at the Royal Exchange' in Munro, *UQP The Writer's Press*, p. 79.

13 Merril Thompson to author, 26 March 2010, pers. comm.

for example, unsettled certainties about British Australian identities and 'exposed a rich vein of material' about 'English and Australian customs'.[14] Thompson himself wrote of two distinct 'Australias'—that of the working people and that of the British Australians. The 1960s saw a flowering of Australian poetry, and the emergence of a powerful international anti-war movement.[15] Other social movements, which were concerned about gender, race and the environment, also crossed national boundaries.

Thompson dissolved 'a number of British-Australian publishing inhibitions' and in doing so UQP's publishing program 'laid the foundations for what has since come to be regarded as a renaissance in Australian literature'.[16] UQP's first wider market than the merely scholarly was a one dollar poetry series. The new generation of poets and readers were well read in international poetry. David Malouf, then working as a poet, encouraged Thompson to take them into account and publish cheap paperbacks editions.[17] Standard British publishing practice was to publish hardback editions first, then follow up with a paperback edition if the hardback had sold well, or been reviewed well. The time lag for the cheaper edition was further drawn out by the complications of government funding. Thompson risked the cash flow early in the year from the sale of textbooks to cover printing costs for a paperback poetry series, and by midyear, in time for accounting, had sold enough to cover the costs. No hardback editions were published nor government subsidy sought. Malouf believed it was one 'of the

14 David Carter, 'They're a Weird Mob and Ure Smith', in Craig Munro and Robyn Sheahan-Bright, eds, *Paper Empires: A History of the Book in Australia, 1946–2005* (St Lucia, University of Queensland Press, 2006), p. 28.

15 'Radical Politics & the University of Queensland: Staff & Student Activism', available at: www.library.uq.edu.au/fryer/radical_politics/page2.html [Accessed 1 February 2010].

16 Ivor, Indyk, 'Magical Numbers' in Katherine Bode and Robert Dixon, eds, *Resourceful Reading The New Empiricism, eResearch, and Australian Literary Culture* (Sydney: Sydney University Press, 2009), p. 145.

17 David Malouf, 'Poets in Paperback', in Munro, *UQP: The Writer's Press*, p. 72.

most brilliant publishing initiatives of the decade'[18] and from that time Brisbane became the 'destination of every would-be young hopeful with a manuscript of poems or stories'.[19]

Primarily through its capacity as an originating press, UQP generated cheap, widely available current literary titles. Quick to follow the poetry Paperback Poets series was its Paperback Prose series made up initially of short-story collections, later longer fiction. The second British-Australian publishing inhibition UQP dissolved was through its focus, nurturance and promotion of artists and writers working in Australia, even those living and working in regional Queensland, long neglected through deference to British literary traditions. Ian Fairweather, for instance, in his final years was living an extraordinarily ascetic life on Bribie Island misrecognised by the local developers. Yet the extraordinary calibre of Fairweather's translations from Chinese and his original illustrations for *The Drunken Buddha* was clear to Thompson, and he negotiated UQP's first joint American creative writing publication with Blair and the MSUP in 1965.

Overcoming a third 'inhibition' in British and Australian publishing, Thompson and UQP were 'equally interested in a wide range of other creators',[20] that is historians, zoologists, women, contemporary writers from Asia, the Pacific and Russia. With his powerful sense of the possible and the aesthetic, and his capacity to recognise this in others to whom he delegated the role of editor of different series, the paradigm shift in values manifesting in the publishing list could be likened to an awakening of Australia's place and responsibilities in the region and the world. Thompson established his first series in new Australian plays and commissioned Eunice Hanger, a UQ drama academic, as editor. He arranged for her selection of three Australian plays to be jointly published with the MSUP through Blair in Michigan.

In the late 1960s and 1970s, 'the settled institutional form' of British and American publishing underpinned by the British Commonwealth Market Agreement, carving the English-speaking world up into

18 Malouf, 'Poets in Paperback', p. 74.

19 McDonald, 'Imbibing Culture at the Royal Exchange', p. 77.

20 McDonald, 'Imbibing Culture at the Royal Exchange', p 76.

exclusive spheres of operation, was being challenged as booksellers, justice departments and publishers sought more open markets.[21] UQP, as an independent Australia-based publisher, was positioned outside exclusive British rights in Commonwealth territories. UQP sought world rights from its authors. By the late 70s, UQP had evolved a strategy for entering the American market. Their best and preferred option was to sell the American rights of a UQP title before publication and for UQP then to enlarge their print run to include an American edition. They had established a precedent with the joint publications with MSUP. It bought printing costs down for UQP. At this stage in the production of the book, innumerable different options were possible and American editions could be packaged with a new cover, bound differently or even produced from UQP flat sheets. Thompson built up contacts beyond MSUP, attending the annual Frankfurt Book Fair to network with representatives from the North American presses, and he also travelled to the US regularly.

The second way for UQP to sell into the North American market was by selling the rights after their Australian edition had been published. Again there were a number of printing options and UQP could sell the American publisher the film, or allow them to re-photograph the book itself for use in their manufacture of the books in the US. The least preferred option for UQP, if the attempt to sell American rights proved unsuccessful, and they had world rights to the book, was for them to go ahead alone and publish the book themselves in America. UQP shipped copies directly across the Pacific to the US for distribution and marketing with 1500 finished copies as the maximum allowed.[22] Marketing for UQP in the US was done initially through Crane Russak & Company. Distribution was through Technical Impex Corporation and UQP set up its own warehouse through them in Massachusetts.

Thompson positioned UQP as not only a seller of rights, but also a buyer of Australasian rights, seeking out joint UQP publication with

21 John B. Thompson, *Books in the Digital Age: The Transformation of Academic and Higher Education Publishing in Britain and the United States* (Cambridge, Malden: Polity, 2005), p 74.

22 To protect the North American printing industry after 1500 copies the book had to be reprinted in the United States.

other presses as the originating publisher. His reports on the Frankfurt Book Fair indicate the extent of negotiations and exchanges taking place. Contacts made at Frankfurt by Thompson were followed up from the press in Brisbane. He developed a close working relationship with the publishing advisors, Crane Russak & Company in New York, who bought and sold rights. They were a small, independent publishing establishment created in 1973.[23] Its two genial directors had recently retired from major American companies seeking to pursue high quality publishing. Ted Crane was a former head of VNR Publishing, and Ben Russak was the former president/founder of the Elsevier Publishing Company. Their initial list consisted of 400 British-import titles for which they had acquired US rights, so they were well positioned to address UQP's needs for both selling rights and direct sales. Through them, UQP had dealings with Humanities Press, Barnes and Noble and other North American publishers.

By 1975 UQP had sufficient turnover of stock in the US to warrant the employment of an agent. Crane Russak recommended Penny Warren. The market for Australian books was growing despite the wider policy of the Australian government that 'the bilateral relationship' demanded no 'special cultural/educational cultivation'.[24] While the Whitlam government had endowed an Australian chair at Harvard University for the US bicentennial, it was a 'very narrow base'. Alongside the efforts of UQP, there were core 'American Australianists' in the US working within the academy. In 1977 UQP published Henry Albinski's book *Australian External Policy Under Labor*. For generating an interest in Australian literature, Nicholas Birns points to the importance of Johanna and Joseph Jones who taught it and edited the series of Twayne monographs on Australian writers, and also Robert Ross, and feminist critics Joan Lidoff and Marian Arkin.[25] Joseph Jones' *Radical Cousins:*

23 Nat Bodian, 'How "A Stress Analysis of a Strapless Evening Gown" Became a Bestseller', *Publishing Research Quarterly* 12.3 (1996): 28–29.

24 Henry S. Albinski, 'Australian Studies in America: Legacies, Promise and Lifelines', *Journal of Australian Studies* 17.63 (1993): 3.

25 Nicholas Birns, '"So Close and Yet so Far": Reading Australia Across the Pacific', *Australian Book Review* (March 2009): 50–51.

Nineteenth Century American and Australian Writers was published by UQP in 1976; Martin S. Day's handbook of American literature the year prior. In 1982 Pennsylvania State University was to open an Australian Studies Centre (Albinski's home university) and UQP jointly published *The Australian–American Security Relationship* with New York based publisher St Martin's Press. With the 'gradual widening' of Australian studies with the centres, staff and other resources, there was a 'catalytic effect of inter institutional connection'.[26] UQP was closely involved with many of these developments, actively seeking links with the University of Texas Press, Penn University Press and the University of New York Press among others once Australian studies centres were established at the associated university.

In a wider frame, American interest in things Australian was taking place across the arts, through the New Age, music and film on the one hand and through US–Australian 'bonding' caused by wartime comradeship, marriage and the modernisation project Australia had embarked on in the 1950s and 1960s on the other. Thompson taught a course in American literature until it attracted too many hundreds of students. Among them was Shapcott who became closely associated with UQP, and he was one among many Australians drawn to the US. New York began to challenge London as the cultural mecca. He travelled there on a Churchill Scholarship in the early 1970s while working on the 'first' transpacific poetry anthology, *Contemporary American and Australian Poetry.* UQP published 1000 copies of the hardback edition and 2500 copies of the paperback in 1977. The hardback edition sold out by 1987; the paperback sold out by 1988.[27] UQP could not find an American co-publisher partly because of the expense of re-negotiating each poet's American copyright, but the anthology remains a landmark in transpacific dialogue.

Penny Warren was employed by UQP as their American agent from July 1975 to September 1978 on a part-time basis. While Thompson met and interviewed her on one of his trips across the Pacific, it was

---

26 Albinski, 'Australian Studies in America', p. 10.

27 Unfortunately there is no indication from the royalty cards how many copies were sold in the United States.

Merril Yule who carried out the extensive correspondence with Warren to establish the process, to develop and sustain the methods of trying to sell the American rights before publication, and if that failed to publish the book in the US themselves. They developed a marketing catalogue, other promotional material, protocols and procedures. The retail price was arrived at by straight conversion plus ten per cent. The two women developed an open channel of communication about financial, intellectual and sales matters and began to include personal information forming an epistolary friendship. By 1976 sales had doubled since the previous year. UQP books were being exhibited, for instance, at the American Library Association meeting (ALA): 'this exposure more important than anything else for us'.[28] UQP catalogues were sent out to 1400 university, 2500 public libraries as well as Junior and Community College libraries. Warren increased the review lists building on those sent out by Technical Impex Corporation. She was involved in a network with other women working in the industry and she told Yule of her lunch dates and conversations with women such as Ellen Wynn from St Martin's Press. Wynn wanted all the 'back-up material' about a book she could get, to make her job of evaluation easier. She told Warren St Martin's were interested in 'Victoriana' and 'Aborigines'. And this personal friendship was productive for UQP.

UQP was finding that as long as texts were not 'too Australian' and in the general field, not fiction, there was the possibility of books being sold in the US. In 1979, significantly, St Martin's Press took their first two pieces of creative writing, that is apart from scholarly and trade books. St Martin's Press was the main publishing house that bought Australasian rights. They took rights for the play, *Struggle of the Naga Tribe*, by the leading Indonesian dramatist, Rendra, translated by Max Lane. Second was Ulli Beier's selection *Voices of Independence: New Black Writing From Papua New Guinea*. Rita M. Troy, St Martin's Import manager, told UQP how:

> Each of these has a political or a cultural angle which gives them some additional selling points beyond their literary

28 Thompson to Warren, 17 May 1977, UQP F 198, Box 210, Fryer Library.

> value. And that's made them work for us, since we don't normally publish original literature on our academic list.[29]

The following year, they co-published Chong-wha Chung's *Meetings and Farewells Modern Korean Stories*. North American publishers were prepared to pay for creative writing from Australia's neighbouring cultures on UQP's publishing program, well before they sought rights to works by Australian novelists on their list.

Novelists in Australia were putting pressure on UQP to find them wider English speaking markets, and the US market was supposedly the largest and most mature in the world. Peter Carey wrote about Australia as a colonised space in his short story 'American Dreams'. Initially the role of the artist and model maker was to provide a mirror 'of our town just for this moment, to let us see the beauty of our town, to make us proud of ourselves and to stop the American dreams we were so prone to'.[30] But the group of these new writers, mostly men, 'mostly young, fed on the first Literature Board Fellowships'[31] who were involved with UQP continued to dream American dreams. With its limited population, the Australian market hardly compared with the possibilities that the North American market might offer. With increasing confidence in part generated by the success of its wider list of academic books in the US, UQP through the agency of Thompson, Yule and Warren, with input from marketing and sales, decided to try to sell the American rights to literary fiction. To keep the loyalty of their authors, Thompson believed, UQP had to develop international outlets. They started with the work of two Australian authors, Carey and Barbara Hanrahan. Warren in New York sent out their fiction to possible American publishers who might buy the American rights.

UQP had world rights to Carey's first book *The Fat Man in History* and also to the hardback version of his second collection of stories *War*

---

29 Rita M. Troy to Pearl Bowman, 11 December 1979, UQP F 198, Box 257.

30 Peter Carey 'American Dreams', in *The Fat Man in History* (St Lucia: University of Queensland Press, 1978), p. 56.

31 Shapcott, *Biting the Bullet*, p. 245.

Crimes.[32] Carey is now an international celebrity author, twice winner of the Booker prize. From the monthly reports Warren sent Yule the progress of his books through the various publishing houses—and their rejection—can be tracked. Readers were responding with enthusiasm to Carey's work in Australia; finally UQP decided to publish *The Fat Man in History* in the US itself, and did so. Soon afterwards Carey's international agent, Deborah Rogers, through her representative in New York, negotiated a contract with an American publisher, Random House, for a new selection of short stories *The Fat Man in History.* Some of these stories were contained in the earlier book already released there. This was in breach of copyright and new legal arrangements had to be drawn up. While Carey was to maintain a commitment to publishing with UQP, the influence of the agent could be rapacious and for Australasian rights to Carey's next novel, UQP had to negotiate with the originating publisher Faber, who also sold Carey's American rights. UQP no longer negotiated directly with Carey himself, or North American presses on his behalf. This was the period of explosion in the scale of agents' activities and the increasing importance of the rights manager in-house.[33]

Barbara Hanrahan was then a mid-career South Australian author first published in London by Chatto & Windus and only later by the University of Queensland. *Where All the Queens Strayed* was UQP's first novel by a woman. UQP negotiated an English edition with Chatto & Windus who insisted on the 'normal British market', which, as this meant traditional Commonwealth rights, included Canada.[34] Thompson refused to let them have Canadian rights because publishers in the US usually asked for Canadian rights. When Warren in New York read Hanrahan's second UQP novel, *The Peach Groves,* she was very enthusiastic. She tried it with Beacon Press, Harper & Rowe, Avon

32 D. Jordan. 'Re-figuring Parallel Importation Restrictions: The Case of Peter Carey's Short-stories', Translegalité Conference Papers, Griffith University CD-ROM, December 2009.

33 Michael Lane, 'Shapers of Culture: The Editor in Book Publishing', *Annals of the American Academy of Political and Social Science* 421 (September 1975): 42.

34 D.J. Enright to Barbara Hanrahan, 8 June 1979, Hanrahan File, UQP Archive.

Books and Warner Books. Then the galley proofs were sent to George Braziller. But despite interest from different American publishers at the Frankfurt Book Fair and in response to Warren's approaches, no American publisher was found for any of Hanrahan's books. Hanrahan was, however, widely translated across Europe, and Chatto & Windus later took up the option of the North American rights.

Malouf's *Johnno* was the first UQP originated novel to find an American publisher, but not until the novel had sold well in Australia. Like Carey, Malouf had been encouraged by UQP as an emerging writer and his importance is now widely acknowledged; in his case, Braziller, the American publisher approached UQP directly. UQP had sold Penguin Australia the Australasian paperback rights in 1976 and it went extremely well. Malouf's second novel *An Imaginary Life* was published by Braziller through his agent, Tim Curtis, with no involvement from UQP. Braziller then approached Curtis for North American and Canadian rights for *Johnno*,[35] who in turn alerted UQP. In 1989, when Braziller reverted the rights of *Johnno*, UQP reprinted a hardback version and sought again to sell the overseas rights. Malouf continued to send his poetry compilations to UQP first for consideration, with Chatto & Windus taking up subsidiary rights when they wanted them.

None of these novels had found joint publication, UQP's preferred strategy and both Malouf and Carey went on to publish their fiction with multinational publishing firms. This changed when UQP did finally sell North American rights for Roger McDonald's first novel in 1979. McDonald had worked at UQP as poetry editor and now, like Malouf, is a widely acclaimed author. UQP sent the jacket blurb, author form and proofs of McDonald's *1915* to Warren who sent them on to St Martin's fiction editor, Les Pockell. Pantheon considered them in April 1979; Viking rejected it two months later; Harper & Row and Farrar Straus followed. Braziller made an offer for 1800 copies of the book and a contract was signed in June 1979 even while Random House was asking for a copy to consider. Braziller also took paperback rights which they then offered to the New American Library, Richard Gallen, Bantam, Washington Square Press then Pocket Books and more who

35 George Braziller to UQP, 24 April 1978, Telex, Johnno File, UQP Archive.

also declined it: 'the reaction is usually that it is too literary a work for the general market in paperback fiction'.[36]

When McDonald's second novel *Slipstream* was ready to publish, UQP was better prepared and the book was feted at the Frankfurt Book Fair in 1981.[37] Knopf, Scribner, Farrer Straus, Braziller, Viking and David R. Godine, all North American publishers, expressed interest in seeing a copy. Braziller was offended when UQP did not give him first option believing it his right after he had published *1915* in the US. However Braziller had not made it easy for McDonald when he wanted to make corrections to *1915* and although they claimed they had paperback rights, never produced a paperback edition or sold the rights.[38] At Frankfurt, Faber bought English volume rights. In this contract, Faber agreed that they would not deal with the author on this book or any other book on rights, but would only deal through UQP. This would prevent the 'end run' of Faber going around UQP for McDonald's next book, as had happened when Faber contracted *Bliss* with Carey for world rights. UQP's American agent finalised a contract with North American Little Brown publishing company in February 1982.

When UQP's agent, Warren, left to take up full-time freelance work, Pearl Bowman, another American, had replaced her in late 1979. Bowman was especially involved in marketing. Her objective was to sell UQP books: 'I knew how to reach the library and specialist markets',[39] she wrote, but not markets for 'exotic' fiction. By the 1980s, UQP had organised a variety of different options and working relations with different North American presses. UQP also did buy in rights to overseas titles; for instance, they bought Australian rights to *The Coup* and *Problems and Other Stories* by John Updike. Thompson wanted Bowman to take on agenting duties for the UQP 'top writers' as part of her brief. She found, however, 'Nothing I have ever done professionally has been as frustrating as sending a manuscript to an editor and having

36 Letitia Burns O'Connor to Yule, 22 May 1989, 1915 File, UQP Archive.

37 Frankfurt Report (1981) UQP F198.

38 Merril Thompson to author, 26 March 2010, pers. comm.

39 Pearl Bowman, 'West 85th Street, New York' in Munro, *UQP: The Writer's Press*, p. 104.

it back a few days later—rejected'.[40] Within a few months Bowman pleaded to be 'let off'. But no one agent could be found to act as a rights person for UQP's entire list, because of its wide range and variety. And worse, it was not worth an agent's time unless they had a sale of 3000 copies.

For the year 1982/83, after Bowman had been with UQP for three years, US sales were budgeted at eight per cent of UQP's turnover. Allocation for these sales was eleven per cent of the sales budget, which was after the export market board subsidy—the Australian government promotional rebate—had been taken into account.[41] The staggering figure and important here in context of UQP's overcoming of British Australian publishing inhibitions, is that US sales were eight per cent of their turnover; the entire rest of the overseas sales was only six per cent, and only had one per cent of advertising monies allocated to them. That is the markets in Britain and Europe, and in South East Asia combined, did not amount to more than the books marketed and sold in the US. The Australian dollar was devalued in the 1980s. Foreign rights sales slowed. With the expiration of the export subsidy in the early 1980s, Bowman acknowledged 'my usefulness to UQP diminished'.[42]

How widespread in the Australian publishing sector were American dreams? UQP was only one among many university presses during the 1970s, just as UQP is only one of the independent publishers in Australia, so remains merely a case study in any wider study of transpacific movement. How do we understand UQP's powerful vision to decentre and decolonise and to sell its diverse works worldwide—even as the increasing transpacific flows were uneven, lumpy, and barely unreciprocated? Even as authors and agents were out of step with UQP and only like to relinquish world rights to UQP in the early stages of their career? UQP was a hub within the wider transnational region, especially through its Asia and Pacific series, networked with other hubs in North America. The foundations had been laid for the successful rights sales to North American publishers in the 1970s and 1980s, even

40 Bowman, 'West 85th Street, New York', p. 105.

41 'Market Report' UQP 198.

42 Bowman, 'West 85th Street, New York', p. 109.

as UQP withdrew its North American office. When Thompson and Yule resigned in 1983, they had already appointed another American, D'Arcy Randall, who was to have such an important role in continuing to open up the production and publication of Australian women's writing in the US in the ensuing decade.[43]

43 This research arises from a wider project on the economies of literary publishing in Australia from 1965 to 1995 with Professor Ivor Indyk, Dr Louise Poland, Craig Munro and others and also from the project on American editions of Australian literary fiction with Professor David Carter. I would like to thank Professor David Carter and Merril Thompson for insight, assistance and comments, and the staff and publisher of UQP for access to and permission to quote from the UQP archive.

22

Transpacific or Transatlantic Traffic? Australian Books and American Publishers

David Carter

Studies of Australian literature concerned with publishing history have, with good reason, focused on the British connection or the related theme of local publishing's emergence out from under the British yoke. As the fiction market expanded in the last decades of the nineteenth century, relations between the British and Australian book trades were newly institutionalised through formal agency and distribution arrangements, price regulation via the Net Book Agreement in Britain, the establishment of cheap Colonial Series, and the emergence of international copyright and trade agreements that cast Australia firmly into the British rather than the American sphere. These developments meant an increase rather than decline in Australian writers' and readers' dependence on British publishing in the decades around Federation; in more positive terms, they meant increased *access* to British publishing.

Either way, as Richard Nile and David Walker put it, London was the 'production centre for Australian literature' and the 'commercial centre of the literary world'.[1] Australian publishing was a 'tale of three

1 Richard Nile and David Walker, 'The "Paternoster Row Machine" and the Australian Book Trade, 1890–1945', in Martyn Lyons and John Arnold, eds, *A History of the Book in Australia 1891–1945: A National Culture in a Colonised Market* (St Lucia: University of Queensland Press, 2001), pp. 3, 7; R. Nile and D. Walker, 'Marketing the Literary Imagination: Production of Australian Literature, 1915–1965', in Laurie Hergenhan , ed., *The Penguin New Literary History of Australia* (Ringwood: Penguin, 1988), p. 286.

cities', with Sydney and Melbourne subordinate to the great London publishing machine. While this claim is undoubtedly valid, indeed fundamental to understanding the history of Australian books, it does ignore New York, the *other* great commercial centre of the Anglophone literary world. Few accounts of Australian book history mention the United States despite the fact that American publication has attracted Australian writers for well over a century. As Laurie Hergenhan argued in his study of the great American Australianist C. Hartley Grattan:

> American editions of Australian works … [are] more extensive than has been realised, for they have been typically overshadowed by interest in … the English aspects of Australian publishing history. Few realise, for instance, that Patrick White's first popular success was the American edition of *The Tree of Man* (the first edition of that novel), that Martin Boyd's *Lucinda Brayford* was a Book Society's choice and bestseller in America or that Eleanor Dark's *The Timeless Land* was also popular as a Book of the Month choice.[2]

While the British connection remains massively determining, once we add America into the picture things start to move—to move outside the framework of the national culture and the singular relationship between imperial centre and colonial outpost. Australia's place in the world republic of letters needs a new trigonometry.

Research to date certainly supports Hergenhan's contention.[3] The bibliographical evidence indicates a long and abundant history of American editions of Australian fiction; this is not a phenomenon that has arisen only in the last two or three decades. A diverse history too. But this diversity seldom adds up to density or continuity. Perhaps only once, in the 1980s, can we talk of 'Australian literature' as such having

---

2 Laurie Hergenhan, *No Casual Traveller: Hartley Grattan and Australia* (St Lucia: University of Queensland Press, 1995), p. 47.

3 Data about American editions of Australian works of fiction have been derived in the first instance from AustLit: The Resource for Australian Literature, available at: www.austlit.edu.au, supplemented by additional bibliographical and archival searches.

a presence in the American book scene. Instead we have a broken and lumpy history, quite different depending on the market segment, and with the American connection having largely to be reinvented for each new generation. Nonetheless the extent and range of American editions is often remarkable, not least for being so little known. To illustrate this fact, let me give a quick survey through to the early decades of the twentieth century.

Australian tales by long-term colonial visitors such as Charles Rowcroft and Henry Kingsley found American as well as British publishers. Rowcroft probably has the honour of coming first, with *The Bushranger of Van Diemen's Land* published by Harper and Brothers in New York in 1846, the same year as in London. The three-volume English edition from Smith, Elder was reduced to 144 pages in double columns for Harper's paper-covered Library of Select Novels, at 25 cents. Subsequent editions appeared in 1855 and 1874. Rowcroft's earlier book, *Tales of the Colonies, or, the Adventures of an Emigrant* (1845), had at least six American editions between 1853 and 1884 under the more dramatic title *The Australian Crusoes, or, The Adventures of an English Settler and his Family in the Wilds of Australia*. Kingsley's *The Recollections of Geoffry Hamlyn* was published on both sides of the Atlantic in 1859, by Macmillan in London and Ticknor and Fields in Boston, the latter having paid Macmillan £50 for proofs in order to establish its exclusive rights to the title as its first American publisher. Later, in the 1880s and 1890s, there were six subsequent editions, from mainstream publishers—Dodd Mead, Scribner's, and Longman, Green—and from pirate publisher J.W. Lovell. To take another case, from the 1870s, after thirteen years in Australia and New Zealand Benjamin Farjeon published a series of convict, goldfields and bushranging tales in the cheap libraries of Harper, Lovell and other American houses: over forty individual titles published in seventy different editions in the final three decades of the century. Based in London, Farjeon, like Kingsley, was hot property in a competitive American marketplace, not least for his Australian tales such as *Grif: A Story of Australian Life* (Harper 1872, Robert M. de Witt 1880, Munro 1882, Lovell 1892) or *The Sacred Nugget* (Munro 1884 twice, Harper 1885, Lovell 1889).

These are scattered and perhaps marginal cases. But as reflected in Kingsley's and Farjeon's careers, the volume of traffic to the US *doubled* decade by decade from the 1870s to the turn of the century, and major authors began to appear regularly in American lists. By the end of the nineteenth century more than sixty Australian novels had been published in American editions, with the bulk of these, over three quarters, appearing in the final two decades of the century. A more generous definition of an Australian novel would raise the total to eighty, perhaps one hundred, American releases.

His Natural Life was published by Harper in 1876, a one-volume 178-page paper-covered edition, making Marcus Clarke the first permanent resident in the Australian colonies to have an American edition. Not unusually for the period, Clarke knew nothing of this publication until he received payment of £15 from Harper. 'Why this curious sum I don't know', he commented, 'I suppose it represents something in dollars—Harper's conscience, perhaps!'[4] But the firm was in fact acting honourably in the circumstances, forwarding a payment to Clarke, albeit a minimal one, when they were under no legal obligation to do so because of the absence of international copyright legislation in the US. The absence of such legislation together with an extraordinary boom in cheap paperback publication from the late 1870s to the early 1890s provides the dynamics for the significant appearance of Australian fiction in the American market before the turn of the century. Two further editions of *His Natural Life* appeared in 1881 in cheap series, and two more in the 1890s.[5]

Ada Cambridge, Rosa Praed, Catherine Martin and Tasma were all published in America. Cambridge had thirteen American titles in multiple editions; Praed, the first Australian-born novelist with American publications, had around twenty, again in multiple editions. All seven of Tasma's books (six novels and a collection of stories) appeared in the US, while Catherine Martin's *The Silent Sea* joined

4 Quoted in Lurline Stuart, 'Introduction', in Marcus Clarke, *His Natural Life*, L. Stuart, ed. Academy Editions (St Lucia: University of Queensland Press, 2001), p. xlix.

5 Stuart, p. l.

Tasma's *In Her Earliest Youth* and Praed's *Rebel Rose* in Harper's Franklin Square Library: no. 728 in this enormously successful series.[6] The presence of these authors in the US was more than negligible: between 1888 and 1898, Cambridge, Praed and Tasma had seventeen titles among the first 250 in Appleton's famous and reputable Town and Country Library (Guy Boothby also had six). Others also prospered in the American market. Fergus Hume began a remarkably successful American career from London with *Madame Midas* in 1888 and *The Mystery of a Hansom Cab* the following year. These were followed by more than fifty American titles. Mary Gaunt had an early novel, *Deadman's*, published in New York in 1899, before she too expatriated herself; four more American titles followed. Louis Becke managed twenty-nine American publications, most through the well-established firm of J.B. Lippincott in Philadelphia. Some editions appeared in America *before* their English release, but the more common pattern until the collapse of the triple-decker in London in the mid-1890s was for the first American edition to appear around the same time as the English one-volume edition (that is, after the original three-volume release), the American edition being set from English proofs. That at least was the common practice among established American houses such as Harper, Appleton or Lippincott; the 'pirate' publishers were another matter.

Rolf Boldrewood's American career, unusually, owed nothing to the cheap paperback reprinters and everything to his publishing arrangement with Macmillan in London. Macmillan had established a New York office in 1869 and by the early 1890s it began acting more or less independently.[7] It is difficult to determine which Boldrewood titles were, strictly speaking, published in New York, but from *Robbery Under Arms* in 1889 it appears that the English editions, which announced both London and New York as place of publication, were sold by the American firm as their own. Boldrewood, like Praed among

6 Publishing information in this paragraph derived from Rosemary Foxton's Introduction to the Colonial Texts Series edition of *The Silent Sea* (Sydney: UNSW Press, 1995), pp: xv–xli.

7 Elizabeth James, 'Letters from America: The Bretts and the Macmillan Company of New York', in E. James, ed., *Macmillan: A Publishing Tradition* (Houndmills: Palgrave, 2002), pp. 170–77.

many others, was keenly interested in the American market and the development of US copyright law. From 1895, after the passage of the International Copyright Act and after Boldrewood had engaged a professional literary agent, A.P. Watt, all his contracts specified an American edition. One book that represents New York as the principal place of publication has been sighted and the evidence suggests others were also published out of New York.[8] Boldrewood was sufficiently well known for his death in 1915 to be reported in the *New York Times*.[9]

The number of Australian works published in the US dropped in the early decades of the twentieth century, but there was nonetheless a steady flow of American editions, more than eighty, again, to 1920. In this period, G.B. Lancaster published the first of nine American titles, Katharine Prichard the first of five, and Henry Handel Richardson the first of seven across the next two decades. Between 1927 and 1929, Bobbs-Merrill of Indianapolis published Martin Boyd's *Brangane*, the first edition of *The Montforts* (as *The Madeleine Heritage*), and *Dearest Idol*; other books followed in the thirties and forties. Also in 1929 Barnard Eldershaw's *A House is Built* was published in the US, to very positive reviews. At a time when his books were banned or likely to be banned in Australia, Norman Lindsay published five novels—and *The Magic Pudding*—in New York during the 1930s, including four first editions. Eleanor Dark's five American titles began in 1936 with *Return to Coolami*, picked up by Macmillan in New York on the personal recommendation of William Collins in London.

Beneath these more familiar names exists a vast undergrowth of little-known books and authors, one-off American titles, and niche successes in specific genres. Between 1900 and 1930, Ethel and Lilian Turner, Louise Mack, David Hennessey, Roy Bridges, Erle Cox, Jack McLaren, Dulcie Deamer, Helen Simpson, Dorothy Cottrell and Marie Bjelke-Peterson, among others, achieved at least one American edition. Given Stanley Unwin's estimate in 1926 that only five per cent

8 *The Crooked Stick; or Pollie's Probation* (New York: Macmillan, 1895). The title-page colophon reverses the usual order, placing New York above the firm's name and London below.

9 *New York Times*, 12 March 1915, p. 11.

of 'ordinary' British books were separately printed and copyrighted in the US (although the percentage was significantly higher for fiction), the numbers in themselves demand attention.[10] More than that, writers such as Cambridge, Praed, Boldrewood and Richardson established reputations as successful, worthy authors in the American marketplace. But what patterns or structures, what connections, transatlantic or transpacific, can be discerned?

Very few if any Australian titles made their way directly to the US from Australia before the 1930s. They travelled via London, either through first publication there or, more rarely, following an Australian first edition. As commodities, then, these books travelled as British books regardless of their stories or settings or the author's residence or birthplace—it is largely a transatlantic not a transpacific story, a trade in literary property that had little to do with any specific interest in *Australian* books or authors. Even Louis Becke's 'South Sea' stories, a popular genre across the Pacific, were mostly published first in London before making their way to the US market. There is little evidence of primary editing or substantial re-editing by American houses until the 1920s or 1930s—with Prichard, for example, whose *Fay's Circus* (Norton 1931), the American version of *Haxby's Circus* (Cape 1930), includes an additional chapter and other substantial variations.[11] And while reviews suggest some interest in Australia as a parallel Anglo-Saxon 'new society', and even something of a market niche for Australian tales of goldfields, bushranging and backwoods romance, these books circulated as contributions to British literature rather than as 'Australian literature' in any meaningful sense of the term.

And yet, to look at the period's publications with America triangulated to Australia and Britain is to be reminded not simply of British domination but rather of the extraordinary mobility of those who belonged to the 'writing classes'; and equally the extraordinary

10 Stanley Unwin, *The Truth About Publishing* (London: George Allen & Unwin, 1926), pp. 69–70.

11 Carol Hetherington, 'Authors, Editors, Publishers: Katharine Susannah Prichard and W.W. Norton', *Australian Literary Studies* 22.4 (October 2006): 417–31.

mobility of texts across national and imperial boundaries. Not only Australian and British, but also British and American, and Australian and American cultures were *closer* than they would become by the mid-twentieth century. This was due partly to shared cultural and racial ambitions, and partly to the legal settings and industry structures that favoured imported British books in the US market for much of the nineteenth century. Here we find a strong case for transnational rather than national literary histories.

This sense of mobility is confirmed by the recurrent patterns of expatriation and imperial commuting among some of the most successful writers—Praed, Gaunt, Tasma, Becke—and by the imperial and Pacific tourism of long-term visitors such as E.W. Hornung, the inventor of Raffles, 'Amateur Cracksman'. Hornung's few years in the colonies in the 1880s were translated into multiple Australian tales that were among his more than twenty American editions. While texts were more or less compelled to travel through London or to originate there if they were to travel at all, in many cases they kept on travelling: London was a relay station, giving texts the power to travel further.

The imperial connection itself was not merely a constraining factor but also a productive force, especially when it intersected with modernity, in this case with the emergence of the new mass-markets for popular fiction generated in the late-nineteenth century in both London and New York. This development in turn produced the boom in American editions of Australian titles. The earlier colonial circuits expanded in the late nineteenth century to form an international Anglophone market for popular fiction. Australian readers and writers, we might say, were subjects not merely of British cultural hegemony but also of an expanding global market for popular entertainment: a modern mass market, not simply a contained colonial one. This market embraced the colonial and exotic romances of a Boldrewood or Praed, but its *future* can be better traced in the careers of the successful genre writers who emerged in this period when the genres themselves emerged into clear definition. Hume and Hornung pursued successful careers across the Empire and across the Atlantic with detective and mystery stories. Guy Boothby too: born in South Australia, Boothby began publishing stories in British magazines before relocating to London just as his first novel was published there in 1894. The novel appeared in Chicago in the same year, the first of almost fifty titles, mainly thrillers, half of which had American editions. James F. Dwyer, NSW-born, pursued a writing career in New York for more than a decade from 1907. Producing mysteries, thrillers and romances, Dwyer had at least nine American titles between 1912 and 1930. Arthur J. Rees moved from Melbourne to London, from where he published more than twenty crime and mystery novels, with sixteen American editions from 1913 to 1938. Ambrose Pratt published popular novels in London, Sydney, New York and Chicago in both the old and new genres—from bushranging to spy stories—with five American titles between 1901 and 1910. This was a truly transnational industry.

Obviously the shifting possibilities for US publication depended upon the situation of the American book trade itself, its internal structures and its external relations, primarily transatlantic. These were governed by informal agreements between publishers and, after 1891, by formal copyright legislation. The rapid expansion of American editions for Australian writers in the two decades from the late 1870s was almost wholly the result of 'the most flourishing, dynamic, and controversial era of paperback publishing' in American history.[12] A cluster of factors including improvements in printing, binding and paper production came together in the 1870s and, in the absence of international copyright law, encouraged new publishing ventures based on 'pirated titles, cheap materials, long press runs, low prices, and nontraditional outlets'.[13] Entrepreneurs such as George Munro and J.W. Lovell produced cheap editions of imported works, mainly pirated British (and hence Australian) novels, typically in series or 'libraries', with new titles appearing weekly or even twice weekly. These 'books in disguise', were printed in magazine format, with two or three columns

12 Kurt Enoch quoted in John Tebbel, *A History of Book Publishing in the United States. Volume II: The Expansion of an Industry 1865–1919* (New York: Bowker, 1975), p. 482.

13 James L. West III, *American Authors and the Literary Marketplace since 1900* (Philadelphia: University of Pennsylvania Press, 1988), p. 35.

per page and paper covers; indeed publishers sought to reproduce the success of the magazines, with regular issue, uniform appearance, numbered series, large print runs, a cheap cover price, convenient size, annual subscriptions, and sales at newsstands.[14] By 1886 there were twenty-six libraries, issuing 1500 titles in that year alone.[15] In order to survive in what became an intensely competitive market, established publishers like Harper and Appleton produced cheap libraries of their own. Competition produced an enormous appetite for non-copyrighted foreign titles. British publishers' lists, serialised fiction, and domestic competitors' lists were systematically raided for next week's new release. Typically for Australian authors, an English edition or an authorised American edition would be followed by a pirated edition, and often multiple editions of the same title from the competing paperback reprinters. Between them, Cambridge, Tasma and Praed had twenty-nine books published in forty different editions in the libraries of Munro, Lovell, Appleton and Harper between 1879 and 1898. Tasma's *Uncle Piper of Piper's Hill* provides a case study of the fate of many Australian titles in the period: first serialised in the *Australasian* in 1888, it had two editions in London in 1899 and then near-simultaneous American editions in cheap libraries from J.W. Lovell, Frank F. Lovell, Harper, and Munro, all in that same year. But Tasma complained, 'How little *material* benefit I have reaped from my work despite the fact that the Americans have issued four different editions of it'.[16]

What allowed this situation was the USA's refusal to legislate for international copyright until 1891. This meant that no payments to foreign authors or their publishers were legally required, although mainstream houses such as Harper, Appleton and Scribner's did pay one-off amounts for plates or sheets or for exclusive rights to an author's work; they worked through London agents and often had well-established

14 Robert A. Gross, 'Building a National Literature: The United States 1800–1890', in Simon Eliot and Jonathan Rose, eds, *A Companion to the History of the Book*, (Malden: Blackwell, 2007), p. 326.

15 Tebbel, pp. 485–86.

16 Tasma's diary, 1 January 1890. Quoted in Patricia Clarke, *Tasma: The Life of Jessie Couvreur* (Sydney: Allen & Unwin, 1994), p. 121.

informal arrangements with British firms. A publisher's investment in a title or an author was protected in the US market by a system known as 'courtesy of the trade', a set of conventions whereby a firm's exclusive right to a book would be recognised by other publishers if that firm was the first to announce its intention to publish the book in the American market. Such a claim was strengthened if payment had been made to the author or English publisher.[17] The pirate reprinters either ignored or deliberately sought to undermine the conventions of trade courtesy, and the inability of publishers like Harper or Appleton to protect their investments led them eventually to support the International Copyright or Chace Act, which became law in July 1891. Cheap paperback series gradually disappeared as the copyright regime and the industry itself stabilised. By the 1920s the structure of the US industry had taken the shape it would retain until the end of the century around the major New York houses such as Scribner's, Putnam, Knopf, Viking, Norton, Simon and Schuster, and William Morrow. Paperback publishers formed a very large second tier. With international rights now at stake, literary agents become an essential part of the relationship between authors and publishers, not least across territorial boundaries. A common dilemma for authors and agents was whether to retain American rights and hope for a separate American edition, which would bring its own advance and royalty payments, or to assign American rights to the British publisher who might then negotiate with an American firm, usually on the basis of a one-off payment split fifty-fifty between publisher and author.

While these settled arrangements made it more likely that Australian writers in the twentieth century could profit from American publication, they tightened the conditions under which this might occur; hence the drop in numbers after 1900. To receive copyright protection, the act required an overseas title to be wholly manufactured in the US and to be published on or before the date of foreign publication (in 1909 *ad*

---

17 Tebbel, pp. 481–511, 634–44; James L.W. West III, 'The Chace Act and Anglo-American Literary Relations', *Studies in Bibliography* 45 (1992): 303–11; Michael Winship, 'The Transatlantic Book Trade and Anglo-American Literary Culture in the Nineteenth Century', in Steven Fink and Susan S. Williams, eds, *Reciprocal Influences: Literary Production, Distribution, and Consumption in America* (Columbus: Ohio State University Press, 1999), pp. 98–122.

interim copyright was introduced, giving American publishers thirty days to register a foreign book and another thirty after that to publish). The manufacturing clause in particular, in place for British books until 1954, made publishing new foreign titles potentially a more complex and costly proposition. Authors, agents and publishers improvised a range of strategies to meet or sidestep its requirements—copyrighting a portion of a book (as Praed did with *Nyria*), printing 'phantom' copies, organising simultaneous publication across the Atlantic, or simply gambling that one's rights to the literary property for which one had paid would be respected by other firms where copyright could not in fact be established. In this context, the number of Australian titles that did get picked up is perhaps surprisingly high. In one sense, publishing was 'normalised'—that is, it operated on a title-by-title basis—but this too could disadvantage Australian authors whose local reputations seldom accompanied their books to the US. By restricting free access to British books, the Chace Act also played a role in the rise of self-consciously American literary traditions and 'nativist' publishing, which could add another barrier for Australian books to overcome.

The terms offered by American publishers in the twentieth century were not necessarily more generous than British terms, but they were certainly attractive to those Australian authors who could obtain only the reduced royalties offered on 'colonial editions' by British publishers. As Carol Hetherington has shown in Prichard's case, many Australian authors saw the American market as an alternative to the 'poor royalty payments, poor marketing and poor supply of books', and in some cases the patronising attitudes towards colonials, they had experienced at the hands of British publishers.[18] The major American houses, by contrast, seemed to promise a different publishing culture—more serious editorial attention and more commercial *nous*—while the US market offered the possibility of many more thousands in sales and subsidiary rights through magazine placements, radio serialisation, Hollywood options, and, best of all, book club and paperback sales.

In 1929 Richardson's *Ultima Thule* became an unlikely bestseller as the first Australian novel chosen as a Book-of-the-Month Club

18 Hetherington, 'Authors, Editors, Publishers', p. 419.

selection. Later selections included G.B. Lancaster's *Pageant: A Novel of Tasmania*, first published in New York, in 1933; Eleanor Dark's *The Timeless Land* in 1941, generating 100,000 in sales and US$25,000 for Dark; and in the 1950s Morris West's *Shoes of the Fisherman* and Patrick White's *Voss*. Book club selection meant guaranteed sales in the tens of thousands, an effect which could be multiplied through subsequent paperback reprints. For most of the twentieth century, paperback publishing in America was undertaken by dedicated paperback houses that would pay a one-off fee to a mainstream hardcover publisher for a license to publish a paperback edition, say for a three-year period (the fee would be split between publisher and author). Although the payments per copy were often small, print runs were very large. West's *The Devil's Advocate*, for example, sold 75,000 copies directly, but book club sales added a further two and quarter million and paperback sales another million plus.[19] After White's 1973 Nobel Prize, rights to earlier novels were licensed to the paperback publishers Avon and Pyramid, producing the biggest sales anywhere and at any time in his career.

The popular fiction market from the 1880s to the 1920s was relatively inclusive. While hierarchies of literary and moral value certainly existed, the market was yet to be conceived primarily in terms of separate and *opposed* strata, as registered, for example, in the highbrow, middlebrow, lowbrow hierarchy that emerged in the twenties (the exception was for dime novels). Cambridge, Praed and Boldrewood were received as both popular and reputable novelists. But this broad market was increasingly segmented between and within publishing houses. By the thirties we can distinguish three separate sectors of the American market in which Australian titles participated: pulp and specialist genre publishers (romance, westerns etc.); mainstream genre publishing (mainly crime and science fiction from hardback publishers); and 'literary' publishing, defined broadly to extend across both middlebrow and more restricted uses of the term.

While specialist romance publishers appeared between the wars, the main pulp genres—crime, war, and westerns—boomed in the immediate postwar decades. The number of Australia-originated titles

19 Publicity material in West's papers, National Library of Australia MS 7171.

published in the US doubled from the 1940s to the 1950s, then doubled again in the 1960s, very largely due to the pulp market. In this field, where high turnover was the norm, the outstanding figures were Carter Brown, with around 150 American titles from 1958 (most with the New American Library/Signet who also published J. E. Macdonnell's war and sea adventures); romance novelist Maysie Grieg with around 120, across five decades; and, under numerous pseudonyms, R. Hunter-Wilkes with over seventy (a mix of crime, mystery, and doctors and nurses romance). Science fiction pioneer, A. Bertram Chandler, had the bulk of his forty or so novels published in the US from 1963 to 1985, most by specialist science fiction publishers Ace and Daw. Leslie Meares and others writing under the pseudonyms Marshall Grover and Marshall McCoy sold westerns (back) into the American market. What is most notable for the present project is that these authors pursued their American careers *from Australia*, without expatriation or British intermediaries. This was made possible by the portability of the genres and absence of national markers in the texts, and by the commercial arrangements in the pulp industry, usually on a fee-per-title rather than royalty basis.

In hardback trade fiction, the first striking figure is Arthur Upfield, with thirty-three novels published in the US between 1929 and 1965, mainly by Doubleday in its Crime series, while Jon Cleary published the first of more than forty American editions in 1947. Cleary's career is one of the earliest examples of an author making a direct approach to the American industry from Australia (earlier Norman Lindsay had travelled to the US with his manuscripts in his suitcase, so too Patrick White with *Happy Valley*). In 1943, following the advice of R. G. Campbell, editor of the *Australian Journal*, Cleary sent a bundle of stories to one of the most famous US literary agents, Paul Reynolds, hoping Reynolds could place them in prestigious and well-paying American magazines. Reynolds' initial success was limited, but he spent a remarkable amount of time encouraging and advising Cleary, an investment that began to pay off when Cleary's first novel, *You Can't See Round Corners*, was accepted by Scribner's. The novel appeared in 1947, a year before its appearance in Australia, and Scribner's followed with *The Sundowners* (1952, with four subsequent US editions). Cleary then followed his editor to William Morrow who published forty-one subsequent Cleary titles. Morris West's story has close parallels to Cleary's, beginning with Reynolds and secured through thirteen titles from Morrow.

Cleary and West represent an important sector of the international fiction market, one we know well as consumers but struggle with as literary scholars. Both wrote 'popular fiction', but the term is too broad to be of much use in defining their work or its place in the market. Although they draw on crime or thriller genres—and Cleary published a series of detective novels featuring the working-class Sydney cop Scobie Malone—for the most part they do not write genre fiction in the sense that Upfield, Chandler or Grieg do. Both authors were serious and professional about their craft, but had little patience with elevated or academic notions of the literary. We do not have an adequate vocabulary for describing this register of 'good commercial fiction'[20] except negatively: it is not simply genre fiction, not quite best-selling or blockbuster in the marketing sense of those terms (although both sold well), not quite middlebrow, but not quite 'literary' either. This was a mid-range, mainstream register that was particularly strong in the American market from the forties to the sixties. It was also the register for James Aldridge, with eighteen novels published in the US since 1942, most with Little, Brown and Doubleday; and for George Johnston, at least before *My Brother Jack*, the last of his twelve American titles.[21] Perhaps Tom Keneally is their rightful heir.

West and Cleary sustained English and American careers from an Australian base (despite extended periods abroad); their international

---

20 Long-time US publisher Al Silverman uses the term in his *The Time of their Lives: The Golden Age of Great American Book Publishers, Their Editors and Authors* (New York: Truman Tally, St Martin's, 2008), p. 12. The term doesn't explain or define but its use indicates a 'self-evident' industry category.

21 Both Aldridge and Johnston began their American careers (from London) with books based on their experiences as war correspondents. Three of Johnston's titles—*High Valley*, *The Big Chariot*, and *The Sea and the Stone*—were co-authored with Charmian Clift. Four were published by Morrow.

careers were *launched* from America; and both were soon in a position to negotiate separate contracts with English and American houses. Reversing the usual equation, their Australian careers were a by-product of their international success, and they have been correspondingly difficult to place in relation to 'Australian literature'. To an extent both traded in international genres, but this is only half the story. Cleary's fiction, in particular, makes little concession to non-Australian readers. After all, *The Sundowners*, his biggest American success, deals with Irish-Australian battlers in the bush, while *You Can't See Round Corners*, like the later Scobie Malone novels, is full of local Sydney references. Cleary made only one concession for his first book, changing the title to *You Can't See Around Corners* on his publisher's advice, in case American readers understood *rounded* corners.

Clearly, in the literary middle ground, expatriation remained an important route to American publication: Praed, Richardson, Lancaster, Boyd and others established careers in England or Europe that then sustained multiple American titles. For a number, America was the place of their greatest critical and sales success. But these writers still travelled largely as English authors, alongside contemporaries such as Galsworthy, Priestley, or Somerset Maugham. Perhaps this began to change in the 1940s when Cleary, West, Johnston and Aldridge joined the successful expatriates *without* established British reputations. A different form of 'post-imperial' internationalism also emerges mid-century with Christina Stead, beginning her American career from Europe with simultaneous publication of her first three books in London and New York, and continuing it when resident in the US for a decade from 1937; and with Patrick White. *Happy Valley*, White's first novel, was published in London in 1939, but once Ben Huebsch accepted it in 1940 Viking became White's primary editorial location until the mid-1970s, after Huebsch's death, when Jonathan Cape assumed the role. The point for the present is that White's literary career, like Cleary's and Stead's, was fundamentally shaped by its American connection rather than the US being merely a site of secondary publication. In Simon During words: 'White's relation with his American publisher secured his career. [His] reputation was originally built in America, and was then transferred to Australia and the UK'.[22]

At the same time a cluster of Australia-based and, in different ways, nationalist-oriented writers appeared in American lists from the mid-thirties. Joining Prichard were Dark, Kylie Tennant, Brian Penton, Xavier Herbert, Leonard Mann, Ernestine Hill, Eve Langley, and Joseph Furphy whose *Such is Life* was published belatedly in 1948 following a campaign by Hartley Grattan. Perhaps for the first time Australian books were arriving in the US *as* Australian books. With the exception of Dark and Tennant, however, these publications were one-(or two) off. In part this reflects the title-by-title nature of *all* literary publishing, although multiplied by what Nettie Palmer called the 'inconsecutive' nature of Australian literary life.[23] But it also reflects the inconsecutive nature of American interest in Australia and Australian literature. There was no follow-up to this mid-century mini-boom, nothing really to support the notion of a surge of American interest in Australia following the Pacific war. Behind the massive export of pulp fiction and the prolific careers of West and Cleary, there *was* a steady increase in the volume of literary fiction picked up in the postwar decades, and some authors, including Ruth Park, Randolph Stow and Barbara Jefferis, managed a sequence of American editions. But 'Australian literature' remained a fitful presence, at least until the 1980s.

For the evidence does support the idea of the 1980s as a boom time. Over the decade to 1988 and roughly in this order the following authors all had at least two American editions: David Malouf, Thea Astley, David Ireland, Christopher Koch, Nicholas Hasluck, Roger McDonald, Rodney Hall, Jessica Anderson, Elizabeth Jolley, Peter Carey, Gerald Murnane, Glenda Adams, Olga Masters, Beverley Farmer, David Foster and Tim Winton. All except Astley and Ireland appeared in US editions for the first time in this period; and for the most part they did so with first or simultaneous *Australian* publication.

22 Simon During, *Patrick White* (Melbourne: Oxford University Press, 1996), pp. 5–6.

23 Letter to Frank Dalby Davison, 10 Aug. 1936, repr. in Vivian Smith, ed., *Letters of Vance and Nettie Palmer 1915–1936* (Canberra: National Library of Australia, 1977), p. 138.

Keneally was a precursor of relationships that would become common by the mid-1980s. In terms of American publication, Keneally's first novel, *The Place at Whitton*, followed the orthodox pattern of publication in London and then New York. But from *Bring Larks and Heroes* in 1967, Keneally's novels were published first in Australia and then in London and New York, with most sold on to paperback houses. Later books were published simultaneously by Collins in Sydney and London and by various houses in the US, so that by the mid-seventies Keneally could achieve separate Australian, UK and US editions for almost all of his more than twenty-five titles, a pattern only confirmed in the US by the success of his American Civil War novel *Confederates* in 1980 and then *Schindler's List* (the American title) in 1982. Keneally has truly had an American *career* not merely American editions. In October 1993 he was inducted into the American Academy of Arts and Sciences, the only Australian fiction writer I suspect to have achieved this honour.

The reasons for the eighties boom include the growth of Australian publishing, the 'multi-nationalisation' of publishing globally, and the collapse of the Traditional Markets Agreement that had confined Australia to the British publishing sphere. Together these developments enabled a new trade in international rights where first Australian publication was no longer the disadvantage it had been since the nineteenth century. The new rights regime created a separate Australasian publishing territory, so authors and agents could negotiate Australasian rights and *then* US or UK rights. Australian publishers themselves began to negotiate for Commonwealth and/or world English-language rights (Penguin Australia doing so facilitated a growth in Penguin/Viking US titles, more than thirty in the decade, as no new contracts needed to be negotiated). In this situation, Australia-based literary agents also became a serious proposition. The most prominent, Curtis Brown Australia, had been established in 1967, but its communications with Curtis Brown London and New York expanded rapidly in the next two decades. By the eighties, established writers often had Australian, English and American agents, each negotiating rights in their home territories.

Australian literature as an entity had never been as prominent in the US market; while less dramatic, it had something approaching the presence of Latin American literature over the same period, with feature articles, for example, in the major books papers. A *New York Times* piece from 1984 spoke of the 'flood from down under', and quoted literary agent Elise Goodman crediting the interest in Australian books to the contemporary success of Australian movies.[24] Publishers often picked up earlier titles when they signed a writer to their list; so Braziller published both *An Imaginary Life* and the earlier *Johnno* in 1978 once it signed Malouf, plus a collection of poems in 1979. By the 1990s, the most successful writers—Carey, Malouf, Winton—routinely had separate Australian, UK and US editions for each title as it appeared, often through the multinational reach of the new media conglomerates. Malouf, for example, has published under a range of local imprints belonging to Bertlesmann/Random House (Knopf, Chatto & Windus, Pantheon, Vintage), although such connections do not guarantee preferential treatment on either side.

But the growth of the 1980s has not been maintained, at least not in literary fiction. The most prominent names remain and new writers have appeared on American lists—Kate Grenville, Andrew McGahan, Richard Flanagan—but the most remarkable fact is the growth in Australia's export of speculative fiction. More than a quarter of Australian titles with American editions from 2000 to 2009 are fantasy or science fiction, slightly more even than in the romance genre. Crime, with its taste for locale, comes a relatively distant third.

While the number of Australian books issued by American publishers has been significant, even remarkable, for more than a century, American interest in Australian literature or the Australianness of any of our stories has been uneven at best. The Pacific war did provide opportunities for increased links and occasional reflection from American critics on our shared histories.[25] A party of American bookmen visited Australia in 1946, the same year in which, with the

24 Edwin McDowell, 'Publishing: Books from Down Under', *New York Times*, 12 October 1984, C30.

25 The *New York Herald Tribune* noted that *The Timeless Land* related an 'historical saga strangely kin to our own', while a review of *The Battlers* remarked how its Australians seemed much more similar to Americans than to the British.

encouragement of New York agent Armitage Watkins, two young women in Sydney established the Noëlle Brennan Literary Agency to feed Australian works to US publishers. This is a poignant moment in the history of transpacific literary relations, as the agency was a total failure. Its great hope, short story writer Art Hausler, made no impression. From New York the hundreds of submissions forwarded were 'not suitable for this country'; they were 'too slight [with] not enough development [and] no characterisation'; they 'lack[ed] the professional polish which our large magazines require'.[26] Without widespread access to the magazine market there could be no concentrated presence for Australian literature—which was not, in any case, the agencies' concern.

Australian literature had its supporters of course, including Hartley Grattan, Henry Seidel Canby, William Norton and later George Braziller. On the occasion of an Australian book display in New York in 1948 Grattan wrote: 'It is surprising indeed how many [Americans] recall with pleasure that they have read a novel or two by H.H. Richardson, Eleanor Dark, Patrick White, Xavier Herbert, Christina Stead, Robert Close, Katharine Prichard, Barnard Eldershaw, Brian Penton, Leonard Mann, Dalby Davison—all of whom have had books published in American in recent years'.[27] But Grattan's view was not widely supported in the trade. More common was the indifference reported to Tennant: 'Perhaps in the near future apathy towards the Australian scene, which few books have been able to hurdle, may be destroyed'; or to Cleary: 'We think too that [*The Sundowners*] may very well break through the apathy towards Australian books (and in fact it isn't strongly "Australian")'.[28] When Angus & Robertson pitched Ion

26 Armitage Watkins to Noëlle Brennan, 12 July 1946 and 27 January 1947, Watkins Loomis Records 1883–1987, Series III, Box 4, Rare Books and Manuscripts Library, Columbia University.

27 Grattan quoted in Press Release, Office of the Australian Government Trade Commissioner, New York, 17 Nov. 1948. C. Hartley Grattan Papers, Harry Ransom Humanities Research Center, University of Texas, Austin.

28 Naomi Burton (Curtis Brown New York) to Tennant, 26 February 1946. National Library of Australia, MS 10043/1/11; Scribner's internal Office Memo, Mitchell Burroughs to Whitney Darrow et al., 21 May 1951, Archives of Charles Scribner's Sons, Author Files III, Box 13, Folder 1, Princeton University Library Manuscripts Division.

Idriess's best-selling titles to US publishers, all were rejected save one, a war story about a dog called *Horrie the Wog Dog* (happily retitled *Dog of the Desert* in America). The comment 'of little interest except to Australians' resounds through the readers' reports.[29] Mary Patchett's 1954 novel about another dog provoked a publisher's reader to say, oddly, 'This is the only book about Australia—which surely must be one of the most fascinating places in the world—that I have ever enjoyed'. Another stated: 'If Australia were a useful handle, [the Australian background] would be fine—but I've never seen much indication of popular interest in the continent. Australian books seem to move in spite of the background, not because of it'.[30] D'Arcy Niland's novels were rejected for republication in 1970 with the comment: 'Australian books never do very well in this country, with, again, very few exceptions'.[31] It is difficult to gauge whether this attitude has changed significantly. But the relationship *is* now primarily transpacific, and the shift in the balance of power in rights negotiations has allowed something of an expanded middle, with greater opportunities for ordinary 'good' novelists to reach the American market.

Perhaps the last word belongs to Gerald Murnane. Filling out his author's questionnaire for George Braziller, who published *The Plains* in 1985, Murnane wrote defiantly: 'Between ourselves, if the US reader expects an Australian novel to be a bulky saga of the Outback, with bushfires and spear-throwing black men, we're in trouble. *The Plains* is, at one of its many levels, an *anti*-Australian novel'. Sadly, they were in trouble. *The Plains* was met with 'almost total silence', and it was the last Australian novel Braziller published.[32]

---

29 Bobbs-Merrill MSS 1885–1951, Box 90, Lilly Lib., Indiana University. Readers' Reports 1950–1952.

30 Bobbs-Merrill MSS 1885–1951, Box 132, Lilly Lib., Indiana University. Readers' Reports 1954 & 1955.

31 Lois Dwight Cole (Walker & Co,) to Jane Wilson (John Cushman Associates), 12 Aug. 1970, John Cushman Associates Records 1965–1978, Rare Books and Manuscripts Library, Columbia University.

32 Murnane, Author's Questionnaire (1985), Archives of George Braziller, Inc., 1960s–1995, Box 30, Folder 14, Princeton University Lib. Manuscripts Division.

Index

A

B

M

S

Y

www.ingramcontent.com/pod-product-compliance
Lightning Source LLC
LaVergne TN
LVHW020040110826
845155LV00029B/569

* 9 7 8 1 9 2 0 8 9 9 6 6 0 *